Africa's Thirty Years War

Africa's Thirty Years War

Libya, Chad, and the Sudan
1963–1993

J. Millard Burr
Robert O. Collins

Westview Press
A Member of the Perseus Books Group

Copyright © 1999 by Westview Press, A Member of the Perseus Books Group

Published in 1999 in the United States of America by Westview Press, 5500 Central Avenue, Boulder, Colorado 80301-2877, and in the United Kingdom by Westview Press, 12 Hid's Copse Road, Cumnor Hill, Oxford OX2 9JJ

Library of Congress Cataloging-in-Publication Data
Burr, Millard
  Africa's Thirty Years War : Libya, Chad, and the Sudan, 1963–1993
/ J. Millard Burr, Robert O. Collins.
    p. c.m.
  Includes bibliographical references (p.) and index.
  ISBN 0-8133-3566-3
  1. Chad—History—Civil War, 1965– 2. Chad—History—Civil War,
1965– —Participation, Libyan. 3. Africa—Foreign relations—1960–
I. Collins, Robert O., 1933– . II. Title.
DT546.48.B87 1999
967.4304—dc21   99-10889
                                                                                                              CIP

The paper used in this publication meets the requirements of the American National Standard for Permanence of Paper for Printed Library Materials Z39.48-1984.

10   9   8   7   6   5   4   3   2   1

This Book Is Dedicated to Two Men for All Seasons
Robert D. Hodson, The Geographer, United States Department of State,
1971–1979
and
Yusuf Ibrahim Badri, 1915–1995
Sudanese Educator, Scholar, and Chancellor of Afhad University
for Women, Omdurman, Sudan

Contents

Maps		xi
Acronyms		xii
Preface		xv

1	Sahara, Sahel, and Sudan	1

Continuities, 2
Crossing the Sahara, 5
The Power of Belief, 8
The Bonds of Blood, 11
Boundaries and Frontiers, 13
Implacable Imperialism, 19
Notes, 21

2	Chad: An African Conundrum	22

France and the Republic of Chad, 24
The Tombalbaye Government, 26
Seeking Support Outside France, 29
Revolt in the B.E.T., 32
Drought and the Insurgency, 34
FROLINAT, 37
A Nasty Little War, 41
Tombalbaye Fights Back, 43
The Return of the French, 46
French Conditions and Tombalbaye's Response, 47
Opposition in France, 49
The French Military in Chad, 50
The Libyan Card, 51
Notes, 52

3	The Sudan and Tombalbaye: Muslims and Christians	55

The Sudan and Chad, 57
Sadiq al-Mahdi and Chad, 60
FROLINAT Attacks, 63

The Sahelian Drought, 64
The Return of Hasan al-Turabi, 66
Turabi and Sadiq, 69
Numayri and Chad, 71
Notes, 73

4   Libya and Tombalbaye: Muslim Arabs and Christian Africans   74

Qaddafi's Game, 76
Geopolitic Visions, 77
The Chad-Libyan Boundary Dispute Revisited, 82
Cartographic and Other Territorial Aggression, 85
Hissene Habre, 88
The Aozou Strip, 90
Drought and Man in the Aozou Strip and the B.E.T., 92
Security for Tombalbaye, 94
FROLINAT in Disarray, 95
L'Affaire Claustre, 96
Notes, 99

5   The Struggle for Chad   102

The United States and Tombalbaye, 103
Tombalbaye Assassinated, 104
The Conseil Supérieur Militaire du Tchad and Felix Malloum, 105
Presidents Giscard and Malloum, 106
Dissension Within the FAN, 108
Qaddafi and the Sudan, 110
The Return of the French, 112
Regional Geopolitics in a Changing World, 113
Egypt, Libya, Niger, and the OAU, 115
Habre Joins Malloum, 116
The Popular Armed Forces on the Offensive, 119
Notes, 121

6   Libya Threatens Chad   123

Habre and the Transitional Government of National Unity, 125
Political Disarray and Violence in Ndjamena, 128
Libyan Intervention and GUNT, 130
France Leaves, Libya Arrives, 131
Habre Is Isolated, 133
Libya Incorporates Chad, 135
The OAU and Chad, 137
The Reagan Response, 138

The OAU and Libya, 139
Notes, 141

7   Habre Brings Order   145

Habre Recovers, 145
Mitterrand Assumes Command, 148
Habre on the Attack, 149
Libyan Troops Depart Followed by the GUNT, 153
Habre Triumphant, 155
The United States and Habre, 157
Qaddafi in Defeat and the Beginning of Organized Terror, 158
Notes, 160

8   The Libyan Counterattack   163

The United States, Chad, and the Sudan, 164
Qaddafi on the Attack, 167
Victories at Ounianga Kebir and Faya, 168
The Gourane Counterattack, 170
Operation Manta, 172
Stabilizing the Red Line, 175
The Vittel Conference, 177
Pacifying the South, 179
Habre's UNIR, Qaddafi's CLN, 180
More Strains Within the Rebel Leadership, 181
From Tripoli to Crete, 183
Notes, 186

9   Famine in the B.E.T.: Instability in Darfur   190

Famine and Western Relief, 191
Instability in the Sudan, 192
Qaddafi Continues to Meddle in Chad, 195
Numayri Is Deposed, 196
The Libyan Buildup, 198
Operation Épervier, 200
The United States Attacks Qaddafi, 202
Sadiq Victorious, 203
Sadiq and Darfur, 205
Notes, 206

10   Habre Victorious   209

Acheikh and the CDR Revolt, 211

Goukouni the Captive, 212
Habre Conquers All, 213
Libya Attacks Goukouni, 215
Qaddafi Attacks "Ibri," 217
Libyan Forces in Darfur, 220
Qaddafi and Khartoum, 223
Victory at Wadi Doum, Darfur, and Ounianga, 223
The Fezzan Threatened and the Hadjerai Revolt, 225
The FANT Invades Libya, 227
Notes, 229

11   Conflict in Darfur   232

Sadiq and the Libyans, 233
Peace in the B.E.T., 234
1988 in Ndjamena, Tripoli, and El Fasher, 235
Deby and the Zaghawa Defy Habre, 239
The Collapse of the Chad-Libya Rapprochement, 242
Tribal Tensions in Darfur, 243
Revolution in the Sudan, 244
Libya-Sudan Brotherhood, 246
The Algiers Agreement and the Aozou, 248
Habre and Deby Struggle for Darfur, 249
Notes, 251

12   Deby Victorious   254

The Libya-Sudan Integration Charter, 255
Deby Takes the Offensive, 256
Reaction in Darfur, 259
Drought in Darfur, 260
Deby Counterattacks Again, 261
The More Things Change . . . , 264
Notes, 265

13   The End of an Epic   267

Regional Realignment, 268
Chad in Political Change, 271
Habre, Hail and Farewell, 273
France, Deby, and Oil, 276
The Aozou Solution, 277
Notes, 279

Bibliography   281
Index   287

Maps

	Chad, Libya, Niger Border Area	xviii
1.1	Chad-Libya-Sudan Triangle	2
3.1	Southern Chad—Sudan Border Area	58
4.1	Selected Libyan Coastal Claims	80
4.2	Chad: The Aouzou Strip and the Toubou Tribal Area	87
5.1	Libya, Niger: Tummo Airstrips	117
8.1	Chad: 1984	174

Acronyms

AEF	Afrique Equatoriale Française (French Equatorial Africa).
AFP	Agence France Press, Paris.
AIC	Anti-Imperialism Center, Libya.
AID	United States Agency for International Development (USAID).
ANI	Armée Nationale Intégrée (National Integrated Army), Chad.
ANL	Armée Nationale de Libération (National Liberation Army), Chad.
B.E.T.	Borkou-Ennedi-Tibesti Prefecture.
CAC	Comité d'Action et de Concertation (Action and Coordination Committee) of the CDR, Chad.
CAR	Central African Republic.
CCER	Centre de Coordination et d'Exploitation du Renseignements.
CCFAN	Conseil de Commandement des Forces Armées du Nord (FAN) (Command Council of the Northern Army Force), Chad.
CDR	Conseil Démocratique Révolutionnaire (Democratic Revolutionary Command), Chad.
CENTCOM	United States Department of Defense, Central Command.
CIA	United States Central Intelligence Agency.
CLN	Conseil de Libération Nationale (National Liberation Council), Chad.
COTONTCHAD	Société Cotonnière du Tchad (Cotton Corporation of Chad).
CRCR	Centre des Recherches et de Coordination de Renseignements (Center for Research and Coordination of Information), Chad.
CTT	Coopérative des Transportateurs Tchadiens (Transporters' Cooperative of Chad).
DDS	Direction des Documents et de Sécurité (Document and Security Directorate), Chad.
DGSE	Direction Générale de la Sécurité Extérieure (General Directorate for External Security), France.
DUP	Democratic Unionist Party, Sudan.
FAC	Front d'Action Commune (Front for Common Action), Chad.
FAN	Forces Armées du Nord (Northern Army Force), Chad.

FANT	Forces Armées Nationales Tchadiennes (National Armed Forces of Chad).
FAO	Forces Armées Occidentales (Western Armed Forces), Chad.
FAP	Forces Armées Populaires (Popular Armed Forces), Chad.
FAT	Forces Armées Tchadiennes (Chad Armed Forces).
FBIS	Foreign Broadcast Information Service.
FDT	Front Démocratique du Tchad (Chadian Democratic Front).
FEWS	Famine Early Warning System.
FLT	Front de la Libération Tchadienne (Chad Liberation Front).
FPL	Front Populaire de la Libération (Popular Liberation Front), Chad.
FROLINAT	Front de Libération Nationale du Tchad (Chad National Liberation Front).
GOFAT	Groupe des Officiers des Forces Armées Tchadiennes (Chadian Armed Forces Officers Group).
GUNT	Gouvernement d'Union Nationale de Transition (Transitional Government of National Unity), Chad.
ICF	Islamic Charter Front (Mithaq), Sudan.
ISA	Intelligence Support Agency (United States, Department of Defense).
JANA	Jamahiriya News Agency, Tripoli, Libya.
MDD	Mouvement Démocratie et Développement (Movement for Democracy and Development).
MDRT	Mouvement Démocratique de Rénovation Tchadienne (Democratic Movement for the Renovation of Chad).
MENA	Middle East News Agency, Cairo.
MNLT	Mouvement Nationale pour la Libération du Tchad (National Movement for the Liberation of Chad).
MNRCS	Mouvement National pour la Révolution Culturelle et Sociale (National Movement for Social and Cultural Revolution), Chad.
MPLT	Mouvement Populaire pour la Libération du Tchad (Popular Movement for the Liberation of Chad).
MPR	Mouvement National pour la Révolution (National Movement for Revolution), Chad.
MPS	Mouvement Patriotique du Salut (Patriotic Safety Movement), Chad.
MRP	Mouvement Révolutionnaire du Peuple (People's Revolutionary Movement), Chad.
MSF	Médecins sans frontières (Doctors without Borders), France.
NAM	Non-Aligned Movement.
NDA	National Democratic Alliance, Sudan.
NFSL	National Front for the Salvation of Libya.

NIF	National Islamic Front, Sudan.
NSRCC	National Salvation Revolutionary Command Council, Sudan.
OAU	Organization of African Unity.
PDF	Popular Defense Force, Sudan.
PLO	Palestine Liberation Organization.
PPT	Parti Progressiste Tchadien (Chadian Progressive Party).
PPT/RDA	PPT/Rassemblement Démocratique Africain (Chadian Progressive Party of the African Democratic Assembly).
RCC	Revolutionary Command Council, Libya.
RCC	(National Salvation) Revolutionary Command Council (NSRCC), Sudan.
RDP	Rassemblement Démocratique Populaire (Popular Democratic Assembly), Chad.
SDECE	Service de Documentation Extérieure et de Contre Espionage (External Documentation and Counter Espionage Service), France.
SNIE	Special National Intelligence Estimate, United States.
SPLA	Sudan People's Liberation Army.
SSU	Sudanese Socialist Union.
SUNA	Sudan News Agency, Khartoum.
TMC	Transitional Military Council, Sudan.
UDEAC	Union Douanière et Economique de l'Afrique Centrale (Customs and Economic Union of Central Africa).
UEAC	Union of Central African States.
UGFT	(Muslim) Union Générale des Fils du Tchad (General Union of the Sons of Chad).
UNT	Union Nationale Tchadienne (Chad National Union), Chad.
UNHCR	United Nations High Commissioner for Refugees.
UNIR	Union Nationale pour l'Indépendence et la Révolution (National Union for Independence and Revolution), Chad.
UNIROUTE	Union Routière Centre-Africaine.
UNT	Union Nationale Tchadienne (Chad National Union).
USAID	United States Agency for International Development (AID).

Preface

This idea for this book began during the years from 1974 to 1986 when Dr. J. Millard Burr served as Political Geographer, Special Assistant to The Geographer, and Acting Director, Office of The Geographer, the United States Department of State. The Office of The Geographer began the production of its respected *International Boundary Studies* series in 1961 with a review of the Algeria-Libya boundary, and its third volume, published in the same year, included its study of the Chad-Libya boundary. For three decades thereafter the Office of The Geographer produced analyses, studies, and background briefs on the numerous issues concerning the differences between Chad and Libya. Dr. Burr monitored the Chad-Libya dispute for more than a decade and prepared a major study on the Aozou Strip and intelligence reports on the struggles within Chad. From 1989 to 1990 Dr. Burr was on assignment in the Sudan with the United States Agency for International Development, during which time he visited Darfur and the western frontier.

Professor Robert O. Collins has written about the history of the Sudan, the Upper Nile, and Africa in numerous volumes published throughout the last half of the twentieth century. *Africa's Thirty Years War* is the second collaborative effort of Dr. Burr and Professor Collins. Like the first, *Requiem for the Sudan: War, Drought, and Disaster Relief on the Nile* (Westview, 1995), this volume brings together their unique spheres of knowledge, diverse perspectives, and different disciplines. It seeks to illuminate the extraordinarily complex events in Libya, Chad, and the Sudan during a generation of conflict from 1963 to 1993, which has not been previously described or analyzed. There will be those who will attempt to compare Africa's Thirty Years War with the one that is better known in the curriculum of courses in modern European history—Europe's Thirty Years War, which took place between 1618 and 1648. There is a temptation to draw dramatic parallels—religion, ethnicity, weapons, personalities, territory—but it would be more contrived than instructive, and therefore, in the judgment of the authors, should be ignored and resisted. The one and only viable consistency between the two is the coincidence that both conflicts absorbed the energies of a generation before the futility of the enterprise resulted in peace.

Spellings

Spellings can be a curse that results in chaos, particularly when the documentation for a book, like this one, comes from four major written languages: Arabic,

English, French, and Italian. Equally important are the African languages, the Adamawa-Eastern of the great Niger-Congo African linguistic family and the Nilo-Saharan of the politically powerful in Chad. As the "lords of the land" in the past and present, each in turn gave their names to those places they controlled in Libya, Chad, and the Sudan. Motivated by familiarity, practice, or ethnic pride, Africans, Arabs, and Europeans have spelled the name of the same person, place, or event in a transliteration that reflects their own parochialism, patriotism, and panache. The result has been confusion rather than clarity. The only legitimate principle is consistency of spelling in the text. Consistency, however, is not a universal virtue and does not always guarantee clarity. In the search for clarity, we have consequently Anglicized or given the English equivalent for place-names and events recorded in a different language. This is not from academic arrogance. It is a practical response for those who wish to understand what we have written; readers can identify with a person, place, or event encountered in wider media than this book. Thus, Tchad becomes Chad; Oueddai, Wadai; Ouadi Doum, Wadi Doum. Place-names are spelled for understanding rather than in the local patois. Personal names are more precisely retained because they are a complex, for everyone spells his or her name to their satisfaction. Like place-names, variety can produce bewilderment for the reader. The sensible rule is, therefore, consistency in the text. The same principle applies for diacritical marks in transliteration. Thus, for consistency, we have not incorporated them in the text for either place-names or personal names. The French marks for accent, however, have been used when it is an established and accepted spelling.

Acknowledgments

This book has been made possible by the records collected over many years by Millard Burr from thousands of sources, both public and private, and the international historical research of Robert O. Collins in the archives of Khartoum, Cairo, London, and the Sudan Archive at Durham University, which is now the repository of his private collection of papers and oral traditions acquired during his years of research in the Sudan and its neighbors. These original sources have been confirmed and supplemented by the published literature in the libraries of Rhodes House, Oxford, the British Museum, the Library of Congress, and the libraries of the University of California.

We wish to acknowledge the many private citizens and government officials who have given their time, support, and information to the authors. Because political conditions within Libya, Chad, and the Sudan remain unsettled, their privacy must be maintained for their personal security. There are those who have served as loyal civil servants and diplomats in the governments mentioned in this narrative and who wish to remain anonymous, but to whom we owe a deep debt of gratitude for their time and wisdom. We hope that they will find gratification in the final product. We have strived to ensure that the quotations supporting this narrative have all been made from the public record and not attributed to any individual.

Special thanks must go the Office of The Geographer and its cartographers, especially William Hezlip and Daniel Kaiser, for their kindness and unstinting assistance. There is also the band of brothers who deserve special appreciation—Nico Cabrera, Alex Tarango, Chris Davis, and Chris Emerson, all led by Joan Murdoch and Paolo Gardinali from the Office of Information Technology in the College of Letters and Science at the University of California, Santa Barbara. They were always available to correct computer mistakes, enjoying our ample supply of oranges as they did so, and helped make this volume a reality.

J. Millard Burr,
Tucson, Arizona

Robert O. Collins,
Santa Barbara, California

Chad, Libya, Niger Border Area

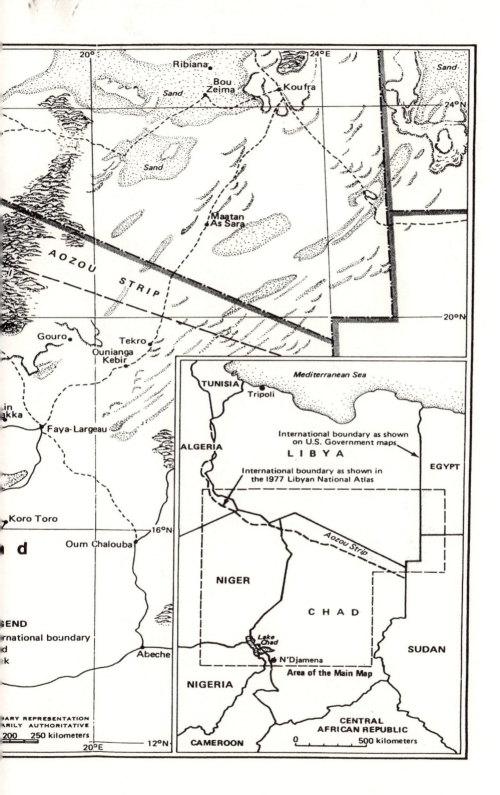

20°   Ribiana•

Sand   Bou
        Zeima•   •Koufra   24°E   24°N

Sand

Sand

Maatan
As Sara•

A O Z O U

S T R I P

20°N

Gouro•
        Tekro•
    Ounianga
    Kebir•

in
akka
        •Faya-Largeau

Koro Toro•

d   16°N

    Oum Chalouba•

GEND
rnational boundary
d
:k

ARY REPRESENTATION
ARILY AUTHORITATIVE
200   250 kilometers
        20°E   12°N

Inset map:

TUNISIA   •Tripoli   Mediterranean Sea

International boundary as shown
on U.S. Government maps

ALGERIA   L I B Y A   EGYPT

International boundary as shown in
the 1977 Libyan National Atlas

Aozou Strip

NIGER   CHAD

Lake
Chad

•N'Djamena   SUDAN

Area of the Main Map

NIGERIA

CENTRAL
AFRICAN REPUBLIC

CAMEROON   0   500 kilometers

1

Sahara, Sahel, and Sudan

The thirty-year struggle for Chad is a melancholy African affair. This conflict is not unique to Libya, Chad, and the Sudan; the same themes that have determined the course of their hostilities have characterized the violence in other regions of Africa during the generation since independence. These themes are, unfortunately, a familiar litany of confrontation between leaders, tribes, regions, races, and religions, of nomad against farmer, of cultivator against city dweller. Unlike other areas of the African continent, Libya, Chad, and the Sudan have historically been more susceptible to drought, insect infestation, and indigenous famine. This vast region of three million square miles forms a right triangle anchored by three capitals: Ndjamena south of Lake Chad on the Chari River, Khartoum at the confluence of the Blue and White Niles, and Tripoli whose waterfront is washed by the Mediterranean (see Map 1.1). The area of this triangle encompasses some of the most desolate landscape anywhere in Africa and the world. Within this wasteland of Sahara, Sahel, and savanna, neither Libya, Chad, nor the Sudan would appear to have much in common except for the lone pillar in the depths of the implacable Libyan Desert where their three boundaries come together. Throughout time, however, these hostile lands have been crossed by their inhabitants, who have fashioned complex and historic relationships that since 1963 have commanded the attention and consumed the energies of African and Arab politicians, regional and international institutions, and the leaders of the West and the Third World.

The history of the past thirty years has been dominated by a score of leading actors in the unfolding drama, some African, some Arab, some both. The struggle for Chad during this time has been defined by the imposition of new technologies commanded by African, Arab, and Western incomers upon a stage of great antiquity. Personal ambition, revenge, greed, and intrigue are as evident at the end of the twentieth century as they were during the previous millennium and have almost invariably resulted in warfare. As in the past, many of those who have participated in the mayhem have failed to justify their actions in the principal events during the thirty years of war, in which there have been few victories

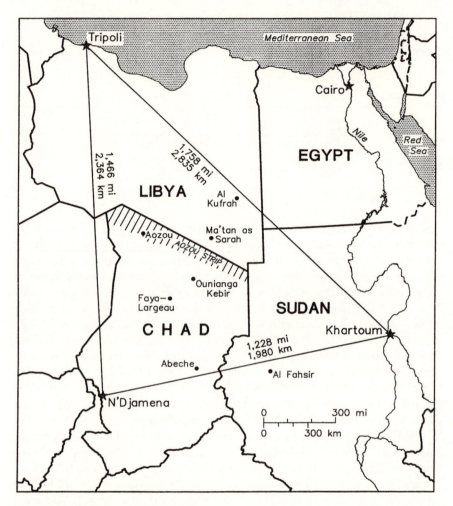

MAP 1.1   *Chad-Libya-Sudan Triangle*

and many, many victims. At high noon in the illimitable panorama of the desert, one must shade the eyes and squint very hard to discern the shadows that give definition to the landscape.

Continuities

Africa's Thirty Years War is the history of Libya, Chad, and the Sudan in the past generation. This period has been sculptured more by geography and history than by ideologies or triumphant technology. The continuity between the past and the present has determined the conflict. The fundamental issues at the end of the twentieth century are the direct descendants of those of the previous two millennia; they have dominated the realities of life in a land characterized by a hostile environment. The drive to acquire space, to dominate people, and to proselytize the faith has changed little in these arid lands in two thousand years. The routes across the Sahara today are the same as they were when the camel replaced the bullock in the fourth century; the four-wheel-drive vehicle is simply a modest improvement at the end of the twentieth century. The passage of people over these routes during the ages produced an intimacy that has resulted in curiosity and customary concern for the spiritual relation of man to his gods or God. The passage of time produced both accommodation and rivalry among the traditional religions of Africa and the monotheistic imports, Islam and Christianity, which has resulted in syncretistic practices, on the one hand, and the determination to pursue the truth faith by any means, on the other.

The caravan routes brought trade and religion that were sealed by the bonds of blood. The allegiance to clan, lineage, and tribe has been the cement of society in the Sahara, Sahel, and savanna throughout the ages. Survival in a hostile environment depended more on kith and kin than in the more fertile lands of other continents. Recognition of and obedience to blood ties has sustained and protected those least tranquilized by the global revolution in communications and transportation. These obligations to belief and consanguinity have been defended in blood throughout a vast frontier in Africa extending from the Tibesti across the Ennedi Plateau and down through the arbitrary boundary between the historic sultanates of Wadai and Darfur to the Congo. Unlike the frontiers that have vanished in the new worlds, no ruler from the Mediterranean, the Nile, or Lake Chad has successfully exerted his authority, in the past or the present, into the abyss of the Sahara, Sahel, and savanna. This failure was not due to the dearth of resources. The geographic isolation of the frontier, which today defines Libya, Chad, and the Sudan, was demarcated by Europeans eighty years ago, but it was irrelevant to the ebb and flow of ancient African traders, pilgrims, and those who lived in the *Bilad al-Sudan,* the Land of the Blacks.[1] The boundary markers of the European imperialists represented a futile exercise that had its beginnings a thousand years before Africa's thirty years war. The markers, now lost in the sands of the Sahara, the scrub of the Sahel, and the grass of the savanna, are a striking example of that imperial exhilaration in conquering marginal lands for disproportionate returns, which was justified by their cartographic sweep on published maps. Each imperialist, from Septimus Severus to Qaddafi, has had his own particular interests, but the drive for control of territory south of the Sahara has been continuous throughout the ages.

There was, of course, new technology that changed the means, but not the motivation, for war south of the Sahara. The pervasive influence of instant communications corrupted and replaced the gossip of the *suq* (the market) and the caravans. The media can now spread dissimulation, and the astonishing efficiency of the automatic weapon to destroy customary relationships between friends and enemies has escalated the price for blood on a frontier where revenge had by tradition a very high price. The more refined combat of the past was now characterized by the unlimited power of efficient weapons and the alarming realization that indiscriminate victory by superior firepower leads only to endless retaliation. All of the unwritten but immutable rules of the frontier to resolve disputes were now dissolved before the new tools of empire.

The dramatic disparity between the firepower of the past and of the present came at the beginning of the twentieth century and the arrival of the Europeans. On the Nile, Kitchener demolished the Khalifa of the Mahdi at Omdurman on 2 September 1898 with his Maxim guns. On the Chari, Major François Lamy destroyed the Sudanese freebooter Rabih Zubayr at Kusseri on 22 April 1900 with his repeating rifles. A hundred years later, the efficiency in defeating the enemy was inhibited only by the instructions on how to use the new imperial automatic instruments of destruction, particularly the Kalashnikov AK-47.

There were also new ideologies in this war of thirty years, but most were old camel saddles wrapped in new sheepskins. The most attractive appeal for late-twentieth-century Arab imperialism was the revival of Pan-Arabism in a variety of manifestations. It has been the secular goal of Muammar Qaddafi to recreate the Pan-Arab socialism espoused by Gamal Abd al-Nasser. The unity of the Arabs has been an inspiration for Arabs since their expansion in the seventh century. The efforts of Muammar Qaddafi to translate this ethnic effusion into an enlarged Arab state by the amalgamation of Arab nationalism and the remnants of European imperialism has met with little success, particularly among his neighbors who are Africans and not Arabs. The mercurial manipulations of Qaddafi to weld the Arabs together could hardly achieve what a thousand years of Arab conquest and culture has failed to accomplish.

His dreams for the resurgence of the Arabs were not improved by his support for international terrorism, which produced only condemnation from the international community and the mobilization of the security forces of the Western world. During this thirty years of war, terrorism became a legitimate weapon in the arsenal of Muammar Qaddafi. Terrorism is as old as history. The revolution in the devices of destruction, communication, and transportation has enabled terrorism to become international in scope, rather than its more local and parochial use in the past. The abduction and murder of the United States Ambassador Cleo A. Noel, Jr. and his Deputy Chief of Mission, George Curtis Moore, in March 1973 by the Palestinian terrorist organization Black September was the most conspicuous act of terrorism in the Sudan. Qaddafi certainly approved of the assassinations in response to the growing rapprochement between President Numayri, of Sudan, and the United States. Indeed, in the following year, 1974, he publicly demanded the assassination of Numayri, and his subsequent threats against the Sudanese president elicited the assistance of the United States security officials to his bodyguards. Hissene Habre was the recipient of numerous threats and attempts on his life that originated in Libya, undoubtedly with Qaddafi's knowledge. In West Africa there was no illusion among its leaders in the 1970s that the numerous warnings against their lives originated in Tripoli.

This is not surprising. The frontier between Libya, Chad, and the Sudan is a hostile environment. Its history, its ethnic loyalties, and its religious commitments have defined the responsibilities of those who, by birth or ability, were expected to lead. As for the chiefs, they often preferred their own survival to that of their followers. Many seized the opportunities, ironically provided by drought and war, to ensure their own advancement and preservation. The prerogative of leadership often involved the irresistible temptation to enrich oneself at the expense of those who had been defeated. The fine line between greed and survival was buried in the sands of the Sahara, the soil of the Sahel, and the loam of the savanna. Historians have been overwhelmed to explain the cataclysms of the twentieth century. The magnitude of the destruction of life and property in the past one hundred years has been attributed to historical factors and pervasive disintegrative forces. This is not true in Africa's thirty years war. This enervating conflict was as much the result of individual initiative, avaricious ambition, and malevolent motives as the more idealized and immutable demands of geography, commerce, religion, and ethnicity. The individuals indeed strut and fret to seek their own advantage and then are heard no more. They have left the stage now filled with death and destruction, "the sound and fury signifying nothing."

Beginning in the 1950s, drought exacerbated the historic isolation of the frontier between Libya, Chad, and the Sudan. Tripoli, Khartoum, and Ndjamena have refused to assume responsibility for providing food for those without. The traditional means for relieving the terror of drought for the peoples of the *Bilad al-Sudan* was destroyed by the same war that had devastated their spiritual beliefs and most certainly their trade. Ever since the end of the Pleistocene Era some five thousand years ago, Libya, Chad, and the Sudan have experienced periodic drought. Whether nature imposed its dearth and discipline upon man in cycles, patterns, or as the result of inexorable climatic change is irrelevant for those whose livelihood depends upon water. However, those who live in the *Bilad al-Sudan* have prepared for times of scarcity to avoid famine. The established means to cope with drought were never absolute, but they were successful for survival. In the past, famine was contained; in the present, the widespread devastation of modern warfare has prevented the flexibility and traditional means to avoid it. War is the principal cause of famine, not drought, whether in the fifth, the fifteenth, or the twentieth century. Unless warfare is resolved, all efforts of the international humanitarian community to alleviate famine will fail.

Crossing the Sahara

The hostile environment of the Sahara has impeded but has never prevented the crossing of the desert from the Mediterranean littoral to the *Bilad al-Sudan*, the Land of the Blacks, along the historic trans-Saharan caravan routes made possible by historic and strategic oases. These hazardous trails were used for commerce but seldom for conquest. The most ancient routes across the Sahara were far to the west: the Walata Road from the Senegal and the Taghaza Trail from the Niger ended in the great commercial center of Sijilmasa in southern Morocco. These were famous and profitable passages, but the three great caravan routes in the east, from the *Bilad al-Sudan* to Tripoli, were equally ancient and even more profitable. Two of them are the same routes Qaddafi's battalions and the Islamic Legionnaires followed into Chad at the end of the twentieth century. As early as 1500 B.C. the herdsmen of the Fezzan in Libya, known as the Garamantes, controlled these routes from their capital at Germa in the Wadi Ajal and used their horse-drawn chariots to raid north to the Mediterranean and south to the *Bilad al-Sudan*. The same routes are now patrolled by the jet fighters of the Libyan air force. By the fourth century B.C., the Phoenician trading cities of North Africa had evolved into independent commercial city-states trading across the desert with the land of the Blacks in Sudanic Africa through Ghadames and further east along the route named for its former rulers, the Garamantean Road.

Relations between the imperialists on the Mediterranean and those of the desert and beyond were no different in the past than at the end of the twentieth century. The control of the land was made possible by control of the caravan routes that passed through it. The Romans secured the routes from their southern frontier by the famous Legio III Augusta, which for two and a half centuries, far longer than Qaddafi's Islamic Legionnaires, kept the peace on the southern frontier of the Roman Empire. Muammar Qaddafi's more recent obsession with the Aozou Strip, his southern border with Chad, was not much different from that of L. Cornelius Balbus, who established a Roman outpost at Ghadames in 20 B.C. after defeating the Garamantes to occupy the Wadi Ajal. By the first century A.D., the Roman legions had secured the Garamantean Road through the Fezzan.

This was a sustained and heroic effort, but the effective control of the trans-Saharan routes was soon dramatically transformed by the camel revolution. The camel, indigenous to central Asia, did not appear in North Africa until the first century A.D. The camel walks at the same speed as man, two and a half miles per hour, thirty miles a day, over reasonable terrain with a load of 350 pounds for ten days without water. By the fourth century, the dependable gait and endurance of the camel had redefined the three traditional passages across the central and eastern Sahara. There was the Ghadames Road from the Niger at Gao up through Ghat and Ghadames to Tripoli. To the east lay the Garamantean Road, also known as the Bilma Trail, which skirted the sands south of Murzuk to pass between the two great mountain massifs, the Alhaggar to the west and the Tibesti to the east, to reach the Kawar oasis. From Kawar the route traversed the great *erg,* the sand dunes of Bilma, and its oasis and salt before reaching the savanna north of Lake Chad. This was the shortest and consequently the easiest route for commerce. Slaves and ivory were exchanged for salt. The most eastern route, the famous Darb al-Arbain, the Forty Days Road, began at Kobbei, twenty-five miles north of

El Fasher in Darfur. From this commercial emporium the route traversed the Libyan Desert to the Wadi Howar, passing through Bir Natrun, an important source for salt that sustained the camel nomads and provided them with an essential commodity to trade with the merchants in Kobbei in Darfur and Asyut in Egypt. This route carried the accumulated commerce of slaves and ivory from central and eastern Chad and Darfur to Egypt for a thousand years but is now a trail of desiccation and drought.

There was a fourth route from Benghazi through the Kufra oasis to Wadai that became an important avenue for trade across the Sahara when the caravan routes in the west were in decline during the nineteenth century. This eastern route across the implacable Libyan Desert was the most recent, having been established as late as 1810 by a Majabra merchant from Gialo (Jalu). The fortunes of these caravans were constrained by the difficult terrain until the Grand Sanusi, the Islamic reformer and entrepreneur and his successors, established their religious hostels and sanctuaries from Kufra and Wadai for merchants and pilgrims seeking the security of their persons and property. The Sanusiyya imposed their authority to settle the terms of trade and secured the route from Libya to Chad, which produced a symbiotic relationship between the merchants and the *talibes,* the students of the Grand Sanusi, through which both they and the brotherhood prospered. From Kufra, the Sanusiyya could control the trade and profit by commerce and revenue collected from custom duties. They also intensified their missionary efforts through the Fezzan, Kawar, Tibesti, Borkou, Ennedi, Darfur, Wadai, Kanem, and as far as Baguirmi. The Kufra Road, like the Garamantean Road (or Bilma Trail), provided an easy passage for the vehicles of Libyan imperialism in the twentieth century.

The three traditional crossings of the desert became regular highways of commerce, culture, and religion for the Arabs, who had come to Libya and North Africa first in the seventh century and later in the eleventh century. They were originally inspired to spread the word of God, but even as masters of the Arabian Desert equipped with the camel, they could not have developed the trans-Saharan crossings without their curious relationship with those who controlled the routes throughout the millennia. In the Sahara west of Chad, the Berbers and the Tuareg dominated the caravans. In the Fezzan and Borkou, Ennedi, and the Tibesti, known in the twentieth century as the B.E.T., the sands, rocks, oases, and the desert crossings are controlled by the Toubou, the descendants of those who lived in the Sahara long before the end of the Pleistocene Era. The Toubou are not Arabs. They speak a language of the Nilo-Saharan linguistic family, unrelated to the Afro-Asiatic languages of the Arabs. The Toubou, not the Arabs, are the cameleers of Africa who control the crossings of the Sahara from Libya, Chad, and the Sudan.

This man is the nomad, the great camel-nomad, grouped into formidable tribes. Each one of which, with no previous training, is a sort of natural regiment, speedy,

elusive, liable to appear at any moment, as unexpected as a catastrophe, from the un-
guarded wastes: a powerful military machine. And this great nomad, inured to the
privations of the desert, is as a result consumed with overwhelming lusts, greedy for
possessions and power; in his wretched poverty, this human savage confusedly
purses a constant dream of pillage and domination.[2]

The Toubou were the shepherds and security guards for the caravans that
passed along the Garamantean and Forty Days Roads bringing slaves and ivory
from the lands south of Lake Chad, for there was no gold. In return came cloth,
hardware, and horses for the cavalry of the Sudanic kingdoms. In the thirteenth
century, the *mai* (king) of Kanem, Dunama Dabelmi ibn Salwa, bragged that he
could put into the field 40,000 mounted warriors but neglected to mention that
no horse will charge massed camels. The most important commodity was not for
show but survival. Man cannot live without salt, and Africa south of the Sahara
has very little, whereas the Sahara has much. The Bilma oasis on the Garamantean Road was one of the great sources for rock salt, blocks of which were carried
by 20,000 camels to Chad in the annual Azalai salt caravan, whose escort was by
tradition the Kel Owi Tuareg. To the east, the salt from Bir Natrun was the principal commodity exchanged for slaves and ivory on the Darb al-Arbain, the Forty
Days Road from Darfur to Egypt.

There have been only two revolutions in technology that have influenced
trans-Saharan travel and been utilized by the Toubou. The first was the arrival of
the camel south of the Sahara, Sahel, and the Sudan in the fourth century A.D.
The second was the introduction during the twentieth century of the Toyota
truck. There is little difference between the two except the former is more disagreeable than the latter.

The Power of Belief

In the seventh and the eleventh centuries the Arabs came to Libya and North
Africa, adding their names to the list of invaders who had come in the past. The
first Arabs were warriors inspired and united by the teachings of Islam preached
by the Prophet Muhammad. He died in A.D. 632, and his followers responded to
his call to spread the word of God by the book, the Quran and, if necessary, by
the sword, the *jihad,* to the Africans beyond the sands of the Sahara. The Arabs
swept all before them across the Mediterranean littoral with uncompromising
speed. In A.D. 642, Cyrenaica was occupied and by A.D. 645, Tripolitania was included in the *Maghrib al-Wasith,* the Middle West of the Arab North African empire. The rapidity, enthusiasm, and unity of the initial Arab conquest in Africa
could not be sustained in the subsequent centuries, which were characterized by
internecine political and religious disputes. The Kharijites, the Ibadites, the Bani
Khattab, the Aghlabites, and the Rustemite family were all active in these early
centuries of Islam, whose Islamic militancy has resurfaced among the Islamists in

Libya and the Nile Valley at the end of the twentieth century. The arrival in the eleventh century of the Bani Hilal and the Bani Sulayman from Arabia by way of Nubia soon eclipsed these religious confrontations. This later wave of invasion was characterized by primitive, predatory Arab warrior tribes from the Hijaz, whose interests were more in plunder than politics or religion. Cyrenaica and Tripolitania were overrun by the Bani Sulayman, who eliminated their Fatimid rivals in order to promote their interests in the interior of Libya and down the routes to the south.

Throughout the centuries, Islam provided the spiritual bond that geographically united those on the Mediterranean shore with the desert nomads and Sudanic aristocracy. By A.D. 641, the Arabs had conquered Cyrenaica and Tripolitania, and from there they carried Islam across the Sahara to the *Bilad al-Sudan* more by commerce and persuasion than by the *jihad* that had characterized the North African conquests. The Muslims thrived among the mercantile communities in the towns whence their influence flowed to the courts of the kings. The Mansa of Mali, the Askiya of Songhay, and the Mai of Kanem and their courtiers, all acquired the prestige that the *Dar al-Islam* conferred upon its members. The rulers of the *Bilad al-Sudan* became members of a larger material and spiritual world through the piety, social order, literacy, and the knowledge of lands beyond the Sahara obtained from the *mallam,* the Muslim learned men.

Islam experienced a great revival in the nineteenth century. After several centuries of decline, this restoration of Islam in the Muslim world was made manifest in Libya, Chad, and the Sudan by two Islamic reform movements. Although the reformers differed in the details of their teachings and in personality, they both sought to sweep away the corruption of Islam by the Turks and the West and to replace it with a reformation based on the Quran, the *hadith* of the Prophet, and the message of the guided ones. In Libya, the reformer Sayyid Muhammad ibn Ali al-Sanusi al Khattabi al-Idrisi al-Hasani sought to carry out this mission on the northern shore of the Mediterranean. In the Sudan, Muhammad Ahmad ibn al-Sayyid Abd Allah, al-Mahdi, sought to restore Islam on the Nile.

Muhammad ibn Ali al-Sanusi was born near Mustaghanim in Algeria about 1787. He founded his Islamic reform *tariqa* (brotherhood), the Sanusiyya, in 1837 at Mt. Abu Qubais near Mecca. Six years later he returned to Africa and settled at Jabal Akhdar in Cyrenaica. Here in the *Zawiya al-Baida,* the White Monastery, his learning and charisma attracted a large following of *talibes* (students) from Arabia, North Africa, and the Sudan. The followers of the Sanusi Order have since been a powerful religious and revolutionary force in Libya, Chad, and the Sudan. Upon al-Sanusi's death in 1859, his eldest son, Muhammad al-Mahdi, succeeded as Grand Sanusi. Muhammad al-Mahdi expanded the brotherhood with the profits from the opening of the Kufra Road, by which the Sanusiyya intensified their missionary and commercial networks throughout the Fezzan, Kawar, the Tibesti, Borku, the Ennedi Plateau, Darfur, Wadai, Kanem, and as far as Baguirmi. Here in the south, in the Sahel and savanna of Chad, the teachings of the Grand Sanusi were unacceptable to the non-Arab, non-Muslim Africans, particularly where they were governed by the Christian French. Not only were the French an immediate challenge to the expanding Islamic empire of the Sanusiyya at the end of the nineteenth century, but their imperial adventures in Chad appeared to represent a revival of a thousand years of Christian and Muslim rivalry for the souls of Africans. The French destroyed the Islamic religious outpost and school *(zawiya)* of the Sanusiyya at Bir Alali in January 1902. In 1906 they took Kawar and Bilma. The following year Ayn Galakka was overrun, and Sidi Muhammad al-Barrani, the most successful Sanusi missionary in the Sahel, died in the fighting. By 1914 the French had successfully terminated the influence of the empire of the Sanusiyya at a time when the brotherhood was equally hard-pressed by the Italians in Tripolitania and Cyrenaica. The Sanusiyya were also beset by internal disputes and probably could not have sustained their political control over such a vast territory even if the Europeans had not coveted the sand, rock, and wind of the Sahara and Sahel. There can be no doubt, however, that the historic crusade by both Christians and Muslims for the control of souls had been firmly implanted in Chad during the first half of the twentieth century, and it would be revived by Muammar Qaddafi in the second.

If the Grand Sanusi represented the continuity of Islam across the Sahara from the Mediterranean, Muhammad Ahmad ibn al-Sayyid Abd Allah, al-Mahdi was the manifestation of the Islamic revival west of the Nile. In June 1881 on Aba Island in the White Nile south of Khartoum, Muhammad Ahmad declared himself to be the "Expected Mahdi" to restore Islam from its corruption by the Turks and to bring peace and justice to the Sudanese. Influenced by the teachings from the Wahhabite movement in Arabia and the Sanusiyya in Cyrenaica, his teachings demanded the reform of Islam by a return to the fundamental tenets of Islam. Like Abd al-Wahhab and the Grand Sanusi, the Mahdi was attracted to Islamic mysticism, or Sufism, which he incorporated into his teachings and which had a compelling appeal to the rural tribesmen from the western provinces of the Egyptian Sudan, Kordofan, and Darfur. Although the Sanusiyya kept their distance from the Mahdists, many of the peoples from the frontier sultanates between Wadai and Darfur were attracted to the Mahdi's teachings, and generally there was respect between the followers of the two Muslim reform movements.

Although the Turco-Egyptian government in Khartoum viewed the Mahdi as only an administrative nuisance, the Baggara Arabs, cattle nomads, of Darfur rallied to him with alacrity and enthusiasm. During the eighteenth century in Chad, the Baggara had employed their military talents as mercenaries for the sultanates in Bornu, Kanem, Baguirmi, and Wadai and helped to subdue and to drive the Africans from the Chad basin. By the end of the century, they and their cattle had wandered eastward to settle in the sparsely populated plains of southern Darfur, where their presence challenged the Dinka to the south and the Fur to the north for pasture and political control. The call by the Mahdi to the *jihad* to restore

Islam proved irresistible. Here was the opportunity to consolidate the Baggara presence in Darfur, to plunder, and to destroy their Turkish overlords all in the service of God. On 5 November 1883 the Baggara were in the vanguard of the *Ansar,* the followers, of the Mahdi that annihilated 10,000 Egyptian troops at Shaykan. Ever since, the western provinces of the Sudan, Darfur, and Kordofan have been the fortresses of Mahdism. Even in the political ferment that led to the independence of the Sudan in the 1956, Darfur and the western frontier were always considered peripheral to the Sudanese in Khartoum and by the Nile. Darfur was ignored, dismissed as the impregnable religious redoubt of Sayyid Abd al-Rahman al-Mahdi, the posthumous son of the Mahdi and the heir to his revolutionary religious tradition. Like the that of the Grand Sanusi, the Mahdi's *jihad* was a driving force of Islamic reform, which a century later has been ruthlessly suppressed by the new reformers, the Islamists of Hasan al-Turabi.

The Bonds of Blood

The conquest of the lands across the Sahara has been dependent upon the fissiparous and fiercely independent desert nomads, the Bedouin, who know no boundaries but enjoy the deep loyalty of their kin, their tribe, who follow its herds. Kinship was the cement that solidified the primitive and predatory Arab tribes of the Bani Hilal and the Bani Sulayman, who overran Cyrenaica and Tripolitania in the eleventh century. The Bani Hilal proceeded into the sunset to the ends of the Maghrib. The Bani Sulayman remained behind in Libya where they eliminated their Fatimid rivals to Arabize and reinforce the early teachings of Islam among the Bedouins, teachings they later imported to the interior of Libya, the Sahara, and the Sahel of northern Chad.

In Libya, Chad, and the Sudan the juxtaposition of mobile desert nomads and sedentary Sahelian and savanna agriculturalists has resulted in a conflict over control of the land and the marketplace, which has been determined throughout the centuries more by kin than religion. The history of the non-Arab, nomadic influence in the Sahel and savanna has been governed by the need of these peripatetic peoples to find space for their herds in a harsh environment. They had the mobility to respond to changing economic and political situations of desert trade, politics, and warfare. To survive the vicissitudes of man and nature required the ability, within the immutable demands of kinship, to maneuver geographically and politically in order to achieve personal security. Territory was of little consequence when compared to personal relationships, the trust in those of shared blood and the unassailable descent from a common ancestor. These were the immutable ties of a nomadic society. These loyalties permitted the seemingly contradictory behavior of collaboration with the enemy, on the one hand, and resistance to him, on the other. Nomadic peoples coalesced and disintegrated less by a commitment to religion than by genealogical disputes, personal greed, or calamities of nature and warfare. All three have forced beleaguered survivors to seek sanctuary with kinsmen or, in time of greater stress, survival within the tribe.

The history of Chad is closely tied to its ethnicity. A state whose territory was defined by European imperialists at the end of the nineteenth century has been determined by ethnic loyalties in the twentieth. There are the Zaghawa from the Sahara, who came to Chad ten centuries ago and who play a prominent role in *Africa's Thirty Years War.* There are the Toubou, members of the Nilo-Saharan linguistic family, the Black nomads whose heartland is the Tibesti massif.

A place of relative amenity and final refuge which, in a largely hostile world, a handful of men may successfully defend. Water is always present, as are thin mountain pastures just sufficient for flocks, if not herds, and upland valleys where a few palms and crops may be tended. "Here, in a remote corner in the depths of the Libyan Desert refuge, a little piece of the ancient negro Sahara has preserved itself more or less intact."[3]

The Tunjur came to Wadai from Darfur and are now forgotten.

Before the arrival of the Europeans there was a second nomadic intrusion into the central Sudan by the Arab Awlad al-Sulayman that contributed to the steady deterioration of the Sudanic states. Claiming descent from the Bani Sulayman, who migrated into Libya from upper Egypt in the eleventh century, the Awlad Sulayman united their fissiparous lineages to confront the imperial ambitions of the Turks and the French. Driven from the Fezzan by the Ottoman Turks in 1842, the survivors went south into northern Chad where they raided with impunity until the arrival of the Sanusiyya. The appearance of the Sanusiyya at the end of the nineteenth century exacerbated the divisions within the Awlad Sulayman, which were soon exploited by the French as they imposed their imperial authority. Although the Awlad Sulayman never constituted more than a third of the inhabitants of northern and central Chad, they represented the Arab in a land of the Toubou. Their presence has led to the vagaries of diplomatic, political, and military loyalties during the thirty years war. The ethnic rivalry between Arab and Toubou, who dominated the lands north of Lake Chad, was ameliorated but never resolved by the tenuous bond of Islam.

The Sara was the last wave in the great Bantu migration from Cameroon. They arrived in southern Chad in the eighteenth century where they established themselves among the disparate cultivators in the valleys of the Chari and Logone Rivers. They had no unifying allegiance except their hostility to the incomers—Arab, Toubou, or European. Each had exploited and oppressed them, the last of whom were the French. They introduced the cultivation of cotton as a cash crop in the 1920s, which evolved into a productive cotton belt, known to the French as the *Tchad-Utile.* Its cultivation, collection, and profits were controlled by the French consortium COTONFRAN, but the Sara, now one-third of the population of Chad, prospered and consequently established political dominance over the more disparate indigenous Africans of southern Chad.

Although the Sara and the linguistically related peoples (Adamawa-Eastern) of the savanna, woodlands, and rivers of southern Chad were admirably suited to their environment, their social, political, and spiritual structure could not accept with equanimity the challenge by the invaders from the north or from the south into the Ubangi-Chari. Their localized societies, identifying with lineage rather than tribe and with the village rather than the state, were unable to repel or to accommodate those organized for expansion. Thus the militant Sudanic and European states readily imposed their authority over these African societies, justifying their conquest and plunder by religious conversion. The cultivators of southern Chad represented a human repository from which the Sudanic kingdoms of the *Bilad al-Sudan* acquired a steady supply of slaves, the most important and profitable commodity of the trans-Saharan trade.

The French administration of the Ubangi-Chari was hardly distinguishable from the *razzia* of the Arabs of the past. It was replaced by the *corvée,* forced labor, to grow cotton or to build the right-of-way of the Chemin de Fer du Congo-Océan, the Congo-Ocean railway to connect Brazzaville with Pointe Noire on the Atlantic. The human cost of its construction was 15,000 dead African conscripts from the corvée.

In Abeche the French had initiated an aggressive policy that had its origins in their Nile policy at the end of the nineteenth century. Its failure had reduced the imposition of their imperial authority to Wadai by a puppet sultan, Adam Acyl, a grandson of the Sultan Muhammad al-Sharif. He could rule in Wadai, despite his illegitimate title, in peace but not in war. During the tumultuous years of World War I, the Sultan in Constantinople appealed to his fellow Muslims on the frontiers of Islam to join the *jihad* against his French and British enemies on the Western Front. Those in Wadai and the frontier sultanates of Dar Masalit, Dar Tama, Dar Sila, and Dar Qimr were attracted to the call of Islam, the intensity of which the French had experienced in the last century in Algeria and the Western Sudan and the British at Khartoum. To assert French authority in Wadai and over the frontier sultanates, the Tirailleurs Sénégalais ruthlessly subdued dissent, as did the British in Darfur. "Between 1913 and 1918" Wadai lost "60 percent of its population, most by starvation, which was a result of the colonial conquest."[4]

Boundaries and Frontiers

A boundary is a stark and precise line delimited either by a ruler on empty maps in a stateroom of a European capital or on the ground by instruments to place markers of metal or stone. The boundary between Libya, Chad, and the Sudan did not exist before the twentieth century and was meant to define national sovereignty, not frontiers. A frontier is a wide swath of land usually contested for control or ownership throughout time. The frontier of Libya, Chad, and the Sudan sweeps across the Sahara of southern Libya and northern Chad, the Fezzan, and the B.E.T. (Borkou, Ennedi, and the Tibesti) to turn south across the Sahel of Darfur and Wadai and the fertile savanna. It ultimately disappears amid the gallery and tropical rain forests of the Congo.

The boundaries to demarcate the imperial conquests of Britain and France between Chad and the Sudan became necessary when France signed the Anglo-French Declaration of 21 March 1899, by which Great Britain and France defined their respective spheres of influence to deny French access to the Nile. France was given Equatorial and Saharan Africa, Chad. Geographically ignorant, the British and French representatives agreed to arbitrary boundaries, the final delimitation of which was not completed for another sixteen years. During 1922 and 1923, the Franco-British Boundary Commission of political officers and surveyors plodded down the elusive frontier between Wadai and Darfur. Their recommendations were subsequently incorporated into the Anglo-French protocol of 10 January 1924, which defines the boundary between Chad and the Sudan to this day.

The personalities of imperialism and the new technology to support their ambitions were part of twentieth-century nationalism. The French came from the south, the British from the east, and the Italians from the north. Although the Anglo-French Declaration of 1899 divided their respective spheres of influence in the *Bilad al-Sudan,* it did not presume to dispose of Ottoman Libya, despite the fact that it was wedged between the French in Algeria and Chad and the British on the Nile in Egypt and the Sudan. There was another party with historic claims to colonial and strategic interests in Libya. Italy had become a unified nation in 1870, and the Italian nationalists regarded Italian imperialism as a verification of Italy as a world power not to be ignored in the partition of Africa. The Italians declared war against Turkey on 29 September 1911. Their ambition was to fulfill *una fatalita storica,* a historic destiny to make the *Mare Nostrum,* the Mediterranean, an "Italian Strait," a narrow channel from the heel of the Italian boot to Libya, "a potential base for the Italian penetration of Africa to Lake Chad and beyond."[5]

Until the twentieth century, modern Libya did not exist. Its western boundary was defined between the Italians and the French in 1919. The eastern boundary was confirmed in the Italian-Egyptian Treaty of 1925. That treaty, however, did not resolve the dispute over the Sara Triangle, a geometric definition of worthless territory claimed by the Sudan and left over from the divisions of Libya, Chad, and the Sudan between France and Britain in 1899. Hungry for any territory, no matter if it contained only sand and gravel, and sand of such poor quality that it could not even make glass, Mussolini asserted his claim as part of the inheritance of Italy to Turkish rights. The British were not about to quibble with Italy over the Sara Triangle. On 20 July 1934 Mussolini acquired more Saharan sands and the oasis of Ma'tan as-Sarra, which was transformed a half century later by Muammar Qaddafi into a major air base, the headquarters for Libyan intrusion into Darfur, and a center for mobilization in the invasion of Chad.

No sooner had Mussolini acquired the Sara Triangle than he demanded Aozou from the French. In January 1935 Pierre Laval, the new French foreign minister, arrived in Rome. He was anxious for a rapprochement between Italy and France, which would confirm his legitimacy as a diplomat and recognize the dynamism of the New Rome of Mussolini. He readily agreed on 7 January 1935 to the rectification of the frontier between Italian Libya and French Equatorial Africa (Chad), which would add 45,000 square miles of sand and a fringe of mountainous desert in the Tibesti to the Italian colony in Libya, a cheap bargain at any price. This treaty was never ratified by the Chamber of Deputies in Paris, but its legacy was a distorted rectangle of worthless territory known as the Aozou Strip, which became the passionate quest for Muammar Qaddafi that resulted in so much bloodshed during Africa's thirty years war. In 1931–1932 Commandant Ogier of the B.E.T. was instructed to delineate a boundary that would safeguard French interests in Equatorial Africa while keeping the Italians "at a sufficient distance from Lake Chad to prevent the possibility of any threat to communications between French West Africa and French Equatorial Africa."[6]

Boundaries define states; frontiers define peoples. The conquest and control of the expansive frontier between Libya, Chad, and the Sudan has been the ambition of Romans, Greeks, Arabs, Turks, Italians, French, British, and Africans. There is no rational explanation for this obsession. The Libya-Chad-Sudan frontier is not only one of the most remote regions of the earth but one of the most worthless. It encompasses little more than sand, rock, and wind interrupted by the occasional oasis or a well-watered wadi in the canyons of the Fezzan, the Tibesti, and the Ennedi Plateau. The great mountain massif of Jabal Marra on the Chad-Darfur frontier is a fertile garden in an arid plain that gradually receives the rain from the south Atlantic to produce more-fertile pastures that extend south into the rain forests of the Congo. These grasslands of the Sahel and the savanna have supported states and sultanates throughout the ages, but they were not sufficient to provide for the state or its inhabitants when a struggle for the finite resources disrupted the profitable routes of pilgrimage and trade. In the nineteenth century the sultanate of Wadai in Chad sought to dominate the frontier as did the sultanate of Darfur in the Sudan. Their rivalry was not only between themselves; it also encompassed their ability to exert their authority over the petty but fiercely independent frontier sultanates of Dar Kuti, Dar Runga, Dar Masalit, Dar Sila, Dar Qimr, and Dar Tama on what ultimately became the imperial boundary. These small and insignificant constituencies derived their disproportionate strength not from their size and numbers but from their ethnicity and an acute ability to play their more powerful suzerains in Darfur and Wadai to their own advantage on a volatile frontier.

In the nineteenth century the sultanate of Wadai in eastern Chad emerged as a dominant power on the frontier to expand west into Bornu and southwest into the decaying frontier kingdom of Baguirmi. The origins of Wadai are obscure, but in the seventeenth century the Maba, like the Toubou, spoke a Nilo-Saharan language and were led by the legendary Abd al-Karim who built his capital at Wara, introduced Islam, and founded a dynasty that ruled Wadai until 1915. After his death, the history of Wadai was characterized by succession struggles and the evolution of an aristocracy under an absolute monarch. The principal preoccupation of both feudal lords and the ruler was the defense of the sultanate and its expansion at the expense of the kingdom of Bornu to the west and the sultanate of Darfur to the east.

Islam was the state religion, but its acceptance among the cultivators and herders was either casual or ignored in preference to the traditional, non-Islamic, and accepted religious rituals. The power of the state depended upon its agricultural and pastoral resources, but its prosperity was derived from the trade in slaves obtained by its own *razzias* and those of its tributaries in order to supply the trans-Saharan caravans with an increasing number of slaves for the Ottoman Empire and Asia. It was no coincidence that Wadai was able to expand its authority on the frontier with Darfur when the new eastern trans-Saharan caravan route from Benghazi to Wadai was opened in the first decade of the nineteenth century to bring firearms for slaves. The eastern route flourished, particularly from 1875 to 1900, in commercial if not religious alliance with the Sanusiyya and, after 1881, prospered from the closing of the Darb al-Arbain, the Forty Days Road, from the Darfur to Egypt by the intervention of the Mahdist state.

The expanding economy of Wadai was mobilized by able and energetic sultans to consolidate their authority against the relentless challenge by the sultans of Darfur. In 1838, a Fur military expedition routed the army of Wadai and reduced the authority of the sultan to that of a tributary subject until the independence and prosperity of Wadai was once again established by Muhammad al-Sharif and confirmed by his successors throughout the nineteenth century. While a young prince, Muhammad al-Sharif had made the *hajj* to Mecca where he met Muhammad ibn Ali al-Sanusi, the Grand Sanusi, with whom he forged a close friendship. He embraced the Sanusi Order and profited from its control of the eastern trade route through the Sanusi strongholds of Jalu and Kufra. The profits for Muhammad al-Sharif enabled him to build a new capital at Abeche in 1850 after his armies had defeated those of the *shehu* of Bornu in 1846. In the south he reasserted his authority over the frontier kingdom of Baguirmi, but relations with Darfur degenerated into raid and counter-raid across the petty frontier sultanates, which only escalated misery for the inhabitants and provided little plunder for the raiders. The sultans of Wadai and Darfur both failed to secure their ambitions to rule when they did not have the power to protect those they sought to tax.[7]

In Chad, the other significant frontier state was the Kingdom of Baguirmi, located southeast of Lake Chad. The people of Baguirmi spoke languages of the Adamawa-Eastern family of southern Chad and the great Niger-Congo family of Africa and had no linguistic and little cultural relation with the Toubou, Fur, and Arabs. The history of Baguirmi has been one of constant warfare to acquire slaves from the south to purchase independence or to pay the demands for tribute from powerful neighbors, particularly Wadai. During the sixteenth century the sun kings, *mbang*, forged an imperial state in which the official religion was Islam. During the seventeenth and eighteenth centuries *mbang* Burkumanda I (1635–1655) consolidated the state, and his formidable armies extended the influence of Baguirmi as far north as Lake Chad. Their revenues came from the tariff levied on slaves sent down the Garamantean Road, or Bilma Trail, to Tripoli. Slaves were the fundamental commodity of the Kingdom of Baguirmi. They were chattels for the trans-Saharan trade, agricultural laborers for local estates, retainers for the *mbang* and the nobility *(maladonge)*, and eunuchs and concubines for the Ottoman Empire. The dependence on slavery and its trade was the principal cause for the decline of the kingdom. In 1805 Sultan Sabun of Wadai launched a brutal offensive against Baguirmi. His army captured the capital of Massenya but, in uncharacteristic fashion, slaughtered the *mbang* and all those inhabitants who were not enslaved. Baguirmi never recovered. It was plundered for slaves by the sultans of Wadai and the Sudanese freebooter Rabih Zubayr throughout the 1890s. In desperation, *mbang* Gaugrang II surrendered his kingdom to the French in 1897 to preserve his authority but in fact to consign it to oblivion for a half century. When the French retired in 1960, their withdrawal revived the long African memories of the Kingdom of Baguirmi, reviving dreams of reclaiming its historic role on the frontier.

The historic confrontation between Wadai and Darfur on this volatile frontier was determined as much by the relations of their respective sultans with their patrons and the petty border sultans and chieftains as by their own armies. During the past two hundred years, the resources for Wadai have come from the north down the trans-Saharan caravan routes. The resources for the Darfur have come from the Jabal Marra massif, which captures the moisture from the south Atlantic to water the fertile farms of the Fur. Their produce provided the resources for the Kingdom of Darfur. The orientation of the sultanate, however, has remained eastward to the Nile, whether through Kordofan to Khartoum or up the Darb al-Arbain to Asyut in Egypt. The relationship between Darfur and the Nile was always as ambivalent as the symbiotic contact with their northern Toubou, Zaghawa, neighbors, who came south in search of pasture and were anxious to trade the commodities of their animals for the produce from the fields of the Fur. The establishment of the Fur sultanate on this isolated western frontier is attributed to a historical leader, Sulayman Solongdungo (c.1650–1680), the founder of the Keira dynasty. Neither the Fur nor the Toubou, both speaking Nilo-Saharan languages, were responsible, however, for the introduction of Islam into Darfur. The conversion of the king and his subjects was the work of the *fuqura*, the holy men from the Nile. They applied their powers of religious persuasion and piety to instill deep devotion to Islam among the peoples of the *Bilad al-Sudan*, committing this western kingdom to the Nile rather than to the Mediterranean. In 1787 Muhammad Tayrab, the seventh sultan, extended the Fur sultanate to the Nile by conquering the Funj province of Kordofan to the east and opening Darfur to the expanding international commerce of the seventeenth and eighteenth centuries.

In 1792 his successor, Abd al-Rahman, founded a permanent capital at El Fasher, which is an emporium to this day for the Ja'alyyin traders from the Northern Sudan, Khartoum, and the Nile.

In the nineteenth century, Darfur began a tempestuous passage through a sand sea of troubles. In 1821 the sultanate was overrun by the forces of Muhammad Ali, the Viceroy of Egypt seeking an empire in the Nile Basin, but Darfur was a remote sultanate whose isolation enabled it to regain its independence within a few years and to retain it for another half century. None of the Turco-Egyptian governors-general in Khartoum were able to exert their imperial authority over the sultanate of Darfur or the western frontier. Their embarrassing impotency in the west was demonstrated by Zubayr Pasha Rahma Mansur, the extraordinary Ja'ali entrepreneur from the riverine Northern Sudan who had built a vast commercial empire in the Southern Sudan for the export of ivory and slaves.[8] In November 1874 he extended his commercial empire in the West on behalf of the governors-general in Khartoum when his private army defeated the Fur at the battle of al-Manawashi. The sultan, Ibrahim Qarad, was killed, El Fasher was occupied, and Zubayr established his authority over the recalcitrant frontier petty sultanates of Dar Masalit, Dar Tama, Dar Qimr, and Dar Sila. This was one of the few brief moments in history when the frontier had been stabilized.

This extraordinary achievement was short-lived. Zubayr was placed under house arrest in Cairo, but his empire in Darfur dissolved not because of his absence. In 1881 the appeal of the Mahdist revolution for religious reform was answered with alacrity and enthusiasm by the Fur and the Baggara alike in order to be rid of the hated Turks and the Ja'ali mercantile imperialist from the Nile. The *Ansar* (followers) of the Mahdi swept all before them in the west. They annihilated an Egyptian army of 10,000 men at Shaykan in Kordofan in November 1883. They then turned Darfur into a violent battleground, not unlike the present, between the Mahdists with their zeal for reform and the Fur, whose traditions of independence and ancestral worship were incompatible with the social pretensions and economic positions of those coming from the Nile. The Mahdists suppressed rebellion in Darfur and on the western frontier, where the opposition to the Mahdists was led by a *faqi,* a holy man, from Dar Tama, Muhammad Zayn, known in history as Abu Jummayza. His army was a haphazard coalition of warriors from the frontier sultanates who were crushed by the *Ansar* outside of El Fasher on 22 January 1889. Thereafter, Mahmud Ahmad, the Mahdist *amir* ruled Darfur until the collapse of the Mahdist state and the return of Ali Dinar Zakariya Muhammad al-Fadl.

Ali Dinar was a dynamic sultan determined as much to secure his own person as that of his subjects. Restored to his inheritance, he revived the power of the Fur as clients of the new British masters on the Nile, which would guarantee them autonomy if not independence. His return fortuitously coincided with the decline of the hitherto dominant influence of Wadai on the frontier with the death of its powerful sultan Ibrahim ibn Yusuf ibn Muhammad Sharif. With Wadai in disarray and Ali Dinar unable to impose his authority beyond Darfur, security on the frontier had to await the arrival of the next wave of invaders, the Europeans. The French occupied Abeche in 1902; the British conquered Darfur in 1916. Both were ephemeral imperial enterprises that intruded upon the ancient relationships of those who lived on the frontier of Libya, Chad, and the Sudan.

Implacable Imperialism

Historically, the motivation for acquiring worthless territory in the Sahara, Sahel, and the *Bilad al-Sudan* has been defined by kings, rulers, chieftains, warriors, *shaykhs,* and *fuqura* (holy men), whether advancing from the Mediterranean, the Chari, or the Nile, as the conquest of Chad. Their motivations throughout two millennia are certainly complex. On the one hand, they appear to be driven by their own personal needs or desires. On the other, their conquests have been rationalized as the pursuit of prosperity as derived through the acquisition of empire. There has always been the determination to enhance prestige, the symbols of which are preserved in the statuary and shrines of the conquerors and the graves of the victims. The conquest, occupation, and presumably the exploitation of these marginal wastelands of the Saharan, Sahel, and the savanna were always disproportionate to the return. Africa's thirty years war in Libya, Chad, and the Sudan was yet another manifestation of this imperial goal. It embodied the exhilaration of conquest and the implantation of ethnic and religious orthodoxy over those who had not been so blessed by a higher civilizing influence. More exciting for the successful participants was the exhilaration of painting their national colors on the maps of sand. Each imperialist had his own particular objectives, but the continuity of their ambitions in Libya, Chad, and the Sudan differed very little throughout the millennia. The Greeks, Romans, Arabs, Berbers, and Turks represent the old imperialism of the ancients. The French, British, Italians, and the Libyans represent the new imperialism of the nationalists. Every imperialist, whether ancient or modern, sought territory, security, or the control of resources, and they differed more by means than by motivation.

The new imperialists in Libya, Chad, and the Sudan consisted of many personalities whose interests were dominated more by personal ambition, greed, and survival than ideology, principle, or self-sacrifice. As chief, *shaykh,* sultan, king, or one of the new European educated elite, they often preferred their own survival to that of their followers. Many seized the opportunities of momentary power, often made accessible by drought or war, to ensure their own preservation and advancement. The prerogative of leadership entitled one to the irresistible temptation to enrich oneself at the expense of those who had been defeated or outmaneuvered in the marketplace. The fine line between greed and survival was buried in the sands of the Sahara, the soil of the Sahel, and the loam of the savanna.

The imperialism of the past and present was certainly driven by personalities and ideologies, but the new imperialism of the nationalists in the twentieth century has succeeded not by charismatic leadership nor an appeal to the Faith, but by the new tools of empire. The new technology of weaponry changed the former conduct of African war to make it more efficient and to confirm upon the imperial condottiere of this century of any ethnicity a moral superiority for their conquests by superior weapons. Their new technology changed the means but not the motivation for war south of the Sahara. The pervasive influence of instant communications corrupted and replaced the gossip of the *suq* and the caravans.

Imperial Italy came from the north in 1911 to revive the empire of the Romans in the sands of the Sahara. The Italians easily defeated the Turks but not the Arab and Toubou until 1931, when they hanged Sidi Umar al-Mukhtar, the lion of the desert and for twenty years the leader of the Sanusi insurgency against Italian imperialism. On 15 May 1936 after the Italian conquest of Ethiopia, Benito Mussolini proclaimed the birth the New Rome and its emperor, King Victor Emmanuel of Italy.

French imperialism in Africa was neither consistent nor formulated in Paris. It was decided by more by the *officiers sudannais,* the headstrong and ambitious French officers in Africa, than civil servants in France. They were men of action equipped with modern weapons and modest intellect who cultivated insubordination to a heroic art in order to carry out a forward policy in the Sahara and the western Sudan. Their campaigns were against those Muslims who had sought to reform Islam in the nineteenth century to repel the European Christian invaders, as had their coreligionists during the Crusades. The defeat of the Sanusiyya by the French was a continuation of this confrontation between Crusaders and Muslims in the African Sahara and Sahel in the twentieth century.

British imperialism had demonstrated its imperial success on the Nile by its victory on the plains of Karari outside Omdurman on 2 September 1898. The British objective was to secure the Suez Canal for their Oriental Empire. The canal, however, was dependent upon Cairo, whose safety could be obtained only by control of the Nile waters and not the acquisition of a remote and well-known turbulent frontier far to the west, which was best left to the traditional ruler, Ali Dinar.

Although it is doubtful that Ali Dinar could have survived long in an imperial age, he precipitated his own downfall by a perilous combination of the arrogance of one from the frontier and the ignorance of one who knows little of the world beyond it. Long suspicious of his loyalty, the British authorities in Khartoum were not amused by his notification that he would no longer pay his paltry tribute. In 1916 there were very heavy casualties and no progress on the Western Front. In the Middle East, the Arab revolt against the Turks in the Hijaz required inspiration from the intricacies of oriental negotiations. Britain and France were quite prepared to give away the sands, the Sahel, and the savanna of Libya and Chad to Italy in return for a military alliance against Austria and Germany. The British authorities in the Sudan were not unlike their French counterparts in Chad. They were imperial, confident in their abilities to govern, and assured in their knowledge of the people they ruled that their administration would prevail and maintain civil and social tranquillity. They were right. On 22 May 1916 at Beringia east of El Fasher, the Fur army of Ali Dinar was decisively defeated. Ali Dinar fled to Jabal Marra where he remained a fugitive until trapped and killed by Major H. J. Huddleston, later governor-general of the Sudan. "We came on a thick-built form, with a strong and dignified face marred only by cruel, sensuous lips, with a bullet drilled through the centre of his forehead. It was 'Ali Dinar."[9]

Only fools would believe that the death of Ali Dinar was the end of the sultans or that the age of imperial ambition was over.

Notes

1. *Bilad al-Sudan* was the name given to the savanna south of the Sahara from the Atlantic to the Red Sea by the medieval Muslim geographers from which the more modern names of states have derived their titles.

2. Quoted in John Wright, *Libya, Chad, and the Central Sahara* (London: John Hurst, 1989), p. 15, from E.-F. Gautier, *Le Passé de l'Afrique du Nord* (Paris: Payot, 1937), p. 209.

3. Quoted in Wright, *Libya, Chad, and the Central Sahara*, p. 19, from E.-F. Gautier, *Le Sahara*, (Paris: Payot, 1950), p. 136.

4. Benyamin Neuberger, *Involvement, Invasion, and Withdrawal: Qadhadhafi's Libya and Chad, 1969–1981* (Tel Aviv: Tel Aviv University Occasional Paper, no. 83, May 1982), p. 13.

5. John Wright, *Libya* (New York: Praeger, 1969), p. 121.

6. Bernard Lanne, *Tchad-Libye: La Querelle des frontières* (Paris: Éditions Karthala, 1982), pp. 29, 129–153. For a text of the Franco-Italian accords signed by Mussolini and Laval on 7 January 1935, known as the Treaty of Rome, and Ogier's delimitation for which he was criticized by his fellow officers for giving away too much, see Lanne, *Tchad-Libye*, pp. 131–135, 152–153; and "Trattato fra l'Italia e la Francia, del 7 gennaio, 1935, per regolare I loro interessi in Africa," *Oriente Moderno* 15, no. 7, Title 2 (Rome: Instituto per l'Oriente, 1935): 308–309.

7. Lidwien Kapteijns, *Mahdist Faith and Sudanic Tradition: The History of the Masalit Sultanate, 1870–1930* (London: KPI, 1985), p. 15.

8. *Ja'ali* is the term used by those west of the Nile for the riverine Arabs who congregated in the villages along the Nile north of the confluence of the Blue and White Niles and who have traditionally claimed descent from Al-Abbas, the uncle of the Prophet. As merchants they represented traditional trade but also the Arab imperialism from the river, whether past or present.

9. J. A. Gillan, "Darfur 1916," *Sudan Notes and Records* 22, no. 1 (1939): 21–23.

2

Chad: An African Conundrum

In September 1958 the few inhabitants of Chad who were eligible to vote under French electoral rules decided that they no longer wished to be a part of any formal French connection. After the polls had closed, 182,000 Chadians had expressed a desire to become a self-governing republic within the French Community, first visualized by General Charles de Gaulle, the leader of the Free French in World War II, and made explicit in his famous Brazzaville Declaration in January 1944. General Charles de Gaulle had preferred strong, centralized postcolonial governments in postcolonial Africa, but the difference in economic and political sophistication within the French administrative units that constituted French Equatorial Africa clearly required reorganization. The Central African Republic sought a loose confederation; Gabon wanted close ties with metropolitan France; the French Congo went one way, French Cameroon another. Chad was the impoverished stepchild. Almost unnoticed, on 11 August 1960—sixty years after the creation of the Territoire Militaire des Pays et Protectorate du Tchad—the Republic of Chad was born.[1]

The Republic of Chad was not only one of the poorest of Africa's new nations, it was a landlocked creation of convenience from the scramble and partition of Africa at the end of the nineteenth century. Of its three and a half million inhabitants only a few thousand were literate, and they mostly congregated in the ramshackle colonial outposts of Abeche and Fort Lamy. Fort Lamy was the capital and administrative center of French imperialism. Its location had been determined more by the triumph of French arms over Rabih Zubayr, one of the last great African warlords, than the fortuitous neutral ground where the Muslim and Arabs from the north had long intermingled with the Christians and Africans from the south. For twenty years Fort Lamy would endure as an island of tranquillity amid a turbulent sea of troubles. The fragile economy required supporting the military administration of the French and consisted of the export of cotton from the fertile and well-watered lands of the south and cattle from the arid Sahel in the north. To transport European merchandise by the railroad from Pointe Noire inland to Brazzaville and then overland by primitive roads to Fort

Lamy required two months. There were a few miles of paved roads outside of Fort Lamy. They soon disappeared into the traditional tracks of the trans-Saharan caravans leading to eastern Chad and the northern wastelands of the Sahel and the Sahara known in the romance of remote outposts as the military administrative region of the Borkou-Ennedi-Tibesti Prefecture, the infamous B.E.T. South of the "unproductive" north were the more "useful" lands where the growing of indigenous cotton was organized and improved with imported strains to create a region that French officials called the *Tchad Utile*. When Chad became independent in 1960, barter was the customary means of business, and after a half-century of French colonial administration the economic return to France was less than the 425 square miles of Martinique, the last bastion of French influence in the Caribbean.

Surrounded by six emerging African states, each with different interests, Chad had no choice but to take an active part in African politics, despite its isolation and vulnerability. Geographically and ethnically, the country was an anachronistic conglomerate composed of competitive rather than integrated interests. Politically, Chad consisted of a handful of minuscule political parties that spanned the spectrum from the reactionary to the revolutionary. There were the conservative chiefs of Kanem, Wadai, Mayo Kebbi, and Baguirmi and their more radical "young Turks," who considered the dominant Chadian Progressive Party (PPT) too conservative, too southern, and too African. There were only a few educated Chadians who could administer the country. There were fewer than three hundred students enrolled in foreign universities, and they were a generation away from establishing their imprint on the governance of an imperial and African conundrum. Given the paucity of leadership, the chief of state, Ngartha (François) Tombalbaye, from southern Chad, appeared justified to assume the multiple portfolios of president of the Council of Ministers and minister of national defense.

Chad decided for independence a decade after King Idris took power in Libya in 1951 and four years after the Republic of Sudan declared its independence in 1956. The three states, for they were more states than nations, appeared to have little in common except for a tripoint where all three came together in the sands of the Libyan Desert. With no window on the sea, Chad had no choice but to align itself with the Francophone states of West Africa. Libyan interests were driven by Mediterranean and Arab North African influences. The Sudan had little to do with Chad and Libya, for its interests have traditionally flowed with the Nile northward into Egypt with whom the Sudanese have always had an ancient but ambiguous relationship, in contrast to the ungovernable inhabitants on their remote western frontier with Chad. Before the discovery of oil in Libya, the Sudan was by far the richest of the three and geographically dominated the vast landmass between the Nile and the Niger from the Mediterranean to the tributaries of the Congo. Its promise of a dynamic parliamentary democracy disappeared in 1958 when a military dictatorship determined to prosecute with great vigor a civil war that pitted the Arab of the Northern Sudan against the African of the south. No one at the independence ceremonies of Chad in 1960 would have predicted that this African conundrum would soon be entrapped in a similar civil war. To protect its interests, France had imposed a confidential understanding with the new government of Chad to provide military support for the president if necessary. The French were concerned about two immediate threats to the new Republic of Chad. The subversion of the government by the revival of Pan-Islam from the north and the equally insidious appearance of communists from the Soviet Union.[2] Within five years Muslim rebels from Chad were active in Wadai and the B.E.T. Their insurgency would involve the French, the Sudanese, the Libyans, and ultimately Egypt, the Organization of African Unity, the United Nations, and as reluctant allies, the NATO states in a struggle for paramountcy in a wasteland about which they knew nothing.

France and the Republic of Chad

In 1958 General Charles de Gaulle returned to power ostensibly to preserve *Algerie Française*. He would, however, soon preside over its dissolution, while simultaneously reconfiguring the French colonial empire in Africa. The Evian Agreements of 1962 ended the war in Algeria that had never had the same appeal for General de Gaulle as had Francophone Africa, particularly the forest, savanna, Sahel and Sahara of French Equatorial Africa that had stood by him in the darkest days of World War II. He had assumed personal responsibility for the "delicate orchestration" of French policy to consummate an unholy marriage between the historic imperial traditions of France and the determination of the Africans for independence. Indeed, as long as President de Gaulle dominated the Fifth Republic, he would endeavor to braid a cohesive French-speaking community bound by political, economic, and military ties to France. By close supervision from the French Ministry of Cooperation and the Council of African and Malagasy Affairs, both created in 1961 to project French interests south of the Sahara, he could circumvent the efforts of French bureaucrats to formulate policy, which he regarded as his personal prerogative. General de Gaulle was willing to provide financial assistance and military security in return for the protection by independent Africans for French commercial and strategic interests. In Chad, France would be generous with its economic assistance as long as the government did not interfere with the export of cotton, which was essential to the treasury of Chad and the textile mills of Marseilles. In order to reorganize the neocolonial empire in Francophone Africa, de Gaulle ordered Jacques Foccart, his associate for many years, the "most faithful among his faithful," as his personal shield-bearer in Africa.[3] "La Foque," as he was known, presided over an informal gathering of officials from the French ministries of foreign affairs, finance, the army, and cooperation, an unofficial cabinet appointed to serve President de Gaulle's personal and often idiosyncratic inclinations as to the future of French Africa. Foccart was in charge of African affairs from 1960 to 1974 and negotiated the most important French African political issues of the time and directed the African activities of the SDECE (Service de Documentation Extérieur et de Contre-Espionnage), the French intelligence agency. He was close to most African leaders, from whom he acquired a steady stream of information, supplemented by the gossip from the small cells of African intellectuals, which was never shared with the Ministry of Foreign Affairs in Paris nor with its embassies in Africa.

In his role as éminence grise, "La Foque" did his job very well indeed, and for more than a decade enjoyed unparalleled access to President de Gaulle and his successor Georges Pompidou. His precise evaluations of conditions in Africa shaped French policy throughout the continent, while his penetrating briefings and analysis on Chad, Libya, and the Sudan not only determined French actions but were selectively shared with the African allies of France.[4] Certainly, the mystique of Foccart was confirmed by his public invisibility, and when he appeared in Africa or was rumored to have appeared, the international media immediately assumed that there was something amiss which required attention, fixing, or resolution.

During the early 1960s France had signed numerous military agreements designed as paternal support for the survival of friendly African governments and to ensure the lasting presence of France in Africa. French military bases in the Central African Republic served as the headquarters from which the French Overseas Army Zone 2 forces could be deployed, but not without the determination of a rapid strike force. In 1961 President de Gaulle approved the creation of a rapid deployment Force d'Intervention Interarmées of the 11th Parachute and 9th Marine Infantry divisions, which could be moved instantly by air to support African leaders whose own Armées Nationales were all trained by the French. The French presence was a European counterweight to the popularity of Egypt's Gamal Abd al-Nasser and the diffusion of his Pan-Arab and Pan-African philosophy and a deterrent to the growing interest and influence of the Soviet Union and the People's Republic of China in postcolonial Africa.

Despite frequent demonstrations by Chadian nationalists for the reduction of French influence, French subsidies were essential for the maturation of the political process and the maintenance of public order in which all the elite had a vested interest. Together, the Chadian gendarmerie and military forces consisted of a thousand men, 10 percent of whom were French. Another 3,000 French troops were garrisoned in Chad, while French military advisers were seconded to command, staff, and training stations to sustain the new Chadian national army. More important, the administration of the B.E.T. remained the responsibility of the French military administration. President Tombalbaye strongly objected, but few Africans from southern Chad were permitted into the B.E.T. This was the homeland, the citadel for thousands of years of the nomads who spoke a Nilo-Saharan language and had a culture with ambivalent and suspicious ties to the Afro-Asiatic Arabs from the north and the Africans in the south. The token African presence in the B.E.T. consisted of a handful of minor officials in unimportant civil and military posts who could only justify their positions to themselves and their kin by a rapid transfer home to the verdant south. Ironically, no sooner had President Tombalbaye sought to assert his independence than he required the support of the Force d'Intervention to secure his government and Chad's independence and to confirm the French "general commitment to the security of Francophone Africa."[5]

The Tombalbaye Government

After independence a small cadre of French-educated southerners, who rarely traveled north of Fort Lamy, acquired the accoutrements of government. Nearly all were born in the Sahel from the right bank of the Chari River to the frontier with the Central African Republic and the Cameroon. The region is dotted by hundreds of villages, which contain half the population of Chad, and is homeland to the first president of Chad, Ngartha (François) Tombalbaye, a forty-year-old Sara who had received a patina of education at French schools. Both friends and enemies would admit that Tombalbaye and his Parti Progressiste Tchadienne (PPT) might govern Chad, but it was French foreign aid, which provided 95 percent of the capital budget of the independent government of Chad and paid for five hundred French financial, administrative, and military advisers, that made possible his rule as a pawn in the designs of President de Gaulle for the historic French *mission civilitrice* in Africa.

It cost France a pittance, $20 million annually, to retain its preeminent influence in Chad. French entrepreneurs and Levantine merchants were encouraged to continue their command of the marketplace; metropolitan French commercial interests were delighted with the semiautonomous status granted to the renamed Société Cotonnière du Tchad (COTONTCHAD) to facilitate the construction of the Fort Archambault-Cameroon railroad to stimulate cotton cultivation. The embryonic financial institutions were the preserve of French bankers; health care and the educational system were dominated by French professionals and teachers. Independence may have come to Chad, but the historic French *mission civilitrice* was to remain in Chad for another generation.

In 1960 Tombalbaye appeared to have no political rivals, but there soon emerged a spate of political parties whose membership encompassed the many and the few and whose rhetoric vibrated from the reactionary to the revolutionary. Among the Muslims were the conservative chiefs of Kanem, Wadai, Mayo Kebbi, and Baguirmi who were opposed by the young, more-educated Muslims discovering their heritage in Pan-Arab and Pan-Islamic themes.[6] Of all the provinces, Wadai on the volatile eastern frontier was the most ungovernable. Historically, any frontier is turbulent, and the borderlands between Wadai and the Sudan are more the rule than the exception. On the frontiers of Islam there were many political malcontents but few charismatic figures. The French had reduced the powers of the *jallaba,* petty merchants, from the Sudan, the Libyan traders from the Fezzan, and the Sanusi and the Mahdist brotherhoods, and last but not least, the Sultan of Wadai. The latter was little more than a French figurehead, for although his title had been fully restored, the French had circumscribed his traditional powers. By 1960 his influence hardly extended beyond the capital, Abeche, which had only replaced the historic capital of Wara in 1850.[7] A hundred years later the population of some 10,000 survived as a trading center for camel and cattle nomads and a way station for pilgrims on their way to Mecca. Sudanese from Darfur, both cultivators and pastoralists, had settled there, and during the French administration, town planning included quarters for new emigrant ethnic groups, the Hadjerai from southeastern Chad, Nilotes from the Southern Sudan, and a few Sara from the southwest. The inhabitants of all ethnicities thrived on political and theological debate, but Wadai and the B.E.T. in the north were, in practice, excluded from political participation in the new Chad. Not surprisingly most of the residents of Abeche continued their close ties to Darfur in the Sudan while the pastoral Baggara in Chad continued to drive their cattle to the Sudan railhead at El Obeid in Kordofan.[8]

The overwhelming French presence in Fort Lamy, renamed Ndjamena on 6 September 1973, did little to dispel the impression, if not the reality, that independence was a sham. In fact, Tombalbaye became an increasingly disobedient French poodle whose distemper toward his masters was fed by the growing nationalist feeling among the small class of educated elite. By 1982 he had become determined to reduce the suffocating French presence, but he also had observed that in Dahomey and the Congo, where French aid had been withdrawn, their governments were summarily overthrown, and France had not lifted a finger to save their protégés. Tombalbaye was certainly unwilling to dispense with the personal and political benefits that he had accumulated from the French connection, and at the advice of Foccart he quietly agreed to give the French *carte blanche* to intervene in Chad should President de Gaulle consider that there existed a clear and present danger to Tombalbaye, his government, or to Chad. According to Foccart, "the General" had a fondness for Chad, and he was convinced that his government would end badly, "*bien-aimé*" Tombalbaye.[9]

Confident of French indulgence and support, Tombalbaye stifled his political opposition in direct proportion to his growing arrogance. Few observers of Chad were surprised when he succumbed to the "African Disease," *hubris*, perhaps imported by Greek traders. Within the year, Chad had become an African dictatorship dominated by French-speaking Africans from the south. In January 1962 all political parties were dissolved and prohibited except, of course, the Parti Progressiste Tchadien (PPT) of President Tombalbaye. A few days later the National Assembly was dissolved. While consolidating his dictatorship, on the one hand, he sought to mollify his critics, on the other, and in the following year he permitted a supervised election that brought into his cabinet a small number of educated Muslim elite from the north. This window dressing could not hide the fact that there was little political blood circulating through the body politic—less than ten graduates studying abroad had returned home—and Tombalbaye publicly admitted that the new cabinet appointments had been necessary to appease the growing discontent from the Pan-Islamic, Pan-Arab center of the B.E.T. in a government dominated by Christian, European Africans from the south.

Many of the young, politically active Chadians had become increasingly disgruntled by the very visible French presence in Chad. Ideologically, it was a blatant symbol of French neocolonialism; personally, it was an imperial stonewall to their own ambitions. Thus, while President Tombalbaye maneuvered to strengthen his personal control, the National Assembly, ostensibly a captive of the political process, began to oppose him. It first demonstrated its growing discontent with the passage of a resolution calling for the reduction of French forces and administrative personnel. The assembly specifically demanded the removal of French military advisers, the reduction of French military personnel, and the expulsion of French officials and civil administrators charged with Muslim affairs, an admission and recognition of the fact that the French military and intelligence advisers were successfully gaining the support of the more conservative elements in the Muslim regions. Not content with insisting upon a reduced French presence within the more active political regions of Chad, the assembly called for an end to the French military presence in the B.E.T., the remote and romantic region in the Sahel and Sahara, for sixty years the administrative prerogative of the Officiers Sudanais and the Foreign Legion, who had struggled to fly the Tricolor from their *beau geste* forts. In Fort Lamy opportunists ingratiated themselves with the nationalists to demand the expulsion of French administrators, and the National Assembly unanimously requested that French forces be withdrawn from Chad within "a reasonable time."

These demands were debated throughout northern, Muslim Chad where its inhabitants considered themselves to be the unfortunate recipients of the imposition of French military and civil administration that now appeared to have been replaced by an even more disagreeable alternative, President Tombalbaye. Among the nomads and village leaders throughout the north, French rule had never been very popular, despite the French insistence that the customary warfare between petty sultanates be brought to an end, which had resulted in a modest increment in the prosperity among the inhabitants of the Sahel and Sahara. The arms trade had been curtailed, the slave raids into the south by Arabs from Baguirmi and Wadai were a fading memory, and the raiding of caravans and extensive camel and cattle rustling had been greatly reduced. No imperial power can rule without order and for the miscreants French punishment had been sure and severe. The French Officiers Sudanais had employed determination and discipline to maintain their military and police forces ready to strike across the sands to keep the peace on the frontier. There were, however, many within all the levels of tribal society that remembered with nostalgia the more rough and tumble and certainly more exciting ways of doing business before the imposition of the French imperialism.

Restless under the *pax Gallica* and infuriated by a government in the south led by an insufferable *abid* (slave) from the African south, the hostility of the northern *shaykhs* turned to fury when they saw their authority being eroded by younger men who were kinsmen but regurgitated the new ideologies of Pan-Arabism and Pan-Islam, which were foreign to those who read the Quran and regarded themselves as devout if parochial Muslims. The French military administrative officers were well aware of this discontent, and it was only with difficulty that Foccart persuaded Tombalbaye not to amend the constitution to eliminate the teaching of Arabic in Chadian schools nor to depose the innocuous Sultan of Wadai, despite that fact that the president had already appointed one of his Sara kinsmen to be the chief administrative officer of Wadai. This egregious insult was further compounded by the appointment of administrators from southern Chad with instructions to collect the taxes with vigor from the Muslim villages in central and northeastern Chad. The insensitivity and ignorance of these tax collectors from the south only convinced the Arabs of central Chad that they were quite correct to despise government tax collections, the ubiquitous tax collector, and the principal perpetrator of their discontent, President Tombalbaye.

As discontent and distrust of Tombalbaye spread throughout central and northern Chad, the Arabs and Muslims turned their resentment against the French, without whom they well knew Tombalbaye could not survive. They strongly opposed the presence of French troops in Wadai, whom they considered to be Tombalbaye's praetorian guard. The president was neither obtuse nor unaware of the dangers in the north, and he launched a campaign in 1963 through his formal report to the Congrès Nationale to promote his commitment to a "Chadian way," an autochthonous response against French neocolonialism. It was not dissimilar to the many other initiatives taken by Africans at the time to steer a distinctive and independent course between the colonial past and the neocolonial future. The 1963 report reviewed those concerns that were particular to Chad, including economic reorganization, farm labor, youth, female emancipation, unions, African unity, tax reform, and party activities.[10] Antigovernment opposition, including Muslim-led riots within Fort Lamy and at Am Timam, had caused more than fifty deaths, but public safety was studiously ignored in the report.

Seeking Support Outside France

During the first three years after independence the Republic of Chad differed very little from colonial Chad. This would change as Chad followed other newly independent African nations to create autochthonous regional organizations designed to stimulate political and economic integration. In addition, there were numerous Third World and African meetings to attend, alliances to be formed in the United Nations and its subsidiary organizations, and an awareness of the very

active Arab, Islamic coalitions, and the growing importance of Third World regional blocs, which spanned the globe eastward from the Atlantic to the Pacific.
President Tombalbaye took full advantage to meet his counterparts from the
Third World who had more resources but similar concerns as those of Chad. His
critics, not surprisingly, found his numerous sojourns excessive, but the peripatetic leader found them useful and exhilarating and enjoyed playing the role
that geography itself demanded. Particular attention had to be paid to all of
Chad's neighbors, especially since a vast array of peoples living within the borders of Chad claimed lineage ties with their kinsmen in the contiguous states.
Libya was the historic land bridge of the trans-Saharan caravans to the Mediterranean, and Tombalbaye hoped that King Idris would allow a free port for Chad
trade goods on the coast. The Sudan was another traditional passage for trade to
the Nile, the Red Sea, and the African end of the important Route of the Pilgrims
that stretched from West Africa through Chad to Port Sudan. Equally important
was the western frontier between Wadai and Darfur, Chad and the Sudan, which
had presumably been settled by Britain and France after World War I but never
accepted by the frontiersmen who had fought for centuries in the border lands.
The boundary between Chad-Niger to the northwest, only an insignificant scrawl
on the map of Africa, was another source of conflict where the traditional rivalries of the Tuareg and Toubou were now confounded by the search for oil and
uranium. There were even greater conundrums to the south. The Central African
Republic was the bridge to the Congo that in 1960 was the richest of African
states. To the southwest, the Chad-Cameroon frontier offered an even better out-
let to the sea than through Nigeria. This was an awesome agenda for one of the
poorest countries with a great landmass, ethnic diversity and division, and no indigenous, compact class to provide the evolution from a colonial conundrum.

There was much to be done, and although thousands of French administrators, teachers, and aid workers had invaded Chad, by 1963 Tombalbaye had
begun to look beyond France for additional economic support not only for development but as a counterweight to a necessary but increasingly embarrassing
French presence. Upon his inauguration in January 1961, President John F.
Kennedy had demonstrated a concern for African affairs. The United States had
discovered Africa in 1960 and with their anticolonial traditions embraced this
newfound continent in the universities, foundations, business, and in the state-
rooms of government. President Kennedy, for political, humanitarian, and romantic reasons, was swept up in the Africa euphoria. The Department of State
was quick to emulate the president's enthusiasm, described by one biographer:
"In no part of the third world did Kennedy pioneer more effectively that in
Africa."[11] Despite the concern of President Kennedy for Africa and his distrust of
French colonialism, for many years after the United States recognized Chad in
January 1961, the U.S. presence at Fort Lamy was hard to find and difficult to understand. West Africa might offer fertile ground for the spread of American in-
fluence, but the State Department had no desire to complicate the increasingly

difficult and deteriorating relationship with President de Gaulle by intruding into a region of no interest to the United States for which General de Gaulle was known to have a historic and romantic affection.

Despite his interest in Africa, President Kennedy could not authorize substantial assistance to Chad or Francophone Africa without appearing to meddle in French affairs—which many French were convinced he had done as a United States senator by openly supporting Algerian independence.[12] Sensitivity to French susceptibilities, however, did not prohibit a harmless assertion of America's discovery of Africa by flying the flag, and in 1962 an impecunious and insignificant foreign aid mission arrived in Fort Lamy. It was as far as the Kennedy administration was prepared to venture into the Dark Continent of Francophone Africa. Impressed, President Tombalbaye requested a major American foreign aid program, which was considered and rejected. The United States Agency for International Development (USAID)—a Kennedy creation—denied Chad's demands; its officials could find few qualified indigenous administrators or technicians. They predicted that any USAID support would only result in disaster in a country where 240 distinguishable ethnic groupings could be expected to demand a disproportionate amount of the very small pie that would arrive from Washington.

Washington was aware that Tombalbaye might soon approach communist nations to reduce his dependence on France, but it was not until the governments in Congo-Brazzaville and Dahomey were overthrown that the State Department became more concerned about Chad. There were those in the Department of State who, in deference to President de Gaulle and the French imperial past, had dubbed Chad "the pivot of Central Africa" but argued forcefully that even if France were to reduce its presence in Chad, it was not in the interests of the United States to assume either a military or an economic role. Foccart was convinced that U.S. officials had demonstrated little disposition to play an important role in Francophone Africa and would not as long as French influence remained decisive.[13]

To diversify its economy and reduce French control, Tombalbaye sought to sell cotton to Yugoslavia where President Tito and Gamal Abd al-Nasser of Egypt had emerged as the leaders in the ideological marketplace of the Third World. Foccart easily discouraged their inept efforts to reduce French interests in COTONT-CHAD. In a defiant attempt to assert his proscribed independence he sent a mission to Brussels, Bonn, the Hague, London, Copenhagen, and Washington in an effort to convince the Europeans and the Americans that Chad was a profitable political and economic investment that required capital grants and skilled personnel. In Washington the Chadian representatives stressed the problems of the rapid urbanization of Fort Lamy and the consequent high rate of unemployment; it wanted an urban development program, which USAID summarily rejected. The U.S. presence in Chad was increased not by a grant in aid but by the call from President Kennedy for volunteers to join a small Peace Corps program, which was authorized in 1966—the same year the government claimed that more than 1,200 officials had been killed by rebels.[14] By then President Kennedy was dead, the United States was sinking into Vietnam, and Washington's interest in Africa had all but disappeared. After five years of pervasive support from the French, Tombalbaye had acquired by persistence the prerogatives of power, most important of which was his control of the secret police recruited from his Sara kinsmen. He lectured his followers to modernize society while his security forces crushed the opposing political parties and the Chadian labor movement. He pledged to transform "the mentality of the masses too often anchored to tradition," through voluble rhetoric inspired by an alcoholic haze. His nondrinking Muslim citizens were not convinced that the "new Chadian man" envisaged by President Tombalbaye would have tolerance for any other race, religion, or political ideology.

Revolt in the B.E.T.

Although the Sahel and Sahara constitute 40 percent of Chad, Tombalbaye, not unlike the French, considered the B.E.T. in the far north to be too isolated to squander the limited resources of Chad on any development schemes. The inhabitants were primitive nomads who had raided into the south for loot and slaves, and its population in 1964 was only 75,000 of the three million citizens of Chad, which would hardly warrant any generous government expenditure.[15] To President Tombalbaye, the B.E.T. was inconsequential and better left to the French Officiers Sudanais, who had kept peace in the sands with their légionnaires and the indigenous Toubou and Zaghawa of the Garde Nomade (the camel corps), and a few selected police from southern Chad.

Although unpopular, the French presence in the B.E.T. had been sophisticated and sufficient to restrain the growing discontent not only against themselves, which was a traditional rite, but more troublesomely against the southerners, the slaves and infidels, who dominated the government at Fort Lamy. The French military advisers who remained after independence were sympathetic with their turbulent wards. They ruled with a loose reign and sensibly refused to hinder the movement of their nomads into Niger, the Fezzan, or Darfur. This imperial ritual, whereby the very independent pastoral peoples were permitted to follow their herds to pasture in return for good behavior, began to dissolve when Tombalbaye insisted that France reduce its military presence in the B.E.T. In 1964 there were 3,000 security troops and gendarmerie in the B.E.T. They were gradually withdrawn to be replaced by southern officials who had no understanding of the culture, history, or environmental needs of the nomadic peoples of the B.E.T. They considered their assignment to the ignorant, Muslim fanatics an opportunity to profit from their consignment to the purgatory of the sands. The withdrawal of the old French devils, unpopular but trusted, began when Tombalbaye received the rumors that dissidents were active in the B.E.T. after an unknown movement calling itself "the Committee of Northern Chad" attacked his policies in a letter delivered to President de Gaulle.[16]

At Abeche, Moussoro, and Fort Archambault, the French administrators were replaced by southern officials of dubious qualifications. Their transfer was soon complemented by the arrival of six companies of French-trained troops recruited from southern Chad, which eliminated the unobtrusive, unpopular, but sympathetic military presence of the French in the B.E.T. It was a great mistake. French officials in the B. E. T. warned that this 1,000-man force had neither the ability nor the sensitivity required to keep the peace. The Toubou were born to quarrel and lived to fight with their allies, the Teda from the Tibesti and the Daza riding out from the Ennedi Plateau. Few of these survivors of the Sahel and the desert have ever agreed on anything. The Teda, camel nomads, had ignored the Turks, welcomed the Sanusi; the Daza, a mixed society of nomads and sedentary agriculturists, had hated the Turks and feared the Sanusi and sought to exclude them both from their cultural heartland in the Faya oasis. As a Sara from the south, Tombalbaye was determined to secure his own personal position without giving obeisance to the chieftains of the north, who throughout the centuries in Chad had destroyed so many before him. They had only a hodgepodge of weaponry, but the French were aware that the Toubou used their muskets and old Statti and MAS-36 rifles with great efficiency.

The revolt began at Bardai within days of the first French withdrawal of their troops. The village, which sheltered a French fort, was a picturesque *beau geste* oasis located among the Tibesti mountains 475 miles northwest of Faya Largeau, the administrative headquarters of the B.E.T. It was the Teda-Toubou cultural center and winter home to hundreds of nomadic families. The crisis began at a dance during which soldiers from southern Chad and local Toubou tribesmen soon clashed; much blood was spilled. There could be no more unfortunate incident for the future of Chad than this brawl, in a remote outpost surrounded by volcanic craters and sulfuric deposits, involving new government troops sent to impose new government taxes determined by the new Sara administrators from the south. Their insensitivity appeared confirmed when the southern officials threatened to impose the "forced" labor of the old French *corvée* to support the government's unrealistic regional agricultural development projects.

If there had been trouble at Bardai, there was certain to be clashes at Zouar, the renowned archaeological site located at the base of spectacular volcanic grottos between Aozou and Faya Largeau festooned with prehistoric rock paintings. It is the home of Wodei Kichidemi, often called the "Sultan of Zouar," who had served since 1938 as the *Derde*, the elected nonhereditary leader chosen from among the nobles of the Tomaghera clan of the Teda and acknowledged as the spiritual head of all the Teda of the Tibesti. The French had worked well with Kichidemi and respected his office; however, once they began to depart the B.E.T., and its administration was transferred from Faya Largeau to Fort Lamy,

Tombalbaye suspended the traditional right of the *Derde* to adjudicate tribal disputes. Trouble at Zouar was soon followed by a pitched battle at Aozou, a village in northwest Tibesti. There, the Daza Toubou from the Garde Nomade attacked and routed the local government forces, who fled to the French administrative headquarters at Faya Largeau. Stung by these reverses, Tombalbaye ordered in July 1965 a government column to reopen the caravan route between Bardai and Aozou. It was ambushed with heavy casualties, the losses of which were suppressed by the government in Fort Lamy, but in Chad and in Africa there are few secrets, and in the capital everyone was well aware there was trouble in the north. Even the foreign embassies knew there was trouble when a forgotten 1960 restriction on travel to the B.E.T. was suddenly reimposed.

In September 1965 the Toubou tribesmen clashed once again with the garrison of southern troops at Bardai, who responded with indiscriminate and brutal reprisals against civilians; infuriated the Toubou charged that the Chad military commanders had unleashed a murderous army of "occupation." Indeed, the presence of soldiers from southern Chad was a recipe for disaster, and the government prefect, Lt. Colonel Negue Djogo, a Sara and former NCO who had served with French forces in Indo-China, was a feckless commander who was unable to contain the protest, which soon turned into open revolt.

During a short visit to the B.E.T. in January 1966, the usually observant anthropologist and explorer Carleton S. Coon observed "the tricolor still flying, and a French lieutenant, who was black," awaiting his party at Bardai.[17] He then discovered a superior rock engraving of a prehistoric human figure, but otherwise the Bedouin of the timeless desert had remained unchanged. Coon flew on to Tripoli to explore southern Libya where he arrived only a few weeks prior to the signing of the 1966 Chad-Libya Treaty of Amity and Good Neighborliness. The agreement would allow the Toubou to trade freely on both sides of the border, but as cross-border movement was limited to very specific trade routes, the Toubou considered the treaty just another intrusion by a despised government and yet another attempt to limit their sacred right to travel whenever and wherever they pleased.

Drought and the Insurgency

Although French advisers in Chad and Foccart in Paris urged Tombalbaye to implement reforms to reduce the tensions in the B.E.T., he refused. And as the French predicted, the Toubou increased their insurgency; sporadic attacks upon caravans and government outposts became more frequent and more violent. The few merchants in the north discreetly decided to leave the B.E.T.[18] In June 1966 the Chad Ministry of Foreign Affairs informed the small diplomatic community that travel in the B.E.T. would be allowed only with "the express permission of the Chief of State." In addition to the approval of President Tombalbaye, all foreigners would also require certification from the prefect at Faya Largeau to travel

north of a line that began at Tarka on the Chad-Nigeria border and drawn eastward to Zouar, Bardai, Yebbi Bou, Gouro, Ounianga Kebir, and Fada and then to
the border with the Sudan. Travel between Chad and Libya was permitted only
along the Zouar-Korizo-Sebha caravan route.

By November 1966 the government's presence north of Faya Largeau had become tenuous at best, impossible at worst. Curiously, as winter approached, the
sniping and skirmishing against the government posts became less frequent and
then ceased altogether; the Toubou vanished from the jagged moonscape of the
Tibesti. The Toubou did not withdraw, however, because of the presence of government troops from the south, whom they despised, or concern over their military strength, which was sustained only by the French, but because of the devastation of their fragile environment by a prolonged drought. They could no longer
continue their rebellion against the central government when they had to devote
all their energies to a desperate search for water and pasture. The failure of the
spring rains in 1966 had been followed by a severe drought during the months
from June to September. Normally in a year of reasonable rainfall the pastoralists
of the B.E.T. would roam some 500 miles in search of the ephemeral pasture
found along the desert fringe between the Sahara and the Sahel. By the autumn
of 1966, however, there was no pasture, and there was little water to be found
from Niger in the west to Darfur in the east. This was the most severe year in a
more prolonged desiccation that began in 1960. Thousands of families were deprived of water from the wells and of grass in the historic pastures. Unknown to
the Bedouins, the *sécheresse* of the 1960s would be the first of a series of widespread droughts to devastate the B.E.T. and the western Sudan during the next
thirty years. After 1960 a year of average rainfall in the Sahel would be the exception rather than the rule.[19]

In the northern B.E.T., the Teda *fazzara* moved to the Faya Largeau oasis to
water their animals and wait out the drought. There, and in the towns of Abeche,
Fada, Kutum, and Geneina, officials of Chad and the Sudan were soon confronted by desperate people seeking food and water. In Borkou and Ennedi, the
drought produced upheavals in the traditional pattern of nomadic life; people
sought relief through migration from the B.E.T. and Wadai into central and
southern Chad. The Ennedi Plateau was probably the most desiccated region, but
the peoples inhabiting the one area are common to the others and over centuries
they have provided mutual support in times of hardship. The Toubou, the Zaghawa, and the Bedeiyat of the Ennedi hills, however, found little help in Abeche
or central Chad and consequently moved east like their grandfathers into Darfur.
In Kutum, El Fasher, and the market towns of Darfur, there was a forced sale of
the camels and sheep from the Chad-Sudan borderlands, which historically have
been highly valued in the riverine Sudan and Saudi Arabia. To *jallaba* and traders
in the *suq,* the center of mercantile enterprise in northeastern Africa, the opportunity to extract a profit from desperation was a normal transaction of the marketplace, but it was a tragedy for those pastoralists from Chad and the Sudan,

who had lost their capital, never to be recovered or forgotten. In the Ennedi Plateau scores of settlements simply disappeared, marked only by the pride and the *revanche* of the dispossessed.

The Toubou rebellion in the B.E.T. began in anger at the new restrictions imposed upon them by southern, African administrators, whom they regarded as slaves, and expanded with the agony of the relentless drought, which destroyed their herds even more than the despised tax collectors. On 1 November 1965 a government "good will visit" was made by Tombalbaye's Minister of the Interior and lesser Chad officials to Mangalmé, a small town located 300 miles east of Fort Lamy and far from the B.E.T., which provoked widespread rioting. The discontent in Mangalmé was the same as in the B.E.T. but without the hardship of drought. The inhabitants were the Moubi, who speak Daju, a dialect of the Nilo-Saharan language of the Sahel, and who have close kinship affiliations with the Arabs of Darfur to the east. Their hostility toward the government was not dissimilar to that of the Toubou in the B.E.T. The arrogance of the new southern administrators, which was compounded by an unreasonable increase in the rate of taxation, the unacceptable contempt of petty Black functionaries sent to impose their authority upon the "savage" inhabitants of the eastern Chad, and the discontent in the north, was more than sufficient to precipitate violent demonstrations from the Moubi. Their allies were the Missiriya Baggara and the Mahamid Arab nomads, who were intermediaries between the Toubou and Zaghawa of the B.E.T. and the Moubi of the Sahel east of Lake Chad. When the crowd surged out of control, the gendarmerie overreacted, and before the rioting could be quelled, the director of the cabinet of the Ministry of the Interior, eight other officials, and more than 500 demonstrators were dead.

The discontent and drought in the B.E.T. now combined with the Mangalmé riots to spread the flames of rebellion throughout central Chad. The Muslims mobilized against the hated Sara tax collectors and their armed guards, who imposed heavy taxes "on cattle and women . . . designed to inflict damage on the pastoral and polygamous Muslims of the North."[20] Muslim leaders in Chad compared their situation with that of their coreligionists in the Sudan, where Muslim Arabs were attempting to impose their religion and rule upon the infidel Africans of the Southern Sudan. And when the day of the riots was over in Mangalmé, the Muslims of Chad declared holy war, *jihad,* against the slaves from the south and its officials who had sought to impose their rule on the *Dar al-Islam.*

After the Mangalmé incident the protest spread rapidly among the Hadjerai villages of Guera and among the Baggara west of Abeche and then to Lake Chad and north and south along the Sudanese border, where small bands of armed men, invariably the Muslims of Chad, found a safe haven in the Sudan from which to attack isolated government outposts on the frontier. Tombalbaye was not unaware of the abuse of his tax collectors, but he argued that insubordinate local chiefs, whose traditional prerogatives had been substantially reduced by both tax and administrative reforms, were the ones to blame for his problems in central, eastern, and northern Chad. The United States embassy, much to its consternation, discovered that the nomads were "forced to pay the animal head tax for both themselves and their animals" in every prefecture visited during the year; thus, "they end up paying five or six times as much as they should."[21] Crushing taxes were collected by those who were despised for their ethnicity and religion during a time of great travail caused by the desiccation of the land; this, combined with the personal limitations of President Tombalbaye could lead only to discontent and rebellion.

In 1967 the Muslim insurgents increased their attacks against the government forces in Wadai. They were no more successful than their compatriots in the B.E.T.; the United States embassy reported that operations were characterized by "inefficiency, reprisals, brutality and by an overall lack of effectiveness."[22] Whether in the B.E.T. or Wadai, the government forces of the Republic of Chad were regarded as an occupying force. To the dismay of the French and the few informed observers of Chad, President Tombalbaye refused to acknowledge that his government could not contend with a serious revolt; his fumbling attempts to disguise the problem only managed to magnify its severity.

FROLINAT

By 1968 the situation beyond Fort Lamy could no longer be ignored by its insecure and inexperienced officials. The National Political Bureau (BPN), which advised the government on political matters, managed to aggravate the growing division between Arab and African in Chad when it issued a mendacious and provocative communiqué: "Despite the rout of the rebel irregulars some time ago, foreign elements, who are hostile to the public order, are continuing to carry out psychological warfare by spreading alarming rumors in Fort Lamy," but the provocateurs had been "identified and are being followed."[23] At Fort Lamy, suspects were rounded up and jailed; in the countryside south of the B.E.T., the security forces, having been given reason to seek and contain those in opposition to the government, roamed indiscriminately to settle old personal or tribal scores and to loot the inhabitants of the nearest village.

Unable to suppress the rebellion in the north, Tombalbaye blamed his inadequacies on the devious designs of Chad's neighbor, the Sudan. To be sure, a succession of Sudanese Arab leaders had provided his political enemies a safe haven in Darfur since 1964 and, by 1966, were providing arms and logistic support to the rebels inside Chad. For Khartoum to send arms to the opposition in Chad was provocative, but to openly support the subversion of a neighboring state with flagrant abandon infuriated Tombalbaye: Despite the ties of race and religion with the Southern Sudanese, he had refused to send aid to their insurgency against the Arab government in Khartoum, which had divided the Northern and the Southern Sudan far greater than the insurrection in the B.E.T. had bisected Chad. On numerous occasions he had bluntly rejected pleas by the Christian leaders of the Anya Nya rebellion in the Southern Sudan for military assistance or a safe haven inside Chad. Indeed, Tombalbaye had restrained his own media when the Sudan government broadcast propaganda calculated to incite his Muslim subjects in Wadai to revolt. He could have made trouble for Khartoum by encouraging the growing discontent among the African ethnic minorities in Darfur and the formidable Nilotes and the Equatorians on the Uganda frontier who were already engaged in a bitter conflict with the Sudan government.

Ibrahim Abatcha was one of the first Chadian dissidents to receive support from Khartoum. Intelligent, charismatic, a born organizer and agitator, he would prove to be a very dangerous enemy for Tombalbaye. He had first emerged in Chadian politics as a Nasserite socialist and leader of the pre-independence Chad National Union party (Union Nationale Tchadienne, the UNT), which was comprised of radicals who objected to any continued association with France. Little was known of Abatcha. He was born at Fort Lamy in 1938 of Bornu immigrants from northern Nigeria and educated in French schools and later employed in the Chad administrative services. He was jailed either for political activities or for "indelicacies" in carrying out his functions.[24] After independence, Abatcha fled Chad but surfaced in 1982 in Ghana where with two other Chadians, Abubakr Djalabo and Ali Mahamat Taher, he began his career as a revolutionary leader of the nascent Chad Islamic Republic in exile. The following year he published a tract, *Toward a United National Liberation Front,* characterized by ill-digested Maoist ideology. He declared war on Tombalbaye, Western imperialism, and French neocolonialism. There would be no acceptance of the COTONTCHAD cotton monopoly, and there would be no place or need for French advice, their advisers, or their soldiers.

Early in 1965 Abatcha was seen in Algiers where the most extreme UNT members had congregated after Tombalbaye proscribed all political parties in Chad. From Algiers, Abubakr Djalabo and Abatcha visited Syria to seek financial and military support while other UNT activists sought converts among Chadians studying in France and Egypt. They made no known converts among the students in Paris, but they were welcomed by many apostate Muslims and Arab socialists studying in Egypt. They had particular success among the Chadian Arabs studying at the Al Azhar University. In Cairo, Abatcha formed a close relationship with other non-Arab Chadian revolutionaries to create a clandestine administrative committee comprising six like-minded revolutionaries. With the aid of the Cameroon Marxists, Abatcha and a handful of the faithful left Cairo in June 1965 for training in North Korea. They returned to Egypt four months later, only a few days before the tax revolt in eastern Chad would explode at Mangalmé.

From Cairo, Abatcha and his compatriots, nicknamed the "Koreans," entered the Sudan in March 1966. Despite their ill-disguised Marxist ideology, Abatcha and his movement surprisingly received considerable financial support from Sudanese groups of differing political persuasions and even from the conservative

Sanusi brotherhood of Libya. From his sanctuary at El Fasher in Darfur, Abatcha began to build a clandestine operation in Chad, whose cells would soon be scattered throughout the Sahel. Until his death, Abatcha himself, and even his more visible followers, remained unknown to either the efficient intelligence service of the French or the less efficient but knowledgeable intelligence service of the government of Chad.

In Darfur the revolutionary triumvirate of Abatcha, Abubakr Djalabo, and Ali Mahamat Taher was joined by Muhammad Al-Baghalani, who was soon ranked fourth in order of importance. There is much information that is contradictory about Baghalani, who was known as a Black Arab from Wadai and who was probably a Zaghawa. Educated in the Sudan, Baghalani claimed to have been a member of the UNT since the early 1960s, but his credentials were subsequently denied by those who were soon to create the Chad National Liberation Front, in which the UNT was incorporated. It was known that he left Chad in 1963 through the Central African Republic and appeared in the Sudan, where in the name of the UNT he began to recruit Chad refugees. Baghalani represented the historic and traditional role of the Muslim *shaykh,* and his Vulcan Force was reputed to have the support of the Muslim Brotherhood in the Sudan, which had been founded in 1954 and was led by Hasan al-Turabi, a Sudanese intellectual educated in the Sorbonne who returned to the Sudan in 1965. The Muslim Brothers in the Sudan had been greatly influenced by the founders of the movement in Egypt. They had the ambiguous support of the Mahdists in the Sudan for Turabi, who was the brother-in-law of their leader, Sadiq al-Mahdi, and the Sanusiyya of Libya, who could not support the cause of religion and reform for the creation of a "Muslim Republic of Chad" that the Sanusi did not dominate. The Africans, of Christian and traditional religious persuasion, were determined to assert their independence after a half century of European Christian imperialism and centuries of Muslim influence from the north.

In El Fasher other Muslim dissidents agreed to join Abatcha. El Hajj Issaka and his small revolutionary force were new to Darfur, but he would prove to be invaluable for his knowledge of the eastern Chad and Abeche. Adam Sanoussi, a Hadjarai from Chad born of a Sudanese Dinka mother, had been trained as an enlisted man in the Sudan Defence Force and had met El Hajj Issaka at Am Timan. Given his military training he was made Chief of Staff of the revolutionary army in preference to the more politically correct but militarily inept "Koreans" and took command of ten armed revolutionary groups, each consisting of ten men.

In Darfur the rebels began to proselytize among the Zaghawa, Masalit, and Toubou with surprising success, but there were few converts from the Hadjerai of Guera prefecture. The Hadjarai, like the Toubou, lived on the periphery of the heartland with an ancient and well-deserved distrust of the Arabs of eastern Chad, Wadai. Both the Sultan of Wadai and the French had experienced mixed success in their efforts to enlist the Hadjarai into their armies and gendarmerie, and they were reluctant to commit themselves to those whose ethnicity and ideology were suspect. After months of recruiting Chadian dissidents and Sudanese converts, Abatcha and his lieutenants founded the Chad National Liberation Front (FLT), at Nyala in Darfur on 22 June 1966, which subsequently became known as FROLINAT, the acronym designed by French intelligence in September 1968 for the conglomerate of Chad dissidents.[25] The Chad National Liberation Front was supported by the Sudan government and received arms from the Egyptians. It was controlled by a Central Committee of thirty members with Abatcha as the secretary general. Its revolutionary objectives were neither surprising nor obscure: the end to the government of President Ngartha Tombalbaye, the end to the French military presence in Chad, agrarian reform, reduced taxes, increased salaries for correct officials, nationalization of the economy, the elimination of illiteracy, but interestingly the acceptance of French as well as Arabic as official languages, and the establishment of diplomatic relations with all countries except Israel and South Africa. There were the usual pious appeals for peaceful coexistence, positive neutrality, assistance to wars of national liberation, and the defense of world peace. Its slogan, "Chad for the Chadians," was not only ambiguous but pretentious for none of the leaders of FROLINAT were from the southern, African Chad.

After the call at Nyala for the revolution the rebels began to proselytize with enthusiasm throughout eastern Chad, particularly in Wadai, only to be betrayed by their own ethnic rivalries, historic confrontations for the limited resources of the land, and religious and political ideologies compromised by the desiccation of the land. Under the umbrella and euphoria of the founding of FROLINAT at Nyala, a few disgruntled former hard-core Marxist members of the UNT combined with the minuscule Chad Liberation Front (FLT) led by Ahmad Moussa to begin the revolution in central Chad. That arrangement would not last long. Ahmad Moussa had recruited his few hundred from those discontented in Wadai with taxes, drought, and insecurity who, in the tradition of their fathers, had sought refuge over the border in Darfur. Consequently, the FLT consisted exclusively of those from Wadai with kinsmen in Darfur who needed neither ideological exhortations, religious sermons, nor the devastation of drought and taxes to demand the end to the African, Christian government of President Tombalbaye and his French masters in Fort Lamy. The FLT had been active along the western frontier between Chad and the Sudan, but historically it was the renewal of the ancient contest for control of the land and the trade by the sultans of Darfur and Wadai. In the volatile borderlands Moussa overplayed his hospitality by recruiting men to fight for the revolution, but against which government was not defined and the Sudanese authorities promptly threw him into jail in Geneina for "illegal involvement in Sudanese politics." When Moussa was subsequently released, he refused to join the FROLINAT, which he now considered an organization controlled by that *abid* from Fort Lamy. He was joined by former FLT members and some Wadai Arabs who opposed the FROLINAT leadership and its ties to Egypt and North Korea. It was the first split in the Chadian revolutionary ranks but certainly not the last.

The FROLINAT insurgents began their operations from the security of southern Darfur by operations across the border into Wadai, but it was not long before the rebel organization began to fracture. Baghalani opposed any dealings with communist nations and even objected to Abatcha's continued contacts with the North Koreans and the Soviets. Dr. Abba Siddiq, the principal theoretician of an indigenous Marxist movement known as the *Jeunesses* and once a friend of Tombalbaye, only complicated matters by his preference for political debate rather than guerrilla warfare in the bush. While the leadership continued to bicker in the Sudan, Abubakr Djalabo and Ali Mahamat Taher moved to Algiers where they opened a FROLINAT office for propaganda and to maintain contact the with Arab states. A second office was opened in Baghdad in December 1966. The FROLINAT office in Algiers contacted the *Derde* who did not need to be reminded of his historic mission to rid the Tibesti of any rule but his own. The *Derde* requested and received arms, while Ali Mahamat Taher took an interest in the Toubou movement and began to incorporate their units within FROLINAT. Taher was ideally suited for this task. The young revolutionary was from Kanem. He could speak both Daza and Teda, and he had made contacts with Toubou studying in Libya. They had divided into a group known as Sebha, which was allied with the *Derde* and other Toubou at the University of Beida. They were in contact with Goukouni Oueddei, the son the *Derde*, who was carving a path independent from his father. Unlike the comfortable safe haven they had found in the Sudan, the FROLINAT leaders and their revolutionary rhetoric were neither welcome in Tripoli nor likely to receive support from King Idris. The direct descendant of the Grand Sanusi would always support the Toubou in the B.E.T. where he, as the head of the Sanusiyya, had historic commercial and religious interests, but he was deeply suspicious of the leadership and the revolutionary appeals of FROLINAT. The king had the more immediate problem of maintaining a distant but correct relationship with Egypt while attempting to reduce the growing influence of Egypt's Gamal Abd al-Nasser in Libya. The FROLINAT was not allowed to organize in Libya, and relationship between the monarchy and the revolutionaries would remain frigid as long as Idris was in power.

A Nasty Little War

By 1967 the revolt in the B.E.T. had spread to the shores of Lake Chad, and when President Tombalbaye refused to admit the presence of armed rebel forces north, east, and west of Fort Lamy, he only succeeded in magnifying their importance. It was not until August 1966 at a press conference in the capital that he acknowledged, for the first time, that rebel activity was "widespread." The President specifically admitted that his government was being challenged in Wadai, Guera, and southern Batha provinces. As in the past, he refrained from acknowledging, let alone condemning, the military assistance coming from the Sudanese in Darfur and passing through the traditional market town of Geneina on the border between the sultanates of Darfur and Wadai.

When FROLINAT patrols operating from Darfur began to harass the Chad police and military forces in Wadai, particularly in the subprovince of Adre west of Geneina astride the historic great west road for trade and pilgrims from West Africa to the Sudan and Mecca, General Felix (N'gakoutou Bey'ndi) Malloum, a Sara and deputy chief of staff, was ordered to suppress the revolt. Tombalbaye could no longer ignore the provocation by the Sudan government giving safe haven for the Chad guerrillas, and after his press conference in August, he used what little leverage he had on the frontier by restricting travel for all Sudanese citizens residing in Chad to within three miles of their residence. Simultaneously, he closed the border and customs posts on the great west road between Abeche and Geneina. Air service between the two countries was prohibited, but this was more an inconvenience than a deterrent. General Malloum increased his patrols along the frontier. In the vast reaches of a remote borderland in dispute between Wadai and Darfur for centuries and the homeland of very independent and sympathetic chieftains and petty warlords, the mobile, lightly armed FROLINAT units easily avoided any contact with the Chad security forces and roamed with impunity as far south as the Central African Republic. All of this activity only succeeded to fortify the Sudanese resolve to support FROLINART, while demonstrating that the movement could not be easily contained.

The efforts of General Malloum to block infiltration of FROLINART across the Chad-Sudan frontier were doomed to failure. Between June and December 1966 the elusive rebel columns engaged the Chad contingents in nine major military battles in Salamat, Wadai, and Guera.[26] Malloum would send patrols of slow-moving military units who were no match for the highly mobile search and destroy assaults from the guerrillas who knew every outcrop and *wadi* of the frontier. In the north, FROLINAT roamed freely through Biltine, a province carved from Wadai in 1959 to reward the sultan of the Mahamid Arabs and the friendly Zaghawa leaders who inhabited Dar Zaghawa, 18,000 square miles of sand, rock, and sparse grazing, which stretched north to Libya and east to the Sudan. Fiercely independent, the Zaghawa had reluctantly accepted the French but had little use for the guerrillas of Hassan Moussa's FLT, who represented FROLINAT in Biltine, when it became known they had arrogantly abused the Zaghawa villagers.

The next center of protest erupted in the Arab quarter of Fort Lamy where hundreds of Arabs took to the streets to demonstrate against taxes and their vigorous collection by the government. During the ensuing riot, heads were broken, shops were burned, and the "Nasserite" agitators, Muslim Brothers, suspicious malcontents, and even holy men, the Muslim *faqi,* were arrested. When the demonstrations continued, more Arab leaders were imprisoned, and African canton chiefs who supported the tax protest were summarily dismissed. The protest against "unfair taxation" could not be contained in the capital and soon spread throughout central Chad, but irrespective of the issue of taxation, the tax revolt confirmed the deepening division between the ruling southern elite and the northern traditional religious and tribal authorities. In the following year, 1967, FROLINAT exploited this spreading discontent to launch forty major assaults against the government, inflicting more than 1,000 civilian and military casualties. The combination of the tax revolt and the widespread insurgency led by FROLINAT in eastern and central Chad were a much greater threat to Tombalbaye and the survival of his government than the furtive revolt of the Toubou in the northern sands.

By 1968 the government had lost control of the Sudanese frontier and much of Wadai, the losses of which were compensated in February when a government patrol ambushed a small rebel unit near Lake Fitri in which the FROLINAT leader Ibrahim Abatcha was killed. The death of this charismatic rebel may have been fortuitous, but the discovery on his body of a cache of secret papers and a Letts Desk Diary with a daily record of all rebel operations was a devastating blow to FROLINAT. The government immediately made full use of this windfall from the vagaries of revolutionary war by circulating throughout the country a photograph of the dead body to dispel the belief widely rumored by FROLINAT that Abatcha had survived. Even more damaging, however, were the rich sources about the movement taken from Abatcha and his lieutenants, which allowed the intelligence services of Chad and, of course, the SDECE to piece together the history of the FROLINAT. The French were able to identify the disparate elements of the movement, their training bases in Darfur, and the location of their operations in Wadai and Guera. The documentation also disclosed not only the weapons that had been provided to FROLINAT but the suppliers and the source of arms in Egypt and eastern Europe. In effect, the captured documents confirmed what had long been suspected but not corroborated: The Sudan was directly involved in an attempt to overthrow the government of Chad. In Khartoum the Egyptian embassy officials, particularly the military attaché, had been working closely with the Sudanese government and its military officers to destabilize and bring down President Tombalbaye.[27]

Tombalbaye Fights Back

At the Sixth Congress of the Parti Progressiste Tchadien (PPT) held in Fort Lamy on 5–10 January 1967, Tombalbaye used the forum to impose a *parti unique* for Chad. He argued that a Tombalbaye dictatorship was necessary at this stage in the political development of Chad, but to numerous observers the meeting was an exercise in the "mystical" rather than the political realities of Chad. Nevertheless,

the congress dutifully confirmed the appeal of the president for a personal dictatorship, while "the protracted conflict and struggle for power between the
Moslem, Arab-oriented north and the animist, Christian southerners" was "relegated to limbo" by the 600 delegates.[28]

Provided with full powers, Tombalbaye outlined his program for the future.
French influence would be further reduced. The government would use its own
true voice in Africa and in the Third World. Specifically, there could be no rapprochement with the Sudan as long as Sadiq al-Mahdi remained its prime minister. This was Tombalbaye's tit for tat with Sadiq, who had publicly declared that
peace with Tombalbaye was impossible as long as Chad used Israeli advisers to
train African personnel and to improve its intelligence service. However, when
Muhammad Ahmad Maghoub replaced Sadiq in May, Tombalbaye sought to
mend fences with the Sudan. He failed to obtain from Maghoub an extradition
treaty that would have required the Sudan to give up Tombalbaye's enemies from
their safe havens. At the same time he vigorously pursued private talks at the
meeting of the heads of state of the Organization of African Unity held in Kinshasa in September 1967 for an understanding between Fort Lamy and Khartoum over a volatile and remote frontier. Mahgoub could not abandon FROLI-
NAT by an extradition treaty, but he did promise Tombalbaye that he would
restrain the dissidents operating from Darfur.

President Tombalbaye returned to Fort Lamy confident that the differences between the Chad and the Sudan had been resolved. With the help of a delegation
from Niger, a Chad-Sudan border commission was convened at El Fasher in early
September, and on the 25th the two governments issued a communiqué to announce the peaceful resolution of their border dispute. Five days later the border
reopened. Despite numerous incidents, which Mahgoub insisted the Sudan army
had strict orders to prevent, the peace on the border continued to be threatened
by the chieftains who believed and were now convinced that they would prevail
in the fullness of time on the frontiers of Islam. The arbitrary border between
Chad and the Sudan had been drawn on the map by a Anglo-French boundary
commission in 1922–1923, approved by their respective governments in 1924,
and promptly ignored whenever practical by those who were the guardians if not
the proprietors of the border.

In the B.E.T., Ali Mahamat Taher and his men had been busy subverting the
Garde Nomade, nearly all of whom rallied to FROLINAT despite their excesses
among the Zaghawa. In Libya, Taher began to provide arms to exiled Toubou
who had congregated at Sebha and in January 1968 began to drift toward Zouar
and Bardai. However, once FROLINAT rebels appeared in the B.E.T. bearing
arms to support the Toubou, the hitherto inchoate Toubou rebellion became integrated within the larger, more organized FROLINAT movement. Thereafter,
Taher would lead the FROLINAT forces in the north while the remnants of
Abatcha's guerrillas struggled in eastern and central Chad. In February 1968 a
combined force from the FROLINAT of Taher, the Toubou, and the renegade

Garde Nomade attacked Ain Galaka in the B.E.T. and threatened the administrative headquarters at Faya Largeau.

Ironically, despite the rebellion on the eastern frontier, the outbreak of troubles in central Chad, and the resurgent Toubou supported by Ali Mahamat Taher, the United States Embassy reported in January 1968 that Tombalbaye was "as firmly in the saddle as ever."[29] Despite the futile attempt by President Jean-Bédel Bokassa of the Central African Republic to mediate between the antagonists, the embassy was pessimistic that the revolt would end as long as Sudanese, directly or indirectly, continued to provide the insurgents with arms. The embassy argued that the survival of the Tombalbaye government depended on "the extent to which foreign powers—France on the one hand and Sudan and the Arab world on the other—wish to commit themselves . . . little is at stake for the United States . . . however, the situation is serious enough to warrant the closest attention by the United States Government."[30]

The attention of the United States government should have been drawn to the FROLINAT flag over Aozou, a remote but strategic oasis in the B.E.T. It symbolized the message that Tombalbaye was losing control in the north and that his southern army could no longer respond to the challenge from the Arabs. Where the rebels were most active, government officials were the most inept, corrupt, or both. By spring 1968 the Tombalbaye government no longer bothered to deny that the insurgency had swept like a *habub*, a storm of wind and sand, from the B.E.T. into the central and eastern Chad, where FROLINAT joined their forces with the rebels. By the summer of 1968 government forces were everywhere on the defensive and increasingly insecure. In the capital, Tombalbaye's security forces arrested seven trade union leaders, including the former secretary of the Chad National Workers Union, on the frivolous charge of distributing antigovernment leaflets. His crackdown on labor leaders may have intimidated the trade union movement, but it demonstrated his dwindling control of the government.

This became all the more apparent when it was clear that Tombalbaye was losing the propaganda war. FROLINAT flyers circulated freely throughout the capital, and Chad students in France distributed broadsides in Paris, with funds and facilities from French parties of the left, condemning Tombalbaye's capricious and dictatorial rule. In response Tombalbaye and his entourage swung through central Chad in March with much fanfare followed by an organized demonstration of 10,000 faithful in Fort Lamy to protest the circulation of antigovernment tracts "posted in Paris." The pamphlet war was astonishingly civil. The protesters demanded only that the government free political prisoners and restore political liberties. There was no strident plea to overthrow the government, but Tombalbaye's response was to stuff his prisons with ever more suspected opponents and to continue his visits into the hinterland, where he "appealed to the people [of Kanem and Ati] not to believe in false revolutionaries" or to be deceived by their populist message or appeals to Pan-Islamic sentiment.[31]

The Return of the French

The traditional enemy of the Toubou has always been the desert and drought, and in 1967 history had not changed for the Toubou insurgents. The Chad security forces were of little consequence compared to the great Sahelian drought, which scattered the Toubou insurgents across the landscape in search of water in the *wadis,* wells, and oases. In March 1968 there were unexpected rains, and the Toubou regrouped from their waterholes to besiege Aozou, which the reluctant, if not mutinous, government forces were unable to relieve. Although there were probably no more than 800 armed Toubou rebels in the B.E.T., they soon drove the government troops into isolated enclaves at Bardai, Fada, and Faya Largeau. By June 1968 the B.E.T. appeared lost, and in a gesture to appease the rebels, Tombalbaye appointed a few Toubou to government positions at Faya Largeau and elsewhere in the B.E.T. It was too little too late.

Tombalbaye had lost the battle for the hearts and minds of his Muslim subjects. He had drank heavily and acted erratically. He understood that to survive he could no longer ignore and insult the French or pander to the grandiose schemes of his neighbor and ally, President Mobutu of Zaire. President de Gaulle was amused; Tombalbaye conveniently forgot the "irreconcilable differences" he had once claimed existed between Chad and France. Swallowing his pride in August 1968, he personally requested that President de Gaulle send French troops to halt the rebel advance from the B.E.T., which had placed "in danger the nation's territorial integrity."[32] With characteristic panache and his affection for Chad, he was willing to forgive a chastened Tombalbaye. He approved the dispatch of 1,500 elite French troops to Fort Lamy in August, who were immediately rushed north into the B.E.T. The French foreign minister, Michel Debré, disingenuously described this dramatic military intervention, a cause célèbre in both France and Africa, as noncombatants "sent under a defense treaty signed after Chad became independent."[33] These "noncombatants" suppressed the rebellion in days, and their mobile patrols forced the Toubou in a few sort weeks to abandon their siege of many months at Zouar, Bardai, and Faya Largeau. In October peace had returned to the B.E.T., and with their mission accomplished, the French returned to Fort Lamy in November and quietly departed for France.

The decision to send French troops to Chad was strongly opposed by the French Socialist Party and its leader François Mitterrand. He and other political opponents of President de Gaulle compared the insurgency in Chad to the debacle of French arms and empire in Indo-China and Algeria. Chad was, of course, not Algeria nor Indo-China, nor were the Chadian rebels the Algerian FLN or the Viet Minh, but these considerations were of little consequence compared to the assumption by General and President de Gaulle of the perdurability of French paternalism in Africa. Neither President de Gaulle nor his prime minister, Georges Pompidou, was much concerned about the political sniping from the left, but they were quite determined to maintain the territorial integrity of Chad and the credibility of France throughout Francophone Africa. Unfortunately, neither the French president nor his representatives in Fort Lamy were able to convince the Sara, southern government of Chad that local self-government in the B.E.T. would be in the best interest of President Tombalbaye. He could hardly refuse, however, the French offer of a military and civilian mission to reorganize the dysfunctional army and bureaucracy of his government.

French Conditions and Tombalbaye's Response

When President de Gaulle decided to send a military relief expedition to support President Tombalbaye, he agreed only "on condition that the Chad Government make extensive and immediate administrative reforms."[34] France heavily subsidized Tombalbaye's government, and in 1968 France would meet its deficit of $9.1 million. Tombalbaye could hardly refuse to accept the French conditions to reform his army and his civil service. This agreement, however, soon proved ephemeral, for once the French special forces had left Fort Lamy, Tombalbaye, now secure, could easily frustrate any French attempts at reform, which would have undermined his paramountcy.

He had no such intention and consequently did nothing to institute political reforms. In December 1968 a National Assembly was elected from a single list of 105 candidates personally approved by Tombalbaye. He studiously ignored the Toubou representatives until Foccart frigidly threatened to reduce the French subsidy unless Tombalbaye met with them. In February 1969 Tombalbaye promised a thorough administrative reform and the replacement of his Sara B.E.T. military administrator with a civilian from the region. Few were fooled by these gestures. While on safari in southern Libya the United States ambassador to Libya encountered a caravan of Toubou "leaving Chad"; they claimed that they had chosen exile because the "Chadian authorities were making their lives difficult" and vowed to avenge the insult. At the remote Kufra oasis, 1,000 miles northeast of Fort Lamy and a million miles from nowhere to all but the Toubou, the ambassador described the Toubou encampment. Here the nomads were captivated by the extensive wheat and alfalfa cultivation made possible by irrigation. Occidental Petroleum, in its search for oil, had struck a great underground aquifer more valuable than oil.[35] The Libyan army followed in the baggage train of Occidental Petroleum with all their modern arms, which the Toubou soon obtained in the traditional ways of barter in the *suq* for camels and other items of commercial exchange.

By spring 1969 the temporary respite achieved by French intervention had vanished. In the B.E.T., Siddi Chahai, a former member of the Garde Nomade, whom Tombalbaye had promoted to prefect of Bardai in 1965, was named governor for the Tibesti to end the remnants of Toubou revolt. He was soon killed in a skirmish on the caravan track between Zouar and Faya in the northern Tibesti. With his death, the efforts of Tombalbaye to recover the B.E.T. dissolved as the southern troops sought sanctuary in Faya Largeau and refused to patrol beyond the perimeter of the oasis. By late February Tombalbaye was seeking military assistance from the French ambassador, who urged Foccart to visit Tombalbaye. Foccart found a desperate and erratic president blaming his predicament on the Soviet Union, the Sudan, Nigeria, and the Congo (Brazzaville)and claiming they were all conspiring to overthrow his government. Once again he requested French intervention to save his government. Foccart returned to Paris where President de Gaulle gave his last major policy decision for French Africa. He approved the use of French troops to defend Tombalbaye and, with his accustomed panache, ordered Foccart to work out the details.

While Foccart was organizing the Force d'Intervention for Tombalbaye, an aging President de Gaulle gracefully resigned after two insignificant parliamentary defeats. It marked the end of an era. Henry Kissinger described de Gaulle as a leader who "had performed the dramatic feats required by the crises that had brought him to power," after which the mundane management of the bureaucratic state was obviously "not for heroic figures."[36] It was time for the mantle of leadership to be passed, and in April Georges Pompidou was expected to continue de Gaulle's policies in Africa. Pompidou did not have the special relationship with Africa that General de Gaulle of the Free French had forged during World War II, nor did he have any special fondness for the romantic wastelands of Chad. Nevertheless, he would honor his patron's last wish to support Tombalbaye.

In May l969 Tombalbaye had completed his second term in office, which he commemorated by another round of suppression of real or imagined dissidents. He was the only candidate on the ballot, and not surprisingly, on June l5th he received the overwhelming approval of 95 percent of the voters and was returned to the presidency. The *New York Times* reported,

> In the opinion of most impartial observers there is no question that the Arabs have been exploited . . . by rapacious tax collectors who triple the rates decreed by Fort Lamy, then pocket the difference. . . . Nearly all prefects in Arab areas are black Christians from the South. Only two Arabs have become officers in the Chadian army, both lieutenants. Chad's own military and paramilitary forces of 4,000 and 5,000 men . . . cope with the rebel challenge . . . by going into villages suspected of sympathizing with the guerrillas and shooting everything that moves.[37]

By summer the cost of living had risen by half that of the previous year. In the Fort Lamy market there was talk that the customs union of the former French Equatorial Africa, the Union Douanière et Économique d'Afrique Centrale (UDEAC), would collapse. The cattle merchants, a reliable barometer of political and economic stability, were threatened with heavy losses in their most important international market, Nigeria. The circulation of FROLINAT pamphlets and rumors of rebel assaults against the security forces exacerbated their concerns. The government response was a nightly curfew imposed on the countryside where the usual transportation—*suq* lorries, buses, and independent truckers—immediately disappeared. Taxes were no longer collected in the rural areas. Guerrilla activity was reported for the first time in the south and into the Sara region. Insecurity on the roads endangered the conveyance of the cotton crop and consequently French economic interests and the principal source of the government's revenue. To protect French investments in the south, the Foreign Legion established a command post at Mongo, the headquarters of the Guera province three hundred miles east of Fort Lamy. Here they represented a military barrier between an estimated 3,000 FROLINAT insurgents in the north and the Chad economic heartland to the south.

The French insisted that Tombalbaye reconstruct his sagging political fences with the northern Arabs, particularly the sultanate of Wadai. In July he welcomed Prince Abdallah Sanusi of Libya.[38] Not surprisingly, the aristocratic Sanusiyya were unimpressed and not about to abandon their historic Islamic traditions to an *abid*, a slave. Whether Tombalbaye liked it or not, France was his only buffer between the demands of the Muslim Arabs in the center and the northern heartland of Chad, on the one hand, and the demands of his African rivals in Fort Lamy, on the other. He had ultimately to admit that his government had "rid itself too quickly of the old colonial administrators," replacing them with kinsmen from the south; "great efforts would be made to correct this error" and reestablish confidence in his regime.[39]

Opposition in France

After the French intervention it was no longer possible to disguise the nasty little war going on in a very large place. In France, debate on Chad and the French commitment to Tombalbaye began to appear in *Le Monde* in September 1969.[40] In articles written by Jacques Isnard, it was concluded that the intervention had reduced the ability of France to act as a "conciliator" between the opposing forces in Chad. The French special forces had fought a major battle in September 1969 at Kidirmi in Borkou, and their intelligence was predicting more bloody engagements. Isnard asserted that the French military intervention had only succeeded to ensnare France in an unwanted conflict in a wasteland to support an unpopular and unjustified political regime. The rebellion was growing in Chad despite Tombalbaye's claims that only bandit gangs threatened the peace. Isnard ominously concluded that the French military commitment was demonstrated by the construction of new barracks and airfields, all of which appeared designed to ensure the permanence of President Tombalbaye.

Military aid to Chad produced a bitter debate in the French Senate, which reached its climax on 18 November 1969. During the debate, senators argued that after the French had intervened in July 1968, Tombalbaye appeared less interested in the Toubou rebellion, ostensibly the cause for French intervention, than the suppression of the Arab rebellion in Guera, Wadai, and Salamat. François Mitterrand, the candidate of the leftist alliance in the 1965 presidential election, was an acerbic critic of French intervention and demanded an official explanation from the president for the French role in Chad. This demand on the Senate floor in Paris produced a violent outburst from Tombalbaye. He denounced Mitterrand's comments as an "intervention" and indignantly insisted that the French politician had "no right to interfere in Chad's internal affairs."[41]

Tombalbaye could not have chosen a worse time to denounce French support for his own unpopular dictatorship in Chad. Confidence in an economy whose external trade was dominated by the French had dissolved into recession at the same time that French experts were finding extensive coal deposits in Bol, geothermal activity in the Tibesti, and gold-bearing quartz in the Iriba. There could be, however, no exploitation of these minerals amid the insecurity of a troubled Chad. The prospects for deposits of coal, steam, and gold were soon overshadowed by romantic rumors of a major uranium find in the Tibesti and the grant of a huge concession to an Iraqi businessman, John Abdulahad, to drill for oil and prospect for gold, diamonds, and tungsten. Not surprisingly, this bizarre concession only confirmed the corruption and instability of the Tombalbaye government.[42] Certainly, the climate for investment in northern Chad was hardly propitious. World cotton prices were falling, a great blow to southern Chad whose revenues had sustained the economy. In the center and north, commerce had come to a standstill. Tombalbaye sought to placate his political and military opponents by permitting village chiefs to reassert their former prerogatives as tax collectors under the French colonial administration in the hope that it might guarantee the flow of revenue to Fort Lamy.

The French Military in Chad

By 1970 French special forces and the Foreign Legion, supported by aircraft and helicopters, had inflicted heavy losses on the insurgents but had not defeated FROLINAT. Ounianga Kebir in the Borkou, which had been occupied by the Toubou in 1969, was retaken by the French in March 1970, during which the Toubou "suffered serious defeats at the hands of the French."[43] During a visit to Togo in May 1970, Tombalbaye accused the press of "tendentious" reporting of the situation in Chad, shortly after which the French forces engaged the FROLINAT in an inconclusive battle at Batha.

Administrative and military reforms in Tombalbaye's government had been the price for French military assistance. These reforms were supervised by Pierre Lami until his return to France in May 1970 following disagreements "with some of Tombalbaye's ministers."[44] Lami's successor, Henri Paillard, arrived in Chad to demand no further procrastination in the implementation of the reforms. In July France began to withdraw the Foreign Legion, which appeared to have no immediate effect on the determination of Tombalbaye to stonewall French implementation of reforms in his government. Disagreements between Tombalbaye and

Paillard continued over corruption, the French subsidies for Chad, and the presence of French troops. The failure to end the insurgency produced endless negotiations at Fort Lamy and discursive discussions in France throughout the summer of 1970. To turn the tide of public opinion running against him in Europe, Tombalbaye visited Paris in August. He did not impress the French nor convince the government to continue support for his regime. Chastened by his reception, Tombalbaye peremptorily ordered upon his return to Fort Lamy that 500 civil servants were to "be retired."[45] By the end of the month 1,300 civil servants had been dismissed to improve efficiency but not necessarily the security of the capital.

The cleansing of the bureaucracy was accompanied by pious pronouncements against corruption. The military, which absorbed a third of the national budget in 1970, remained at full strength with no reductions in personnel. Meanwhile, the French military presence in Chad was reduced in October to 2,300 men consisting of a small air detachment and an even smaller unit of marines under the command of Brigadier Édouard Cortedellas. This detachment of marines was the military descendent of the famous marine artillery, which had conquered the western Sudan for France at the end of the nineteenth century. In that heroic tradition Cortedellas's men hunted numerous FROLINAT *facila*, mobile guerrilla units, usually thirty men who were "untiring marchers, but poor marksmen." In defeat, with heavy losses, even the most dedicated *facila* refused to fight against the French. They would return to battle only in the familiar territory of eastern Chad to fight its army, whom they despised.[46]

The Libyan Card

Despite the support of France, the determination of President Tombalbaye to continue to rule in Chad was suddenly made more difficult by the overthrow of King Idris of Libya in September 1969 by a cabal of junior officers of the Libyan armed forces led by an unknown colonel, Muammar Qaddafi. Qaddafi came from a Bedouin tradition, and in his revolutionary enthusiasm for the Pan-Arabism of Gamal Abd al-Nasser he supported the Toubou in the B.E.T. with light machine-guns and mortars. In December 1970 forty well-armed Toubou, including members of the Toubou guard that had served King Idris in Libya and who had been "expelled" from Libya in June, were killed near Fada in a firefight with French Legionnaires.[47]

Brigadier Cortedellas launched Operation Bison into the Tibesti in January 1971, and after a defeat at Gouro, the Toubou, in the tradition of desert warfare, retreated into Libya; once again the French occupied the Tibesti. The government forces also had minor success in Guera, which led the government to believe that the insurrection would soon be suppressed. Paris was also optimistic; Jacques Foccart reported after a visit to Fort Lamy: "More than ever we have confidence in the outcome of Chad's difficult situation, but it is going to improve and I hope things will return to normal."[48]

Despite the success of French arms, Tombalbaye was alarmed at the selected withdrawal of French military units. In summer 1970 the Foreign Legion 2nd Parachute Regiment departed before any agreement had been reached between the governments of France and Chad. As Tombalbaye discovered, Georges Pompidou did not have General de Gaulle's *beau geste* love for Chad. The cost of the military operations in Chad was increasingly difficult to justify in the Chamber of Deputies and to the French public, who had become tired of Africa. Moreover, the reduction of its military presence was the only leverage that France possessed to force the erratic and unreliable Tombalbaye to either depend on his own undependable army or negotiate with the rebels. Surprisingly, Tombalbaye tried the latter course. In September 1970 he declared a unilateral cease-fire in central and eastern Chad. In December the president continued his peace offensive by offering amnesty to the rebels, replacing the unpopular Chad armed forces with local militia units, and promising funds for economic development. In 1971, many Moubi chiefs and tribesmen, who had been among the first to join the revolt against Tombalbaye, declared their allegiance to the government. Those who came in to give the *baya*, the Muslim oath of allegiance, did not, however, surrender their arms. Indeed, during this period of "no war, no peace," the southerners expressed consternation at the announcement of the departure of the Foreign Legion 2nd Parachute Regiment; by 1972 only 800 army and 1,000 air force personnel were based in Chad.

Notes

1. E. S. Furniss, Jr., *Troubled Ally: De Gaulle's Heritage and Prospects* (New York: Praeger, 1960), pp. 440–455.

2. For the "secret agreement," see J. Foccart and P. Gaillard, "Foccart Parle," *Jeune Afrique* 1 (1995): 275; Chester Crocker, "France's Changing Military Interests," *Africa Report* 13 (June 1968): pp. 16–41.; *Revue de Defense Nationale* (October 1960).

3. Samy Cohen, *Les Conseillers du président Charles de Gaulle á Valéry Giscard d'Estaing* (Paris: Presses Universitaires de France, 1980), pp. 154–156.

4. When Foccart determined that it would be in the best interests of France to share matters of common interest regarding Chad with the Americans, the appropriate information was made available to the United States embassy in Fort Lamy. This was particularly crucial for an early American appreciation of the Toubou revolt in northern Chad and the activities of the FROLINAT rebels in the east.

5. John Chipman, *French Power in Africa* (London: Basil Blackwell, 1989), p. 126.

6. For a history of Chadian political parties see: Jacques Le Cornec, *Histoire politique du Tchad de 1900 à 1962* (Paris: Librairie Générale de Droit de Jurisprudence, 1963).

7. Chambre de Commerce d'Agriculture et d'Industrie du Tchad, *Tchad 1962* (Monaco: Éditions Paul Bory, 1962), p. 54.

8. J. A. de C. Hamilton, *The Anglo-Egyptian Sudan from Within* (London: Faber and Faber, 1935), p. 302.

9. Jacques Foccart to Philippe Gaillard, in Foccart and Gaillard, "Foccart Parle," pp. 275, 300–305.

10. F. Tombalbaye, *Rapport moral du President François Tombalbaye, Congrès Nacional, Fort Archambeau, January 15–20* (Fort Lamy, 1963).

11. Arthur M. Schlesinger, Jr., *A Thousand Days* (New York: Crown, 1965), pp. 551–584.

12. Alistair Horne, *A Savage War of Peace* (New York: Viking Press, 1978), pp. 245–247, 417.

13. Foccart and Gaillard, "Foccart Parle," p. 227.

14. Reports from the U.S. Embassy argued that Chad should be divided into the north and the south, "White and Black" spheres. U.S. Embassy, Ndjamena, Airgram A-111, 11 May 1967. For the murder of government officials see D. G. Morrison et al., *Black Africa: A Comparative Handbook* (New York: Free Press, 1972), p. 208.

15. Service de Statistique, *Enquête démographique au Chad 1964*, 2 vols. (Paris: Government of France, 1966); Le Cornec, *Histoire politique du Tchad*, p. 92.

16. Arnold Rivkin, *Nation-Building in Africa* (New Brunswick, N.J.: Rutgers University Press, 1970), p. 178.

17. Carleton S. Coon, *Adventures and Discoveries* (Englewood Cliffs, N.J.: Prentice-Hall, 1981), pp. 380–385.

18. R. Buijtenhuijs, *Le Frolinat et les revoltes populaires du Tchad, 1965–1976* (The Hague: Mouton, 1978).

19. Richard A. Kerr, "Fifteen Years of African Drought," *Science,* 22 March 1985, p. 1454.

20. Benyamin Neuberger, *Involvement, Invasion, and Withdrawal: Qadhafi's Libya and Chad, 1969–1981* (Tel Aviv: Tel Aviv Occasional Papers, no. 83, May 1982), p. 17.

21. U.S. House of Representatives Subcommittee on Africa, *Report of Special Study Mission to West and Central Africa, March 29 to April 27, 1970* (Washington, D.C.: Government Printing Office, August 1970).

22. U.S. House, *Report of Special Study, 1970.*

23. U.S. Embassy, Fort Lamy, Airgram A-117, 8 January 1968.

24. See Buijtenhuijs, *Le Frolinat.*

25. The Chad dissidents had used many acronyms, as political groups were more cells than parties in the Western definition. There were the conservative Muslim Union Général des Fils du Tchad (UGFT) and the Mouvement Nationale de Libération du Tchad(MNLT), in addition to the Chad National Liberation Front (FLT).

26. Buijtenhuijs, *Le Frolinart,* p. 138.

27. Egyptian efforts to penetrate the Sudan Defence Force had not ceased since the conquest of the Sudan in 1898 and were continued with vigor after independence in 1956. See Dispatch 210, U.S. Liaison Office, Khartoum, 10 May 1955. Egypt provided military assistance to the independent Sudan (Dispatch 146, October 1956) and thereafter has been closely involved with military assistance to successive Sudanese governments, which have never appreciated and often objected to Egyptian influence.

28. "Turning Point for Tombalbaye?" *West Africa,* 21 January 1967, p. 67.

29. U.S. Embassy, Fort Lamy, Airgram A-117, 8 January 1968.

30. U.S. Embassy, Airgram A-117; and Charles E. Bohlen, *Witness to History* (New York: W. W. Norton, 1973), p. 520.

31. "Chad: Speaking to a Meeting of Workers in Fort Lamy on February 25," *West Africa,* 9 March 1968, p. 294; "Chad: A Demonstration of over 10,000 People Was Held in Fort Lamy," *West Africa,* 16 March 1968, p. 326.

32. Buijtenhuijs, *Le Frolinat,* p. 153.

33. "Chad: President Tombalbaye," *West Africa,* 23 November 1968, p. 1391.

34. U.S. House, *Report of Special Study Mission, 1970*, p. 4.

35. "American Ambassador Visits Libyan Sahara and Tibesti," U.S. Embassy, Tripoli, Airgram A-18, 3 February 1969.

36. Henry A. Kissinger, *White House Years* (Boston: Little Brown, 1979), p. 388.

37. *New York Times*

38. "More Amnesties," *West Africa*, 12 July 1969, p. 820.

39. "Chad: President Tombalbaye," *Africa Digest* 17, no. 5 (October 1970): 87–88.

40. Jacques Isnard, "Un pays déchiré, Le Chad: La Rébellion s'organise," *Le Monde*, 23 September 1969, pp. 1, 7; Jacques Isnard, "Des ressources qui s'amenuisent," *Le Monde*, 24 September 1969, p. 7; and Jacques Isnard, "Le Pari de la France," *Le Monde*, 25 September 1969.

41. "Chad: President Tombalbaye," *Africa Digest* 17, no. 5 (October 1970): 87–88.

42. *L'Économie Africaine, 1971*, vol. 3 (Dakar: Société Africaine d'Édition, 1971), p. 109.

43. U.S. House, *Report of Special Study Mission*, p. 27.

44. "Chad: President Tombalbaye," *Africa Digest* 17, no. 5 (October 1970): 88.

45. "Chad: Civil Servants Retired," *West Africa*, 29 August 1970, p. 1011.

46. *Guerres et Conflits d'Aujourdhui* 8 (1985): 14–27.

47. "Chad: Legionnaires Killed," *West Africa*, 12–18 December, 1970, p. 1463.

48. Ibid.

3

The Sudan and Tombalbaye:
Muslims and Christians

On 1 January 1956 the Anglo-Egyptian Sudan became an independent republic, an inchoate democracy of sectarian parties, who promptly failed to govern and accepted with alacrity and ill-disguised relief a peaceful coup d'état in November 1958 led by the commander-in-chief of the army, General Ibrahim Abboud. Abboud was a fatherly figure, but this did not prevent him from imposing a monolithic military dictatorship for the next six years. The Sudan had already become embroiled in a civil war between the northern Muslim, Arab Sudanese and the Southern Sudanese of Christian and traditional religious persuasions. The conflict had actually begun six months before independence, and it remains a violent confrontation between north and south to this day. Although there was a brief respite in the fighting between 1972 and 1983, it was more an armed truce than a resolution to the tragic cultural confrontation between the combatants. The war was prosecuted by both civilian and military governments with inconclusive vigor and was conducted by both sides with increasing ferocity proportional to the passing years. It has produced a deep and wide river of hostility across which no leader from either the north or the south has been able to build a bridge. Ironically, in the Sudan the Arabs of the north have sought to dominate the Africans of the south; in Chad, the Africans of the south have attempted to assert their authority over the Arabs of the north. Tragically, in neither nation has there been any resolution to the spiral of violence and the clash of cultures.

The Sudanese officers who became rulers under Abboud had been greatly influenced during their years as junior officers by the Egyptian Revolution of 1952 and the dynamic Arab socialism preached by Gamal Abd al-Nasser. In fact, Egyptian manipulation and subversion of Sudanese officers had become a way of life after the Anglo-Egyptian Condominium secured British supremacy in 1898, but its overt manifestation was the 1924 mutiny by junior officers from the military academy in Khartoum. The mutiny was summarily suppressed, and the Egyptian troops were immediately removed from the Sudan to be replaced by an

independent Sudan Defence Force. The loss of their presence in the Sudan army
did not deter the Egyptians from clandestine efforts to influence the Sudanese in
the officer corps with only modest success, however, until the Egyptian Revolution of 1952. That revolution "signaled the first spark in the African awakening,"
and Cairo had become "the breeding ground of all African movements of liberation well before they attained independence and recognition."[1] The Anglo-Egyptian Agreement of February 1953, which made possible self-government for the
Sudan, opened the floodgates for unlimited and visible Egyptian influence in
which the Sudanese army and particularly its intelligence services were the principal recipients.

Thereafter, Sudanese military intelligence established a fraternal relationship
with its Egyptian counterpart, the *Mukhabarat,* while the more political aspects
of military affairs were carried out by the powerful military attachés attached to
the Egyptian embassy in Khartoum. By 1955 the Egyptians made no attempt to
conceal their seduction of the Sudanese by "Unity of the Nile Valley." The slogan
was accompanied by a "great deal of Egyptian propaganda and money" lavishly
spread around the Southern Sudan to convince its Africans to join with their
Arab brothers in a political union. The declaration of an independent Sudan on
1 January 1956 by Prime Minister Ismail al-Azhari, himself an ardent unionist,
was a crushing defeat for Egypt, Pan-Arabism, and the unity of the Nile dominated by Egypt. It did not, however, discourage Egyptian efforts to influence the
Sudanese when and wherever they could not assert outright control. The
Mukhabarat redoubled its efforts to consolidate relationships with their Sudanese
counterparts in military intelligence and throughout the army. In June 1957 the
Sudanese prime minister, Abdallah Khalil, a leading figure in the Umma Party,
the traditional and implacable opponent of Egypt in the Sudan, narrowly escaped being captured in an attempted coup d'état supported by Egypt. A year
later the Egyptians were rewarded for their unremitting effort when Abdallah
Khalil quietly turned over his ineffectual government to General Ibrahim Abboud. After Gamal Abd al-Nasser seized the Suez Canal in 1956 to consolidate his
leadership of the Pan-Arab world, the Sudan became more a nuisance to be controlled than the historic defender of Egypt's southern frontier. He had come "to
dream of a union, which would embrace Egypt, the Sudan, and the Congo and so
create a superstate, with Cairo as its capital, stretching from the Mediterranean
and the Red Sea across to the southern Atlantic."[2] Egyptian agents were everywhere, and between 1956 and 1966 more than thirty Egyptian "diplomats" were
expelled from African nations.

Abboud's military government, like all those that have succeeded his, was bewildered and hopelessly incapable of dealing with the insurgency in the Southern Sudan. It appeared as if the Sudd, the great swamps of the Nile, had swal-
lowed up his government. When confronted by a popular front of professionals
and trade unionists, Papa Abboud dissolved his government on 26 October 1964.
A civilian transitional government organized the elections in the spring of 1965

for the parliamentary government that replaced him. Unlike the military, the successive civilian governments were deeply suspicious of the Egyptians, but the two dominant parties in the parliament, the Umma and the DUP (Democratic Unionist Party) were deeply committed to Islam rather than the secular heresies of Nasser. The Umma were the political heirs of the Islamic religious reformer, Muhammad Ahmad, al-Mahdi, whose forces had destroyed Egyptian rule in the Sudan at the end of the nineteenth century. The DUP was the political manifestation of the Khatmiyya brotherhood with historic ties to Egypt, which had become somewhat frayed by an independent Sudan but which was most certainly Arab and Muslim. Whether the Umma or the DUP controlled the Sudanese government, its Muslim leaders perceived that to support the Chadian rebels operating from Darfur would certainly improve their ambiguous and strained relations with Egypt. The genuine efforts of Tombalbaye to court the friendship of the new civilian, Muslim Sudanese leaders appeared hopelessly naïve to sophisticated Arabs and even confirmed their conviction that the Blacks were indeed *abid*, slaves. Psychological perceptions were reinforced by pragmatic considerations. The Sudanese government and certainly the Sudanese Muslims west of the Nile, the Baggara and particularly the non-Arab Fur, considered Wadai as an extension of their historic patrimony. Tombalbaye, the Sara from the far south, was not only an interloper but also an African, a Christian, and a Francophile. He was an *abid* to be dismissed.

The Sudan and Chad

Tombalbaye made every effort to avoid a quarrel with the Sudan or Egypt and appears to have hoped that the relations with his neighbors would be the result of cooperative consultation on the frontier, as in the past between Britain and France and between France and the Sudan.[3] He had proscribed the activity of the Southern Sudanese rebels in Chad in good faith and felt betrayed when Abboud, who had promised that the Sudan would not interfere in Chad's internal affairs, permitted the elusive "warriors" of the "Islamic Republic of Chad" to proselytize freely in Darfur. From there they could pass with impunity over the border assisted by kinsmen and the traditional freedoms of the frontier. The presence of a handful of messianic evangelists preaching the overthrow of a secular government was not new in the *Bilad al-Sudan,* but the availability of modern arms was a more serious development. When the Sudan realized in 1964 that it was no longer to its advantage to ship arms stored in the warehouses of Khartoum up the Nile to the insurgents in the Congo, the government could not resist the requests from their Muslim Arab brethren from Chad.

The support of the Chadian Arabs by the Sudan was not simply motivated by prejudice or practicality. During the half century of French rule, the economy of Wadai had deteriorated, and many Arab inhabitants immigrated east to join the Sudanese army, labor in the cotton fields of the Gezira south of Khartoum,

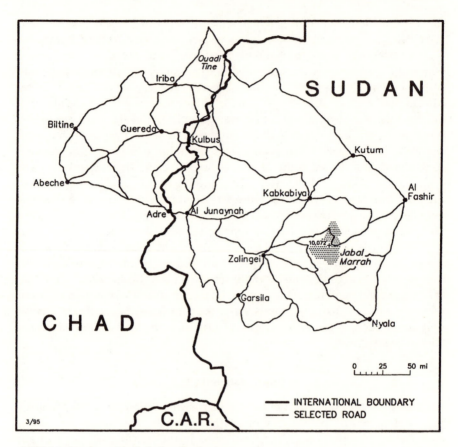

MAP 3.1 Southern Chad–Sudan Border Area

and moved on to settle as menial workers in Saudi Arabia. There were few opportunities for education in Wadai, and the most promising students from the
khalwa, the Quranic elementary schools, were sent to the Sudan and then to
Cairo to continue more advanced academic or theological studies. Like most immigrants, those from Chad retained strong political and theological ties to their
homeland and opposed with dismay the encroachment into Wadai and the B.E.T.
of a government dominated by Africans.

In 1960 the Arabs from Wadai constituted a majority in the Association of
Chadian Students in Cairo. Like Arab students everywhere during those years,
they were obsessed by the Pan-Arab program of Gamal Abd al-Nasser and were
inspired by his message to confirm the revival of the Arabs and the resurgence of
Islam. They regarded themselves as the harbingers of a new political role for the
Arabs and the reformers of Islam in Chad if not throughout the Third World. At
Al-Azhar the students from Chad were deeply influenced by a controversial octo-

genarian, the intellectual Aboubakr Abd Al-Hakim originally from Wadai. As a professor at Al-Azhar, Al-Hakim appears to have had ties with the *Mukhabarat,* who were interested in the association of his more radical Chadian students with students from other African nations, especially those who volunteered for military and political training in North Korea.

Although Al-Azhar had become the center and sanctuary for the opposition to the government of Chad, Tombalbaye did not expect that his invitation to visit Egypt in 1964 would be anything other than a pleasant meeting of heads of state. He was, consequently, both surprised and perturbed to be greeted upon his arrival in Cairo by a violent protest of Chadian students studying in Cairo. The Egyptian police handled the demonstration with deliberate inefficiency followed by appropriate apologies and sumptuous Egyptian hospitality. The incident was largely forgotten, but it was the first indication of the growing unrest among the exiled Chadian Arab population and an ominous omen of darker days on the horizon for President Ngartha François Tombalbaye.

If President Tombalbaye was unprepared for the hostile reception he received from the dissidents in Cairo, he was well aware of the Chadian rebels congregating in Khartoum and raiding into Chad from the frontier with Darfur. He warned Prime Minister Ahmed Mahgoub that if the Sudan did not cease its support for rebel harassment from Darfur, he would have to reconsider his expulsion of the "black Sudanese and Christians [supporters of the Southern Sudanese insurgents, the Anya Nya]" who had sought refuge in Chad.[4]

Tombalbaye was not the only one who knew about the complicity of the Sudanese government. When officials of the U. S. Agency for International Development arrived in Khartoum in January 1966 to negotiate the terms for a modest assistance program, they discovered, upon examining the Sudanese budget the transfer of substantial funds from civilian to military accounts. After close scrutiny the source of these funds were the Persian Gulf states making grants presumably for development projects. Upon further investigation the embassy officials traced the money to a large Chad community in a northern suburb of Omdurman known to the Sudanese as "Little Chad." The "mayor" of Little Chad was Pierre Elisende, Territorial Commander, and Mosambe N'Gakatou, Deputy Commander, of a rebel force soon to be absorbed within FROLINAT. Both were Africans, not Arabs; they were Barma from the former kingdom of Baguirmi, the traditional enemies of Tombalbaye's Sara. In the open society of the Sudan after the fall of General Abboud, the Americans had little difficulty following the money trail to fourteen training camps for Chadian rebels scattered across the Sudan from the Red Sea to Darfur.[5] Supplied with details by Chadian and Sudanese informants, Roy Harrell, Director of USAID in Chad, and Cleo Noel, Deputy Chief of Mission of the U.S. Embassy, Khartoum, pieced together a history of the activities of the Chad rebels in the Sudan and Darfur, and rebel incursions across the border that had begun two years before Ibrahim Abatcha resurrected FROLINAT in June 1966. Raids, skirmishes, and *razzias* in the borderlands were traditional, but the first attack by insurgents determined to overthrow the African government of President Tombalbaye took place in May 1964, when men of Elisende's 2nd and 4th "brigades" attacked Adre. They had trained at Hajar Banda in the Sudan, but the report of a "brigade" was a euphemism for a unit similar to the *faoudj* of the Algerian FLN consisting of only a dozen well-armed men. The *razzia* into Chad continued; there were seventeen engagements in 1965 and another thirty-five in 1966.

Sadiq al-Mahdi and Chad

In July 1966 the government of Muhammad Ahmed Maghoub was defeated in a crucial parliamentary vote and was succeeded by a coalition government led by Sadiq al-Mahdi. Although only thirty years old, the minimum constitutional age for the prime minister, Sadiq was destined for political leadership. Despite his age and relative inexperience, many Sudanese believed that he could lead the Sudan out of the civil war between north and south to a new age of national unity, peace, and prosperity. Although he spoke of peace and accommodation with the Southern Sudanese, he refused to abandon the Islamic mission of his great grandfather. The civil war would, therefore, continue perhaps not with the determination of Abboud or Mahgoub but in a desultory and debilitating fashion.

In late June 1966 FROLINAT, now officially organized, launched its first assault from Darfur against a government post in Chad. This attack was not a border skirmish by Elisende's raiders but the incursion into Chad's sovereign territory by a liberation movement. Tombalbaye publicly accused the Sudan of allowing and supporting FROLINAT to operate freely in Darfur and in Chad. Only a few weeks in office, Sadiq denied the allegation, "admitting only that it had given medical aid to the wounded."[6] Tombalbaye did not believe the platitudes from Khartoum and promptly closed the border with Darfur and ordered his security forces to harass the Arab Sudanese and *jallaba* traders residing in Chad. Sadiq was a bundle of ambiguity. Young, educated at Oxford, and determined to assert his own authority as the descendant of his charismatic great grandfather, Muhammad Ahmad, al-Mahdi, who had founded the Mahdist state in the Sudan at the end of the nineteenth century, Sadiq welcomed the independence of Chad but not by an African who challenged the followers of his religious faith and the brotherhood, the *Ansar* in Darfur. The *Ansar* was the name given to those who had followed the Prophet Muhammad in Mecca and given to those Sudanese who had followed the Mahdi. They now flocked to Sadiq with the *baya*, the oath of allegiance, and spread from the heartland of his heritage in the western Sudan into Wadai and beyond into central Chad. He could not abandon them. His heritage also required that he assert his independence over any Egyptian influence against which his great grandfather had rebelled at a time when the Arab socialism of Nasser was incompatible with the Islamic traditions of Mahdism. To confound these dilemmas was the "problem of the Southern Sudan," the civil war, now ten years old, against peoples whom Sadiq could not accept as equals in a united Sudan. When Tombalbaye closed the frontier and restricted the activities of the Northern Sudanese in Chad, Sadiq continued Abboud's efforts to overthrow Tombalbaye.

The political schizophrenia of Sadiq was demonstrated by his radio address in December 1965 in which he warned that the cancer, "regionalism" in the Southern Sudan, could spread to Darfur. His appeal symbolized his personal and political dilemma. On the one hand, the western Sudan, Kordofan and Darfur, was the home of Mahdism from which had been recruited in the nineteenth century the shock troops of the Mahdi's revolutionary army, the Baggara, who had remained loyal to the call to reform the Faith. On the other, the westerners, the Baggara and the non-Arab Fur, had historically been hostile to the *Awlad al-Balad*, the more sophisticated inhabitants of the villages and the urban Arabs of the Nile. The pastoral peoples and those with cultivated fields in Darfur regarded with suspicion and frequently open hostility the *jallaba* traders from the river, who struck sharp bargains in the *suq*, and the officials from the river, who arrogantly displayed their marginal literacy among the illiterate rustics of the borderlands. The sophisticated Sadiq was well aware that his support for the Chadian rebels could destabilize the fragile political and economic ties that bound the *Bilad al-Sudan* and Darfur with Khartoum.[7] Consequently, it is not surprising that tradition prevailed over modernity. In September 1966 his minister of defense requested more than £S6 million for the Chad insurgency; Sudanese military helicopters began to ferry men and materiel to the frontier, and the Sudanese air force made airdrops inside Chad. These activities did not go unnoticed by U.S. officials in Khartoum, who reported on the clandestine support for FROLINAT by the Egyptians and the more obvious military movements of the Sudanese. None of this information was particularly welcomed at a time when the United States was seeking to improve its relations with the Sudan. It was diverted to the Department of Defense and buried.

The opening of the Sudan after the restrictions of the Abboud regime produced the most free press anywhere in Africa. The critics of the foreign policy of Maghoub and then of Sadiq vigorously denounced the hypocrisy of a government that supported African secessionist movements in Eritrea and Chad but denied the same privilege to the Southern Sudanese. The Sudanese government argued that the insurgency was an internal matter in which any foreign intervention would be a violation of the sovereignty of the Sudan and the constitution of the Organization of African Unity, which reaffirmed noninterference in the internal affairs and the territorial integrity of any independent African state defined by the existing colonial boundaries.

After Tombalbaye closed the border in August 1966, relations between the Sudan and Chad rapidly deteriorated. The great west road between Geneina in Darfur and Abeche in Wadai was a historic route for commerce and pilgrims. The hazards of the border crossing were not improved by the Anglo-French demarcation of the frontier in 1922, whose boundary markers were studiously ignored by the inhabitants who continued to play one sovereignty against another, whether that of the sultans or the pretensions of the new imperialists from Lake Chad and the Nile. Patrols from the security forces of both Chad and the Sudan crisscrossed the frontier with abandon and the good sense not to become involved in any compromising circumstance. Nevertheless, the Sudanese army was committed to supporting FROLINAT, which introduced a new dimension to the accepted rules of behavior on the frontier. The Chadian army in Wadai was a border gendarmerie ill prepared for a guerrilla war, let alone the Sudanese army. By late 1966 the skirmishing in the borderlands had escalated beyond the control of the governments far away in Fort Lamy and Khartoum, when President Hamani Diori of Niger offered to mediate the dispute. Both Tombalbaye and Sadiq welcomed the intervention of a third party in a quarrel that neither desired but that neither could abandon without protest from constituents.

In October 1966 President Diori succeeded in resolving the immediate differences between Sadiq and Tombalbaye: Sudanese bank accounts in Chad were freed; the Sudanese in Chad were permitted freedom of movement; and Sudan Air could resume its service to Fort Lamy. Tombalbaye demanded that the Sudan extradite his many enemies among the "political refugees" from Chad in Khartoum and Darfur; Sadiq agreed to extradite only criminal offenders. These issues were peripheral to the central question of security on an ungovernable frontier, which both Chad and the Sudan, at the suggestion of President Diori, sought to resolve by a joint border commission. This was a convenient device for international political absolution contemptuously ignored by those committed to historic feuds on a border that suddenly had assumed more ideological and national concerns than the traditional *razzia*.

The lull in activities by the Chad insurgents lasted no longer than a midsummer shower in the Sahel. By autumn the Chadian dissidents were freely operating across the border and throughout Darfur; "clandestine" offices were opened in Geneina and El Fasher. In Omdurman the FROLINAT leadership operated from a very visible enlistment office, and the recruits were housed in Sudanese government quarters. By winter the movement opened several other offices in the Khartoum metropolitan area, the conspicuous activities of which were easily monitored by the foreign intelligence community. Their locations were, of course, under constant surveillance by the Embassy of Chad, whose watchers reported frequent visits by diplomats from the People's Republic of China, occasionally by Soviet officials, and even by a trade delegation from Albania. Indeed, the rebels were honored guests; in October high-ranking officials in the Ministry of Defense warmly received Chadian dissidents from Darfur arriving at the central railway station in Khartoum. In Spring 1967 El Hajj Issaka led a more formal FROLINAT delegation, which was greeted with all the ceremony usually reserved for a diplomatic mission from a sovereign state.

FROLINAT Attacks

Tombalbaye's reaction to all these Sudanese activities in support of his enemies was anger and frustration. He ordered the public arrest of the more prominent Sudanese merchants in Fort Lamy, which threatened to undo Diori's mediation and nullify the efforts of the border commission to the disadvantage of the Sudan. Khartoum immediately responded with a gesture of goodwill in April by expelling selected "bandits" to their homes in Chad. In return, Tombalbaye ceased to harass the Sudanese community in Fort Lamy and moderated his criticism of the Sudanese government and its leaders. The rhetorical fencing, however, could not disguise the realities of Sudan's determination to support FROLINAT. In the spring of 1967 a French advisor to the Ministry of Finance and the Minister of Defense in Fort Lamy informed U.S. officials that "extra support" would be required for "additional military activities that will be intensified beginning in May 1967."[8]

Among the most conspicuous revolutionaries operating from Sudan was "Colonel" Ibrahim Ouarnang, a commander in Moussa's liberation front. His main base, according to the Sudanese government, was "somewhere" in Darfur, but in reality he operated from the sanctuary of the historic Sudan border town of Geneina. Moussa had under his command 200 men, most of who were subsequently killed in a battle with Chad security forces at Katafa in June 1967. Ali Arabi Daoud led a second force. He first appeared in December 1965 when he led an assault on Chad units at Um Guereda and Tachana. Daoud's men also fought with Ibrahim Ouarnang at Katafa where they suffered heavy losses. Adoum Nimr, a member of the FROLINAT politburo, also operated from Geneina. Like the others who flaunted their prowess as heroic border chieftains, he made no attempt to disguise his intentions, and even the Sudanese officials could not tolerate his arrogance; he was firmly ordered to leave Geneina and disappear beyond the eyes of Sudanese intelligence. Perhaps the most dangerous of the "colonels from Chad" was Mahamat Saoun. He had replaced Ibrahim Abatcha upon his death as the commander of the FROLINAT forces in Chad. He had a reputation for daring and a sinister proclivity for "violence" in Salamat and Guera where his men behaved with more ruthlessness than was customary in border wars. These frontline "colonels" presumably answered to the official FROLINAT political commandants who moved in and out of the Sudan. El Hajj Issaka was in charge of Salamat, and Bahar Dannah commanded the "Dankar" detachment in Batha. To the pastoralists of the Sahel and those who cultivated the soils around its villages, the appearance of armed men refreshing themselves by the fire was neither new nor an imposition on their customary hospitality, but their ideological convictions made little sense to those who had led the *razzia* for profit or vengeance.

During 1967 the FROLINAT forces were engaged in at least thirty battles with the government forces, but none were more than 50 miles west of the

Chad-Sudan boundary. Despite the unusually heavy casualties, these encounters appeared to many civilians in the border towns an unfortunate escalation of the traditional *razzias* associated with the volatile life of a tempestuous frontier. A few of the insurgents penetrated as far west as the Batha and Chari-Baguirmi prefectures, but they were contained by the French-trained reinforcements of the Chad security forces. The FROLINAT offensive was launched by a paper campaign of tracts proclaiming that FROLINAT controlled much of Chad, from which the Western press reported that, indeed, President Tombalbaye was now confronted by a civil war.

At the Sixth Congress of the ruling party in Chad, the Parti Progressiste Tchadien (PPT) convened in Fort Lamy in January 1967. Tombalbaye sought to stem the tide of the FROLINAT insurgency and to consolidate his control of the government by appealing for a *parti unique* for Chad. Threatened from without and within, the salvation of the nation was to invest President Tombalbaye with complete and unquestioned authority to confront the foes of Chad. The six hundred party members, mostly Africans and predominately Sara from the south, dutifully accepted his proposal. "The protracted conflict and struggle for power between the Moslem, Arab-oriented north and the animist, Christian southerners" was "relegated to limbo."[9]

There would be no rapprochement between Chad and the Sudan as long as Sadiq al-Mahdi remained prime minister. However, when Mohammad Ahmed Maghoub replaced the young Sadiq in May 1967, he used the annual meeting of the Organization of African Unity (OAU) in Kinshasa in September 1967 to discuss privately with Tombalbaye the means whereby these disruptive border disputes could be contained. Neither Tombalbaye nor Mahgoub wanted an international incident on their frontier that would compromise them before their respective religious constituencies. Maghoub was a lawyer, a prominent member of the Umma Party, and a realist. He was prepared to crack down on the dissidents operating in Darfur, whom he personally regarded as bandits, but he was not about to extradite his fellow Muslims to the Christian Sara authorities on the Chad-Sudan frontier. Moreover, Mahgoub was not prepared to sign Tombalbaye's extradition treaty, which had been approved in May 1967 by a docile Chad National Assembly. Consequently, Tombalbaye sought support from his allies in Zaire and Niger to bring pressure to bear on the Sudanese to resolve the differences. President Diori responded in September with his Niamey Communiqué, which absolved both parties, for neither Tombalbaye nor Mahgoub wished to be embroiled in a frontier squabble that threatened the stability of their respective governments, the participants of which had nothing but contempt for one another.

The Sahelian Drought

During the 1960s the great African drought had spread throughout the Sahel from the Atlantic to the Red Sea and determined, like previous droughts, the pattern of the historic *razzia* and now the rebel activity in the B.E.T. The instincts and the lessons taught by the Sahelian drought sent the Toubou, Zaghawa, and Bedeiyat into eastern Chad and Darfur, for they had never known boundary markers during their search for grazing for their herds and food for their survival. In Darfur the Chadian insurgents who had been evicted by the Sudanese authorities for "arrogant behavior" now sought to return. Whether infiltrating into the towns or congregating around the depleted water holes in the countryside, the FROLINAT guerrillas became an unwanted infestation of predators that aroused the fury of the Fur and their representatives in Khartoum. The distress in the west, Darfur, was not the result of any immediate frontier dispute with Chad. Most controversies were skirmishes in the historic rivalry for the frontier lands; they were not motivated by any exhilarating response to the ideology of Arab and African socialism. They responded to the historic distrust between the *Awlad al-Balad*, the riverine inhabitants of the Nile Valley, and the proud cultivators and pastoral peoples of the great plains of the west. The urban communities of the Nile Valley represented a learned and sophisticated tradition that was not appreciated by their dynamic but rustic brethren from the steppes. This fundamental cultural dichotomy has defined the ambivalent and frequently hostile relationship between those from the west and those from the Nile Valley that has not been resolved to this day.

Darfur was the forgotten region of the Sudan. During the Anglo-Egyptian Condominium, the province had received no more attention than the Southern Sudan. At the end of World War II, the "problem of the Southern Sudan" dramatically came to the attention of the Sudanese government after the Juba Conference in 1947. Everyone rushed to provide assistance to the Southern Sudan and completely forgot Darfur. It had received little from the development funds that had come in the aftermath of the Allied victory in World War II. This neglect of the west only reinforced the historic distrust between the rural and the urban societies in the Sudan. Its poverty was soon confirmed by drought. Drought was not unknown to the peoples of the Sahel. When the rains had failed in the past the westerners had sought to ameliorate the worst ravages of dearth from drought by many traditional means. Petty wars on the frontier never violated the wells or the wadis. The new ideological warfare was as devastating as the new drought in the west, for its advocates were often contemptuous of the inviolable customary agreements.

Next to the southern provinces, Darfur was the most poverty-stricken region in the Sudan, and it was about to become poorer as the land suffered an environmental catastrophe of unheard of proportions. From north to south in Chad and Sudan there was a creeping impoverishment of villages and grazing lands and their peoples. Drought turned topsoil to dust to be blown away by the wind; stable sand dunes along the northern edge of the Sahel moved south into the pastures. The fallow season was shortened, which accelerated the decline in soil fertility and decreased the crop yield. The great Sahelian drought of the twentieth century reached its depths in Wadai and Darfur in 1966, but the rains would not return to normal for another two decades.

In Darfur the deterioration of the Sahel was most noticeable in districts like Umm Kaddada into which many Gourane from Chad had moved in search of

water after the drought had destroyed the pastures in the Erdi Hills. Although in
the rain shadow of Jabal Marra, Umm Kaddada had received sufficient rainfall
during the first half of this century to produce an abundant harvest. Grain was
purchased by the Gourane in the large *suq* to the north at Jabal Meidob and
transported along the ancient caravan route west to the villages of Dar Zaghawa
in Chad for a profitable resale. Now ravaged by drought, Umm Kaddada and sur-
rounding districts in Darfur could not grow sufficient food for themselves, let
alone for sale. In search of survival, tens of thousands of the inhabitants of the
Sahel in Chad, particularly Wadai, and in the western Sudan, particularly Darfur,
began to move east to the Nile for water and work. Not all the victims went east.
The more hardy sons of the Gourane, Zaghawa, and Bedeiyat reverted to that traditional occupation of hard times, banditry, and during the next two decades of
drought in the Sahel there was no security throughout the borderlands of Chad
and the Sudan for merchants or pilgrims and even the unwary soldier.

   The governments of both Chad and the Sudan initially responded to the
drought by initiating extensive well-drilling programs. Most of the well-drilling
projects were an ecological disaster and a political mistake.[10] The deep wells, not
surprisingly, attracted large numbers of camel and cattle nomads desperate for
water. Large herds could not be restrained and invaded the cultivated lands sur-
rounding the villages where the sedentary farmers were dependent upon seasonal
rainfall for the success of their crops and their survival. Ironically, the drought
turned farmers into shepherds. Their fields now filled with only stunted and
shriveled stubble, the villagers reluctantly bred the few sheep and goats kept by
every household in the Sahel into large flocks of eatable and milk-producing animals who could now drink from the deep wells drilled by the government and
decimate with vigor and in an ever-expanding circle the limited pastures sur-
rounding the village. Gazelle, rabbit, and fox disappeared. As the drought deepened there was now intense and often violent competition between the sheep and
goats of the villages and the camels and cattle of the nomads for the overgrazed
pastures. The centuries of tribal and ethnic disputes had always been tempered
in times of plenty. They were now revived in times of dearth. Past animosities
demanded settlement or vengeance in order for the parties to survive in the
present, and the traditional means to reconcile disputes and the authority of
the traditional leaders to settle them evaporated in the desiccation of the implacable drought. Throughout Darfur, eastern Chad, and the B.E.T., society reverted to a Hobbesian state of man against the elements and against one another
for survival.

The Return of Hasan al-Turabi

At the end of the nineteenth century the *jihad* of the religious reformer
Muhammad Ahmad al-Mahdi drove the Turks and the Egyptians from the
Sudan in 1885 to end the colonial rule of Muhammad Ali, the Viceroy of Egypt

and his Khedivial successors. The Mahdi established the first independent state to rule most of the modern Sudan, but the religious war of liberation against the hated Turks and the subsequent military campaigns to consolidate the Mahdist state and to pursue the reform of Islam beyond the frontiers of the Sudan resulted in heavy losses. The dislocation precipitated by constant conflict was soon compounded by a debilitating drought at the end of the 1880s and the beginning of the 1890s, similar to the drought that was to decimate the Sudan some seventy years later. War and drought at the end of the nineteenth century resulted in widespread death and depopulation just as they did at the beginning of the 1960s. The conquest of the Sudan by the Anglo-Egyptian forces was led by General Kitchener, and the British subsequently established rule under the anomaly of the Anglo-Egyptian Condominium, whereby sovereignty, but not authority, was legally shared by Great Britain and Egypt. Under British rule, peace and prosperity returned slowly but steadily to the Sudan, particularly in the Nile Valley, and the cultivation of cotton expanded in the great Gezira scheme on the lands between the Blue and the White Niles south of Khartoum. This was the home of the riverine Arabs, who not only prospered but also became the heirs of the British in an independent Sudan. Although the Arabs in the Sudan constituted only 40 percent of the population, they not only controlled the wealth and the government, but their affluence was in contrast to the poverty of the large majority of rural Sudanese who lived on the vast plains of the Sahel and in the verdant grasslands and forest of the south. The growing disparity between the river and rural during the twentieth century only exacerbated the historic relationship between the *Awlad al-Balad* and the Sudanese of the countryside, a relationship characterized by deep suspicion at best, bitter distrust at worst. Independence removed the paternal protection for the rural Sudanese by their British guardians to expose them to the Arabs from the Nile, whose contempt for their more rustic brethren appeared to confirm a historic incompatibility.

When Hasan al-Turabi returned to the Sudan from his studies in Paris, he immediately emerged as the intellectual leader of the conservative Sudanese elite, who envisaged the future of the Sudan as a consolidation of their religion and their position as Arabs in a multicultural Sudan. Hasan al-Turabi was the son of a *qadi* (Islamic judge), born on 1 February 1932 at Kassala near the Ethiopian border. He was a brilliant student, and at an early age he was attracted by the teachings of the Muslim Brotherhood in Egypt (Majallat al-Ikhwan al-Muslimin). His sympathies were reinforced by the Muslim Brothers who fled to the Sudan after their failure to assassinate President Gamal Abd al-Nasser in 1954; he participated as a student at the University of Khartoum in the first congress of the Muslim Brothers of Sudan in 1954, and as a student he attracted considerable attention for his brilliant academic performance. During the next decade he disappeared into Europe, where he pursued his studies with determination, receiving advanced degrees from the University of London in 1957 and the Sorbonne in 1964. Returning to the Sudan as Dr. Hasan al-Turabi, he devoted his learning, political acumen, and organizational abilities to a Muslim renaissance. His formal training in London and Paris had been primarily legal, which, of course, included Islamic law and theology. As a lecturer in the School of Law at the University of Khartoum, his charisma and learning attracted a large following among the students and the sobriquet *ulama* (theologian). He impressed Sudanese and foreigners alike with his enthusiasm, learning, and sense of humor. His lectures, commentary, and numerous writings on religion and political affairs increased his influence and the grudging respect of his opponents as one of the most perceptive interpreters of Islam.[11]

Upon his return from Paris in 1964, he not only took up his lectureship at the university but immediately entered politics to translate his teachings into political action as the leader of the Islamic Charter Front (ICF). The military government of General Ibrahim Abboud had collapsed in October 1964 and was replaced by a transitional government whose responsibility was to organize elections for a representative government to rule the country and to devise a constitution by which it should be governed. The transitional government of Sirr al-Khatim al-Khalifa achieved the first but failed, as have all subsequent governments in the Sudan, to devise a constitution acceptable to all the Sudanese. The winter of 1964–1965 was a time of euphoria for the Sudanese seeking a constitution for their new government after the experiment with the military pragmatists who had become dictators. The Islamic Charter Front proposed an Islamic constitution written in polished Arabic and adhering to the code of Islamic laws derived from the Quran, the *Shari'a*. Turabi disclaimed the authorship, but there were few in the Sudan who could have produced such an elegant codification based on the enormous body of Islamic jurisprudence and legal interpretations to establish the legal foundations for the Islamic state. His Islamic constitution would effectively dismantle the secular legal structure introduced by the British at the beginning of the century. The Turabi constitution was to secure the place of Arabs and Muslims in the Sudan and would "clearly and specifically state that the Sudan is an Islamic Republic."[12] Since two-thirds of the inhabitants of the Sudan were non-Arabs and a quarter were non-Muslims, the prospect of an Islamic constitution would reduce them before the law, if not in society, to second-class citizens. In the heated debate over this constitution, Turabi and his Islamic Charter Front had to settle for a rhetorical compromise: "a Democratic Socialist Republic based on Islam," a platitudinous aphorism made all the more appealing by its vacuity.[13]

Dominated by the riverine Arabs, the members of the Islamic Charter Front and the Muslim Brotherhood were determined to secure their political power in the governance of the Sudan. They had little interest in their rustic Muslim, non-Arab brothers in the country, west to Darfur and east to the Red Sea Hills; they had less concern for the Africans of customary and Christian religions in the south. Neighboring states inhabited by peoples of similar persuasions surrounded these enemies of Islam and the Arabs within the Sudan. The followers of Turabi perceived their duty not only to consolidate the Islamic kingdom in the

Sudan but to reform, by subversion if necessary, their citizens as part of the global renewal of Islam and the mission, now centuries old, to bring Islam to the Africans. There followed a host of incidents of Muslim proselytizing. In April 1965 an ICF minister was "accused of being involved in the smuggling of arms" to the Arabs in the Eritrean Liberation Front, then at war with the Christians in Ethiopia.[14] When Haile Selassie, the Christian emperor of Ethiopia, visited Khartoum in 1967, the Muslim Brothers embarrassed the government by raucous street demonstrations. During these same formative years for the Islamic Charter Front, there was sympathy and support, both material and influential, within the Sudanese government for the FROLINAT Arab, Muslim rebels. The ICF supplied direct cash payments to the Chadian rebels in Khartoum and wrote supportive articles for the Sudanese newspapers it controlled, as well as offering financial incentives for propaganda in those it did not.

Turabi and Sadiq

Although brilliant and charismatic, Hasan al-Turabi did not have the prestigious patrimony of his rival, Sadiq al-Mahdi. They were the same age and curiously much alike. Both were the heirs to an Arab and Islamic tradition. Both had been educated in the West, Sadiq at Oxford, Turabi at the Sorbonne. Both had come of age in the euphoria of a Sudan independent from British, Christian, alien rule. Both were determined to lead the nation into a new age untrammeled by an imperial past, whether Egyptian or European. Both were prepared to achieve this goal by using the political means at their disposal. Sadiq had only to call upon the past, the *Ansar* of his great grandfather and the Umma of his grandfather, to reassert the greatness denied by Kitchener's armies on the plains of Karari in 1898 and by the British rejection of the ambition of his grandfather, Sayyid Abd al-Rahman, al-Mahdi, to be king of the Sudan. Turabi possessed none of this ancestry, but his power emerged from his own talents and the twentieth-century revival of Islam, whether in the manifestations of the Muslim Brothers or of the riverine Arabs of the Sudan. He promptly cemented his legitimacy among the patriarchs by marriage to Wissal al-Mahdi, great granddaughter of Muhammad al-Mahdi, sister of Sadiq al-Mahdi, who was now his brother-in-law and rival. The marriage was not simply a morganatic arrangement. The heir to the mantle of Mahdism had similar objectives to those of the Islamist. Sadiq argued that "the concepts of secularism, humanism, nationalism, materialism, and rationalism, which are all based on partial truths, became deities in their own right; one-eyed superbeings. They are responsible for the present Euro-American spiritual crisis. The partial truth is [that] all these powerful ideas can be satisfied by Islam."[15] The only difference between the two were the ambiguities about the future of a multicultural Sudan, which haunted Sadiq but never troubled Turabi.

As the young and inexperienced leader of the *Ansar* and Umma, Sadiq was the leader in charge of the Sudanese government. Turabi meanwhile only had to orchestrate the score for the Islamic Charter Front. The conservative patriarchs of the Mahdiya hoped that the historic traditions founded by the Mahdi would be fused with the modern, militant Islamic message from the Islamists led by Turabi. The result was constitutional chaos. Between July 1966 and May 1967 Sadiq called upon his heritage as the descendant of the Mahdi to be the champion of a permanent constitution with an Islamic orientation.[16]

The debate in Khartoum over an Islamic constitution was not lost on those non-Muslims in the Southern Sudan nor upon those Muslims in the west and east who had ancient grievances against the patriarchs and now the Islamists in Khartoum. These smoldering animosities produced alienation, on the one hand, and ingratitude, on the other; this was confirmed when in November 1966 Sadiq approved a new law that defined any demand for self-determination by any region of the Sudan as treason. During the annual meeting of the Organization of African Unity held at Addis Ababa in November 1966, he replied to his critics: "There are major tribal groups as well as small ones; if we grant them the right to self-determination, nothing would be left to us."[17]

After the parliamentary manipulation that ended Sadiq's short tenure in office in May 1967, Mohammad Ahmed Mahgoub returned as prime minister after the elections of 1968, but he presided over an unstable government characterized by interminable disputes over the constitution and the continuing conflict in the south and dissatisfaction in the west. He also suffered a heart attack, which immobilized him for three months.

Despite the strong opposition by the Christian Nilotes from the Southern Sudan and the Muslim Fur from the west, a new constitution was presented to the Sudan's Constituent Assembly in January 1968. It proposed to change the government from a parliamentary to a presidential system to the obvious advantage of the riverine Arabs. Article 1 of the draft constitution repeated the former compromise that "the Sudan is a Democratic Socialist Republic founded on Islamic Faith." The controversy over the Islamic constitution has never been resolved in the Sudan, and the vehement debate continues in Khartoum to the present. This interminable constitutional discourse was suspended, to the relief of many Sudanese, by the coup d'état of Colonel Jaafar Numayri in May 1969. His coup was as bloodless as that of Abboud, but ironically it preempted a planned attempt to seize Khartoum by a ragtag coalition of country folk composed of the Fur from the west, the Funj from the Blue Nile borderlands with Ethiopia, the Nuba from Kordofan, and the Beja from the Red Sea Hills. These rebels traced their lineage to Dr. Adam Ahdam's Black Block, founded in 1938 to represent the non-Arab Sudanese in the Anglo-Egyptian Sudan. It was just another dissident and marginal group of the disgruntled that the British quietly discouraged and it had no political constituents and posed no threat until the 1960s.[18] Their first public demonstration took place in February 1965 to coincide with the visit of Queen Elizabeth to the Sudan. The Sudanese displayed their well-known generous hospitality to the queen, but the government also used the occasion to convene a gathering of the sultans, nazirs, and chiefs from Kordofan and Darfur to demonstrate its concern for the drought and insecurity in the western Sudan. The meeting was an opportunity for the government to show the flag and solidarity; it became, instead, a platform for the westerners to reject the arrogance of their Arab brothers from the Nile Valley. The Muslim Arabs from the west now joined with the non-Muslim Nuba and non-Arab westerners to demand that their representatives in the national parliament in Khartoum should sit only for the interests of Kordofan and Darfur, not the Sudan. Many outspoken independents argued that a Fur could be a nominee from one of the national parties, but above all he must represent the Fur nation. The regionalism and rural interests of the western countryside were deeply rooted, but the Baggara Arabs did not desert their Arab, Mahdist traditions. As the shock troops of the Mahdi, they had been in the vanguard of every battle during the *jihad;* they were determined to remain loyal as *Ansar* and Umma to the Mahdi's great grandson. The Nuba, who had suffered from Baggara raiders long before the message of the Mahdi had diverted their proclivity for the *razzia* to the more profitable towns along the Nile, now formed their own coalition, which left the west divided not only by geography but by ethnicity.

On 25 May 1969 the commander of the Khartoum garrison, Colonel Jaafar Muhammad al-Numayri, seized control of the government. The Free Officers led by Numayri had little in common with General Ibrahim Abboud and his officers, who were the military heirs of the British. They were the Sudanese replicas of Nasser's Free Officers who had carried out the Egyptian Revolution in 1952. Numayri and his fellow conspirators had been reluctant to wait seventeen years, and he himself had been suspected of plotting a coup d'état in 1957 and 1966. If the Free Officers were new men, their coup d'état was precipitated by the same disillusion with parliamentary institutions that had led to the peaceful transfer of government to General Abboud in 1958. Disenchanted with democracy, mismanagement, corruption, and especially with the politicians, the Sudanese Professionals' Front, supported by a huge popular demonstration by civilian citizens, had ended Abboud's military dictatorship in 1964. Personal interests and political apathy soon dissipated the euphoria produced by people power. Thus, when Colonel Numayri seized the government on 25 May 1969 no blood was shed, no demonstrations threatened the soldiers, and no anxieties spread among the citizenry, who appeared resigned and relieved that the transfer of power had been swift and painless. Now a Major General, Numayri brought an end to democracy, a free press, and political parties. He was promptly declared president of the Democratic Republic of the Sudan, which was neither democratic nor a republic.[19]

Numayri and Chad

Numayri immediately consolidated his control over the vocal but impotent opposition. Hasan al-Turabi vociferously condemned the presence of communists among the Free Officers and was promptly sentenced to seven years imprisonment.

Sadiq al-Mahdi's criticisms were more moderate, but when it became apparent that the leader of the Umma was not about to commit his support for the regime, he too was jailed in June. Throughout 1969 and the spring of 1970, Numayri's principal opposition came from the *Ansar* and the Umma with their political and military strongholds in Kordofan and Darfur. After Sadiq was placed under house arrest, the mantle of leadership passed to the Imam al-Hadi, grandson of the Mahdi, who denounced Numayri and openly defied his officers by retiring to the holy origins of Mahdism on Aba Island, 150 miles south of Khartoum. Here the Imam surrounded himself with thousands of the faithful, many heavily armed to defend the Mahdi's mission. On 27 March 1970 Numayri confronted the *Ansar,* and in a fierce engagement the Sudanese army of the Free Officers, presumably representing the progressive future against the traditional past, killed the Imam and 12,000 *Ansar.* Sadiq fled into exile.

Numayri's violent victory at Aba Island appeared to consolidate his authority. In fact, it merely shifted the struggle for control from his enemies without to his officers from within, who were divided among leftists, those in the middle, and the Islamists sympathetic to Turabi. These internal power struggles were never fully resolved, but they were at least postponed until after the communists were eliminated from the government in the summer of 1971, leaving the secular officers of the middle in the majority. Meanwhile, Turabi counseled the conservative Muslims officers to be patient, to accept the new order of President Numayri, but to begin the systematic recruitment, instruction, and infiltration of the officer corps from the students in the military academy and the University of Khartoum. All of these domestic considerations and conflicts conditioned President Numayri's policy toward his neighbors and particularly Chad. He had successfully crushed the Mahdists, but it served no purpose for him to seek further retribution against the *Ansar* and Umma in their geographical and religious strongholds of Kordofan, Darfur, the borderlands, and Wadai. Increasingly suspicious of the communists within his government, he was not about to encourage the leftists of FROLINAT. He quietly circumscribed the hitherto open activities of FROLINAT in Khartoum and Omdurman and was rewarded by a grateful Tombalbaye with the Grand Cross of the National Order of Chad. He returned the compliment during his visit to Chad in February 1971 by signing an agreement to improve commercial transfers between Chad and the Sudan. Six months later he rid himself of the communists in his government and seized the occasion to proscribe FROLINAT members in Darfur as communist fellow travelers. He strengthened his armed forces against the Mahdists in Darfur. No government from Khartoum, whether Turk, British, or Sudanese, had ever firmly controlled the western frontier, but like the British before him, Numayri was able to bring stability to a volatile frontier. He received the gratitude of those trying to manage a subsistence living in a region ravaged by drought and, of course, of President Tombalbaye. Law and order, or what passed for it in Darfur and the Sudan borderlands, was followed by the People's Local Government Act of 1971, an ephemeral attempt at administration, which ultimately created twenty-two rural councils in a gesture to return the administration of government to the people. It appears to have been a genuine attempt by Numayri to devolve the institutions of government, but the proliferation of administrative units bound together by the single political party, the Sudan Socialist Union, created a bureaucracy controlled by insensitive officials from the Nile. It infuriated the traditional authorities and intruded upon the historic independence of the villagers and nomads in the west.

Notes

1. Raphael Israeli, *"I Egypt": Aspects of Anwar Al-Sadat's Political Thought* (Jerusalem: Magnus Press, Hebrew University, 1981), p. 114.

2. Anthony Nutting, *Nasser* (New York: E. P. Dutton, 1972), p. 290.

3. For frontier affairs see *Report on the Administration of the Sudan in 1951/52* (Khartoum: 1952), sections 501–529 and subsequent reports of later years.

4. Arnold Rivkin, *Nation-Building in Africa* (New Brunswick, N.J.: Rutgers University Press, 1970), p. 38.

5. A list of military units, locations of their training camps, and dates of skirmishes and battles across the border in Chad were prepared by U.S. Embassy–Khartoum officials Roy Harrell and Cleo Noel. Roy Harrell had been the director of USAID-Chad and was seconded to the Sudan from August to November 1966; Cleo Noel was the deputy chief of mission at the U.S. Embassy in Khartoum. Noel was appointed Ambassador Extraordinary and Plenipotentiary of the United States of America in December 1972; he was assassinated in Khartoum on 2 March 1973 in the Saudi Arabian Embassy by Black September terrorists who had seized the embassy.

6. Mohamed Omer Bashir, *The Southern Sudan: From Conflict to Peace* (Khartoum: Khartoum Bookshop, 1975), p. 28.

7. Gabriel Warburg, *Islam, Nationalism, and Communism in a Traditional Society: The Case of Sudan* (London: Frank Cass, 1978), p. 115.

8. U.S. Embassy, Fort Lamy, Airgram A-111, 11 May 1967.

9. "Turning Point for Tombalbaye?" *West Africa*, 21 January 1967, p. 67.

10. Hassan A. El Manouri, *Umm Kaddada District* (Khartoum: U.S. Agency for International Development, September 1985).

11. U.S. House Foreign Affairs Committee, Africa Subcommittee, *Hearings on the Sudan*, 20 May 1992.

12. Bashir, *The Southern Sudan*, p. 29.

13. Bashir, *The Southern Sudan*, p. 33.

14. G. H. Jansen, *Militant Islam* (New York: Harper and Row, 1979), p. 126.

15. Sadiq al-Mahdi, "The Concept of the State," *The Challenge of Islam* (London: Islamic Council of Europe, 1978), p. 2.

16. "Government Drafts Treason Law, SF Policies All Victims of the New Law. Calls for Plebiscite, Self-Determination, and Separation Are Criminal," *The Vigilant* (Khartoum), 4 November 1966, pp. 1, 4; Saddik Rejects Self-Determination at OAU," *The Vigilant* (Khartoum), 13 November 1966, p. 3; and *Africa Confidential*, 26 December 1966, p. 5.

17. *Africa Confidential*, 13 August 1965, p. 6.

18. Edgar O'Ballance, *The Secret War in the Sudan, 1955–1972* (Hamden: Archon Books, 1977), p. 47.

19. Anthony Sylvester, *Sudan Under Nimeiri* (London: Bodley Head, 1977), pp. 65–69.

4

Libya and Tombalbaye:
Muslim Arabs and Christian Africans

FROLINAT suddenly and unexpectedly discovered a new and more committed patron than the unreliable politicians and the new military dictator in Khartoum. On 1 September 1969, only three months after Numayri had come to power, another group of Free Officers led by Colonel Muammar Qaddafi, almost as unknown as Numayri, engineered a military coup to depose King Idris of Libya. The efficient and peremptory seizure of the government by young army officers in Egypt, the Sudan, and now in Libya was not simply a testament to their vision for the future but a statement of their disillusion with a past preserved by tradition and religion for the elite. After seizing power, Qaddafi justified his leadership as a reformer for "Libya, Arabism, and Islam." His radio appeal was not that of the charismatic Islamic theologians and reformers of the nineteenth century, al-Hajj Umar or the Grand Sanusi, but the progressive path of the Free Officer Movement proclaimed by Gamal Abd al-Nasser in 1952 for the Arabs and Islam. Unfurling the banner of "Freedom, Socialism, Unity," Qaddafi and his Revolutionary Command Council (RCC) promised to free the Libyan people from the oppression of tradition made corrupt by the acceptance of Muslim *shaykhs* and kings of the Christian colonial capitalists from the West.

Like Nasser in Egypt, Numayri in the Sudan, and Tombalbaye in Chad, Qaddafi considered political parties an intolerable nuisance. None of these revolutionary leaders were democrats, and indeed the fragility of democracy and parliamentary institutions in their countries had only confirmed their conviction that military discipline was the only means to achieve a social revolution. Like Nasser and Numayri, Qaddafi placed his confidence in a cabal of military friends; dissident officers in the army were summarily dismissed. The disorganized Libyan domestic opposition was quietly silenced, and the convening of a General People's Congress of People's Committees was organized to present a facade of civilian participation as powerless as its presence provided legitimacy for the Free Officers. The Muslim brotherhoods had to be immediately contained, for in

Libya the Sanusiyya had been the historic inspiration for resistance against the Italians. The Sanusiyya, or the Muslim Brothers, who had sought to overthrow the Sanusi King Idris, were excluded from the government and their activities closely circumscribed. Muslim teachers and scholars, the *ulama*, were cautioned to be politically correct, and the conservative holy men, the *faqura* (sing. *faqi*) were quietly but firmly warned not to use the mosque to speak against the new order.

Qaddafi was full of youthful energy and ideas that tumbled out in long speeches at odd hours and at odd times. He insisted he was a Muslim revolutionary, presumably in the tradition of the Islamic reformers of the nineteenth century, without their learning or piety. His oratory was digressive; his ideology imprecise and incomprehensible to his illiterate constituents. His ramblings often led to depression, during which he flirted with apostasy, when his inadequate knowledge of Islamic theology failed to resolve the future of Libya with an Islamic past that could not be dismissed. Insecure, if not paranoid, he had the good sense to surround himself with an entourage of close friends from the Free Officers and relatives.[1] His relatives and Bedouins provided personal bodyguards, and only very close personal friends were admitted into his ruling circle. His director of military intelligence was a personal confidant, al-Khuwaylidi al-Humaydi; the head of civilian intelligence was a relative, Ahmad Qaddafi al-Dam. His cousin, Colonel Hassan Ishkal, commanded the armed forces.[2] The Arab Socialist Union, like Numayri's Sudan Socialist Union, was the only political party in Libya, the management of which was entrusted to Qaddafi's close friend and conspirator Abd al-Salam Jalloud. As Deputy Prime Minister, Minister of Interior and Local Government, Jalloud supervised the organization of Arab socialism in Libya and prepared all government documents for Qaddafi's signature as Chairman of the Revolutionary Command Council and Prime Minister.[3]

Despite his frequent capricious and eccentric behavior, Qaddafi's foreign policy was surprisingly consistent having been shaped by the Pan-Arab views of Gamal Abd al-Nasser transmitted by transistor radio throughout the Arab world when he was an impoverished student outside Tripoli. He absorbed Nasser's *Egypt's Liberation: The Philosophy of the Revolution* and adopted its geopolitical concept of three concentric circles—Arab, Islamic, and African. Like his hero, Qaddafi would dream of a single, united Arab nation stretching from "Sind [Pakistan] to the Atlantic Ocean." If Nasser believed the Sudan to be the vanguard of the Arabs on the Nilotic frontier of Islam, Qaddafi was convinced that Chad should be the Libyan extension of an Arab, Islamic frontier into the Sahel, savanna, and forests that stretch from the Sahara into the heart of Africa.

Qaddafi soon refined these fundamental principles into axioms for action. Governments with significant Muslim minorities and led by African Christians or practitioners of traditional religions were infidels to be replaced by Muslims, preferably Arabs. Those multicultural African states where Arab Muslims ruled, like the Sudan, were to be supported. Young, impressionable, and impetuous, he vehemently denounced colonialism, publicly flaunted his anti-Semitism, and spoke of the extermination of Israel. He soon became a captive of his own hatred against the West and Israel, the rhetoric of which was to be translated into internal subversion, military attack, or arming indigenous rebels, FROLINAT, and to be carried out by any means necessary including terrorism.

Qaddafi's Game

No sooner had Qaddafi secured his control of the Libyan government than he met with his idol, Gamal Abd al-Nasser, to propose an Arab union of Egypt and Libya. Nasser was taken aback. The gesture appeared impetuous and naïve. To Mohammed Heikal, the sophisticated Egyptian journalist, the offer by this very unsophisticated Libyan revolutionary was "shockingly innocent and scandalously pure."[4] Nasser graciously declined the union as inspirational but premature. Ironically, Nasser might have been well advised to accept a union with Libya rather than to contain his astonishment at the political immaturity of the one who proposed it. The vision of a great North African Arab nation had inspired the Arab captains who had come out of Arabia after the death of the Prophet. The unity of the Arab world of antiquity could now be resurrected by the oil revenues of Libya, which could offset those lost by Egypt in the Six-Day War of 1967. Here in Libya were the resources to modernize Egypt, but Nasser was ill, and his failing energies were required to rebuild Egypt's strength and prestige, not to embroil himself in yet another adventure in the ephemeral search for Arab unity. He would humor Qaddafi, but he never took him seriously.

Nasser's polite rejection of his proposal for the union of Egypt and Libya did not deter Qaddafi's enthusiasm in the pursuit of Pan-Arabism. His Tripoli Unity Charter proposed a Federation of Arab Republics of Egypt, Libya, and the Sudan. The reaction of President Numayri was not unlike that of President Nasser. Astonished, Numayri rejected the prospect of unity with Libya with less grace than Nasser. The Unity Charter languished until revived during the negotiations in November 1970 between Egypt and Syria for the Federation of Arab Republics when Anwar Sadat and Syrian president Hafez al-Assad considered adding Libya and the Sudan. Nothing came of these negotiations when Jafaar Numayri refused to become involved in any federation dominated by his more powerful neighbors. The vision of the Pan-Arab state may have faded but had not entirely disappeared when President Sadat met with Qaddafi in 1972 and signed the Benghazi Declaration. Its appeal for a Pan-Arab nation was more gratuitous than sincere and subsequently vanished when the referendum for its approval never took place.

Having failed to consummate his dream of a Pan-Arab nation, which had enormous appeal but little pragmatism, Qaddafi had even greater difficulties in introducing domestic reforms. The Zawara Declaration of 15 April 1973 suspended the secular law and instituted the Islamic *Shari'a* law; simultaneously,

Qaddafi outlawed the communists, the Baathists, and the Sanusi and Muslim brotherhoods. He then reorganized the government bureaucracy, demanded the end to Western influence in education and the media, and armed a "popular" defense force. Revolutionary committees were created, consisting not of the traditional and "reactionary" authorities but of young intellectuals who were trained in seminars and special camps in the principles, objectives, and defense of the revolution against its enemies.[5] Members of the revolutionary committees took their place in the General People's Congress, which theoretically was the new institution determining the future of the government of Libya. In fact, the Congress was controlled and orchestrated by the Chairman of Libya's Revolutionary Command Council, Muammar Qaddafi.

Geopolitic Visions

Qaddafi was consumed by geopolitics. He adopted Mussolini's African design for the New Rome, and he was captivated by the bizarre geography of Libya, which embraced the empires of the Phoenicians, Greeks, Romans, Arabs, Turks, and Italians along the Mediterranean shore. The sand and rock, the oases and wadis of the interior, are the historic magnets, which have drawn man into the desert to protect the fertile littoral and the routes of many ages across the Sahara to the wealth of Africa. The bones of man and his animals mark the passage of the great trans-Saharan caravans coming out of Africa through the wastelands to Tripoli in century after century. This was the barren homeland of Qaddafi's ancestors; once seen, it can never be forgotten. He may have failed to interest his neighbors in Arab unity, but the idea of a Greater Arab Libya and a new Islam for new times of incredible wealth were not incompatible with his vision, now more modest, to follow the Muslim merchants and holy men, the *faqura,* across the Sahara and to continue the historic mission of the Arab on the frontiers of Islam. Here in the Sahel, the historic forward course of Islam, denied by the Christian colonial powers in the nineteenth century, would now prove irresistible in its progress among the Africans in the twentieth.

These objectives, however, lay in the future. His immediate hostility to colonialism, forged from the long and bloody Italian imperialism in Libya, was now translated into an ambiguous relationship with the West. Without the enormous revenues from Libyan oil produced by the skills of the West, his ambitions were little more than the traditional self-interest of a desert *shaykh.* This dependency only made it all the more despicable. He could, however, assert his independence by demanding the removal of the real and symbolic facilities of the Western presence without jeopardizing its nonmilitary beneficence. He demanded that the British evacuate their military bases, which they had held since liberating the Libyans from the Italians and Germans, by March 1970. He was less preemptory with the Americans, who were aggressively developing Libyan oil and producing the revenues he needed. The United States, however, was deeply embroiled in Viet

Nam and was not prepared to defend the Wheelus Air Force Base, which was no longer worth its marginal strategic utility in return for future American oil interests. The departure of the paternal imperialists permitted the arrival of the adventurers. Qaddafi was young, impetuous, and unpredictable; he was delighted to receive the arms, which had vanished with the departure of the British and the Americans, but he was not going to sell himself or his revolution when his treasury was overflowing. Consequently, when President Georges Pompidou sought to reassert the historic presence of France on the southern shores of the Mediterranean by presenting Libya with forty French Mirage jets, which had already been sold to Israel, in return for oil, Qaddafi could hardly refuse. This seedy transaction was not made more acceptable by President Pompidou giving a lecture in the United States in February 1970 on the need for realpolitik and commenting that "there was a vacuum to fill" in Libya and it was in the historic interests of France to fill it.[6] To those in Washington who remembered their history, France had never demonstrated this much interest in Libya in the past. Throughout the twentieth century there had been interminable boundary rectification between the French and Italian spheres of influence, particularly on the Tunisian frontier, but in 1935 the French foreign minister, Pierre Laval, made it quite clear that Libya was part of the *Mare Nostrum* of Mussolini's new Roman empire. The Mirage fighters did indeed fly over the sands of Libya and over the waters of the Mediterranean, provoking sorties from the American Seventh Fleet. Qaddafi's interest was not in the waters but the oil-bearing sands and the historic routes across the Sahel and the Sahara, where France had interests it never pretended to possess at Tripoli or in Cyrenaica.

During the second anniversary of the transfer of Wheelus Air Force Base to Libya, Colonel Qaddafi delivered his speech before a large gathering, which included the diplomatic corps. He announced that he was sending "arms, money, and volunteers" for the Sinn Fein liberation struggle against the British forces in Northern Ireland and the to Muslim freedom fighters in the Philippines. Libya would also use its wealth to support the seizure by Iran of strategic islands in the Persian Gulf, which was the sovereign territory of the United Arab Emirates. Perhaps carried away by his own rhetoric, he declared that he would "fight Britain and the United States on their own lands," for the United States was the enemy who had guaranteed the Israeli occupation of Arab lands. His determination to assist in the liberation of the oppressed would include the African-Americans struggling against "American arrogance." His vehemence and conviction for the revolution appeared no longer to be the infatuation of an impetuous young colonel with an unlimited bank account, but of a dangerous member of the community of nations advocating terrorism as acceptable means for achieving revolutionary goals. When his speech exceeded civil and diplomatic propriety, the ambassadors from the United Kingdom and the United States walked out in protest. His determination to support movements of liberation, revolution, or terror soon had no frontiers, and when he turned his attention to Latin American, the United States immediately withdrew its representatives in protest and threat-ened to break all diplomatic relations.[7] At the time, Qaddafi's pledge of volun-teers and money for Palestinian guerrilla groups fighting Israel and his promise to pay to train and equip volunteers from any Arab country was more ominous than his bizarre support for fanatical Christians in Belfast.

Qaddafi was emboldened by his own rhetoric. He had extracted favorable terms for oil exploration, particularly from Occidental, the renegade of the oil cartel, resulting in a treasury bulging with wealth for which no disposition had been contemplated. He first sought to demonstrate his aggressive foreign policy by asserting a "historic" claim to the Gulf of Sidra, whose waters constituted the vast indentation of the southern shore of the Mediterranean formed by a straight line drawn at 32° 30′ north latitude (approximately Tunis to Benghazi). This "gulf closing line," in effect, extended Libyan territorial waters two hundred miles into the Mediterranean incorporating shipping lanes for commercial vessels and the sea for warships of any nation sailing the international waters (see Map 4.1). Libya's assertion that Sidra was her "historic" right not only challenged the naval forces of the Mediterranean states but the powerful fleets of the United States and the Soviet Union. Moreover, Qaddafi's demand was an egregious embarrassment to the United Nations, whose members had made substantial progress to codify the Law of the Sea. They argued that Libyan pretensions to the gulf did not have "any historic or legal justification and as illegally restricting freedom of naviga-tion on the high seas." The United States, which has consistently demanded recognition of the traditional twelve-mile limit for jurisdiction by any nation off its coastline, argued that Libya had not exhibited the "continuous and unchal-lenged" control over the waters within the gulf closing line "for an extended pe-riod of time." Consequently, the waters could not be considered an extension of the Libyan landmass. Qaddafi refused to withdraw his claim; the United States re-taliated by instructing the U.S. Navy to conduct annual operations south of the line and throughout the waters of the gulf.[8]

Nasser died in 1971, but Qaddafi continued to support his successor, Anwar Sadat, in the expectation that he would persevere in the cause of Pan-Arab na-tionalism and prevail in restricting the Egyptian communists and the "Nasserite elements" who had promoted the presence of the Soviet Union in Egypt. Sadat was not Nasser but a realist who had little use for his idealistic and mercurial ally. When Qaddafi visited Egypt in June 1973, he embarrassed his host by publicly chastising the passive response by Egypt to the Israeli occupation of the Sinai Peninsula. Not satisfied by humiliating Sadat in Cairo, upon his return to Tripoli he impetuously organized a "unity march" on Egypt to demonstrate support for the Arab federation and encourage Sadat to behave with the courage and deter-mination that Qaddafi expected from the leader of the Arab world. Not surpris-ingly, this bizarre affair, more a tantrum than an episode, failed ignominiously. Furious, Sadat ordered his troops to stop the Libyan convoy at the Saloum bor-der crossing and ridiculed Qaddafi's attempt to achieve a federation, let alone a

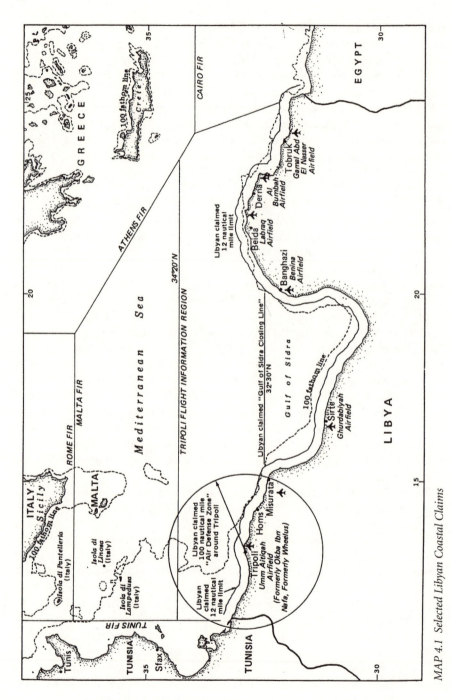

MAP 4.1 Selected Libyan Coastal Claims

cultural revolution in Egypt.[9] Qaddafi's behavior was all the more infuriating, for unknown to him, Sadat was energetically planning a major offensive across the Suez Canal against the Israeli positions in the Sinai. He never again took Qaddafi or his pronouncements seriously.

Rebuffed by Egypt, Qaddafi turned his attention to the Sudan. The Sudan was not the ideal partner in his search for either Arab unity or the chimera of federation. The Sudanese, particularly their politicians and military officers, had possessed an ambivalent relation with the Egyptians. On the one hand, the power and resources of Egypt in the Nile Valley could not be ignored; they required from the Sudanese polite recognition, mutual protestations of brotherhood, and close cooperation on common concerns. On the other, the Sudanese educated elite, both Arabs and Africans, deeply distrusted Egyptian influence south of Aswan. Even Qaddafi realized there could be no union with the Sudan without the concurrence of Sadat, whom he had alienated. This, however, did not inhibit his support for Numayri's suppression of the Mahdists, *Ansar* and Umma, whom he regarded as a deviant Islamic sect not unlike the Sanusiyya of Libya, nor his critical assistance to Numayri when he was challenged by the well-organized Sudanese communists. During February and March 1971, Numayri had publicly accused the communists of subversion and appealed to the Sudanese to destroy them. On July 19th the communists led by Major Hashim al-Ata staged a coup d'état. They briefly captured Numayri, who escaped to rally his supporters backed by Sadat's Egyptian troops on the frontier and the dramatic intervention of Muammar Qaddafi. Major Hashim had inadvisably precipitated the overthrow of Numayri when two of the principal communist leaders were away in London. They immediately flew to Khartoum to participate in the formation of the revolutionary government, when Qaddafi, with his now expected flair, ordered his Mirage fighters to intercept and force the BOAC airliner to land at Benghazi in a flagrant act of air piracy. The coup collapsed, and "the coup's two leaders were arrested and were sent later to Sudan to be executed."[10]

Qaddafi was more than willing to help Numayri eliminate communists in the Sudan, but he was not about to recognize the non-Muslim Africans of the Southern Sudan when Numayri signed the Addis Ababa agreement in 1972 that ended seventeen years of civil war in the Sudan. The difficulty for Qaddafi was not so much the peace agreement but the terms, which accepted an autonomous, regional self-government for the Southern Sudan. The agreement recognized the reality of the African presence and domination in the Upper Nile Basin, which was neither Arab nor Islamic. Qaddafi regarded Numayri's accommodation with the insurgents, the freedom fighters, as a betrayal of Islam. When the Sudan subsequently adopted a constitution that retained a secular educational and legal system, Qaddafi, who had contributed to the rescue of Numayri from oblivion in 1971, was rewarded by the recognition of the Africans south of the Sahara, whom he despised. Ignored by both Egypt and the Sudan, Qaddafi was further humiliated when Sadat launched the Yom Kippur War in 1973 without informing him of the Egyptian plans or requesting Libyan financial assistance. In the spirit of Arab solidarity, Qaddafi offered Egypt the use of the Libyan air force, which was politely declined, and made intolerable remarks when Egypt suspended its attacks on Israeli positions in the Sinai and opened negotiations. Only the spiraling revenues from Libyan oil would assuage his rejection and isolation.

In 1973 the price of oil on world markets escalated to unprecedented levels, precipitated by the war between Egypt and Israel. During the war Libya played no significant military role, but in its aftermath it became one of the principal producers of oil in the Arab world and an influential desert state of wealth. Hitherto dismissed as a petty and impoverished kingdom, Qaddafi's claim to be the leader of a pan-Arab, Islamic state could no longer be treated with disrespect. Qaddafi, the Muslim, Arab nationalist and revolutionary, used the proven oil reserves of Libya to nationalize the British concessions and to force Occidental Petroleum to increase its payment for every barrel of oil pumped from the Libyan sands. Once the accepted international price per barrel of crude had been revised to the advantage of Libya, the producers had little choice but to accept Qaddafi's terms if they wished to exploit their Libyan concessions.[11] However, there was no literate or sophisticated population in Libya to manage these incalculable resources. Until the discovery of oil, Libya's principal export and source of foreign exchange was scrap iron salvaged from the wreckage of the British and German armies during the desert campaigns of World War II. The thin line of the Libyan educated elite was rapidly absorbed by the oil industry; the nomads and desert people discovered munificent employment from the massive requirements of the oil companies. Neither the educated nor the nomads where about to abandon new opportunities for ideological or Islamic adventures. To continue the revolution, Qaddafi used his treasury to create an "Islamic Legion" from the influx of Africans recruited to produce Libyan oil.[12]

The Chad-Libyan Boundary Dispute Revisited

None of the rulers of Libya, let alone Qaddafi, have ever accepted its ephemeral boundaries. The constancy of this admirable defense of sovereignty appears all the more perverse when these historic, often violent, disputes were over sand and rock, not fertile valleys or green pastures. The rulers of Libya—Romans, Greeks, Berbers, Arabs, Turks, the Sanusiyya, and the Italians—all sought to expand their control of the hinterland in order to secure the coast, to protect the trans-Saharan caravan routes for trade, and to acquire territory for imperial gratification. It was now the turn of Muammar Qaddafi to revive the moribund and disputed southern boundary of , whose antiquity was confirmed by its impermanence.[13] Like Mussolini, Qaddafi refused to recognize the boundaries established by Great Britain and France after World War I. And like Mussolini, his appetite for territory and prophetic ambition would lead him to stimulate, sponsor, and support a "Greater Libya" into distant Africa. He visualized an "Islamic State of the Sahara" to be part of a larger Pan-Arab union from an Iranian "Arabistan" to the Maghrib that would swallow the Sahel and Equatorial Africa. Even Septimus Severus, the greatest Roman emperor to come from Libya, never dreamed of such conquests.

The problem was Qaddafi's mercurial personality. Within weeks of taking power he was considered the most voluble statesman in the Arab world. He had a tendency to think aloud and to broadcast his opinions with little thought as to their consequences. His speeches often became diatribes that divided the African community into two camps. His friends were the radical states that practiced and supported "liberation." His enemies were the reactionary states who practiced and exported "imperialism." Definitions, however, became obscured in the rhetoric, and friends became foes, as Numayri discovered after he declined to become involved in Libyan unification schemes or campaigns to destabilize Chad.

Rebuffed on the Nile and repulsed on the waters of the Gulf of Sidra, Qaddafi was determined to extend his imperial religious message to the sands of the south. King Idris and his Sanusi supporters had feared the FROLINAT and had expelled its leader, Dr. Abba Siddiq, whom Qaddafi, after seizing power, immediately invited to return. The "first permanent base" of FROLINAT was opened in Tripoli in November 1969.[14] No longer welcome in the Sudan, FROLINAT now depended upon Qaddafi for support and sanctuary in Libya. Despite his deep antipathy against communism and his critical intervention in 1971 to assist Numayri's suppression of the Sudan Communist Party, he responded with characteristic inconsistency by taking a personal interest in FROLINAT, presumably to seduce its Marxist leaders while their comrades where being indoctrinated in North Korea and Palestine.[15]

Qaddafi soon discovered to his dismay that FROLINAT was composed of rival factions and that his confidant Jalloud was entangled in a web of internal squabbles precipitated largely by Abba Siddiq's uninspired leadership. Although firmly supported by Qaddafi, Siddiq's political disquisitions infuriated the Chad revolutionary students in Libya. Wodei Kirchidemi, the *Derde* (spiritual and traditional "Sultan of Tibesti"), despised him and "accused Siddiq's forces of leaving behind [his] wounded Toubou guerrillas" to the tender mercies of Chadian troops.[16] Qaddafi promptly placed the *Derde* under house arrest, for Abba Siddiq had made himself more useful than the independent and contentious sultan. He fabricated charges that the United States was secretly establishing a military base outside Faya Largeau, the Chad administrative headquarters of the B.E.T., and was supplying arms and money for counter-insurgency training for Chadian forces in Zaire and Liberia. Moreover, he spread rumors that the U.S. Central Intelligence Agency (CIA) had infiltrated the government of Chad and that the air base at Goz Beida, sixty kilometers from the Sudanese border, was an Israeli camp for training Southern Sudanese insurgents, the Anya Nya. None of these accusations were ever substantiated, but Qaddafi gratefully used them to inflame public opinion in Libya against the United States and his archenemy, Israel.

Despite his ancestry and instincts, Muammar Qaddafi preferred to become the patron of FROLINAT rather than the patron of the Toubou of the Tibesti. He could control the former but not the latter. Moreover, his Bedouin background was replete with the folklore of the treacherous *zurqa*, a pejorative term used by Arab Bedouins to describe the non-Arab Gourane of Libya, Chad, and the Sudan, who were by their Toubou culture, language, and politics implacably independent and the aristocracy of southern Libya and the B.E.T.[17] They were not to be trusted, and Qaddafi systematically reduced the Toubou influence in Libya. The Beida (Bardai) Toubou who had served in the bodyguard of King Idris were expelled from Libya; the Toubou of the Kufra oasis, their historic headquarters, were warned not to rally to their Sanusi patrons, particularly the nephew of King Idris, Abdallah Abd al-Sanusi. Known as the "Black Prince," Abdallah was actively seeking mercenaries from the Toubou in northern Chad and southern Libya against Qaddafi, whose security forces retaliated by driving a thousand Toubou from the Fezzan in 1970.

There was much confusion within the international community over whether Qaddafi would support the Toubou, FROLINAT, or both.[18] Whether Qaddafi still supported the Bedouins or was having second thoughts about FROLINAT, there can be no doubt that he was determined to overthrow Tombalbaye. He terminated a proposed telecommunication link between Chad and Europe through Libya and denied any further negotiations on a free port for Chad on the Mediterranean that King Idris had promised Tombalbaye. Qaddafi's bizarre behavior was again characterized by his public offer "to act as mediator between the Chadian Government and the rebels," while privately working to destroy the government of Chad. Tombalbaye, of course, rejected this egregious offer, which provided Qaddafi the opportunity to denounce him and unleash the Libyan media against the "tyrant of Chad." In November 1969, *Al-Youm*, the influential Tripoli daily, published a series of articles describing growing tension between the northern Arab, Muslims and the southern African, Christians, along with the accustomed accusation that Tombalbaye was a French "stooge." This press campaign appeared to confirm Qaddafi's support for FROLINAT, complete with photographs of rebels in Chad. The Chadian ambassador to Libya, Bashir-Sow, himself a Muslim, responded with great vigor that his coreligionists were not being persecuted in Chad and singled out Abba Siddiq for dissimulation and provocation against his government. His diplomatic outburst precipitated a vehement public debate between the two protagonists to the delight of the press if not the edification of the citizens of Tripoli.[19]

The most vitriolic denunciation of Chad was reserved not for its ambassador but for its relations with Israel.[20] Six months after Qaddafi had seized power, his Ministry of Unity and Foreign Affairs officially protested to the Chadian ambassador in April 1970 remarks made by President Tombalbaye in Fort Lamy in which he reportedly said, "Judaism differs from Christianity . . . Islam is against Christianity." Tombalbaye approved of the Exodus during which "the Israelis had been seeking for a long time to return to the land of their forefathers," and they had "now returned there with the help of the great powers." Qaddafi considered the first statement an insult, the second an unbearable affirmation of Israel's right to exist. The Libyan ministry claimed that both statements "undermine Libya's efforts to achieve true friendship and cooperation with its neighbor, Chad."[21] Thereafter, anti-Semitism became a cornerstone of not only Qaddafi's personal philosophy and of Libyan foreign policy but also of the commentary from the Libyan media. Chad was "neocolonialist" and "pro-Zionist," and President Tombalbaye, the pawn of Semitic imperialism, must be overthrown. Ironically, Qaddafi's tirades against Tombalbaye were perceived by François Mitterrand as an opportunity to consummate his promises made during the elections of 1965 to reduce the French presence in Chad. On the floor of the French Senate he demanded an official explanation of France's role in Chad. Desperate for French military assistance, Tombalbaye reacted strongly, arguing disingenuously that the French president had no right to interfere in the internal affairs of Chad.[22]

After this brief storm, Tombalbaye visited Paris in August 1970 in search of military assistance against the growing insurgency in the north. Information about these meetings is obscure, but the French troops who remained in Chad intercepted FROLINAT forces in the Batha prefecture, and after the skirmishes they captured arms and messages that confirmed support from Libya. While the French reluctantly agreed to continue to protect 800 French army and 1,000 air force personnel based in Chad, Tombalbaye sought military assistance from the United States. The U.S. embassy in Tripoli had warned Washington that the Libya-Chad alliance between King Idris and President Tombalbaye had dissolved. There were, however, no illusions in either the U.S. Department of Defense or Department of State about the danger of Qaddafi. Not only was his behavior erratic, but he had the oil revenues to satisfy his ambitions.

Cartographic and Other Territorial Aggression

Throughout history rulers have sought to acquire by the cartographic rearrangement of boundaries what they could not achieve by conquest. The wastelands of Libya, Chad, and the Sudan are no exception. The frontier between Libya and Chad was as worthless as the imperial designs of those who had sought to claim it throughout the millennia. The most avid collector of the Sahara and the Sahel in this century was Benito Mussolini, who as *Il Duce* sought to revive the ramshackle collection of Renaissance states that constituted Italy at the end of the nineteenth century into the New Rome of the twentieth. The granary of the old Rome had been the Mediterranean littoral of Libya; it would now become the granary of the new. Mussolini and his fascists, however, had more ambitious visions. Libya was to be the pillar in the west, Ethiopia the pillar in the east of the new Roman Empire, whose heartland would be the deserts between them.

This heartland of sand and rock and wind were defined to Mussolini's satisfaction by an agreement signed in Rome on 7 January 1935 by the representatives of France and Italy. The frontier between Libya and French Equatorial Africa (Chad) was moved southward sixty miles to add a strip of territory, some 43,000 square miles in area, consisting of wasteland and a fringe of mountainous desert known only to the Toubou. It was to become famous thirty years later as the Aozou Strip.[23]

The acquisition of Libyan sands appeased Mussolini for the moment, but when the French Senate refused to ratify the agreement, the transfer of the Aozou Strip was never consummated. In December 1938 Italy officially informed France that it did not consider the 1935 agreement to be in force. If Qaddafi could claim the waters of the Gulf of Sidra why not the sands of the Aozou Strip as reparations for a hated Italian imperial adventure. Control of the Aozou Strip would frustrate Toubou irredentism south of the Tibesti and would create a base from which to advance the revolution into the Sahel and savanna of Chad. Not surprisingly, Qaddafi rejected the boundaries of imperial Italy, but his cartographers diligently confirmed that Mussolini's demarcation of the Aozou Strip and a slice of sand from the Republic of Niger belonged to Libya (see Map 4.2).[24]

Seizure of the sands by cartography infuriated Tombalbaye not so much for any loss of wasteland and rebellious subjects but because the colonial boundaries were enshrined by Article 2 of the constitution of the Organization of African States. In 1963 none of the African states were prepared to encourage instability by opening a Pandora's box of readjusting arbitrary frontiers. By March 1971 aggression by cartography and the resurrection of imperial claims to the Aozou Strip had seriously eroded relations between Chad and Libya. In a dramatic gesture President Tombalbaye and El-Hajj Arabi Elgoni, Chairman of the Chad National Assembly, traveled to Tripoli to meet privately with Libya's Deputy Prime Minister Major Abd al-Salam Jalloud. Two months later the Chad delegation was still in the Libyan capital, where Tombalbaye's representatives were attempting to convince the *Derde* to return to Chad as "the Sultan of the Tibesti" and bring peace to the B.E.T.

Tombalbaye was willing to recognize the *Derde* in order to make peace in the north, but these overtures were no guarantee for Tombalbaye's personal security. In August 1971 Tombalbaye's French advisors prevented an attempted assassination. The plot was the inspiration of Ahmad Abdallah, one of Tombalbaye's closest advisors, and during his interrogation he revealed the names of his fellow conspirators. He also substantiated government intelligence reports that Libya was the source of arms for Muslim insurgents in Chad. This was corroborated by another rebel who claimed "he had been trained in Libya and that the aim of the coup was to regain Chad for the Muslims."[25] Tombalbaye promptly expelled the Libyan diplomats from Fort Lamy and denounced them in the media for sponsoring a coup that would impose Islam and its legal code, the *Shari'a,* upon the

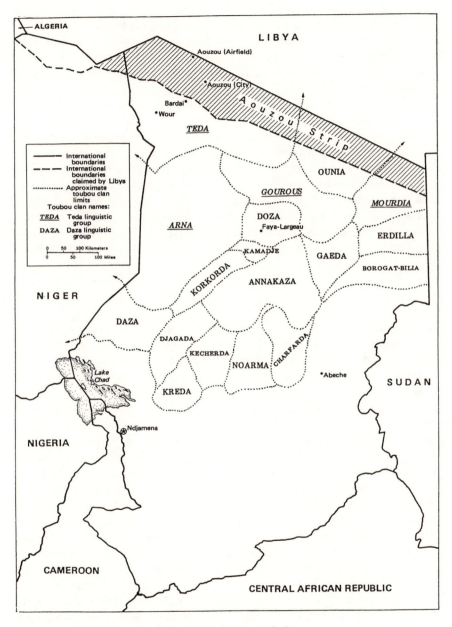

MAP 4.2 Chad: The Aouzou Strip and the Toubou Tribal Area

non-Muslims of Chad. Tombalbaye attacked Qaddafi's "religious and racial fa-
naticism," Libyan "imperialism," and "expansionism." He predicted a Libyan in-
vasion and appealed for the French to reconsider their withdrawal.[26] He offered
Libyan exiles a place to live and promised to protect the Toubou of Chad in the
B.E.T. He claimed the Fezzan, the only ruler from the savanna pastures of Lake
Chad to do so since Idris Alawma, the powerful sixteenth-century *mai* (king) of
Kanem-Bornu.

At the United Nations and in the Organization of African Unity, diplomats
from Chad carried out a vigorous campaign to alert their members to these
Libyan threats. The Chad delegations were sent to Arab and African nations to
warn them of Libyan intrusions into Chad and its implications for the solidarity
of the OAU and its commitment not to rearrange African boundaries. In October
1971 the Chad representative to the UN General Assembly formally complained
that Libya interfered in its internal affairs. He reported that insurgents were being
trained in Libya and that the National Radio of Libya was broadcasting support
for FROLINAT. Finally in a cartographic drama of delimiting deserts, he placed
on the table an official Libyan map, which included the Aozou Strip in "Greater
Libya."

Hissene Habre

The attempted assassination of Tombalbaye in August 1971 coincided with the
emergence of Hissene Habre, a Daza Toubou, who despite his nonaristocratic
patrimony was able to unify the fiercely independent Toubou clans. Known to
the Libyans as "the strange personage," Hissene Habre was born in Faya Largeau
in 1942, the same year as Qaddafi. Like him, Habre grew of age during the reconstruction after the World War II that nurtured many liberation movements from
European colonialism throughout the Middle East and Africa. He attended a
French-sponsored primary school and entered government service. His education led to his appointment as subprefect in Faya Largeau at the age of twenty-
two, where he acquired an interest in politics and a large circle of friends. In the
company of strangers his taciturnity and offhand manner disguised an innate intelligence that soon came to the attention of the well-informed and perceptive
French officials in the B.E.T. "Perhaps, because he was incorruptible," he was selected to attend the Institute de Droit Publique in Paris from which he obtained
the equivalent of a secondary school degree and was then enrolled in the elite Institute des Sciences Publiques.[27] Although he never obtained a degree, upon his
return to Chad in 1971 he possessed more impressive credentials than most.

Despite his education, or perhaps because of it, Hissene Habre has remained
an enigma for friend and foe. His first appointment in government service was
subprefect at Moussoro in Kanem, a post from which he soon disappeared. He
would later claim that President Tombalbaye had sent him on a secret mission to
Libya, but he certainly left Chad and in October 1971 was seen in Tripoli. He met

Abba Siddiq and Goukouni Oueddei, the son of the *Derde*, the Toubou "Sultan of Tibesti," at the time when relations between FROLINAT and the Toubou were rapidly deteriorating. Only two months before, at a conference in Benghazi, Qaddafi had personally chosen Siddiq to lead the revolutionary armies against Chad. Unpopular and contentious, Qaddafi's investiture of Siddiq immediately produced dissension within the rebels, especially among the Toubou. Qaddafi sought a rapprochement during a second conference at the Kufra oasis. He was only partially successful. The Arabs of FROLINAT and the non-Arab Toubou of the desert agreed to a "strategic alliance" that was meaningless since each insisted on maintaining the independence of their respective military units. Thereafter the FROLINAT forces were composed of two separate "armies," which were allied together in theory but not in practice. The First Liberation Army led by Siddiq operated in central Chad; the Second Liberation Army under the command of Goukouni remained in their mountain sanctuaries of northern Chad. Neither cooperated with the other. Habre appears to have played no role in the internecine rivalries nor to have met Qaddafi or his senior military leaders. He did, however, refuse the invitation of Abba Siddiq to spend six months at the FROLINAT office in Algiers. Elusive and mysterious, he next appeared in the B.E.T., where he offered his services to the Second Liberation Army of Goukouni Oueddei and his Toubou. There were reports that he was embittered upon learning that Tombalbaye's security police had arrested members of his family, but such rumors were the coinage of Chad.

Despite his education in Paris, the French in Fort Lamy at first thought he was one of the FROLINAT "Maoists" trained in Korea. Habre soon proved, however, that he was no romantic political theoretician but a Daza Toubou pragmatist born in the desert at Faya Largeau and educated by the French institutes concerned with the practice of law and administration. Substance, not theory, was the means by which he sought to acquire power for his own advantage. In Toubou, "Habre" means stubborn; he was also brave, a characteristic recognized by the French and indispensable for any leader of the Toubou. His Toubou rival, Goukouni Oueddei, contemptuously dismissed Habre as not a real "Tou," not a man of the Tibesti. He was no *abbala*, a camel nomad, nor a Teda, the ancestral ruling clan that dominated the Tibesti Mountains and the oases of Kufra, Sebha, Gatroun, and Murzuk in southern Libya. Habre was an Anakaza of the Daza Toubou, the nomads of the plains who ruled the lands between the Ennedi Plateau and Faya Largeau. Indifferent Muslims, the Daza recognized neither the religious patrimony of the Grand Sanusi nor the *Derde* of the Tibesti. In contrast to the Teda, whose authority among the Toubou emanated from the wadis and wells of the Fezzan, the Daza roamed south from the Sahara across the pastures of the Sahel. Here they had encountered Africans from the south to absorb through the centuries a more expansive appreciation of the world beyond the B.E.T. Here in the markets of the Sahel, the exchange of merchandise between the pastoral nomads from the north and the cultivators from the south has taken place throughout the millennia. Their principal predators were the petty warlords, whose pretensions were only exceeded by their greed, and the frontier sultans, whose historic claims to rule were forever exposed by their inability to do so.

Hissene Habre was the illegitimate son of Habre Mishetemi, a small herdsman who tended his flocks of sheep and goats on the fringe of the oasis at Faya Largeau. Like many other Anakaza Daza living on the desert margin, he lost his independence when the pastures disappeared and his animals died in the drought that imprisoned him as a sedentary caretaker in the groves of date palms that stretched for fifty miles from Yen to Faya Largeau.[28] Despite his humble background, Habre could not be ignored upon his return to the B.E.T. He had long talks with the *Derde,* who, sufficiently impressed, appointed him to command the FROLINAT Second Liberation Army. The *Derde* may have been fascinated by the intense determination of Habre, but he used the promotion of Habre to rebuke his son, Goukouni Oueddei, for the defeat the Ounia Toubou had suffered at Ounianga Kebir in March 1970 and the extensive damage by the French to this strategic oasis. This paternal manipulation was further complicated when Muhammad Idris, second in command of Siddiq's FROLINAT First Liberation Army, challenged Habre's leadership of the Second Army. Neither the Toubou of Borku nor those from the Ennedi Plateau, undoubtedly responding to instructions from the *Derde,* where about to join Idris, which precipitated the collapse of the insurgency against Tombalbaye and his Africans in Fort Lamy. When Siddiq sought to establish a "Ho Chi Minh Trail" from the Kufra oasis through Ennedi into Wadai, Habre and his Second Army moved south and east to frustrate the attempt by Idris to gain control of the frontier from Dar Zaghawa to Libya.[29]

The Aozou Strip

In February 1972 a FROLINAT First Army column advancing from southern Libya into Chad along the ancient caravan route, the Garamantean Road, was intercepted at Amdagachi by units of the French Force d'Intervention, which was supporting the Chad regular army. Like many desert forays, the firefight was a fierce encounter during which both sides suffered heavy casualties. The French battalion commander was killed, but the FROLINAT rebels retreated in disarray leaving their dead and many modern weapons supplied by Libya. The dogs of war had been loosed across the Sahel to bay at the dawn of a new and more brutal violence. The battle of Amdagachi demonstrated President Pompidou's determination to defend Chad against any designs by Qaddafi for a greater Libya, while French officials, led by Jacques Foccart, were quietly negotiating a rapprochement between Qaddafi and Tombalbaye. The result of the French mediation remains unclear. On the one hand, the Libyan government reduced its support for FROLINAT and offered substantial economic assistance for Chad.

On the other, the FROLINAT defeat at Amdagachi and French diplomacy presented Qaddafi an opportunity to placate the conservative Muslims with a public statement of his support for them.

Announcements by Qaddafi in Tripoli were not, however, commensurate with his actions on his southern frontier. He strengthened the Libyan army units encamped within the walls of a former French fort that overlooked the six small villages of the Aozou oasis. A desolate island of brackish water and palms in a sea of sand, Aozou nestled in an ancient wadi fifteen miles north of the boundary between Libya and French Equatorial Africa, defined in the agreement of 7 January 1935 between France and Italy, and forty miles northeast of Bardai, the northern outpost of Chad in the Tibesti. The addition of this territory, the Aozou Strip, to Libya in 1935 was as bizarre as it was worthless. Pierre Laval, the French foreign minister, could afford to be generous with the sands of the Sahara. Well aware of Mussolini's territorial aspirations south of the Tibesti, the French had carefully prepared a concession to Italy, which would do the least possible harm to their interests in French Equatorial Africa. In 1931–1932 Commandant Ogier of the B.E.T. was instructed to delineate a boundary that would safeguard French interests in Equatorial Africa while keeping the Italians "at a sufficient distance from Lake Chad to prevent the possibility of any threat to communications between French West Africa and French Equatorial Africa."[30] Laval would later boast to the American ambassador in Paris that "he may have lost his shirt" to Mussolini, but the Aozou Strip was a region where "Mussolini could not raise a dozen bananas on the 117,000 square kilometers of African soil." He even seemed pleased to be free of any French role as the policeman of the Aozou and the wretched Tibesti, particularly when he believed to have come away with "Mussolini's shirts and studs."[31]

The colonial patronage of the past was only of interest to Qaddafi when it suited him to advance his own imperial frontier. The presence of Libyan regulars in the Aozou Strip was not simply a dispute over boundaries in the sand but the support for the Arab, Muslim politicians and their suspicious non-Arab Toubou allies against the Black, African traditionalists and Christians who controlled the government of Chad. Not surprisingly, the government of Chad filed a complaint with the Organization of African Unity (OAU) stating that Libyan military forces had occupied the sovereign territory of Chad in the Aozou Strip. The protest was not welcome in Addis Ababa, the headquarters of the OAU. One of the immutable principles of the organization defined in Article 2 of its constitution is the recognition of the colonial boundaries inherited at their independence from the European imperial powers. Any readjustment of boundaries in a worthless desert would establish a precedent for frontier rectification in the more fertile and populous lands to the south, which would precipitate unwanted disputes. To everyone's relief, Chad's concern for its sovereignty could best be resolved after Tombalbaye restored diplomatic relations with Libya, despite reports that the Aozou Strip contained "substantial uranium and magnesium deposits."[32]

These reports were the result of cursory surveys by French geologists and were soon magnified beyond belief and given greater credence by Qaddafi. He ordered prospecting for uranium in the Murzuk depression, founded an atomic energy commission in 1974, and in another of his mercurial inspirations was rumored to have approached Argentina to carry out uranium prospecting in the Aozou Strip.[33] In October, Abba Siddiq moved his office from Algiers to Tripoli predicting that Tombalbaye's days were numbered and only the Christian, imperial French remained to thwart the triumph of FROLINAT in Chad.

Drought and Man in the Aozou Strip and the B.E.T.

Siddiq was so absorbed by the Pan-Arab revolution that he neglected to observe the realities of the great drought. More than revolutionary rhetoric, appeals to Arab solidarity, the call of the *muezzin* to Islam, or the uninhibited distribution of automatic weapons, the return of the drought throughout the Sahara and Sahel reduced to dust the petty plans of men. In summer 1972, from the mountains of the Tibesti Plateau to the Ennedi Hills and from Lake Chad to Darfur, the land of Chad was once again ravaged by drought. That biblical horseman of the apocalypse had reappeared on the frontier of nature, Islam, and the inviolable pastures of the free peoples of the Sahel. In a good year the rains from July to August yield fifteen inches. In the 1960s the rain in the Tibesti was sporadic, in the Ennedi Hills, ephemeral, measured by drops not inches. The search for water to sustain human life and to replenish the animals would not be fulfilled in political theory or personal ambition.

By midsummer 1972, the drought had caused the FROLINAT Second Army of Hissene Habre to disperse. The Toubou could no longer depend upon the supplies from their kinsmen in the Sahel and now ranged widely in search of water and pastures in the B.E.T. The people and rebels in the east, particularly in Wadai, were also seeking water and forage while avoiding government patrols shadowed by the French special forces. By 1973 some 70 percent of the cattle in Chad had been slaughtered or had perished. The militant cattle-Arabs, the Baggara from Wadai and the Sudan, were impoverished and angry. The robust, traditional cattle markets of central Chad, Wadai, and Darfur were now the *suqs* for desperate sales, foreclosures, and extortion by the *jallaba* merchants from the Nile, which would not be forgotten by the rustics of the west, then or now.

Despite this disaster, Chad was the last state in the Sahel to declare a national emergency. This only exacerbated the hostility of the pastoral Arabs and nomadic Toubou against Tombalbaye and his southerners. The French displayed nearly as much lethargy as the government of Chad. By June the French foreign ministry requested 50,000 tons of food for Chad and Niger, an amount far beyond the capabilities of a corrupt, unsympathetic Chad bureaucracy and the vast distances needed to be traversed along ancient caravan routes. Moreover, the Cooperative des Transports Tchadiens (CTT) initiated a slowdown to extort higher rates for their truckers and to obscure the embarrassing fact that CTT did not have the trucks necessary to move relief supplies from the stocks in Cameroon and southern Chad.[34] The failure to transport food to the Arabs and Toubou of the north was not, however, simply the failure of Chad's infrastructure. CTT had been founded in 1955 by small African entrepreneurs and predominately Sara truckers to contest the lucrative monopoly that transported Chad's cotton, held by the Union Routière Centre-Africaine (UNIROUTE), an expatriate company controlled by the Rothschild holding company, the Société Mory et Compagnie. With the support of Tombalbaye and his entourage in the Parti Progressiste Tchadien, the CCT broke the monopoly of UNIROUTE and brokered an agreement in 1957 with Nigeria whereby 85 percent of the massive tonnage hauled between Fort Lamy in Chad and Maiduguri would be carried in Chadian trucks. The windfall profits produced enormous returns for the southern truckers and the politicians from the PPT who had wisely invested or were paid off for their interest in kin and country.[35] There was certainly no incentive for the African truckers of CTT to risk the lucrative and secure transport in southern Chad by hauling supplies across the hazardous trans-Sahelian routes to alleviate the distress of traditional enemies in the north. It was more sensible, profitable, and politically correct to divert the food, now rotting in the open awaiting shipment north, to the Sara markets in the south. When no food reached Dar Zaghawa or the Ennedi Plateau, thousands of Arab and Toubou fled into Darfur, complicating the erratic relief program of the Sudan government. The depth of bitterness by the abandoned Arab and Toubou confirmed their beliefs, their history, and their convictions about relationships on the frontiers of the *Bilad al-Sudan* between Arab and African.

The drought not only destroyed cultivation and the pastures, it diminished the fervor of revolution. Tombalbaye and his government never seemed more secure. The revolt in the north had been contained by the drought, but Foccart and the French officials in Chad recognized that their influence and advice was replaced by a clique of disreputable advisors from the Caribbean and Africa. A series of unseemly scenarios soon followed. The president ordered the arrest of several well-established French businessmen in Fort Lamy. Protests by the French embassy were dismissed by orchestrated media attacks against French "neocolonialism" in Chad and its architect, Jacques Foccart. President Pompidou warned Tombalbaye that he had seriously jeopardized the "special relationship" between the governments of France and Chad. Tombalbaye ignored that rebuke and flew to Tripoli in November to announce that he and Qaddafi had reached an agreement: Chad would receive economic assistance and Libya would reduce its support for FROLINAT. Tombalbaye would terminate his relations with Israel.[36] This rapprochement with Qaddafi may have been a snub to the French, but it spread deep concern among Tombalbaye's supporters and the faithful in the PPT. They had no use for his new advisors from abroad, and his abrupt termination of the Israeli connection disturbed those who had personally benefited from the relationship and had sought Israeli assistance as a counterweight to their mutual enemies in the African Sahel. Cynical rumors, more *suq* gossip than reality, were widely circulated that Tombalbaye had sold the Aozou Strip to Qaddafi for the Agreement on Friendship and Cooperation, by which Libya pledged $60 million toward Chad's economic development.[37]

Security for Tombalbaye

Tombalbaye closed the Israeli embassy and issued ambiguous statements for the press in support of the Palestinians. The French said little and did nothing despite the concern expressed by the Chadian foreign minister, Wadal Abdelkader Kamougue, that modern weapons were being distributed to FROLINAT by the Libyans. More ominous was the departure on 1 September 1972 of General Edouard Cortadellas, the French commander-in-chief of the Franco-Chadian forces in Chad. He left behind a military establishment presumably to defend France, Chad, and Tombalbaye. In fact, his legacy and that of Foccart and France was a hodgepodge of ethnic, historic, and personal rivalries institutionalized by titles and confirmed by modern weaponry. The Chadian security forces numbered 14,000 men, each unit inveterate rivals for power and patronage, including the Garde Nationale et Nomade, 4,000 men who were to police the countryside and secure its buildings. The Garde was commanded by Major Camille Gourvenac, a French expatriate with a reputation for brutality and a close advisor to President Tombalbaye. His power came from his position as the Director of the Centre de Coordination et d'Exploitation du Renseignement (CCER), the Chad secret service and military intelligence, whose more sophisticated methods were quietly concealed by the more rustic ambiance of the Garde Nomade.

Another thousand men were recruited, mostly from the Sara, into the benign Sûreté National. The Sûreté, originally civil police responsible for immigration, criminal records, and smuggling, were transformed in 1967 by security specialists from Morocco into an imperial guard, the Compagnies Tchadiennes de Sécurité, under the command of Colonel Salebiani under the direct orders of the president. Colonel Salebiani's responsibilities were to prevent the overthrow of Tombalbaye, from within or without, through which he and his men became greatly feared by the people, their politicians, and their competitors for control of Chad security. When General Cortedellas retired he also left behind the Gendarmerie Nationale, which had been established after independence under the command of Colonel Mamari Ngakinar Djimé and French regimental officers. The 4,000 men of the Gendarmerie Nationale were organized into mobile units to maintain security in southern Chad, which required little effort and provided the opportunity of kinship with the president to obtain preferential treatment and the most modern weapons. All of these special forces outnumbered the regular army of Chad, which had neither prestige nor sophisticated arms and in

1973 only two Arab officers. It was not, however, without political power, for its veterans of the French foreign wars, mostly Sara, had fought in the Western Sahara, Indo-China, Algeria, and had gone north with Leclerc against the German Afrika Korps in Libya. They were now the proud French pensioners in Chad, all 15,000 in the Association des Anciens Combattants du Tchad, most of whom claimed kinship with the president.

FROLINAT in Disarray

In December 1972 the FROLINAT First Army under Siddiq, and the second under Habre went their separate ways. Siddiq retained his command of the "original army," now a rump, while Habre reorganized the Toubou into the Northern Army Force (FAN). Habre was president of the FAN Command Council; Goukouni Oueddei, the son of the *Derde,* was vice president, and Adoum Togoi was the military commander. The dissolution of FROLINAT was not surprising. Habre had not disguised his contempt for its leadership. He personally despised Siddiq, and in March 1973 the two rival groups fought several skirmishes for control of the strategic Ennedi Plateau. Unable to compete with Libyan arms, Habre and Goukouni retired to their sanctuaries in the Tibesti and Borkou. Once in control of the Ennedi, Siddiq finally opened what he called his "Ho Chi Minh Trail" between Kufra in Libya and Abeche in Wadai. The route was not one of the ancient trans-Saharan caravan. It had only been established in 1811 and had none of the historic infrastructure of the classic desert crossings nor the traditions of trade and all the exposure to Toubou harassment from the west.

The success of the FROLINAT First Army in the Ennedi was short-lived. Among Siddiq's officers were those of the Awlad al-Sulayman, the last of the Arab clans to immigrate into Chad during the mid-nineteenth century, whose expansion was accompanied by great brutality. When they attempted to collect tribute from the Missiriya Baggara (cattle-owning) Arabs, moving their herds through the Ennedi from Biltine to Salamat, the Missiriya assaulted the FROLINAT camp at Amdan in August 1973 killing more than a hundred and capturing large quantities of arms and ammunition. The survivors were subsequently intercepted by government patrols supported by French advisors who inflicted more casualties and captured more weapons.[38] The division and defeats for FROLINAT produced the illusion in Fort Lamy, renamed Ndjamena on 1 September 1973, that Chad had nothing more to fear from the FROLINAT insurrection. Surrounded by sycophants and fawning kin, Tombalbaye not only proclaimed victory but sought to demonstrate his independence from the French by ignoring their support and personally belittling the role of Foccart in the affairs of Chad in his presidential address before the National Political Congress.

The French were not amused. When Tombalbaye refused to attend the first Franco-African summit conference in Paris, his erratic and egregious behavior had become self-evident. The conference was held in November 1973 as a symbolic and historic meeting of the African heads of state with the president of France to confirm the enduring ties between France and Africa. It was conducted with all the ceremony and panache of an imperial and colonial past and an emerging cultural relationship between France and Francophone Africa. Sustained by his solid support in the south, Tombalbaye not only insulted the French but ignored the drought, inflation, and the flag of the Libyan Arab Republic raised over the ramshackle remains of the former French fort at Aozou in the presence of Goukouni Oueddei and Hissene Habre. Gouara Lassou, a young lieutenant in the Chadian army, succinctly summed up this transfer of power: "Libya hoisted its flag and began to issue identity cards to Chadians living in the Aozou region."[39] Having snubbed President Pompidou and publicly berated Foccart, Tombalbaye continued private outbursts against his French advisors and the French presence at the Sahr air base. After the ceremonies to rename Fort Lamy in September, he demanded the withdrawal of its French garrison to be replaced by the Gendarmerie National, not the regular army. France was spending 30 percent of its military aid for Africa in Chad, for which President Pompidou had been repaid with insults that the French public seemed to resent more than their president.[40]

L'Affaire Claustre

While Hissene Habre and Goukouni were rallying the Toubou of the Second Liberation Army, which numbered no more than five hundred warriors, Siddiq was reorganizing FROLINAT after its defeat at Amdan. In consultation with Qaddafi's advisors at Abtouyour and with Libyan money, Siddiq pretentiously divided the FROLINAT First Liberation Army in January 1974 into seven military provinces, each with its own military council. This paper organizational chart for insurgency resulted in feeble skirmishes against the Missiriya, who had defeated them in August, and against Muhammad Al-Baghalani, a rogue and self-styled "general," who was a casual member of FROLINAT and a proficient bandit. By April FROLINAT had neither consolidated its organization nor won supporters from the Zaghawa and Bedeiyat on the eastern frontier.

The exasperation and frustration of President Pompidou with Chad ended with his death from cancer. His successor, Valéry Giscard d'Estaing, was less inclined to tolerate President Tombalbaye's idiosyncrasies. Foccart was immediately sent to Ndjamena to convince Tombalbaye of the importance of the French connection. He failed. Despite his diplomacy and knowledge, he could no longer command Tombalbaye, who had surrounded himself with a cabal of sinister and corrupt advisors. They could mobilize 100,000 faithful for demonstrations against "La Foque" when he arrived in Ndjamena to plot against the "security and happiness" of Chad.[41] Although the Chad National Assembly unanimously passed a resolution denouncing Foccart, news from the north quickly eclipsed the tantrums from the capital.

On 21 April 1974 the Northern Army Force, led by Hissene Habre, overran Bardai, a small oasis of some 800 inhabitants surrounded by spectacular cliffs, craters, gorges, and hot springs. It was the headquarters of the subprefecture of the Tibesti in the B.E.T. 275 miles from Faya Largeau, but only 50 miles from Aozou and 30 miles from the Aozou Strip as defined in the Franco-Italian accords of 1935. The reverberations from the Toubou occupation of Bardai had little to do with its spectacular scenery and a great deal to do with the relations between Libya, Chad, and the Sudan. The dramatic Toubou victory at Bardai infuriated Qaddafi, who appears to have realized that he could no longer manipulate or purchase Habre and confirmed his distrust of the Toubou. Thenceforth, Habre was "enemy number one."[42] And enemy number one he instantly became, not because of Bardai, but because of a coincidence by which Europeans became his hostages. Suddenly, they were the source of instant attention by European governments and the international media. Habre's knowledge of Saharan remains was rudimentary at best and unimportant for the cause of revolution. He had no intention of kidnapping the internationally known French archaeologist Françoise Claustre or Marc Combe, an innocuous French foreign aid official, but he very much wanted to capture Dr. Christian Staewan of the Federal Republic of Germany. Staewan had lived in Bardai for five years, and the FAN believed he was an informant for the governments of both Chad and France. Habre and his five hundred warriors needed arms, and they could be bought with the ransom for his three hostages.

L'affaire Claustre symbolized the folly of its principal participants, Libya, Chad, and France, in the pursuit of imperial ambitions to acquire vast wastelands more useful to their few nomadic inhabitants than to the newly independent states of Africa. The fundamental issue was the control of the Sahel and the Sahara and their ancient trade routes. This historic objective was now hopelessly exacerbated by a hostage situation, the visibility and the emotion of which was confounded by the unreliability of the participants seeking to release the hostages and to remove an embarrassing source of tension among them.

The government of Chad had, of course, to secure the release of the hostages. The Compagnies Tchadiennes de Sécurité subsequently interrogated members of Habre's extended family in Faya Largeau. It did nothing to free the hostages, embittered Habre, and convinced the skeptical Toubou to throw in their lot with the FAN. Ironically, President Giscard d'Estaing was under greater pressure than his nemesis in Ndjamena. The incarceration of a prominent French female scholar in the sanctuaries of the Bedouin in a desert oasis provided an irresistible story for the French and European media, particularly when one of the hostages was German. President Giscard d'Estaing could hardly ignore the public demand for action. Despite Tombalbaye's misgivings, Giscard d'Estaing sent Captain Pierre

Galopin to negotiate the release of the hostages. Captain Galopin appeared to be the consummate intermediary. He had served in the B.E.T. and in 1968 prepared the "Galopin Report," which, not surprisingly, was kept secret for many years, for he revealed the gross abuse by southern Chadian officials, both civilian and military, against the Toubou. He reported the inflated and illegal taxes imposed upon the Toubou for the profit of the collectors of the government of Chad. The Toubou were not unaccustomed to a rapacious government; but they could not tolerate its brutal methods, the humiliation of their traditional leaders, and the indignities imposed upon their women.[43] His secret report written in 1968 was, of course, unknown to Habre and his Toubou in 1974, but in the interminable intrigues of the Tibesti, Goukouni had implicated Galopin in the death of his brothers. His past closed in on him when he failed to have the hostages released. His close association with Camille Gourvenac, director of Chad's secret service and military intelligence, the enmity of the dynasty of the *Derde,* and Habre's ambivalence brought him before a people's court of the FAN. He was "executed as a war criminal" on 26 December 1974.[44]

These personal interventions and petty intrigues could not disguise the need of Hissene Habre to acquire arms. When the plight of the hostages was given greater coverage by the international media, Habre demanded not only weapons but also reparations for damages incurred by French forces during their occupation of Chad after World War II. A FAN manifesto seeking reparations was published in *Die Deutsche Welle* in June 1974, after which Habre was paid the ransom in German marks, a currency he could not easily exchange except in Libya. Staewan was released, but Habre refused to surrender Françoise or her husband, Pierre Claustre, who had rushed to the Tibesti in August 1975 to free his wife only to be added to Habre's hostages for weapons. Françoise and Pierre Claustre were finally released in Tripoli in January 1977 after the inveterate rivalries of the Toubou had taken their course with the falling out of Hissene Habre and Goukouni Oueddei. It was the end of a bizarre, romantic interlude in the long history of Libya, Chad, and the Sudan. The reality of *L'affaire Claustre* was not the hostages' privations amongst the Toubou but the seizure of Bardai by Habre and his Toubou warriors. The FAN demanded the publication of the FROLINAT manifesto in Ndjamena and freedom for political detainees in Chad. Habre dictated the terms of ransom, and when France refused to pay, he demanded weapons. He received in return not weapons from the French but a more powerful weapon, priceless publicity, which exposed the incompetence of President Tombalbaye to govern. His dictatorial rule and the inefficiency and corruption of his government, in which the president and his family were the principal beneficiaries, were now exposed to the international community. Tombalbaye could denounce the French; he could conjure up the threat of Arabs; he could rant against the predatory Toubou, but when he called his military leaders expensive, incompetent, and expendable, he had laid the groundwork for his own demise.

Notes

1. Lisa Anderson, *The State and Social Transformation in Tunisia and Libya, 1830–1980* (Princeton, Princeton University Press, 1986).

2. Ishkal died mysteriously in November 1985. See "Fanatico, mistico, visionario, guia revolucionario, loco: Gaddafi," *Ya* (Madrid), 20 March 1986, p. 1.

3. I. W. Zartman and A. G. Kluge, "Heroic Politics: The Foreign Policy of Libya," in *The Foreign Policy of Arab States,* ed. Bahgat Korany and Ali E. Hillal Dessouki (Boulder: Westview Press, 1984), pp. 183–184.

4. "Creator of Rivers, Makers of Waves", *Times* (London), 2 September 1984.

5. David Blundy and Andrew Lycett, *Qaddafi and the Libyan Revolution* (Boston: Little, Brown, 1987), p. 87. Qaddafi vehemently opposed the Muslim Brothers for more than twenty years, jailed most, and hung many. See *Al-Watan Al Arabi* (Paris), 22 January 1993, pp. 118–121.

6. Anthony Sampson, *The Arms Bazaar* (New York: Viking Press, 1977), p. 171; Henry Kissinger, *White House Years* (Boston: Little, Brown, 1979), p. 565.

7. G. Gera, "Libya and the United States: A Relationship of Self-Fulfilling Expectations?" in *The Middle East and the United States,* ed. Haim Shaked and Itimar Rabinovich (New Brunswick, N.J.: Transaction Books, 1980), p. 200.

8. "Navigation Rights and the Gulf of Sidra," *Gist,* Bureau of Public Affairs, Department of State, Washington, D.C., December 1986.

9. Walter Laqueur, *Confrontation: The Middle East and World Politics* (New York: Bantam Books, 1974), pp. 51–53.

10. M. G. El Warfally, *Imagery and Ideology in U.S. Policy Toward Libya* (Pittsburgh: University of Pittsburgh Press, 1989), p. 59; Gabriel Warburg, *Islam, Nationalism, and Communism in a Traditional Society: The Case of the Sudan* (London: Frank Cass, 1978), pp. 201–204.

11. For the intricacies and drama of oil negotiations, see Leonard Mosley, *Power Play* (New York: Random House, 1973), pp. 350–357.

12. Stephen Ellis, ed., "People, Policies, and Institutions," *Africa Now* (London), April 1985, p. 14.

13. Bernard Lanne, *Tchad-Libye: La Querelle des frontières* (Paris: Éditions Karthala, 1982). C. G. Widstrand, ed., *African Boundary Problems* (Uppsala: Scandinavian Institute of African Studies, 1969) argues that the boundary was not a problem until after Qaddafi's coup.

14. Benyamin Neuberger, *Involvement, Invasion, and Withdrawal: Qadhafi's Libya and Chad, 1969–1981* (Tel Aviv: Tel Aviv University Press, Occasional Paper no. 83, May 1982), p. 25.

15. *The Libyan Problem,* Bureau of Public Affairs, U.S. Department of State, Special Report, no. 111, Washington, D.C., October 1983.

16. Neuberger, *Involvement,* p. 26.

17. See Michael Asher, *In Search of the Forty Days Road* (Harlow, Essex: Longman, 1984).

18. "Civil War in Chad," *Africa Digest* 17, no. 1 (February 1970), p. 18.

19. *Al Youm* (Tripoli), 3 December 1969, p. 1.

20. Golda Meir, *My Life* (New York: G. P. Putnam's, 1975), pp. 317–337; Benyamin Beit-Hallahmi, "In and Out of Africa," in *The Israeli Connection: Who Arms Israel and Why?* ed. Benyamin Beit-Hallahmi (New York: Pantheon Books, 1987), pp. 38–75.

21. Text of Statement by Libyan Ministry of Unity and Foreign Affairs, Tripoli, 28 April 1970. Document in authors' possession.

22. For the Chadian reaction, see articles on Chad appearing in *West Africa* during February 1970.

23. Bernard Lanne, *Tchad-Libye: La Querelle des frontières* (Paris: Éditions Karthala, 1982), p. 29; Douglas Porch, *The Conquest of the Sahara* (London: Jonathan Cape, 1985), p. 127; and the text of the Turkish notes concerning the frontier in Ettore Rossi, *Storia di Tripoli e della Tripolitania delle conquista araba al 1911* (Rome: Instituto par l'Oriente, 1968), pp. 341–342.

24. *Africa,* Foreign Broadcast Information Service, no. 975, 22 December 1970.

25. Neuberger, *Involvement,* p. 26; "Chad: President Tombalbaye," *Africa Digest* 17, no. 5 (October 1970), p. 88.

26. Robert Buijtenhuijs, *Le Frolinat et les revoltes populaires du Tchad, 1965–1976* (The Hague: Mouton, 1978), p. 243.

27. "El Testarudo Rey del Desierto," *Apsi* (Chile), 6 September 1987. A Spanish translation of an undated article in *Le Nouvel Observateur* by Jean-Paul Mari.

28. "El Testarudo Rey del Desierto."

29. This bizarre analogy for the creation of a "Ho Chi Minh Trail," which was hacked out of the tropical rain forest of Indo-China, with the desert caravan routes across the Sahara from the Kufra oasis to Wadai and central Chad preoccupied the revolutionary leaders during their meetings throughout August 1971.

30. *Bulletin of International News,* 1935, 8; Lanne, *Tchad-Libye,* pp. 129–153. For a text of the Franco-Italian Accords signed by Mussolini and Laval on 7 January 1935, known as the Treaty of Rome, and Ogier's delimitation for which he was severely criticized by his fellow officers for giving away too much, see Lanne, *Tchad-Libye,* pp. 131–135, 152–153; and "Trattato fra L'Italia e la Francia, del 7 gennaio 1935, per regolare i loro interessi in Africa," *Oriente Moderno* 15 (no. 7), Title 2 (Rome: Instituto per L'Oriente, 1935), p. 309. For a legal commentary on the Treaty of Rome and a map of the demarcation, see Ian Brownlie, *African Boundaries: A Legal and Diplomatic Encyclopedia* (Berkeley: University of California Press, 1979), pp. 121–126.

31. *General, Near East, Africa,* vol. 1, *Foreign Relations of the United States* (Washington, D.C.: U.S. Department of State, U.S. Government Printing Office, 1935), pp. 173–175.

32. United Nations General Assembly, 26th Session, 1955th Plenary, New York, 6 October 1971.

33. See "Colonel Bogey," *Times* (London), 5 January 1987, 17; and Oye Ogunbadejo, *The International Politics of Africa's Strategic Minerals* (Westport, Conn.: Greenwood Press, 1985), pp. 148–149.

34. "Chad," *Marchés Tropicaux et Méditerranéens* (Paris), 19 October 1973, p. 1425.

35. Samuel Decalo, *Historical Dictionary of Chad* (Metuchen, N.J.: Scarecrow Press, 1977), pp. 88–89, 291.

36. "Libyan Designs on Egypt, Sudan Feared," *Los Angeles Times,* 5 July 1983; Neuberger, *Involvement,* p. 60.

37. "The Desert Storms Choking Mussolini's Heir," *Economist,* 4 April 1987, pp. 27–28; the subject of Aozou is discussed at length in Lanne, *Tchad-Libye.*

38. *Guerres et Conflits d'Aujourd'hui* 8 (1985): 14–27.

39. See speech by Gouara Lassou to the OAU Ad Hoc Committee on Chad-Libya, Libreville, 28 April 1987, in "Kamougue, 'Aouzou est Tchadienne,'" *Jeune Afrique,* 26 October 1983, p. 37.

40. M. P. Kelley, "Weak States and Captured Patrons," *Round Table* 296, October 1985; *L'Aurore* 4718, September 1973.

41. Decalo, *Historical Dictionary,* pp. 122–123.

42. Pierre Biarnes, "Un nouveau dirigeant se félicite du rôle de certains Français dans le coup d'état," *Le Monde,* 26 April 1975, p. 5; "Les Rebelles toubou: Un millier d'hommes sous les armes et un embryon d'administration," *Le Monde,* 12 September 1975, p. 8; "Hissène Habré," *Le Monde,* 12 September 1975, p. 8; for this period see also *Jeune Afrique,* 28 September 1975.

43. Decalo, *Historical Dictionary,* p. 132.

44. *Facts on File,* 21 June 1975, p. 441.

5

The Struggle for Chad

Tombalbaye was determined to consolidate his control of the government of Chad by an African bureaucracy and security forces dominated by his Sara kinsmen from the south. This not only offended the Muslims but also angered the Christian community, for he demanded proof of initiation into *yondo,* as a prerequisite for government employment. *Yondo* was the ritual ceremony of manhood for young males from the numerous tribes of southern Chad, particularly the Sara, and Dr. Vixamar, a Haitian intellectual and physician who became Tombalbaye's confidant and principal advisor, designed the strategy for the Africa "authenticité" campaign symbolized by adherence to the *yondo* rite. Tombalbaye's decree required government officials and civil servants to undergo the *yondo* rite, and one much publicized *yondo* ceremony took place at Tombalbaye's hometown of Bedaya in 1973 with 1,000 initiates. The Christian church, both African and expatriate, had long condemned the practice of *yondo* as barbaric, pagan, and an apostasy. Tombalbaye denounced his Christian opponents at his independence-day speech in 1973, declaring that *yondo* was "the basis of our traditional education with its principles of charity, austerity, renunciation, obedience, and humility."[1] The African Christians and their foreign missionaries who opposed *yondo* were persecuted; some were tortured; others died as martyrs. When the opposition continued to condemn *yondo,* Tombalbaye retaliated by expelling the missionaries and demanded that all Chadians abandon their corrupt religious practices and values to follow him in the search for a more African "Tchatitude."

Tombalbaye did not reserve his condemnations solely for the Christians of Chad. Despite the advice of his friend President of Niger Hamani Diori, he spurned any rapprochement with the dying Pompidou or with his successor Valéry Giscard d'Estaing. Under pressure from Diori, he did agree to join the "States with Saharan Responsibilities," an informal association consisting of Algeria, Mali, Mauritania, and Niger, until he learned that Libya was not invited. Tombalbaye refused to abandon his erstwhile ally and refused to meet with his fellow African presidents. He did not appear to have realized the contradiction between his search for

Libyan financial support and his campaign for African authenticity for which Qaddafi had nothing but contempt. He himself led the African authenticity campaign by taking the name of Ngartha, "True Chief." In January 1974 new passports and identity cards with "African" names were issued to all citizens of Chad, and a series of government decrees, derived from those of President Mobutu Sese Seko of Zaire, demanded absolute obedience to his personal leadership. Like Mobutu, Tombalbaye "Africanized" the Parti Progressiste Tchadien (PPT) in September 1973 by purging the party's cells and reconstituting the party as the Mouvement National pour la Révolution Culturelle et Sociale (MNRCS).

It is quite impossible to determine which ingredients produced Tombalbaye's *authenticité* campaign. There was his own cheerless personality, the political philosophies of his Caribbean and West African coterie, and the stream of advice from President Mobutu. The pudding, however, proved bitter to the taste and ritually impure for Muslims in the north and center of Chad as well as the Christians from the south. Their distaste turned to detestation for the government corruption that characterized the international relief effort for the Muslims of the Sahel. Despite the unpopularity of his *authenticité* campaign, Tombalbaye persevered, surrounded by his few "advisors" in the MNRCS Executive Committee. In April he announced to an audience of party faithful: "We have never ceased to struggle against the rapacity of 'Dopele' [Jacques Foccart], the king of the *mafiosi*, who has made fourteen attempts to bring down our policies and substitute his . . . [and] never forgiven us for working out a political system different from the one he wants to see here."[2]

In April 1974, President Diori was overthrown in a coup d'état for many of the same reasons that bred dissension in Chad—personal rule, corruption, indifference and political isolation, and the failure to provide relief to the victims of the Sahelian drought. Tombalbaye never appeared to have understood the folly of his flirtations with Qaddafi while simultaneously pursing a campaign of Africanization hostile to Muslims. His vehement diatribes against "Dopele" were useful for his cultural revolution, if not personally gratifying, but more the fantasy of independent Africa than the reality of survival provided by France. Pompidou displayed little interest either in Africa or for the Francophiles, such as Hamani Diori, and was concerned only for the interests of France, not for the behavior of those whom he ignored.

The United States and Tombalbaye

By 1975 Tombalbaye had few faithful in Chad and even fewer abroad. He had received little economic aid from Libya, and although the Arab League approved several million dollars in loans, Tombalbaye was unable to attract private Arab capital. Thus, like the Sudan and other African states seeking assistance in a cold war of international rivalries, Tombalbaye would eventually play the American card. During the traditional Fourth of July celebrations in Ndjamena, over which the

American ambassador presides, officials from the government of Chad, the diplomatic corps, and American expatriates gathered in 1975 to enjoy a festive occasion accompanied by speeches polite and political. On this Fourth of July, Justice Minister Joseph Brahim Seid, Chad's most famous intellectual, orator, and least influential member of Tombalbaye's government, delivered eloquent praise for the "Pax Americana brought to the world following World War II." American officials were astonished. Most Americans who represented the United States in Chad were stuck at the end of a career languishing in a post at the end of nowhere, 150 miles from N'Gouandéré, the terminus of the Transcamerounian Railroad to Douala on the Atlantic. Within the sphere of French interests and in a cauldron of domestic turbulence, this calculated praise reopened the somnolent interest of the United States embassy. Its principal role was to report on domestic politics and regional insurgency. There were some 2,000 rebels in the west and north, but they appeared to be "no cohesive opposition" to endanger the government, and there were only some 10,000 Chadian security forces who might represent a potential threat to Tombalbaye. There was no illusion among the American officials in Ndjamena that Chad was "without great strategic assets or interest to us . . . far from having attractive qualities . . . [for economic growth was] probably less than zero."[3] The American embassy had always presented a low profile in deference to the French and as a result of indifference in Washington. The Peace Corps program flourished, and in 1974 the U.S. Agency for International Development pledged $1.5 million for drought relief in the Bardai, Mongo, and Biltine prefectures. This was a very modest presence, but after Brahim Seid's speech, the embassy received the gratuitous personal attention of President Tombalbaye. He did not, however, convince the embassy to recommend that the United States support the Tombalbaye regime. The Department of State agreed.

The State Department had not expressed any particular concern about the opening of the Chad-Libya Development Bank in Ndjamena in January 1974 by the Libyan chief of staff Abu Bakr Younis. Washington was of the opinion that Tombalbaye would receive no real benefit from the bank. Its presence, however, required close surveillance not out of any consideration for Tombalbaye but for the deterioration in relations between Libya and the United States. Qaddafi's claim to the Gulf of Sidra, his inflammatory speeches, and his support of international terrorism culminating in the implication of the Libyan government as an accessory in the assassination of the U.S. ambassador to the Sudan, Cleo Noel, by the Black September organization in Khartoum. Cables intercepted by the United States implicated Qaddafi; the plot had occurred after the Sudanese leader had rejected a merger with Libya and was seeking closer ties to the United States and Egypt.[4]

Tombalbaye Assassinated

Isolated by the international community and the domestic opposition against his *authenticité* campaign, Tombalbaye was haunted by the *L'affaire Claustre*.

Even more alarming, the Chad military and security forces had not received their pay, promotions, or an explanation for arbitrary arrest of a popular officer, General Felix Malloum, for "political sorcery." His attempts to reduce French influence, his cultural revolution, the corruption, the widespread discontent, all contributed to the demise of Ngartha Tombalbaye, but his "further purges of [the] officer corps" brought the end of an African episode.[5] On the evening of 12 April 1975 troops of the regular army under the command of Brigadier General Milarew (Noel) Odingar, the army chief of staff, assaulted the president's residence in Ndjamena killing Tombalbaye and ending his fifteen years of rule in Chad. Few African leaders had managed to last as long, and few had met such a bloody end. The Chad embassy in Washington announced that the National Army had clashed with the Presidential Guard, the Compagnies Tchadiennes de Sécurité, in a five-hour battle with many casualties. The leader of the coup was Brigadier General Odingar, a professional soldier and, like Tombalbaye, a Sara. Trained in the 1950s at the École Général Leclerc in Brazzaville, he later served in the B.E.T., where he earned the respect of the Toubou. Tombalbaye had ordered his arrest in March 1975, which undoubtedly galvanized his determination to end the longest-reigning chief of state in Africa.[6]

The Conseil Supérieur Militaire du Tchad and Felix Malloum

General Odingar represented the Groupe des Officiers des Forces Armées Tchadiennes (GOFAT), which carried out the coup, abolished all political parties, and suspended the constitution; the Executive Council and National Assembly were prorogued. General Felix Malloum, the former commander-in-chief of all Chad's armed forces, was released from prison. He immediately reassumed his command of Chad military forces, and not surprisingly, he was the overwhelming choice of GOFAT to be the head of state and president of the Conseil Supérieur. Malloum was neither a politician nor a diplomat. He was a soldier, born in 1932 to a Sara father and a mother from the north. Like other able, young Sara, he was selected by the French to attend the École Général Leclerc in Brazzaville and the Fréjus military academy in France. His abilities and combat experience in Indo-China and Algeria secured him a lieutenancy in the French army. Upon his return to Chad in 1961 he experienced a meteoric career commanding Chad forces in Kanem, Guera, and Baguirmi and became the head of Tombalbaye's military cabinet, chief of staff of the army, and in 1972 the commander of all Chad security forces.[7]

Unlike the other members of the Conseil Supérieur Militaire, Malloum had a greater understanding of Chad's "Northern Problem." His mother was northerner and he had commanded Chad security forces against FROLINAT. One of his first acts had been to appeal to the rebels to lay down their arms and work with the government for a new Chad, but Abba Siddiq and his FROLINAT refused Malloum's gesture. His reputation and integrity, however, convinced the

Derde to end his self-imposed exile in Libya and return to Chad. Despite these positive initiatives, he made a terrible blunder by confirming the sinister and Major Camille Gourvenac as director of Chad's secret service and military intelligence. A confirmed opportunist, Gourvenac may have established his legitimacy with Malloum by failing to warn Tombalbaye of the coup, but this Machiavellian oversight did nothing to assuage the deep hatred for him by Toubou and Arab. Certainly, Malloum was disposed to institute a rapprochement with France, but the appointment of this duplicitous Frenchman to the most powerful agency in Chad simply confirmed to many cynics the continuing influence of Jacques Foccart and the French presence in the management of government in Chad.

Presidents Giscard and Malloum

Valéry Giscard d'Estaing succeeded President Georges Pompidou in April 1974 and was delighted to recognize Malloum and his government. Nevertheless, he was not going to continue the *France-Afrique* traditions of de Gaulle or Pompidou. Giscard sought to chart a course that would allow the French ship of state to navigate more easily through the shoals of neocolonialism that troubled Francophone Africa. Partnership would replace paternalism; cooperation would replace coercion. The beginning of this brave new world had been outlined at Bangui in the Central African Republic only days before Tombalbaye's assassination. Here the heads of state from eight Francophone countries continued their discussions begun in their informal meetings Tombalbaye had spurned when Qaddafi was not invited. They publicly endorsed Giscard's intention "to increase the effectiveness of French aid" in support of the Lomé Convention by which European nations promised African states substantial economic assistance and trade concessions. Although brief and informal, the Bangui meeting proved to be a milestone in the metamorphosis of the economic role of France in Africa.[8]

While he was offering economic assistance to Francophone Africa, Giscard was disengaging France from political entanglements where "French military solutions could not hope to bring any sort of permanent political settlements in areas [like Chad] where conflict was endemic."[9] It was in the interest of France to establish more cordial relations with Muammar Qaddafi, but any rapprochement with Libya could hardly be contemplated in Paris if the Force d'Intervention was to be employed to suppress the Muslims of northern Chad.[10] Moreover, Giscard's new African policy of quiet economic assistance to replace visible military presence in Africa would have to compete with Qaddafi's avowed interest in Chad. Qaddafi would not abandon FROLINAT or the Aozou Strip to any government of Sara southerners at Ndjamena. As Giscard's new African policy eroded the French connection with Chad, Malloum began to search for an alliance with his neighbors to contain Qaddafi's ambitions on their respective frontiers. Qaddafi had broken with Sadat and Numayri; Tombalbaye was dead; and perhaps mutual interests could be achieved to strengthen Malloum's beleaguered government and maintain the territorial integrity of Chad.

All these larger issues were complicated by the determination of the French government to secure the release of Françoise Claustre, who had now been held captive for eighteen months by Hissene Habre. *L'affaire Claustre* had generated a great deal of publicity and embarrassment for the French government, and no sooner had the Malloum government been installed than Giscard sent Brigadier General Auffray, a former commander of French forces in Chad, to Ndjamena. He failed to convince President Malloum to accept Habre's demands for ransom. The French government then sought to end this wretched affair at any price. The French envoy, Stephane Hessel, arrived in Bardai to promise Habre both cash and military equipment; in September, a priest, Louis Morel, who claimed to have known Habre in France, delivered four million francs and promised French arms. When the French complied with airdrops of shabby supplies, the rebels were furious and the hostages remained at Bardai.

These secret negotiations enraged Malloum. By dealing directly with Habre and Goukouni, the government of France had treated Chad with utter contempt, made all the more intolerable by Malloum's deep sympathies and loyalty to France. He rationalized French arrogance as the work of a cabal of left-wing French determined to support radical revolutionaries in the former French colonies. The activities of the French left-wing intellectual Régis Debray in Bolivia had convinced him that this small circle of French leftists was transporting its unsuccessful attempts at destabilization from Latin America to Africa. He ordered all French military units out of Chad.[11] Giscard was delighted to terminate the French military connection, and in October 2,000 French troops were withdrawn.[12]

Humiliated by the *L'affaire Claustre* and Giscard's lack of enthusiasm for Chad, Malloum was further frustrated when rebuffed by Qaddafi. In August 1975 the Libyan Council of Ministers formally annexed the Aozou Strip and incorporated it into the Mirzuq province of Libya. A census was conducted in the villages of Arbi, Aoumshi, Fazoundi, Aozi, and Arouah within the strip and reported in Tripoli news to confirm that 6,000 Libyans lived in the Aozou "Region," where they had been "shamefully neglected." They had been promptly issued Libyan identity cards and "for the first time" were now "conscious of their belonging to their homeland" and "confirmed the desire of the September 1 Revolution that the Libyan Arab man enjoy his humanity . . . and that he be guaranteed a happy life."[13] Despite official objections from Ndjamena, the reaction from the international community was surprisingly indifferent to Libya's "historic" claim to the Aozou. *The Times* of London and *The Washington Post* did not contest the Libyan occupation; *The New York Times* explained that Libya had become "interested in the land last year after geological investigations showed that [there] might be an extension of a uranium belt running through Niger and Mali further west."[14]

President Felix Malloum considered the Libyan annexation of Aozou a declaration of war. He ordered the reconnaissance flights that reported the construction of buildings at Aozou village, an airstrip, and a road from the Chad-Libya frontier through the Korizo Pass. Within six months a modern road had reached Bardai. A second all-weather road was under construction from Kufra to Jabal Uwaynat, the 6,000-foot cones rising out of the Libyan Desert where the borders of Egypt, Libya, and Sudan meet. Jabal Uwaynat may have been the mythical lost oasis of Zerzura, but it was most certainly a strategic sentinel and watering place from which Libyan forces could operate into Darfur and El Fasher to the east and across the Ennedi Plateau to Abeche and Wadai to the south. The construction of a Libyan base at Uwaynat could hardly go unnoticed by Egypt and the Sudan as at least three Libyan convoys a month passed from Kufra through Uwaynat to the Ennedi with supplies for FROLINAT.

Dissension Within the FAN

The annexation of the Aozou Strip by Colonel Qaddafi upset not only his neighbors but also its inhabitants. The Toubou *shaykhs* would never regard themselves as Libyans, and amongst the warriors of the Northern Army Force (FAN) there were deep divisions that defined and differentiated Qaddafi's friends and enemies. The first disagreement between the two leaders of FAN, Hissene Habre and his deputy, Goukouni, took place at an isolated camp sixty miles west-northwest of Ounianga Kebir amidst the hills overlooking the desolate Gouro salt pans. Here these two dissimilar Toubou warlords debated the future of the FAN. Goukouni approved the Libyan annexation of the Aozou Strip; Habre refused to accept any Libyan role in Chad and certainly not its occupation of the Aozou. Goukouni opposed Malloum's efforts to reconcile the warring parties in Chad; Habre argued that both could benefit from discussions with Malloum who knew the north. Goukouni wanted to end the *L'affaire Claustre;* Habre argued that it was the only means to acquire resources without having to go to Qaddafi. Not surprisingly, there was no agreement, but they and their entourage departed in peace. Goukouni retired into his sanctuaries in the Tibesti; Habre settled in Gouro, an oasis in Borkou.

Despite the tension among the states of the Sahel and Sahara and internecine strife within the governments of Chad, the Sudan, and amongst the rebels, the *L'affaire Claustre* continued to haunt them all. Once again the French government intervened to release the hostages without informing President Malloum. The International Red Cross was inveigled to send "observers" to the Tibesti, precipitating a furious warning from Malloum for them to stay clear of the B.E.T. The minister for foreign affairs, Wadal Abdelkader Kamougue, promptly announced that the government of Chad had taken charge of the negotiations to free the Claustres. The *Derde* would act as intermediary.[15] Kamougue had been one of the leading architects of the coup d'état and had led the firefight against Tombalbaye's loyal bodyguards, the Compagnies Tchadiennes de Sécurité, for which he was rewarded with the foreign ministry. Arrogant, inflexible, and malicious, he had quickly emerged as one of the strongest personalities on the Conseil Supérieur Militaire.

Months passed during which neither Kamougue nor Malloum were able to secure the release of the Claustres. Frustrated Giscard now sent the French prime minister, Jacques Chirac, to Tripoli in March 1976 to urge Qaddafi to intercede with Habre. Chirac flew on to Ndjamena where he informed Malloum of the French direct initiative to use his enemy, Qaddafi, to release the hostages.[16] The efforts of President Malloum and his foreign minister to end the wretched *L'affaire Claustre* had succeeded only in pressing the French into a more intimate relationship with their enemy in Libya. This became apparent when Malloum pressed Chirac for assistance in the B.E.T. only to be rewarded by a convention in which Article 4 stipulated that France would not become involved in military activity in Chad nor to "maintain or reestablish" the government. After sixteen years, *France-Afrique* in Chad appeared to be over.

The French decision to abandon Chad appears to have been deeply influenced by the deteriorating military situation in the B.E.T., which had prompted Malloum's request for an affirmation of the French connection and Chirac's reason for ending it. In February 1976 Habre had led a surprise assault against Faya Largeau, the administrative capital of the B.E.T. His hundred Daza Toubou and Zaghawa warriors of the Northern Frontier Army overran the somnolent defenders, seized the airport, and looted the ammunition dump. They held off the government forces for another twenty-four hours before vanishing into the desert. Habre was an immediate hero throughout the oases and villages of the B.E.T. He was suddenly the reincarnation of the romantic Bedouin warrior of the desert, but like his legendary predecessors his success brought not only fame and followers but also the enmity of his rivals. Goukouni could not hide his jealousy, which had festered since his father, the *Derde*, made no secret of his admiration for Habre's military prowess. These petty rivalries, intrigues, and betrayals had little to do with the larger ideological or religious issues or the control of the Aozou Strip or the B.E.T., but they represented the traditions of centuries by those who lived on the edge of survival in an inhospitable land.

Qaddafi immediately saw an opportunity to divide the FAN between Goukouni's Teda Toubou and the Daza of Habre to further his own ambitions in the Sahara and Sahel. He organized a gathering of the rebel "chiefs" at Aozi village in the Aozou Strip in March 1976. The gathering itself was orchestrated by six of Qaddafi's most trusted officers. Adoum Togoi, military commander of the Second Liberation Army represented FROLINAT. Habre's senior officers represented the First Liberation Army from FAN. The Libyans demanded the release of the Claustres after which Habre would receive a substantial shipment of arms. Neither Habre nor his representatives at Aozi trusted Qaddafi in particular and Libyans in general. He demanded first the weapons and then the release of the hostages. This distrust was not simply the traditional caution of the Bedouin but a historic hostility toward those who encroached into the B.E.T. from the north.

The Daza Toubou from the Tibesti and the Zaghawa from the Erdi Hills had never accepted Libyan promises. Why should they accept them in the present from the Libyan Arabs who considered the dark-skinned Toubou "little better than slaves or sub-humans."[17]

When Habre proved intractable, the Libyan emissaries proposed a personal meeting in May. He failed to appear at the rendezvous, a calculated insult that Qaddafi never forgot. Relations between them continued to deteriorate. In late July a Libyan force attempting to raise the Libyan flag at Omchi, a small oasis in the Aozou Strip thirty-three miles northwest of Yebbi Bou, was attacked by Habre's Toubou from the FAN. Three Libyans were killed, seven wounded, and sixteen Libyan prisoners now joined the Claustres as the news of yet another victory by the warrior Habre swept through the B.E.T. He sought to capitalize on his military success with a diplomatic initiative. In June 1976 a delegation from Habre appeared without warning in Khartoum. Not quite knowing what to make of this surprise visit, Sudanese officials, met in secret with Habre's representatives to learn that they sought to reclaim the German marks the West German government had sent to win the release of Christian Staewen. Habre's courier had received the funds in Khartoum, but passing through Darfur on his way to Chad he was intercepted and relieved of the funds by Sudanese army officers. Habre's representatives were willing to accept the loss of the cash in return for arms. Numayri with Sudanese aplomb and courtesy made good Habre's loss by a donation of substantial arms with little consideration for his relations with President Malloum.

Qaddafi and the Sudan

While haggling over money and arms, the Habre delegation in Khartoum encountered Muhammad al-Baghalani and his deputy Mahamat Nouri, who were being escorted from Geneina by the Darfur police. Baghalani was the commander of the FROLINAT Eastern Liberation Army, which was more a euphemism for banditry than revolution. In 1974 he had been chased into Darfur by Chad security forces where Jaafar Numayri, beset by more pressing problems in Khartoum, was content to provide sanctuary for him and his men as long as they did nothing to embarrass the Sudan government. Basking in security but inactivity in Darfur, Baghalani was infuriated by Habre's success in the B.E.T. He threatened to strike across the frontier with his Vulcan Force as he called the Eastern Liberation Army. This was more the bombast of a bandit than the calculation of a revolutionary, but the embassies of France and the United States warned their nationals in the area of the danger. It convinced Jaafar Numayri to rid himself of a troublemaker. Baghalani and his associates were given tickets and Sudanese passports and peremptorily flown to Tripoli in July when Habre was unceremoniously expelled from FROLINAT.

Numayri had every reason not to antagonize Malloum. Qaddafi had provided a sanctuary for his principal enemy, Sadiq al-Mahdi, and had supplied Sadiq's

Ansar with arms to overthrow his secular government. In 1972 Numayri had accepted the differences between the Africans of the Southern Sudan and the Arabs of its north by making peace between them at Addis Ababa in 1972. Qaddafi could not accept the peace accords that Numayri had signed with the Southern Sudanese, who were Africans, like those in Chad, over whom he wished to extend Pan-Arab ideology, Islam, and the historic control of the trade across the Sahara. Qaddafi thus established a base at Jabal Uwaynat and Ma'tan as-Sarra in the Sara Triangle from which to launch a strike force to overthrow Jaafar Numayri in Khartoum. The Sara Triangle was ceded to Italy by the British and Egyptian rulers of the Anglo-Egyptian Condominium in 1934. It was regarded by both the Egyptians and the British as a worthless piece of sand; a cheap concession to Mussolini's atavistic desire for sand and his passion to reconstitute the new Roman Empire in Africa. Situated 200 miles south of Kufra in the Libyan Desert, Ma'tan as-Sarra was a dismal and isolated oasis seldom visited by the Toubou or Zaghawa and a perfect place to stockpile arms. From Ma'tan as-Sarra insurgents could strike west into the Aozou Strip, south into the Ennedi Plateau and Wadai, and southeast across the sands of northern Darfur to the Nile and Khartoum. The few palms and brackish water of Ma'tan as-Sarra made possible the last trans-Saharan caravan route established in 1811 to link the North Africa of the Sanusiyya with Wadai and the Sahel. With his unlimited oil resources and the huge underground aquifer discovered by Occidental Petroleum at the Kufra oasis, Qaddafi could embark with greater confidence than Mussolini on a forward march across the sands of the Sudan to the Nile at Khartoum. In July 1976 a thousand Sudanese followers of Sadiq al-Mahdi trained in Libya left Ma'tan as-Sarra and crossed the northern sands of Darfur and the plains of Kordofan to storm Omdurman and Khartoum. Numayri was now confronted by a more implacable enemy than the communists were in 1972, and after three days of bloody fighting he was rescued by a tank battalion that drove into Khartoum to restore order. After the fierce combat in which some 3,000 Sudanese were killed, a deep resentment spread throughout the Sudan against Qaddafi's violent intervention. It effectively ended any accommodation between Libya and the Sudan. Numayri never again trusted Qaddafi. FROLINAT was no longer welcome in Khartoum as a sanctuary in its insurgency against Chad.[18]

Frustrated in the Aozou Strip by Habre and repulsed in Khartoum by Numayri, Qaddafi rallied his surrogates to pursue his ideologic, religious, and imperial ambitions south of the Sahara. FROLINAT was his most logical but ineffective agent. In July he called Abba Siddiq, Baghalani, Goukouni, and other rebel leaders to Tripoli to reorganize FROLINAT. The rebels, however, were unable to establish a united front. Abba Siddiq had little credibility with the Toubou "chiefs" and less with their men, who were more amenable to the discipline of the desert than his political ideology. Goukouni, the only surviving son the *Derde*, was cursed by his father's admiration for Habre, his own inadequacies, and his failure to establish his legitimacy as the hereditary leader of the Toubou.

The meeting ended in disarray, but the dissension within FROLINAT was public knowledge and disillusioned followers, particularly in Wadai, surrendered to Malloum's forces. Undeterred, the Libyan government issued maps in September 1976 that incorporated the Aozou Strip within Libya.[19] Chad closed its border with Libya, froze Libyan bank accounts, and prohibited Libyans from leaving Chad. This was a dramatic but futile gesture of defiance that simply convinced President Malloum and his opportunistic foreign minister, Wadal Abdelkader Kamougue, that the government must deal with reality in the north. They were both "in complete agreement with Hissene Habre. . . . His attitude toward the problem has always been clear—he opposes the [Libyan] occupation."[20]

Habre remained defiant. He rejected a rumored offer to govern a "Toubou Protectorate" on behalf of Libya and declared that he would fight Goukouni and moved his FAN from Borkou into the Ennedi Plateau on the Sudan frontier. Goukouni remained in Libya, discomforted by the denunciations of his father, the *Derde*, and his praise for Habre. Meanwhile, Secretary General of the United Nations Kurt Waldheim sent a special representative, who finally managed to secure the release of the Claustres in January 1977 to everyone's relief. Habre also released his Libyan prisoners but kept all the captured arms and ammunition.

The Return of the French

Despite the attention by the international media with *L'affaire Claustre* and the Libyan occupation of the Aozou Strip, President Malloum still found time to govern. Civil servants and the military were paid. Foreign investment was encouraged. The Continental Oil Company had positive reports of oil from a well 180 miles north of Ndjamena. Foreign Minister Kamougue grandly announced in November 1976 that "undoubtedly" there was oil in Chad, and the wealth anticipated from oil grew proportionately with the passing months. Neither the prospects of petroleum nor the economic stability produced by Malloum's austerity program could resolve the rebellion in the north. During the ceremony celebrating the first anniversary of the military coup, the rebels launched grenades at the officials. Shaken, Malloum sought to open direct negotiations with their leaders offering amnesty for their followers and meaningful participation for them in his government. Goukouni refused. He was now completely dependent upon Qaddafi, who had seduced him with the governorship of a Toubou Protectorate that included parts of Tibesti, eastern Niger, and Libya's Fezzan. Habre was the only rebel leader willing to agree to reconciliation. He had publicly terminated his relationship with Qaddafi in July, repudiated the Libyan occupation of the Aozou Strip, and denounced the construction of the new Libyan base at Yebbi Bou, a strategic Tibesti oasis situated 200 miles northwest of Faya. The Libyan base was constructed just south of Aozou Strip and commanded the northern approach to the mile-high Mohi Pass.[21]

His failure to persuade the rebels to resolve their differences with his government convinced Malloum that he could not survive without the French. He immediately set about to mend the fences that Chirac had demolished in March 1976. He appeared with humility at the Third Franco-African Conference of heads of state in May, the first leader of Chad to attend. The French were very pleased, which did not go unnoticed in Ndjamena. Rifts resulting from *L'affaire Claustre* were quietly ignored, and a new military pact was concluded. The Chirac protocol was unceremoniously abandoned, and France agreed to provide military assistance if needed. In return, Malloum allowed France to resume operations at the Ndjamena airport that had served as a strategic support facility for French bases in the Central African Republic. With no publicity a French contingent of the Force d'Intervention was stationed in Wadai where Baghalani's Vulcan Force had become increasingly active.

Concerned by Malloum's overtures to France and the return of French special forces, Qaddafi impetuously arrived with little notice in Ndjamena where he lectured about French neocolonialism and ignored Malloum's pointed questions about his own imperialism in the Aozou Strip. The bluster became bizarre when he sought to convert the president of Chad to Islam. Qaddafi returned to Tripoli to approve further fortification of Libyan installations in the Aozou, which coincided with the publication of his *Green Book,* a long essay incorporating Qaddafi's reflections on Islam. This "Third International Theory" was to be a contribution to the renewal of the Faith by a return to the fundamental teachings in the Quran perceived through his own personal, mystical, theological, and political interpretations. Conservative Muslims strenuously objected to his argument that the Quran alone represented the foundations of Islam to which the law, the *Shari'a,* and the sayings of the Prophet, the *hadith,* were subordinate. In his appeal for a return to the fundamentals of the Quran in Islam, he was following in the tradition of many Sudanic Muslim reformers but without their learning. Hundreds of thousands of copies, however, were distributed in Libya and throughout Africa, by the Da'wa Islamiya (Islamic Call Society), which he had established in May 1973 to supervise religious affairs in Libya and among the hundred million Muslims in sub-Saharan Africa. In little more than a decade the Da'wa would create 132 centers in Africa including a half dozen in central and eastern Chad.[22] The society was especially active in Darfur, Africa south of the Sahara, and among Muslims in France and West Germany. Not surprisingly, the officials of the Da'wa began to influence Libyan foreign policy. Ahmad Shah, the first director of Da'wa, was made head of the Foreign Liaison Office, and cultural attachés in Libyan embassies were expected to promote Da'wa Islamiya and to distribute the *Green Book.*

Regional Geopolitics in a Changing World

When the forces of Sadiq al-Mahdi, supported and financed by Qaddafi, had failed to overthrow Numayri's government in Khartoum in 1976, the Libyan premier, Abd al-Salam Jalloud, denied that the rebels had been trained in Libya or that Kufra and Ma'tan as-Sarra had been used to strike into the Sudan. Qaddafi piously claimed that no Libyan funds had been spent to support the Sudanese insurgents. Numayri denounced Qaddafi as a split personality, "both evil." He immediately signed a defense treat with Egypt and sought to strengthen his ties with Africa. He had achieved international acclaim in 1972 by signing the Addis Ababa accords, which ended seventeen years of civil war between Arabs and Africans in the Sudan. He now used his position as Chairman of the Organization of African States to establish a friendly understanding with President Malloum in order to stabilize their western frontier and support his demands that Qaddafi withdraw from the Aozou Strip.

When Libya continued to construct all-weather roads across the Libyan Desert from Kufra to Jabal Uwaynat and southwest toward the Ennedi Plateau, the Sudanese army was ordered in January 1977 to interdict the flow of arms from Kufra.[23] Military roadblocks were established around the Bir Natrun oasis in northern Darfur, and the minister of the interior prohibited civilian vehicles from traversing the established caravan routes, including the Darb al Arbain, the famous Forty Days Road from El Fasher to Asyut in Egypt. This restriction was to last for many years long after the Sudan Camel Corps had tired of patrolling the wastelands from Natrun to Jabal Uwaynat. Qaddafi denied but could not disguise his support for Sadiq al-Mahdi's attempt to overthrow Jaafar Numayri, which galvanized the Sudan, Egypt, Chad, and Niger into a loose entente against Libya's cartographic aggression into the Aozou Strip. Each insisted that Libya supported political agents, ethnic minorities, and religious leaders opposed to their governments. They were all deeply concerned about Libyan advocacy of international terrorism and the influx of foreign advisors from Cuba, Palestine, and Russia to train dissidents from Chad and the Sudan in skills of terrorism.[24]

In July 1977 President Anwar Sadat of Egypt narrowly escaped an assassination supported by Libya. The Egyptians reacted with fury and during the four days of July 1977, Egyptian tanks roamed through eastern Libya demonstrating their maneuverability in the "Sand War" dramatized by the destruction of a Soviet radar installation at Tobruk. Concerned that the Egyptian assault would lead to Soviet intervention, the U.S. Department of State urged Sadat to withdraw. He did, claiming Egypt's invasion was the result of political and military provocation, but Sadat's contempt for "Libyan sands" was confirmed by his dramatic visit to Jerusalem and peace with Israel. Qaddafi was stunned, but Sadat's perfidy appears to have convinced him to equip his own army with the most sophisticated weapons from the Soviet Union. Humiliated he readily agreed to finance the "Rejection Front"—Libya, Syria, and the Palestinian Liberation Organization (PLO)—to frustrate Sadat's peace effort with Israel. Sadat was demonized as were Numayri in the Sudan and Malloum in Chad.

The hostility between Qaddafi and Malloum became internationally visible during a verbal brawl between the delegations from Chad and Libya during the Fourth Franco-Africa Conference of heads of state in Dakar in April 1977. The French had specifically invited Qaddafi with a conceit that they could manage a rapprochement to end a contentious quarrel that threatened their deteriorating influence in Francophone Africa and involved France in unwanted commitments. The acrimony between the Chad and Libyan delegations was soon transformed into action. In June a combined force of Goukouni's Toubou and the FROLINAT Second Liberation Army under the command of Ahmat Acyl, supplied and supported by Libyan military advisors, overran the Chad army bases at Ounianga Kebir and Kidmi in Borkou. The following month a Libyan detachment under the command of Captain Ali Hireimi attacked the Chad garrison at Bardai, secured a small but strategic oasis situated between the Sunni Plateau and the Aozou Strip, and cleared the way for Acyl's Second Army to seize the Bardai Valley. Routed and in disarray, the Chadians fell back on Faya leaving the northern B.E.T. to the Libyans.[25]

The occupation of Bardai was not only a victory for FROLINAT but also the beginning of Qaddafi's determination to extend Libyan control over the B.E.T. Henceforth, FROLINAT was to become more an instrument of Libyan imperialism than Pan-Arab socialist revolution. The Libyan army had overpowered Malloum's troops, compensating Qaddafi for his humiliating reverse at the hands of the Egyptians. The sympathies of Habre were more with Malloum than Qaddafi, but the centrifugal cultural pull of the northern Arabs and Toubou, now awash in Libyan resources, was too great to overcome. When the north was lost, the center could not hold. If France refused to save his government, Malloum and his army could be broken and two decades of rule by southerners would come to an end in Chad.

Egypt, Libya, Niger, and the OAU

Thoroughly alarmed by Libyan aggression, Egypt supported the determination of the government of Chad to present the Libyan seizure of the Aozou Strip to the Organization of African Unity (OAU) at its annual meeting of the heads of state held in Libreville, Gabon, in July 1977. As the leader of the Pan-Arab world, Egypt's influence was pervasive but quiet, leaving the discussions before the OAU to those most threatened. The Libyan delegates described Chad's allegations as a "campaign by world imperialism to smear the Great 1 September revolution." They argued that Ndjamena was using Libya as a scapegoat for its domestic difficulties. Chad's frontier dispute over the Aozou was dismissed as a "purely technical" matter confirmed by the existence of "many maps and different historic attitudes."[26] When the Libreville talks appeared not to resolve but to exacerbate the dispute, Presidents Kountche of Niger and Obasanjo of Nigeria offered to mediate.

Qaddafi was interested in neither mediation nor the African mediators, but he could hardly ignore the Nigerians. Obasanjo had no quarrel with Qaddafi. Nigeria's enormous oil resources permitted it to play a major role in the political issues that affected its neighbors. Nigeria itself had survived a bloody civil war,

1967–1970, during which France had provided direct support to the Biafra rebels, and it was no secret that the Nigerians welcomed the declining influence of France in Chad. Obasanjo also had no quarrel with Malloum. After the fall of Tombalbaye, Nigeria had begun to finance modest development projects in Chad, but to placate Nigerian Muslims, Obasanjo made no attempt to restrain the activities of the Popular Movement for the Liberation of Chad (MPLT). The MPLT operated from eastern Nigeria where their influence was modest and was more a nuisance than a threat to Ndjamena.

The mediating presence of Niger, regarded as hostile to Libya, was not lost on Qaddafi or Obasanjo. Niger possessed uranium mines that France considered vital to its national security. Uranium had been discovered in northern Niger in the early 1960s and processing the ore began in 1968. Niger became an important source of the "yellow cake" for the French nuclear energy program, the Commissariat de l'Énergie Atomique, which operated a concession at Djado.[27] Although Libya became one of Niger's best customers and paid a premium price for the yellow cake, Qaddafi had claimed the Tummo Triangle, a wasteland of sand and rock with an oasis, Tummo Wells, which had been ceded to Libya by the Franco-Italian Treaty of 1935 (see Map 5.1). Qaddafi suspected that the Tummo Triangle might hide the uranium, which had yet to be discovered in the Murzuk Basin or the Aozou Strip.[28]

More disturbing were reports of Libyan weapons for the Tuareg, the desert predators whose raids into the *Bilad as-Sudan* were remembered throughout centuries rather than generations. President Kountche perceived that the Libyan dispute with Chad was not simply a frontier quarrel but a regional threat to his own government, whose security could be best insured by the OAU. An ad hoc committee of Arab and African members—Algeria, Senegal, Cameroon, Nigeria, Mozambique, and Gabon—was duly appointed upon his request. The committee convened at Libreville in August and was immediately divided by ideological and ethnic interests. Mozambique and Algeria respectively supported FROLINAT; the more conservative, Francophone states, Senegal, Cameroon, Gabon, and Nigeria, were sympathetic to the government of Chad. When political stalemate occurs, the solution is usually to appoint a committee of experts. The ad hoc committee thus established a technical committee to investigate the legal and geographical aspects of the dispute. Libya rejected its report and the subsequent effort of President Omar Bongo of Gabon, ironically a recent convert to Islam, to convene a larger conference of experts at Libreville.

Habre Joins Malloum

While the OAU sought to resolve the Chad-Libya dispute, Qaddafi complained that Egypt was "flying arms to Chad," and when Vice President Hosni Mubarak led an Egyptian delegation to Ndjamena, the Libyan media called it "foreign aggression." It denounced the visit as "a declaration of war on Libya."[29] Within days,

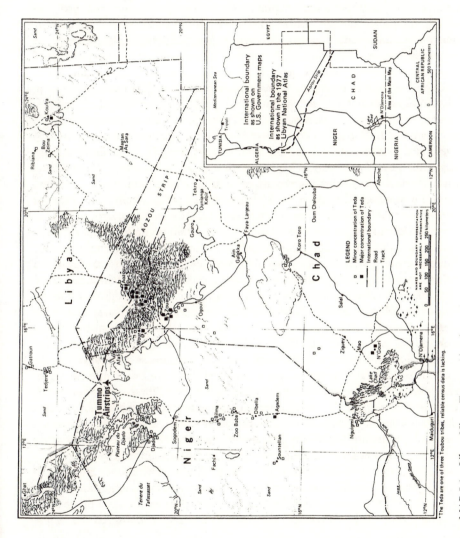

MAP 5.1 *Libya, Niger: Tummo Airstrips*

* The Teda are one of three Toubou tribes; reliable census data is lacking.

President Carter of the United States promised to provide Egypt $200 million for aircraft and equipment to modernize its rapid airlift capacity to protect Egypt's border with Libya and to give the Egyptian air force the ability to support Numayri in the Sudan. The Carter administration also dispatched a team to the Sudan to study its military requirements for defense. Washington also considered arms for Chad, but any overt gestures would most certainly offend the French at a time when American African policy was to "let Africans solve African problems."[30]

Having overcome the challenge from his political left and right and established peace on the southern frontier, Numayri now had to bring peace in the west on the turbulent frontier between Wadai and Darfur. This was the land of the independent petty sultans of Dar Tama, Dar Qimr, and Dar Masalit who had maintained a great deal of independence by manipulating their erstwhile overlords in Wadai and Darfur. It was now territory disputed between Arabs and Africans, traditionalists and revolutionaries, and cultivators and pastoralists. With the surprising support of Muslim conservatives, Sadiq al-Mahdi and Hasan al-Turabi, whom he had enticed back to the Sudan in a spirit of reconciliation, Numayri hoped to provide stability on his frontier and in the *Bilad al-Sudan* by an alliance between Malloum and Habre. He presided at a conference in Khartoum in September 1977 during which President Felix Malloum and Hissene Habre signed a "Fundamental Charter" that designated Habre as prime minister to President Malloum in an agreement to share power. Habre's FAN and Malloum's armed forces of Chad were to be integrated. Habre was given responsibility for the defense of the Ennedi Plateau and Wadai.[31] Numayri, with more assurance than reality, announced that "Sudan and Egypt would act as guarantors of the implementation of any agreement resulting from the talks" and would extend to Chad all assistance to promote national unity and economic and social progress.[32]

The Khartoum agreement not only conferred upon Hissene Habre the legitimacy that had eluded him during his journey from the Tibesti wilderness to the center of power in Ndjamena but proved a watershed in the history of modern Chad. Malloum's French advisors vehemently objected to the arrangement. Some were influenced by Habre's behavior during the *L'affaire Claustre;* others realized that this accommodation would undermine the authority of Felix Malloum and France. It precipitated a review in Paris of its Chad policy from which foreign minister Guiringaud resolved that France should avoid any entanglement in the dispute over the Aozou Strip. Henceforth, France would insist on neutrality. The indifference of President Giscard was a contemptuous gesture for the political demise of Malloum.[33] When Malloum accepted Habre as an equal, his national army was twice the size of Habre's FAN. His southern troops of the Gendarmerie Nationale and the regular army had suffered humiliating defeats and were in disarray. Habre commanded only 1,000 men, hardened Bedouin whom he had transformed into disciplined soldiers. He believed in the unity of Chad. To achieve this he could be ruthless. His alliance with Malloum was, of course, directed at the Libyans in Aozou and the FROLINAT in the B.E.T. Avoiding Habre's Toubou, the FROLINAT Second Liberation Army concentrated their attacks on the demoralized units of the Chad army. Their defeats during innumerable skirmishes depressed President Malloum, who was "falling under the influence" of Wadai Kamougue. The foreign minister had his own political ambitions to achieve by dividing President Felix Malloum and Prime Minister Hissene Habre.[34]

The Popular Armed Forces on the Offensive

The reaction of FROLINAT to the Habre-Malloum alliance was to attack before Habre and Malloum could be supplied and rearmed with Egyptian weapons. Supported by Libya, the FROLINAT attacked Faya Largeau in February 1978. The assault signified a dramatic change in Sudanese warfare. Hitherto the fighting had been between mobile columns moving through the Sahara and Sahel with small arms. The government forces at Faya were now confronted by sophisticated heavy weapons—including anti-aircraft artillery and Libyan air cover and logistical support. The garrison was decimated; Faya was isolated. The French could not ignore Malloum's pleas for help after such a dramatic defeat. Over 2,000 troops of the Force d'Intervention, accompanied by helicopters, Jaguar jets, and Breguet reconnaissance planes, were rushed to Ndjamena. The French established a defensive perimeter from Moussoro to Ati to protect Malloum and the heartland of Chad and rejected Malloum's pleas to recapture Faya.[35] In the B.E.T. only Habre and his FAN represented the government from their strongholds in east and central Chad.

Elated by the victory at Faya, Qaddafi held a general war council in Tripoli to reconstitute FROLINAT as the Popular Armed Forces (FAP) of Chad. The FROLINAT First and Second Liberation Armies, the "old" Vulcan Force of Muhammad Baghalani and the "new" Vulcan Force of Ahmat Acyl were now placed under the command of Goukouni Oueddei.[36] It was a ramshackle military organization, but FAP represented a Libyan attempt to coordinate the rebels for a concerted attack on Ndjamena. The rebels were also reorganized politically. The direction of the war effort was assigned to a Democratic Revolutionary Command, Commandement Démocratique Révolutionnaire (CDR), composed of thirty members selected from each rebel command. Although nominally independent, the CDR, like the FAP, was an instrument of Libyan imperial policy supplied by the government of Libya and personally directed by Colonel Qaddafi.

After Faya the FAP moved quickly south. Its forces threatened to cut the crucial road connecting Ndjamena and Abeche and assaulted the FAN near Ati. Here they were turned back by the intervention of the French jets, which pounded their positions in response to frantic appeals from Habre and Malloum. The FAP retreated north where the leadership dissolved into recriminations as Goukouni blamed Ahmat Acyl not only for the defeat but also for the careless abandonment of so many weapons. Their followers supported their own leaders, but the Libyans quietly began to shift their support to Acyl. During the fighting around Ati, Malloum had launched a diplomatic campaign against Qaddafi. Libyan diplomats were declared persona non grata; the accounts of the Libya Arab Bank were frozen and its Libyan employees expelled. Despite objections from the OAU, which wanted African disputes to be resolved by Africans, Chad took its complaint to the United Nations. In February 1978 the representative from Chad submitted a report to the Security Council that provided a detailed history of the Libyan occupation of the Aozou Strip and its subsequent "intervention in the internal affairs of Chad."[37] Chad had sought without success "to find a basis of understanding with Libya," which had resulted in conflict in the B.E.T., invasion by large numbers of Libyan troops, and the provision of weapons to rebel forces. Moreover, Libya had established military training camps for Chad nationals in Benghazi, Tarhouna, Gouro, and Aozou. The rebels had had the use of Radio Tripoli since October 1977 to unleash a stream of hostile propaganda against the government of Chad. "Yesterday it was Bardai, Zouar, and Ounianga; today Faya and Fada are being attacked. What does tomorrow hold?"[38]

Mutual recriminations between Chad and Libya were exchanged at the United Nations. Libya dismissed the charges as moot, for they dealt with a matter internal to Chad. Chad was prepared to withdraw its complaint in return for a cease-fire by the insurgents.[39] The impasse was broken by the intervention of President Giscard d'Estaing, who persuaded Malloum to withdraw his brief in return for Qaddafi engaging in direct negotiations.[40] The Chairman of the OAU and President of Gabon, Omar Bongo, agreed to host a meeting of Qaddafi and Malloum during the OAU summit conference to be held at Libreville in March 1978. Qaddafi agreed to give the proposal his serious consideration.

A flourish of diplomatic activity followed, having more to do with the venue for the meeting than the substance of the issue. No one appeared interested in negotiating in Libreville amid all the other items on the agenda and in full view of every African head of state. Numayri offered Khartoum; Qaddafi insisted upon Tripoli. Malloum at first refused, but after further pressure from President Numayri, he agreed to send a Chad delegation to Tripoli, and the two parties issued a feeble communiqué on 18 February 1978. The rebels would consider a cease-fire; Chad would work to restore diplomatic relations and continue discussions at Sebha, Benghazi, or anywhere that Qaddafi might suggest, to resolve its territorial dispute with Libya. Qaddafi received the only tangible reward. Chad withdrew its complaint before the Security Council, which seriously undermined Malloum in Ndjamena. When the discussions opened at Sebha on 21 March, Malloum found himself isolated. Without French diplomatic support and with his neighbors, Sudan and Niger, urging him to be conciliatory, he accepted the Commandement Démocratique Révolutionnaire (CDR) in return for a cease-fire. Giving the Chad rebels official recognition for a tenuous armistice provided little security for his beleaguered government.

Notes

1. Robert Jaulin, *La Mort Sara: L'Ordre de la vie ou la pensée de la mort au Tchad* (Paris: Librairie Plon, 1967), p. 2.

2. U.S. Embassy, Ndjamena, Airgram A-24, April 1974.

3. Comments of a U.S. diplomat who was present in Ndjamena. Personal report in the authors' possession.

4. P. Edward Haley, *Qaddafi and the United States Since 1969* (New York: Praeger, 1984), pp. 42–43.

5. Samuel Decalo, *Coups and Army Rule in Africa: Studies in Military Style* (New Haven: Yale University Press, 1976), p. 21.

6. Embassy of Chad, Note no. 206/A/RT/W, Washington, D.C., 23 May 1975.

7. Samuel Decalo, *Historical Dictionary of Chad* (Metuchen, N.J.: Scarecrow Press, 1977), pp. 185–186.

8. Victor D. DuBois, "Former French Black Africa and France," *American Universities Field Staff,* West Africa Series, vol. 16, no. 3 (June 1975).

9. John Chipman, *French Power in Africa* (London: Basil Blackwell, 1989), pp. 243–248.

10. *Jeune Afrique,* 16 May 1976, pp. 24–25.

11. Although significantly reduced, the French continued to provide 80 million and 70 million francs in 1976 and 1977 respectively. M. P. Kelley, "Weak States and Captured Patrons," *Round Table* 296 (October 1985): 329.

12. *Facts on File: World News Digest,* 21 June 1975, 4 October 1975; "Prisoner of Chad," *Newsweek,* 22 September 1975, p. 22.

13. *Al-Fatih* (Tripoli); "North Africa," *Foreign Broadcast Information Service* (FBIS), 8 September 1975, p. 11.

14. *Washington Post,* 8 September 1975, p. A18; *New York Times,* 8 September 1975; *Times* (London), 8 September 1975. In April 1975 Qaddafi claimed that Libya would become a "nuclear state," but that Niger, not the Aozou, would be Libya's "yellow cake."

15. *Facts on File,* 4 October and 6 December 1975; "Prisoners of Chad," *Newsweek,* 27 September 1975; *Economist* (London), 4 October 1975.

16. Claude Wauthier, *Quatre présidents et l'Afrique,* (Paris: Éditions du Seuil, 1995), pp. 326–338.

17. François Soudan, "Hissein Habré dit tout," *Jeune Afrique,* 5 October 1983, pp. 24–27.

18. *Middle East Annual Review 1978* (London: Middle East Review, 1978), pp. 359–360; *The Libyan Problem,* Bureau of Public Affairs, U.S. Department of State, Special Report no. 111, Washington, D.C., October 1983.

19. "3 Neighbors Lose Territory in Libya," *Washington Post,* 10 September 1976, p. 21.

20. "Winning Over Adherents Every Day," *Jeune Afrique,* 10 September 1976, pp. 34–35; "Libya: The Great Test Ahead," *Middle East,* October 1976, pp. 26–29.

21. "Libyan Designs on Egypt, Sudan Feared," *Los Angeles Times,* 5 July 1983.

22. "North Africa," *FBIS,* 30 June 1977, p. 12; *Al-Bayader Al-Siyasi* (Jerusalem), 28 September 1985, p. 34.

23. Omdurman Domestic Radio (in Arabic), 1300 GMT, 20 January 1977.

24. Claire Sterling, *The Terror Network* (New York: Holt, Rinehart and Winston, 1981), pp. 258–271.

25. United Nations Security Council, document S/PV.2060, New York, 17 February 1978.

26. "North Africa," *FBIS*, 31 January 1984, p. Q1, from Paris Domestic Service in French, 1824 GMT, 30 January 1984.

27. "North Africa," *FBIS*, 30 June 1977, p.12, from Tripoli ARNA, 34; S. Koutoubi, "Uranium in Niger," Uranium Institute, Fourth Annual Symposium, London, September 1979.

28. Oye Ogunbadejo, *The International Politics of Africa's Strategic Minerals* (Westport, Conn.: Greenwood Press, 1985), pp. 148–153.

29. M. G. El Warfally, *Imagery and Ideology in U.S. Policy Toward Libya, 1969–1982* (Pittsburgh: University of Pittsburgh Press, 1989), p. 98.

30. "Coming Political Problems in Black Africa," *Africa and the United States: Vital Interests* (New York: New York University Press, 1978), pp. 96–97.

31. For events during 1977–1979, see Virginia Thompson and Richard Adloff, *Conflict in Chad* (Berkeley: Institute of International Studies, University of California, 1981). On the charter of 17 September 1977, see Michel N'Gangbet, *Peut-on encore sauver le Tchad?* (Paris: Éditions Karthala, 1984), pp. 109–110; and United Nations Security Council, document S/12888, New York, 9 October 1978.

32. Anthony Clayton, "Foreign Intervention in Africa," in *Military Power and Politics in Black Africa,* ed. Simon Baynham (New York: St. Martin's Press, 1986), p. 210.

33. Bernard Lanne, "Conflits et violences au Tchad," *Africa contemporaine,* 4th Quarter (1996): 58.

34. Christian Bouquet, *Tchad: Genèse d'un conflit* (Paris: Éditions L'Harmattan, 1982), p. 152; "The Libyan Connection," *Economist,* 4 August 1979, p. 39.

35. *Guerres et Conflits d'Aujourd'hui* 8 (1985): 14–27.

36. Jean Chapelle, *Le Peuple Tchadien* (Paris: L'Harmattan, 1980), pp. 284–285.

37. United Nations Security Council, document S/12554, 1978.

38. United Nations Security Council, document S/12560, 13 February 1978.

39. The documents submitted in these exchanges are include in "Chad-Libya Arab Jamahiriya," *Index to Proceedings of the Security Council* (New York: United Nations 1978), pp. 6–7.

40. United Nations Security Council, documents S/12568, 18 February, and S/12570, 21 February 1978; U.S. Embassy, Ndjamena, Cable 0733, 21 February 1978.

6

Libya Threatens Chad

President Malloum had sought to purchase peace in return for his acceptance of the Commandement Démocratique Révolutionnaire (CDR). He was wrong. Recognition did not reduce Libya's military activity in Chad, and the proposed cease-fire was never implemented. The Sebha-Benghazi negotiations, in fact, provided the CDR time to settle internal disputes that divided Arab and Toubou, characterized more by malice, resentment, and jealousy than mutual ideological or material concerns. Self-interest dominated every faction of the CDR, and only the prospect of victory convinced the captains of the Popular Armed Forces (FAP) to set aside their differences and to test the strength of the government and the French south from Faya and in Biltine, the gateway to Wadai. On 27 April, one month after the communiqué from Benghazi that proposed a cease-fire, the FAP attacked Chad garrisons at Salal and Kanem on 15 April and at Arada and Biltine two days later. Reports of these assaults were officially sent to the UN Secretary General Kurt Waldheim by the Chad foreign minister giving details of FAP weapons of the "most sophisticated kind." The skirmishes in Kanem, however, were the responsibility of the small and shadowy Forces Armées Occidentales, the Western Armed Forces (FAO), often called the Third FROLINAT Army. It was, in fact, yet another ragtag gang, more bandits than rebels, which received military support from Nigerian military officers who sought to control the profitable commercial transactions along the Chad-Nigeria frontier. More immediate and more ominous was the advance by Ahmat Acyl down the Bahr al-Ghazal, the great dry depression extending from the shore of Lake Chad northeast through Kanem all the way to Faya Largeau. A traditional route for trade and invasion, the Bahr al-Ghazal was the highway into central Chad for Ahmat Acyl. In desperation Malloum called on the French government to meet its treaty responsibilities to defend Chad. Although President Giscard had ordered additional support in March for French forces in Chad, he had come under severe criticism in the media and the Chamber of Deputies for his indulgence of Qaddafi, presumably in return for oil.[1] Giscard d'Estaing could not abandon Francophone Africa, however, and he responded with "Operation Tacaud." In May 3,000 French troops supported by armored cars, helicopters, and Jaguar jets arrived in Chad. The Legionnaires fought at Ati in May and Djeddah in June. They immediately brought a halt to the FAP offensive by securing the high road down the Bahr al-Ghazal and by reopening the Ndjamena-Ati-Abeche corridor. The Force d'Intervention had accomplished its mission on the ground, but the most effective weapon in the vast arid lands of Chad were the Jaguar jets from which neither the forces of Ahmat Acyl nor those of Goukouni could hide. The French intervention and the defeat of his surrogates infuriated Qaddafi. He hired American and French mercenaries to destroy the French Jaguars at Ndjamena, but their failure only exacerbated conflict among all the participants in an ugly war for a wasteland considered to be of little utility.[2]

The exercise of French power pleased neither Malloum nor Giscard, but it appeared to have momentarily frustrated Libyan ambitions south of the Sahara. As for Qaddafi, time and patience appeared on his side, particularly after his confidant, Abd al-Salam Jalloud, made a clandestine visit to Paris precipitating rumors of an "understanding" between Giscard and Qaddafi, despite the fact that SDECE was quietly assisting Libyan dissidents in Egypt.[3] Certainly, these speculations confirmed the determination of President Malloum to enlist the support of the Sudan and particularly the OAU. His success was more apparent than real. The exercise of French power satisfied neither Malloum nor Giscard, for the French military presence resolved nothing except the division of Chad. Malloum tried once again to involve the Sudan and the OAU.

The chairman of the fifteenth assembly of heads of state and government of the Organization of African Unity in July 1978 was Jaafar Numayri. Among the leaders of Francophone Africa Numayri was well regarded, for he had supported Malloum and despised Qaddafi, who had supported the attempted coup d'état by Sadiq al-Mahdi and his *Ansar* in 1976. However, Numayri was not the mediator needed to reconcile the problem of Chad. He was, in fact, personally and politically in debt to Anwar Sadat, whose intervention had assisted him in the past, but at the same time he could not ignore his Sudanese opposition loyal to Sadiq al-Mahdi and his future brother-in-law, Hasan al-Turabi. Both of these conservative Islamic leaders were committed to the advance of Pan-Arab Islam in Africa. During the period of reconciliation initiated by Numayri to incorporate these powerful dissidents into the Sudan, he sought their advice and counsel. They urged him to reconcile his differences with Qaddafi despite the past.[4] But Numayri was not about to abandon Malloum, and to resolve his immediate dilemma the OAU adopted the benign "Khartoum Resolution," by which Libya and Chad were to seek "an equitable solution" to their dispute.[5] Libya refused to be bound by the resolution; the heads of state quietly returned to their capitals and the OAU officials to Addis Ababa to record the resolution.

Habre and the
Transitional Government of National Unity

Having received only rhetorical support from the OAU, the discussions of Malloum with Habre and the members of the Command Council of FAN (CCFAN) became crucial for the survival of his government. Despite the agreements reached at Khartoum in 1977 and later at Geneina, the Toubou had never been offered any significant role in the government until Malloum's forces were threatened with defeat. On 19 August 1978 Habre and Malloum agreed to yet another "Fundamental Charter." This time Hissene Habre was named vice-president in a new Transitional Government of National Unity (GUNT). The FAN would remain under Habre's control and he was promised substantial French weaponry. In return, the FAN would clear the Erdi Hills and northern Wadai of the Vulcan Force then under the command of Abdoulaye Adoum Dana.

From its inception the GUNT was a fragile creation. Its governing council consisted of nineteen members, most of whom were pro-Malloum, while its Council of National Union, a larger consultative body of representatives from the prefectures and Ndjamena, was evenly divided between Malloum and Habre supporters.[6] Colonel N'Ganikar, a Malloum man, became minister of defense and Lt. Colonel Wadal Abdelkader Kamougue, the former minister of foreign affairs became the new police commissioner. These appointments were balanced by that of Mahamat Nouri, Habre's friend and the inspector general of the Command Council of FAN, who was appointed to the critical post of minister of the interior, despite his well-known Toubou contempt for the Africans of southern Chad. Ironically, Habre, once the enemy of France, was now allied to its "friendly" forces in Ndjamena. To be sure, Habre had been responsible for the execution of the French intermediary, Captain Pierre Galopin, but Habre's Toubou were the only indigenous force capable of stopping the Popular Armed Forces equipped by their Libyan controllers.[7]

Malloum argued that the reorganization of his government had recognized the place of the Toubou and the northerners to achieve "national reconciliation." National reconciliation, however, was immediately compromised by the massacre of 10,000 Muslims in central and southern Chad by government troops, who were ostensibly seeking out FAP sympathizers but who were also venting frustration over their defeat in the north.[8] Despite the deepening fissures between north and south, Christian and Muslim, President Malloum and Hissene Habre continued to divide the spoils of government between them. Ahmat Acyl and Goukouni Oueddei, in their Libyan sanctuaries, became convinced that the fragile reconciliation between a Toubou Muslim northerner and a Christian southern African *abid* would fail in the fullness of time.

Rearmed by Libya after the defeat at Ati, Acyl and Goukouni aggressively pressed to extend their control throughout the B.E.T. and, of course, denounced the formation of GUNT and refused to negotiate until all French forces had left Chad. Since neither FAP nor GUNT in their reorganization were anxious for a confrontation on the field of battle, the conflict became a desultory tit for tat at the United Nations. The GUNT denounced Libya in a communiqué on 12 September and appealed to all peoples to "rejoin the great family of Chad." Libya, finding the language objectionable, immediately submitted a complaint to the United Nations Security Council. This conflict was a civil war. Chad was not "the victim of Libyan aggression." "Chad [was] trying to use Libya as a scapegoat."⁹ Habre addressed the people of Chad for the first time on 25 September to confirm his support for the government and to condemn Libyan imperialism. This public pronouncement produced yet another document: "Contrary to the assertions in the Libyan letter, the Government of Chad has never denied the existence of internal difficulties [which was] why the Chad Armed Forces put an end, on 13 April 1975, to the regime which had created those difficulties." Libya had occupied Aozou and provided arms to "one of the armed opposition factions . . . [for] the purpose of Libyan expansionism to annex the . . . Borkou-Ennedi-Tibesti and Kanem, or approximately one-half of the national territory." Chad "appealed to all factions of the opposition" to end the bloodshed . . . [that was] "simply the logical consequence of Libyan policy aimed at the destruction of Chad."¹⁰ This exchange of official charges aroused little enthusiasm at the Security Council and certainly none in Paris. There was no interest for France to become involved in a desert war when their surrogates were expensive and unpopular.

The French commander in Chad, General Raoul Bredeche, was a soldier in the tradition of General de Gaulle. He had advised a strike from Faya against FROLINAT and was promptly replaced by General Louis Forest, a more cautious and political commander who would not commit France to military adventures in the sand. By 1979 the French government had tired of its role as peacekeeper in Chad by the Abeche-Bol line and sought the reduction of the French military mission in Ndjamena. Like Tombalbaye, Malloum had few friends in France. As president by a military coup d'état, he had enemies on the French left who were now in bed with French capitalists, the former seeking to improve the subsistence way of life of those who lived in Chad, the latter anxious to profit from its resources. To the embarrassment of the humanitarians and the capitalists, their potential investments, whether human or monetary, were dependent upon French troops.

Chad had not recovered from the great drought that had damaged the cotton crop and dramatically reduced the revenue from Chad's principal source of foreign earnings. Moreover, there was the massive loss of livestock, from 4.7 million head in 1972 to 2.9 million in 1974, ending the profitable cattle exports to Nigeria and the Sudan.¹¹ By 1979 cattle exports were only just beginning to revive and cotton exports were on the increase. Overall, however, warfare in the north and guerrilla activity in the center and south led World Bank analysts to calculate that Chad was still among the half-dozen poorest nations on earth. To sustain their historic presence in Africa, France had been willing to subsidize their poverty-stricken surrogates in Chad. The civil war had challenged their presence, which had become for President Giscard d'Estaing an anachronism to be removed by diplomacy or duplicity, neither of which envisaged a French commitment. Giscard suggested a federal solution that would give equal representation to both north and south in a government of Chad. This proposition was made persuasive by French advisors in Malloum's entourage, but it was met by implacable opposition from Habre and his advisors, who resisted any convenient federal solution to solve the problems of France and Malloum but not those of Chad. Habre represented the interests of many ethnicities on the African frontiers and believed the diversity of Chad could only be contained by a strong central government. This was not an idle dispute. The diversity of ethnic, cultural, and commercial interests along the frontiers of Islam, from the Atlantic to the Red Sea, remains the fundamental cause of conflict in the Sahel.

Consequently, when President Giscard d'Estaing urged a federal solution to resolve the civil war in Chad, Malloum was forced to listen, for he had come to depend on French advisors and perceived that he could not survive without the French military umbrella. Thus, when French interest in his government began to wane, his days were numbered. In contrast, Habre would not give an inch and rejected the federal solution that France proposed; a supporter of a strong central government, he urged Malloum to seek not a French solution but a Chadian solution to Chadian problems. To emphasize his determination, he threatened to attack the FROLINAT and to ignore the de facto line of separation. Malloum, too indecisive by far, was unwilling to do anything that might diminish French support and thus appeared content with the situation of "no war, no peace."

In 1979 Chad was ruled by an uneasy coalition in which Malloum and Habre would inevitably have a falling out. Habre and the FAN were openly recruiting Toubou and Zaghawa deserters from FROLINAT, while southern units of the Chad army were decimated by the disappearance of its demoralized troops. Malloum retained his authority as long as 3,000 French troops remained in Ndjamena and at their defensive perimeter in central Chad. In Ndjamena no one could explain the Byzantine politics that appeared to be manipulated by the few for the many. In Paris, the French government had difficulty explaining its commitment to Chad. As the weeks passed, Giscard was determined to escape from the sands of Chad. Trade with Libya had expanded, as had the sale of sophisticated weaponry. Cheap and accessible petroleum was exchanged for fifty F-1 Mirage jets, helicopters, ten missile boats, and French approval for Niger to sell uranium to Libya.[12] He did not consult with West African leaders nor use his considerable influence to reconcile the discord between Habre and Malloum. His activities implied a France-Libya entente, on the one hand, and a reluctance, on the other, to spend more French money on a military operation in Chad that appeared to have no resolution. The World Bank had promised $21.7 million to Chad in 1979 but was now reluctant to commit it. The European Community had promised $6.8 million "as compensation for export earnings shortfalls" but was now hesitant.[13] Among the foreign investors in Chad, only the consortium of CONOCO and Chevron Overseas Petroleum envisaged any future when they struck light crude from a well in southern Chad "not large enough to justify commercial production because of the remoteness of the region," but sufficient to continue exploration.[14]

Political Disarray and Violence in Ndjamena

The Transitional Government of National Unity dramatically dissolved in 1978 when Habre "ordered the arrest" of its president, Muhammad Saleh, the Malloum figurehead of GUNT.[15] In January the labor movement hostile to Malloum called a general strike to protest economic conditions in Chad, which contributed to the process of political disintegration. On 12 February Habre's forces attacked the government radio station and within hours fierce fighting erupted throughout the capital between Habre's Gourane and Malloum's regulars. Not surprisingly, the Toubou easily routed the southerners, who, battered and bloodied, fled to their kin and the safety of southern Chad. Anarchy in Ndjamena and chaos in Chad deeply concerned its neighbors—Nigeria, Niger, Cameroon, and the Sudan—who could not afford instability in Chad and certainly not the demise of Malloum by Qaddafi's surrogates. They demanded that the OAU resolve a dispute that could easily spill over into their own fragile governments to result in an unwanted regional crisis. In March 1979, under the auspices of the OAU, Malloum, Habre, and Goukouni arrived in Kano for a Conference of National Conciliation.[16] The Kano Accords were hailed as a great victory for African diplomacy by which the antagonists agreed to accept a cease-fire, demilitarize Ndjamena, create a Provisional State Council, and permit an African peacekeeping force of 3,000 troops to guarantee the agreement. French diplomacy had been quietly pervasive, for the prospect of 800 Nigerian troops in Ndjamena would permit Paris to withdraw their troops and end "Operation Tacaud."

Kano was a crushing defeat for Malloum. Convinced that France had betrayed Chad to its enemies, he spurned any post in the new government and departed into exile leaving the leaders in southern Chad deeply apprehensive. They had always dominated the government of Chad, controlled the economy, and prospered from the *France-Afrique*. Now their former persecutors and current protectors were leaving them to the tender mercies of the northern Muslim, Arabs, and Toubou. No sooner had Malloum left than those who remained began to jockey for survival or power. Colonel Wadal Kamougue, the head of Chad's security forces, quickly observed the political winds shifting to the north and secretly approached the Libyans to ensure his survival. The leaders of the former FROLINAT, now the Popular Armed Forces (FAP), sought the spoils of victory over which each was soon quarreling with the other, and all were complaining of the intervention by the Nigerian peacekeeping force. Clearly, neither Nigerian influence nor Nigerian troops could instill the "spirit of Kano" in Ndjamena.[17]

In order to restore stability and reduce the embarrassment of failure by the Kano Accords and their peacekeeping troops in Ndjamena, Nigeria opened a second conference at Kano in April. Ahmat Acyl, Adoum Dana, Kamougue, al-Sanusi, and Abba Siddiq were invited as was Mahomat Lol Choua, the leader of the Popular Movement for the Liberation of Chad (MPLT), Nigeria's representative and bandit on the Lake Chad frontier. Both Goukouni, who sought to demonstrate his independence from Libya, and Habre, who sought to replace Malloum, refused to sit at the same table with their FROLINAT adversaries. Consequently, Kano II failed and, apparently, so had Nigerian diplomacy. Upon their return to Ndjamena, however, the individual participants continued the bizarre and strange entanglements. Meeting among themselves under conspiratorial circumstances, these arrogant personalities of limited education, responsibility, and vision agreed to form their own government free of Nigerian or Libyan interference. With the panache of the frontier, freebooter Mahomat Choua ignored his Nigerian patrons and became president. His enemy, Goukouni, was named vice president. Negue Djogo, a Malloum man, was made the minister of internal affairs, and Habre, the minister of defense. This strange collection of *tragédienne*, masquerading as patriots, lasted only a few weeks, for these bitter rivals in this *comédie drame* reached an elusive compact that angered Qaddafi, infuriated the Nigerians, and tempted the French to make a tenuous offer of economic and military support for the Choua government.

The two Kano conferences had promised much but achieved little; there were too many ambitious Chadians to make them a reality. The Nigerian peacekeeping force had been unable to maintain order in Ndjamena or ensure its demilitarization. Many policemen had fled to the south, which only contributed to the degeneration of security into total anarchy. When Choua found that he could not rule, he turned to Lagos for help. The government of Nigeria then called for yet another conference of Chadian leaders at Lagos in May. Like the two in Kano, the Lagos conclave proved an even more dismal failure when only Siddiq and al-Sanusi appeared. Their only contribution was a communiqué condemning French duplicity. Frustrated and diplomatically exhausted, Nigeria turned to the OAU to bring peace to Chad.

The volatile politics of Chad would again frustrate the diplomacy of the OAU. During that turbulent spring of 1979 Mahomat Choua, whom no one appears to have taken seriously, disappeared as president of the Provisional State Council, and the GUNT was reorganized. Goukouni became president, Kamougue vice president, and Habre and Acyl now served as government ministers. This cosmetic surgery could not change the leopard's spots. Kamougue, who had assumed the mantle of southern leadership, was rebuilding the Chad armed forces with southern recruits, on the one hand, while dealing with the Libyans and Habre, on the other. This dissimulation could not remain secret in Ndjamena. Its exposure was characterized by clashes between Kamougue's Forces Armées Tchadienne (FAT) and the FAN of Hissene Habre. These petty squabbles by those who possessed the guns without any understanding ended the façade of a cease-fire and spurred the creation by Habre and Goukouni of a new Provisional State Council purged of southerners, ending their influence in Ndjamena. Kamougue had not been idle. After meeting with the Libyans, he successfully restrained his troops from harassing Muslims in southern Chad and then turned their hostility against the units of Habre's Northern Army Force (FAN) which had moved south of Ndjamena. Habre was furious. The southerners were routed, and Kamougue fled into exile to appear in Tripoli as the guest of Colonel Qaddafi.

Libyan Intervention and GUNT

No sooner had the negotiations at the second conference at Kano concluded in April 1979 with no resolution than a Libyan motorized column of 3,000 troops left Kufra. It traveled swiftly down the trans-Saharan caravan route 350 miles to the defensive perimeter established by the French in Wadai from where it could threaten central Chad and the petty sultanates on the Wadai-Darfur frontier. Habre, the acting minister of defense in the purged Provisional State Council, advised the bewildered Nigerian troops in Chad to mobilize against the Libyans and ordered his FAN to attack. The Libyans were overrun at Ounianga Kebir, Gouro, Zouar, and Sherda. Large quantities of weapons were captured; scores of Libyan and Arab Legionnaires were taken prisoner. Habre's Gourane continued to harass the retreating Libyans "wherever they fought a battle," humiliating Qaddafi and driving his army in disarray to Bardai, Aozou, and their strongholds in the Aozou Strip.[18] These dramatic victories, like his earlier triumph at Bardai that had won him fame among the Toubou, convinced some FAP and most chastened southerners that Habre was their best hope for peace.

President Obasanjo in Nigeria did not welcome Habre's success. Using the OAU, he convened another conference at Lagos in August to include the representatives from southern Chad and ten Muslim factions. It was the fourth attempt by Nigeria to cobble a government in Chad acceptable to Nigeria, and new negotiations were concluded on 21 August by the signing of the Lagos Peace Accord. Each of the rival factions in Chad agreed to yet another Transitional Government of National Unity (GUNT), which would create a new national army and prepare for elections within eighteen months. After four meetings, characterized by unhelpful contributions by experts to resolve "the problem of Chad" and the rancor and rivalry between the Chadian factions, the transitional government was born on 11 November 1979. It was a fragile and contrived collection of a score of men dominated by ambition and envy, and each was prepared to reject the "pending elections" to which they had agreed.

The Nigerians supported Goukouni for president, in the mistaken belief that he would abandon his close ties with Libya, and Colonel Wadal Kamougue as vice president, who remained the dominate spokesman for the south despite his transparent dealings with Tripoli. Despite Nigerian hostility, Habre demanded and was made minister of defense. This was perhaps an inevitable but curious choice. The Lagos Peace Accord specifically provided for the demilitarization of

Ndjamena, the withdrawal of all foreign troops—including French forces in Chad—and the unification of the various rebel units into a national army. Habre was the only leader in Chad who could mobilize 5,000 disciplined warriors; well equipped and victorious in battle they despised the martial qualities of those who followed Goukouni and Kamougue.

The Lagos Accord of August was no more permanent than the ephemeral arrangements contrived in the spring. Within three months Goukouni and Kamougue had joined an unholy alliance against Habre and his FAN, which effectively dissolved the restored GUNT. Political maneuvers were replaced by military confrontation in February 1980 when the FAN of Habre and the Vulcan Force of Ahmat Acyl began to battle for control in Wadai. Within a month the skirmishes on the frontier moved to the capital. On 20 March the forces of the FAN and GUNT met in a violent contest for control of the capital. To oppose the FAN Goukouni mobilized 5,000 men commanded by Adoum Togoi, supported by units from Ahmat Acyl's Vulcan Force. Togoi also had several hundred unreliable residuals from the gang of Abubakr Mohamed Abderahman and leftovers from the former "original FROLINAT" led by Abba Siddiq. The French foreign minister, Claude Cheysson, described the violence as *la guerre de chefs* as fierce fighting spread throughout the capital for ten days. Hundreds were killed and more than 3,000 wounded in the first ten days of the battle for Ndjamena and Chad. Adoum Togoi's military leadership had much to be desired. Born at Fada in the Ennedi, he achieved fame by embezzling funds from his bank for the FAN. When the FAN dissolved, he followed Goukouni, and after the FAP was organized in Tripoli in 1978, he was named chief of staff. As the battle for Ndjamena continued, both sides suffered heavy casualties, and the foreign nationals scurried to Cameroon and safety. Habre bitterly criticized Libya and France not only for arming Goukouni but also for refusing to intervene to prevent the destruction of Ndjamena.[19]

France Leaves, Libya Arrives

Giscard could hardly ignore the carnage in Ndjamena, but even French diplomacy could not assuage the passions of the *guerre de chefs* and military intervention would have been a domestic disaster. Giscard was convinced that the interests of France were best served by a dignified withdrawal. Rene Journiac, who had succeeded Jacques Foccart as the president's special advisor on African affairs, was to orchestrate the French retreat. Journiac had been involved in Chad since *L'affaire Claustre,* and he sought to use the abortive Lagos Accords to provide a semblance of legitimacy to the French military withdrawal from Ndjamena.[20] The subsequent departure of the Force d'Intervention to their base at Bouar in the Central African Republic convinced the dwindling number of Chad Francophiles that *France-Afrique* had come to an end. The continuing violence in Ndjamena appeared to confirm this conclusion.

In Ndjamena the FAP of Goukouni were on the defensive. His opportunistic companion in arms, Wadal Kamougue, could not effectively deploy his artillery from the former army of Chad, and after his forces had suffered heavy casualties, he retired without warning to his sanctuaries in the south. Habre and Goukouni were now left to fight in a conflict that was no longer south or north, Muslim or Christian, Toubou or Arab, Libya or Chad, for the warriors followed their chiefs into battle. Their heroic commitment was confirmed if not sanctified by their humble contribution to a contest that provided them with an identity beyond the demands of ethnicity or religion. The battle for Ndjamena continued throughout the ides of March 1980 with extensive carnage. The number of casualties will never be known, but there were more than 3,000 killed and 7,000 wounded. One hundred thousand civilians fled into the countryside or across Chad's borders into neighboring states. The Popular Armed Forces (FAP) of Goukouni were decimated. They fought the FAN by day and by night; their wounded were ferried across the Logone River to medical facilities in Cameroon.[21]

The fighting continued throughout the spring. Habre sent his second in command, Idriss Miskene, to an OAU conference in Lagos to challenge Goukouni's credentials without result. The OAU had never evinced any sincere commitment to the dispute in Chad. The West African leaders, led by their intellectual idol, Leopold Senghor of Senegal, were now more concerned about Libyan imperialism than the French. Concern was turned to fear when France appeared ready to abandon Chad. For their own preservation they found the French unilateral abrogation of its historic mission in Chad deeply disturbing. Still, none of the heads of state were inclined to become involved in a dispute that appeared to add additional difficulties to their own. Habre's attempt to seek diplomatic support from the neighbors of Chad in the OAU was a chimera. Diplomacy had been tried in the past at Kano and Lagos and had failed. Hard pressed in a war of attrition at Ndjamena, Goukouni went once again to his patron, Colonel Qaddafi, with whom he signed a treaty of friendship on 15 June 1980. The agreement permitted Libya to intervene in Chad, train the army and security forces, and "consolidate the peace." The personal animosity between Goukouni and Habre was now translated into an accord that acknowledged Goukouni's subordination to Qaddafi. The June agreement convinced the beleaguered FAN to fight on with renewed determination.[22]

When the OAU leadership gathered for the seventeenth meeting of African heads of state and governments at Freetown from 1–4 July 1980, they once again had to consider the Chad issue. The debate was acrimonious, and the acting OAU chairman, President Senghor of Senegal, the distinguished scholar and spokesman for Francophone Africa, accused Libya of interference in the internal affairs of Chad, Senegal, Mali, and Niger. In Senegal Qaddafi had been financing the Hizboulani Party, whose activities particularly enraged Senghor who warned his colleagues at Freetown that Qaddafi was determined to create a "Great Saharan Republic."[23] He had been insulted when Libya closed its embassy at Dakar a few days before the seventeenth summit was convened, and he scornfully denounced Qaddafi's contemptuous assertion that the independence of the Francophone

African states was a "fiction." In a closed session even Egypt's mild-mannered foreign minister, Boutros Boutros Ghali, angrily admonished the Libyan delegate: "You will not convince us that your visions and hallucinations and your crude ideologies have the slightest chance of being accepted by an African country—despite the lure of your petro-dollars."[24] The OAU could reach no agreement to halt the fighting that had destroyed much of Ndjamena. Many of its members wanted to send another peacekeeping force, but the experience of the Nigerians was hardly encouraging. Indeed, the Chad problem not only emphasized the split between what were loosely known as the moderates and the progressives in the OAU, but it had become its most divisive issue since the special conference in January 1976 to consider the civil war in Angola.

When the OAU refused to intervene, Goukouni's FAP continued to suffer very heavy casualties and Goukouni appeared to have little recourse but to capitulate to Habre's FAN or retire in disarray. This was an intolerable embarrassment for Qaddafi and he was determined to prevent it. He immediately ordered a Libyan column to move from the Aozou south through Faya and down the Wadi Bahr al-Ghazal toward Ndjamena. Here 4,000 Libyan troops secured the roads into Ndjamena, and Libyan Antonov–26 transports discharged soldiers and materiel at the Dougia airstrip forty miles north of the capital in July.[25] The arrival of the Libyans and their weapons dramatically changed the balance of power in the capital. During the battle for Ndjamena, Habre had prevailed for two months in a cruel campaign against Goukouni, but with Libyan intervention, his FAN was now outnumbered and outgunned. He ordered his forces out of the city to their strongholds in the east. As quiet settled over Ndjamena, Goukouni remained to claim that at heart he was a patriot, but in reality he was caught in a web of intrigue and ethnic and religious rivalries between Kamougue's southerners and the Vulcan Force of Ahmat Acyl, both of whom had supported direct Libyan intervention. Goukouni insisted that he had called for French intervention but having received no response, he had requested Libya to save the duly constituted government of Chad. The West African heads of state, particularly President Leopold Senghor of Senegal, were furious at the Libyan invasion. None of them believed Goukouni's assertion that he had no alternative but to turn to Libya. Senghor knew very well that Giscard despised Goukouni, but it did not restrain his condemnation of the French for not restoring peace to Chad and for not restraining Libyan "imperialism."

Habre Is Isolated

In order for the invasion and occupation of Chad to be successful, Qaddafi had to crush Habre and his Northern Army Force. This could only be accomplished, if ever, by massive firepower in the vast sand seas, mountain massifs, arid plateaus, and hidden wadis of Chad. Qaddafi had been humiliated within his own natural desert sanctuary by the air power and tanks of the Egyptians.

Perhaps he could now achieve a similar triumph by using his own formidable arsenal in Chad to eliminate Hissene Habre. Libyan forces poured into Chad. Three Libyan airfields at Aozi, Fada, and Dougia daily received materiel and troops; T-55 tanks moved through Faya to Salal, and armored columns moved south along the Wadi Bahr al-Ghazal. Other troop columns drove down the caravan route from Kufra to Abeche in Wadai to sever Habre's route of retreat from Ndjamena to his sanctuaries in the Ennedi Plateau. By September Libyan tanks and troops had turned the tide, and once more victorious Goukouni, the head of government of Chad, flew to Paris.

His presence was not welcomed. On 17 September he met with President Giscard d'Estaing, who had just suffered a crushing election defeat to François Mitterrand with whom Goukouni met the following day. In Paris the French military and intelligence communities were furious at Libyan aggression and had been urging President Giscard to take a strong stand against Qaddafi. At the time of the Libyan invasion of Chad, Giscard was in the middle of a contentious election campaign and was not about to become involved in another foreign adventure.[26] Mitterrand had made his first extensive tour of Africa in 1949 as the overseas minister, and his findings confirmed his conviction that France had little or no national interest in Chad. He certainly was not about to jeopardize his popularity with the supporters of Francophone Africa in France or his own "Africans" in his Socialist Party. He promised Goukouni little. Jean Pierre Cot, his minister of cooperation and development and advisor on African affairs, would formulate an African policy to "decolonize relations between Africa and France" to demonstrate that the Mitterrand government would not interfere in the internal affairs of its former French colonies. Military arrangements would be renegotiated, and the French military presence reduced. The Africans, not the French directors of its African policy, Foccart, Journiac, or de Marenches, would determine their future.

Any French disengagement from their past in Africa and their obligations to Francophone Africa was not that simple. President Mitterrand could not ignore French intelligence reports that Qaddafi and his agents were involved in activities to destabilize West African governments. The Libyan presence in Chad could not be resolved by the departure of the French. Jean Pierre Cot had to admit: "We have duties toward Chad, if only because we behaved there badly in the past."[27] The duties of France in Chad, whatever they might be, were obscured by the Libyan presence. Habre's battered forces retiring from the Battle of Ndjamena were increasingly isolated and harassed by the Libyans. Libyan TU-22s regularly bombed Habre's positions east of the capital, and some FAN units in Wadai began to seek sanctuary in Darfur.[28] Goukouni arrived triumphant in Tripoli, where in a broadcast on 7 November 1980 he thanked his Libyan allies for their timely military assistance, dismissed Habre as a sometime "law graduate from the University of Montpelier," and predicted that the problem of Chad would soon be resolved.

Africa, not France, was the first to denounce Libyan aggression in Chad. At a meeting of the representatives of the Francophone states in Lomé in November there was much indignation but no resolution as to a course of action.[29] Their impotence was made all the more embarrassing when Habre appeared. He declared at a press conference that Goukouni might accept the Libyan presence in Chad, but he never could. It would be a crime of "*lèse-Chad* as well as a crime of *lèse-Afrique*."[30] The Libyan response to this feeble rhetoric was to deploy two battalions of Libyan troops supported by sixty Soviet T-54 and T-55 tanks to occupy Ndjamena.[31] Neither Goukouni nor Qaddafi feared French intervention, particularly after the Mitterrand government had sententiously declared that there was no "legal basis" for intervention. Unable to force a passage through the Libyan cordon to his sanctuaries in the Ennedi Plateau far to the east, Habre and his close associates crossed the Chari River to Cameroon determined to continue the fight for Chad.[32] Libya now dominated Chad. Qaddafi had ignored the OAU, reduced Goukouni to subservience, and humiliated France. In Tripoli a GUNT spokesman warned France against any intervention in Chad, where they would have to meet the might of Goukouni's ally.

The indifference of President Mitterrand to Chad may have made political sense in Paris, but those of *France-Afrique* bitterly argued that French impotence "underscored in the most unequivocal and dramatic fashion the total bankruptcy" of its policies in Chad.[33] Qaddafi had, of course, expended enormous financial and military resources to occupy Chad, including his army of some 80,000 men and another 6,000 from the Islamic Legion supported by an arsenal of more fighter aircraft and tanks than France. This formidable military presence, however, was deceptive. The army had no tradition, little training, and unreliable discipline. The air force and tanks could not have been sustained without the well-paid foreign mercenaries who had no interest in Qaddafi's ideological or imperial interests. The tradition of desert personal warfare, man to man, warrior to warrior, no longer applied in the streets of Ndjamena, given the impersonal technology of Soviet tanks and the all-seeing one-eyed Libyan pilots.

Libya Incorporates Chad

Despite their diplomacy and peacekeeping efforts, the leaders of West Africa had failed to either isolate Qaddafi or prevent his military invasion south of the Sahara. Now that Hissene Habre was in exile and Goukouni a subservient surrogate, Qaddafi could complete his imperial, religious, and territorial ambitions.[34] In January 1981 he proclaimed the "complete unity" of Chad and Libya. Any attack on Chad would be an attack on Libya and now the united Chad would join Libya in the struggle against colonialism and Zionism and the "insidious reactionary forces" destroying Africa, the Arab homeland, and the world.[35] The unification of Chad and Libya was his sixth proposal since 1969 and appeared to be his most successful attempt to create a larger Arab, Islamic, territorial union.

In fact, Libya had instantly doubled its population and its size, and Libya-Chad was now the largest territorial state in Africa, stretching from the Mediterranean to the equator. Qaddafi proclaimed that Libya was no longer "a nation of three million" but "the heart of the Arab nation" and the "trustee of Arab unity." "Chadian soil" was "an extension of Libyan soil."[36]

This was heady stuff incorporating historic traditions. The trans-Saharan routes of great antiquity, the great medieval kingdoms of the Sudan, and the advance of the Muslim heritage on the frontiers of Islam were now all part of Libyan imperialism. Over two thousand years the relations between those who came from North Africa and those in the great states of the Sudan had been conditioned by mutual respect in which the trade in slaves was practiced by all as a commercial commodity. The coming of the Arabs after the seventh century was one of accommodation to the African societies south of the Sahara. Muslim rulers in the Sudan and Muslim merchants had always tolerated African cultures and religions and ethnic, economic, and political diversity in return for political stability, commercial profit, and continuity. This relationship was historic but fragile. Nowhere was this ambiguous relationship more real and historic than in Chad, now complicated by Qaddafi's adventure in historic perspective. "For the first time in 400 years an Arab power had advanced once again into Black Africa."[37] The French were shipping weapons to Tripoli and concluded "a major prospecting contract between the French national oil company [Elf Aquitaine] and Libya."[38]

His unreliable and often independent subordinates compromised Qaddafi's acquisition of Chad more than the African or international community. The leader of the old FROLINAT, Abba Siddiq, emerged to denounce Goukouni and his fiscal patron: "African states, which believe Muammar Qaddafi poses no danger, are deceiving themselves. . . . As long as the Libyan expeditionary troops will not withdraw from Chad no peace will be possible."[39] Perhaps embarrassed by their failure to act at Lomé in November 1980, six West African states now condemned Libya not for the acquisition of Chad but for subversion. Gambia, Ghana, Mauritania, Niger, Nigeria, and Senegal "had found evidence of Libyan interference in their internal affairs."[40] President Seyni Kountche rejected Libyan overtures to join the Organization of Saharan States (Algeria, Libya, Mali, Mauritania, and Chad) because of Qaddafi's pronouncement in a speech at Benghazi in October 1980 that "Moors and Arab-Berber people were 'persecuted and oppressed' in Mali and Niger."[41] He was more troubled, however, by reports of Libyan agents among the Tuareg and Libyan plans to construct a road from Sebha to the Tummo Triangle.

There were more troubling concerns about Libyan imperialism south of the Sahara. The historic commercial and religious relationships between North Africa and the Sudan were now challenged by the resources and ambitions of Qaddafi to spread his revolution beyond the deserts of Libya, the Sahara, and the Sudan to the larger world beyond the sands. This could not be accomplished by

Libyan legions, too few and much involved in conquests in Chad, but by revolutionaries trained in Libya for the destabilization of fragile states and the erosion by terrorism of those more stable. Libya became "the Makkah for Third World revolutionaries."[42] Revolutionaries were trained in Libya. The Islamic Legion had conscripted hundreds of the Faithful to work in Libya. The international intelligence services, particularly the Central Intelligence Agency of the United States, began to monitor the training of international terrorists at twenty Libyan camps for agents from Mexico to Mindanao. The camps at al-Judda'im and Ma'sar Ra's near Tripoli had been the training grounds for the Sudanese *Ansar* of Sadiq al-Mahdi, who failed to overthrow Numayri in 1976.[43]

Sheltered by Egypt and the United States, Numayri had no fear that Libyan tanks would trundle into Darfur after the invasion of Chad. Numayri, however, was more concerned that the Libyan presence in Chad would lead to subversion among the Sudanese tribes in the "poor and neglected part of [Western] Sudan," who had an ancient hostility toward the Sudanese of the Nile Valley, the *Awlad al-Balad.* Moreover, Zaghawa and Bedeiyat, now armed by Libya, had made northern Darfur insecure. As always the Egyptians were concerned about any attempt to destabilize the Sudan not so much because Libyan "inroads" would provoke "tribal unrest" in Wadai and Darfur, but because if Qaddafi managed to subvert the western Sudan, Libya could "threaten the flow of the Nile, Egypt's lifeline."[44]

The OAU and Chad

Although Numayri was concerned about the invasion of Chad by his Libyan neighbor, who had also supported an attempt to overthrow him in 1976, President Seyni Kountche of Niger was even more vulnerable and consequently more alarmed. Together they demanded an emergency meeting of officials from the OAU. Nigeria, which had reestablished a civilian government in 1979 after years of military dictatorship, was strongly supportive and used their influence to convince a reluctant Siaka Stevens, president of Sierra Leone and the OAU chairman, to organize and chair an OAU Committee on Chad composed of twelve West African leaders.

The result of their deliberations was a reincarnation of the past at Lomé and Lagos. The committee reaffirmed that the Lomé Communiqué defined the dispute to be "clearly and primarily within the purview of the OAU" and that the Lagos Accord on National Reconciliation in Chad of August 1979 remained legally binding. The "proposed union of Chad with Libya had violated the spirit and letter" of that accord. The signatories concluded that the GUNT representatives at Lagos had not the "authority to enter into basic agreements of this scope on behalf of the Chadian people."[45]

The OAU publicly demanded the withdrawal of all foreign troops from Chad and privately informed the Libyan representative to "get the hell out of Chad."[46] They warned Qaddafi that his well-known ambition to become the next chairman of the OAU and to hold the 1982 annual summit meeting in Tripoli could be seriously compromised by his invasion of Chad. Qaddafi refused to be intimidated. He castigated neighbors and admonished his friends. "We consider them [Niger] second in line after Chad. Even their fate and security are connected with our fate and security." Moreover, Libya would "reexamine the program of aid to a number of African states, including Niger," for "we possess oil and it is a weapon we will use. . . . Libyan existence [is] provisional. Libyan existence is linked to Arab destiny. . . . It is wrong to look upon Libya simply as just Libya. Libya cannot be viewed except through the Arab nation."[47]

President Seyni Kountche retaliated by halting the sale of Niger's uranium to Libya, breaking off diplomatic relations, and reinforcing its close ties with France. The government of Nigeria was furious and instructed its ambassador in Tripoli to inform the Libyan government that any threat to Niger was a threat to Nigeria. Both Niger and Nigeria bitterly complained that their citizens employed in Libya had been involuntarily drafted into the Islamic Legion, an accusation that Qaddafi imperiously dismissed. Libya had the right to mobilize African migrants into their armed forces "once these people enter Libya."[48] President Numayri was equally disturbed by Qaddafi's challenge to those on his frontier. Radio Omdurman regularly denounced Qaddafi and vehemently protested against the illegal enlistment of Sudanese in the Islamic Legion. The entente between Egypt and the United States protected the Sudan, but Numayri's policies were continually being eroded by the insidious machinations of Sadiq al-Mahdi and Hasan al-Turabi in Khartoum, which he could not ignore. He, therefore, stopped short of open opposition to Libya, offering a policy of containment by Arab Africa while working quietly with President Daniel Arap Moi of Kenya to frustrate Qaddafi's known interests in East Africa.

The Reagan Response

The reaction of the United States to the Libyan threats to Africa was at first tepid. In 1980 Libyan terrorists had assassinated ten Libyan exiles in Europe, but the United States was much too preoccupied with Iraq, Iran, Afghanistan, and Nicaragua to devise any strategy to contain the Libyan threat. "Kaddafi's ambitions pose[d] no direct threat to vital U.S. interests" but were regarded as "a threat to the Sudan, Cameroon, Nigeria and other friendly pro-Western countries in the region."[49] That was probably the last official statement during the 1980s declaring that the United States had no vital interests in the region. Two weeks before Ronald Reagan became the president on 20 January 1981, Colonel Qaddafi announced the union of Chad and Libya. The new president gave a very determined, even belligerent, response. He broke diplomatic relations with Libya, closed its embassy in Washington and the United States embassy in Tripoli. All Americans were advised to leave Libya, and the CIA declared that Qaddafi was "the most prominent state sponsor of and participant in international terrorism."[50]

Others in Washington thought Qaddafi's occupation of Chad "was seen by many in the West, and in sub-Saharan Africa as the first step toward a Qadhafi-led 'Sahara Islamic Republic.'"[51]

President Reagan and his director of the CIA, William J. Casey, were convinced that Qaddafi's ambitions must be opposed, not merely contained.[52] Indeed, the very first Special National Intelligence Estimate (SNIE) was devoted to Libya's "aims" and "vulnerabilities." It was reported that Libya's aims and aggressive policies were "a growing challenge to U.S. and Western interests . . . [and that the] chances for an incident of Libyan involving the U.S. are relatively high." The Sudan had already approached the United States to request support for Habre's FAN, who had retreated into Darfur and were receiving supplies and arms from "Morocco, Egypt, Sudan, and France."[53] The U.S. campaign to isolate Libya and, if necessary, to challenge its military forces received strong support within the Department of State, which regarded Goukouni as a Libyan puppet. President Reagan's advisors had already taken an active interest in Habre. The Department of Defense was less enthusiastic about any forward policy against Libya. The navy, surprisingly, demonstrated little interest in supporting the policy of the Department of State to challenge Libya's claim of sovereignty over the territorial waters in the Gulf of Sidra, which had been proclaimed by Qaddafi in 1973. One observer reported that officials from the Department of State and Libya had confirmed that after bilateral talks the Carter administration had formally used the "32 degree 30 minutes line" as the southernmost boundary for American naval and air exercises.[54] Nonetheless, in 1981 both the Departments of State and Defense rejected the legality of the 1973 line. The Department of State repeated its protest, which happened to coincide with the successful conclusion of a treaty by the United Nations Law of the Sea Conference that, after years of negotiations, defended the fundamental principle of freedom of the seas. Accompanied by the moral support of the United Nations, President Reagan personally decided that the United States Navy "should resume what had been a matter of practice with the 6th Fleet" in the Gulf of Sidra.[55]

The OAU and Libya

While the United States was taking a strong stand in the Gulf of Sidra, its ambassadors in Africa were actively seeking to mobilize a coalition against Qaddafi in the OAU. In May 1981, acting on instructions from the Department of State, they informed their respective African governments that it would be difficult, if not impossible, for the United States to work with the OAU if Qaddafi were made chairman and host of the OAU annual conference in Tripoli. The GUNT leaders and its governing body, the CDR, had welcomed the occupation by Libya of the Aozou Strip to demonstrate friendship with Libya but not accept Libyan domination. Qaddafi did not understand that it is the minor differences in people, who are otherwise alike, that breed hostility. To Qaddafi and to many, it seemed logical that a country as poor as Chad with a per capita income in 1981 of $110 would welcome the resources of a rich Libya, whose revenues were $20 billion in 1980.[56] These revenues, however, had provided him the resources for a massive military machine to threaten the African states of the Sahel. They were now implacably opposed to his Chadian adventure as were their allies and supporters in the West. In East and West Africa, in the Sudan, and now in Washington, the hostility to the integration of Chad and Libya could no longer be ignored by Qaddafi. He began to speak less about the "organic unification" of Chad and Libya, asserting that "critics wrongly translated the Arabic word for 'merger' which was meant to convey 'a union between two fraternal and neighboring peoples, and not organic unity between two states, still less annexation.'" His foreign minister announced that "free elections" would be held in Chad concerning a merger to be "followed by the formation of a government."[57]

These appeals had little impact upon the African leaders exhausted and suspicious of Qaddafi's pronouncements. He had challenged them and the OAU. They were now prepared to challenge him.[58] Having failed in March, the timid chairman of the OAU, President Siaka Stevens of Sierra Leone, called yet another conference to meet at Ndjamena in May. President Moi and the other African leaders of the OAU Committee on Chad were determined that the "Ndjamena Summit" should achieve the immediate withdrawal of Libyan forces. In the midst of their discussions, Muammar Qaddafi himself made an unexpected appearance to defend his actions. To everyone's astonishment, particularly Kamougue, Ahmat Acyl, and the Chad leaders, Goukouni addressed the conference to admit that he had requested Libyan intervention and saw no reason why his forces should depart. Qaddafi then informed the conference that he refused to withdraw his troops unless requested by the government of Chad. Nigerian President Shehu Shagari, who was committed to the prompt departure of Libyan troops, countered with a plan for an OAU peacekeeping force to replace the Libyans. Qaddafi strongly objected. Two days of intense discussion and debate followed.

The conference ended in acrimony and with no resolution or communiqué. This did not discourage President Stevens from inviting the twelve-member Committee on Chad, which had met in March to no avail, to convene again in Freetown on 30 May. All those present at Ndjamena were also invited to join the Committee on Chad, including President Numayri from the Sudan, who had been absent. Negotiations rapidly shifted from the congenial conferences that had characterized the efforts of the OAU to resolve the Chad crisis at Lomé, Lagos, and Ndjamena. Consensus by conference was now replaced by individual initiatives—each with a specific agenda and motivation.

The most aggressive initiative was offered by President Shagari of Nigeria. "He had come to the summit believing that Colonel Qaddafi had agreed in principle to withdraw his troops."[59] President Shagari employed personal diplomacy to support Qaddafi for the presidency of the OAU in 1982 in return for the withdrawal of Libyan troops from Ndjamena by mid-June. The Nigerian peacekeeping force would permit Goukouni to hold elections and allow the Libyans to depart with honor; the initiative would spare Qaddafi any embarrassment at the forthcoming OAU summit meeting by ensuring the success of his presidential campaign. Qaddafi appeared ready to accept this compromise and to order the withdrawal of Libyan forces as the quid pro quo for his leadership of the OAU. He had tired of Goukouni, labeling him an incompetent, and exhorted the Chadians to choose another leader. It was rumored that Qaddafi favored his former school chum, Abdalkadar Sanussi, a "black Libyan" of Chad origin and the head of the Libyan-Chad Friendship Society. Goukouni could no longer depend on Libyan support and would have to turn again to France and the OAU in his pursuit of survival.

The East Africans were the neglected participants in these musical chairs, which had been cause for alarm because of Qaddafi's commitment to the advance of Islam along a sensitive frontier in the Upper Nile Basin. Kenya had no reason to support Libya, for Qaddafi would most certainly cause problems with the Muslim minority in Kenya as he had done in Uganda. Moreover, President Moi had strong support from numerous states, ten of which had no diplomatic relations with Libya. None of them wanted the seventeenth OAU summit to be held in Tripoli, especially Egypt, but if Qaddafi withdrew his troops, no African government was prepared to host the next summit meeting of the OAU. Yet no African leader was interested in openly contesting Qaddafi's presidential aspirations; his mercurial and vindictive behavior could lead to unnecessary and unwanted reprisals. In Chad the Libyan troops were no longer welcome. The Imam Musa Ibrahim denounced Qaddafi in the mosque "as an assassin of Muslim youth, both Libyan and Chadian."[60] Kamougue had left Ndjamena for the south in May 1981. Hadjaro Sanussi, who had succeeded to the leadership of the original FROLINAT, admitted that he had served the Libyans and received their money but now denounced them. Mahamat Abba Said, an influential FROLINAT commander and GUNT interior minister, broke with Goukouni after his troops had become embroiled in a shoot-out with Libyans in Abeche. And last but not least Hissene Habre had revived, and his forces, who had retired into Darfur, were now rearmed and prepared and eager to attack the GUNT and the Vulcan Force along the historic, long, and always volatile western frontier somewhere between Darfur and Wadai.

Notes

1. France had spent 200 million francs in military aid to Chad between 1978 and 1980. M. P. Kelley, "Weak States and Captured Patrons," *Round Table* 296 (October 1985): 329.

2. Joseph C. Goulden, *The Death Merchant: The Rise and Fall of Edwin P. Wilson* (New York, Simon & Schuster, 1984), pp. 232–233, 240–249.

3. *Le Point*, 14 August 1978.

4. Raphael Israeli, "Between Arabism and Africanism," *Middle East Review* (Spring 1979): 39–48; "Quarterly Economic Review of Sudan," *Economist Intelligence Unit* (London),

2nd Quarter (1979); Dunstan M. Wai, "Revolution, Rhetoric and Reality in the Sudan," *Journal of Modern African Studies* (March 1979): 71–93.

5. For the "Khartoum Resolution" see OAU Document A/33/235, July 1978.

6. P. E. Haley, *Qaddafi and the United States, 1969* (New York: Praeger, 1984), p. 102.

7. "France's Forgotten War in Chad," *West Africa*, 2 October 1978, pp. 1945–1946.

8. "Rebel to Rule," *Economist*, 9 September 1978.

9. United Nations Security Council, documents S/12810, S/12889, 28 September 1978.

10. United Nations Security Council, documents S/12870, 28 September 1978, S/12889, 9 October 1978.

11. "Quarterly Economic Review of Gabon, Congo, Cameroon, CAR, Chad, Equatorial Guinea," *Economist Intelligence Unit, Annual Supplement*, 1983.

12. Claude Wauthier, *Quatre presidents et l'Afrique* (Paris: Éditions du Seuil, 1995), p. 333.

13. "Quarterly Economic Review," *Economist Intelligence Unit*, 1983.

14. *Wall Street Journal*, 3 March 1978, p. 20.

15. *Africa South of the Sahara, 1979–1980* (London: Europa, 1979), p. 279.

16. The Kano Accords, 14 March 1979, proposed a cease-fire, general amnesty, and political reconciliation. See Michel N'Gangbet, *Peut-on encore sauver le Tchad?* (Paris: Éditions Karthala, 1984), pp. 111–113.

17. "The Ploy That Failed," *Economist*, 24 February 1979.

18. Michael Goldsmith, *Associated Press* (Ndjamena), 28 July 1979.

19. Paris Domestic Service, 1100 GMT, 9 April 1980.

20. Journiac died in a plane crash in February 1980 en route to Gabon to discuss with President Bongo the "continued presence of French troops" in the Central African Republic. Journiac may have been involved in covert operations in the CAR, including the demise of Emperor Bokassa in 1979 (*Associated Press*, 7 February 1980).

21. Hissene Habre, *Pensées et citations* (Ndjamena: Direction de la Presse Présidential, 1984), p. 21.

22. "Qaddafi's Assault on Chad Causes Fear of More to Come," *New York Times*, 14 August 1983; N'Gangbet, *Peut-on encore sauver le Tchad?* pp. 115–116.

23. "Africa's Troublemakers," *Daily Telegraph* (London), 26 November 1980. For Libyan activity see "Kadhafi a l'assaut de l'Afrique," *Le Matin* (Paris), 25 November 1980.

24. Mohamed A. El-Khawas, *Qaddafi: His Ideology in Theory and Practice* (Brattleboro, Vt.: Amana Books, 1986); "The 1980 Summit of the OAU," *African Institute of South Africa Bulletin* 20, no. 9, 1980.

25. *Associated Press*, 22 July 1980. The U.S. Department of Defense confirmed its estimate of 4,000 Libyan troops supporting Goukouni's FAP (*Associated Press*, 22 August 1980).

26. Count Alexandre de Marenches, the Director of SDECE, reported a "dramatic encounter" with President Giscard, who "refused to order a bombing raid against a Libyan column marching into Chad." M. A. Ledeen, *Perilous Statecraft* (New York: Charles Scribner's Sons, 1988), pp. 4–5; Count de Marenches and D. A. Andelman, *The Fourth World War* (New York: William Morrow, 1992), pp. 196–197.

27. "Western Europe: France," *Foreign Broadcast Information Service (FBIS)*, 12 November 1981, pp. K2–5, from *Le Matin*, 3 November 1981, p. 8.

28. "Libya Sets Off Alarm Bells," *Africa Digest*, 5 December 1980; *Associated Press*, 26 November 1980.

29. "Francophone Black Africa Since Independence," *Conflict Studies* 130 (May 1981): 18.

30. "Evacuation of Europeans and Chadians," *Associated Press*, 26 November 1980; "Libya's Qadhafi Strengthens Forces Fighting in Chad War," *Washington Post*, 7 November 1980, p. A29.

31. "Qaddafi on Verge of Significant Military Win in Chad," *Washington Post*, 25 November 1980.

32. Tripoli JANA Radio in English, 0900 GMT, 15 December 1980; "Qaddafi Scores Victory," *Washington Post*, 17 December 1980.

33. R. Lemarchand, "Chad: The Roots of Chaos," *Current History*, December 1981, p. 414; "Libyan Soldiers Said to Be Fighting in Chad," *Baltimore Sun*, 21 November 1980.

34. Yonah Alexander and Kenneth A. Myers, *Terrorism in Europe* (London: Croom Helm, 1984), p. 61.

35. See the Chad-Libya Accord in N'Gangbet, *Peut-on encore sauver le Tchad?* pp. 115–117.

36. "Qaddafi Explains," *African Index*, 23 March 1981, p. 15; "North Africa," *FBIS*, 2 September 1981; Tripoli Radio, 1744 GMT, 1 September 1981.

37. "Die Vereinigung vom Libyen und Tschad," *Der Spiegel* (Hamburg), 12 January 1981.

38. "Libya, Chad, and France," *Baltimore Sun*, 12 January 1981.

39. S. K. Gyamara, "After Chad—Libya Plans Further Expansionism," *Free Press* (Accra), 2 April 1981.

40. "Libya and American Foreign Policy," *Middle East Journal* (Autumn 1982): 516–534.

41. *Le Continent* (Paris), 24 February 1981; "Libya Sets Off Alarm Bells," *Africa Economic Digest*, 5 December 1980.

42. *Le Nouvel Observateur* (Paris), 18–24 April 1986.

43. "The Secrets of the Unsuccessful Plot Against the Sudan," (in Arabic), *Akhir Sa'ah* (Cairo), 9 March 1983.

44. "Egypt Wants a Meeting on Chad," *New York Times*, 12 January 1981.

45. *Africa Index*, 23 March 1981, p. 13. Benin, Congo, Cameroon, CAR, Sierra Leone, Ghana, Niger, Nigeria, Ivory Coast, Togo, Guinea, and Senegal were the member nations that signed the report.

46. This pithy comment is attributed to Daniel Arap Moi. Personal information.

47. Speech at Sebha, Libya, 2 March 1981, *Africa Index*, 23 March 1981.

48. "Qadhafi Now Threatens Niger," *Nigerian Observer* (Lagos), 8 April 1981; "Chad Another Afghanistan," *Daily Star* (Kaduna), 11 May 1981; "Need to Stop Gaddafi's Territorial Ambitions," *Sunday Star* (Lagos), 7 June 1981.

49. "Qaddafi Explains," *African Index*, 23 March 1981, p. 15.

50. Christopher Dobson and Ronald Payne, *The West's Battle Against Terrorists* (New York: Facts on File, 1982), pp. 51–76.

51. L. Anderson, "Libya and American Foreign Policy," *Middle East Journal* (Autumn 1982): 516–534.

52. William J. Casey, *Scouting the Future: The Public Speeches of William J. Casey, 1981–1987* (Washington, D.C.: Regnery Gateway, 1989), p. 119.

53. Robert Woodward, *Veil: The Secret Wars of the CIA, 1981–1987* (New York: Simon and Schuster, New York, 1987), pp. 94–97. Woodward had access to classified reports on Libya including a study by J. Millard Burr.

54. Claudia Wright, "Libya and the West: Headlong into Confrontation," *International Affairs* 58 (1982).

55. President Reagan, Press Conference, 9 April 1986. Various aspects of United States policy regarding Libya and the Gulf of Sidra were given further explanation at this time.

56. *Actuel Development* 56/57 (1983): 9.

57. *Africa Index*, 23 March 1981, p. 13.

58. "Africa Outraged by Qaddafi's Chad Adventure," *New York Times*, 2 March 1981.

59. "Libya Wrecks Chad Summit Meeting," *London Times*, 25 May 1981; "Silent Partner," *Economist*, 30 May 1981.

60. "Libyan Puppet Leader for Chad?" *Daily Times* (Lagos), 9 September 1981.

7

Habre Brings Order

When Habre left Ndjamena, he crossed the Chari River to Kousseri in Cameroon, while the remnants of his followers beat an orderly retreat eastward to Wadai. After an unsuccessful stand at Abeche against a Libyan-GUNT force commanded by Colonel Radwan Saleh of the Libyan army, Habre's troops, accompanied by their families, retired across the border to the safety of Darfur in the Sudan as their ancestors had done in the past. In December 1980 another 8,000 Chadians crossed the frontier along the traditional routes and more were to follow.[1] Despite his flight to Cameroon, however, Habre once again proved he was a survivor. From Kousseri he went to Lagos and then to Morocco where King Hassan helped him reach Egypt. Here President Anwar Sadat met with Habre at Aswan in January 1981 after which he issued a communiqué declaring that Egypt would "provide military aid to any African country" that would "help defend Sudan against Libyan attack."[2] A few days later Habre appeared in Darfur with his FAN to receive Egyptian arms and ammunition.

Habre Recovers

When Habre's troops crossed the Sudanese border the great drought had impoverished the peoples of the frontier. Villages located in the Dar Zaghawa, Dar Masalit, and the borderlands around Geneina had little food.[3] Not surprisingly, the arrival of a horde of refugees from the war in Chad created even greater hardship on kinship and traditional hospitality. Made destitute by drought, many fled south to Raga in the western Bahr al-Ghazal and as far east to the Blue Nile.[4] Nearly two decades of drought had driven the Baggara, the cattle Arabs of southern Darfur, to raid their non-Arab Fur cultivators to the north for food, while the Zaghawa and the Bedeiyat began to pillage Arab and Fur north of El Fasher. Customary banditry had now become a *razzia*, for the Sudan army rarely patrolled north of El Fasher, and even the redoubtable Sudan Camel Corps could no longer maintain the peace. The frontier peoples were arming themselves with more sophisticated weapons now available not only for protection against known brigands but against the influx of newcomers, Habre's troops and their Libyan enemies.

Sadiq al-Mahdi in Khartoum and his *Ansar* in Darfur had remained hostile to President Numayri, whom they had sought to overthrow in 1976, but Numayri was confident that the United States and Egypt would provide adequate protection for him in Khartoum. In Darfur, however, no government in Khartoum had ever exercised control, whether under the Turks or Mahdists in the nineteenth century or the British in the twentieth. Numayri's government was no exception. The central government could not provide security, let alone relief for the nomad tribes and villagers surviving on the northern margin of the Sahel. In 1981 the Zaghawa and Bedeiyat warriors were the shock troops of Habre's army and, with the Toubou, constituted the vanguard of the FAN army. Historically, the Zaghawa and Bedeiyat were unpredictable allies, but their martial reputation had convinced Goukouni, Habre, and Qaddafi to recruit them. Numayri despised them. Known as the *zurqa,* a pejorative name for peoples of black skin from the west, considered no better than the African *abid* (slave) of southern Chad and the Southern Sudan. Their camel and cattle rustling, which accompanied the arrival of the FAN in Darfur, was not so much the result of drought and war but the noble vocation of frontier banditry, to the exasperation of the beleaguered ruler in Khartoum. It was a reflection of the historic contempt by the more sophisticated *Awlad al-Balad* of the villages and towns along the Nile for the rustic country folk from the plains of the Sahel and savanna of the west.

Despite Numayri's contempt and concern, his governor of Darfur was more realistic. He understood that the region was threatened by an even greater danger than Habre, whom he considered just another rebel from Chad, who would come, like those in the past, to loot and then leave. The danger was not from bandits or warlords but from the "poor, disaffected tribal people who love guns and will not refuse money, both commodities which Libya can supply in plenty."[5] Raiding and petty wars on the frontier had subsided during the Pax Britannica in Darfur and the Pax Gallica in Wadai, which produced thirty years of peace in the borderlands. After the independence of the Sudan, the traditional turbulence of the borderlands revived, but these historic rivalries were now made more violent by the introduction of automatic weapons and made more accessible by the trading networks established beyond the ancient routes of the camel caravans by the *jallaba* merchants. Their *suq* lorries could traverse the arid plains of Darfur and Wadai more quickly than any racing camel and were protected by Kalashnikov AK-47 automatic rifles.

The Fur blamed the Libyans for the influx of modern weapons, which had added a terrifying new dimension to an old problem. Ironically, the Fur did not consider the Zaghawa to be a serious threat despite their warrior reputation; it was the Baggara Arabs encroaching from the south who were most feared. The Zaghawa were few, widely dispersed, and often dependent upon the settled Fur for food for themselves and water for their camels. There had long been a symbiotic relation between the Zaghawa and the Fur preserved by the amicable exchange of complimentary goods in the *suq* and secured by marriage. The Baggara, however, were numerous, concentrated, and independent of the Fur marketplace. In the well-watered savanna of southern Darfur north of the Bahr al-'Arab, they grazed their cattle and practiced their limited cultivation. Self-sufficient by subsistence, the Baggara had long augmented their worldly goods with plunder from their neighbors. Slaves and ivory were taken from the Nilotic and Bantu peoples to the south; firearms, cloth, and hardware was obtained from the Fur to the north. Fur communities in the Wadi Azum, a heavily populated area that stretched from Zalingei to Murnei on the border with Chad, had long been subjected to the *razzia* of the Rizayqat, the largest and most dangerous of the Baggara. The Rizayqat, the Ta'aisha, and the Missiriya Baggara had all raided Fur villages as far north as Jabal Marra. These customary forays were normally more symbolic skirmishes than damaging raids until these years of drought and war made them more predatory and relentless. The Fur, not surprisingly, mobilized to protect their lands, pastures, and above all their settlements. Throughout Darfur, the herders, cultivators, and traders purchased arms from anyone whom would sell. The FAN, which had begun to receive arms from Cairo and Khartoum, were not about to part with their weapons. The Libyans were another matter. They had an abundance of the most sophisticated automatic firearms and no families or land to defend. They bartered, sold, and made expansive gifts of arms, of which the Sudanese authorities on the frontier were aware but had little inclination and fewer forces to intervene. They were customary transactions in which everyone benefited— Arab, Fur, and Toubou.

Capitals, whether on the Chari or the Nile, have never controlled the borderlands between Darfur and Wadai. This has been as true in the twentieth century as in the past. Inhabited by diverse peoples under fiercely independent rulers of petty fiefdoms, these marginal lands had become impoverished by a decade of drought that had eroded the authority of the chiefs and sultans. Their followers had moved by the thousands to find food and water in central Darfur, while others traveled up the ancient caravan routes to find relief in Libya. They had been encouraged to abandon their desiccated homelands by Libyan *faqura* (holy men) preaching the message of the *Green Book* and promising employment in the oil industry.

The Libyan agents were given orders by a triumvirate. The leader was Colonel Abd al-Hafiz Massaoud, head of Qaddafi's personal security, commander of the Sebha military district, and married to a niece of Goukouni Oueddei. Abdallah Zakariya Idris, a Sudanese living in Libya and acting chairman of the exiled Sudanese Popular Socialist Front, and Musa Kusa, director of the International Center for Revolution in Libya completed the committee.[6] The Fur considered Kusa the most dangerous of the three, for he was responsible for Libyan propaganda and the distribution of the *Green Book* and enlisting Sudanese into the Islamic Legion. In Abeche his agents had some success recruiting the Sudanese *jallaba* made destitute by drought and the dearth of trade, but like their kinfolk in Darfur, they began to mistrust Qaddafi.

The sedentary Fur and the Berti around El Fasher had no illusions and no sympathy with the North Africans. On the frontier there were few boundaries of ideology but firm definitions of kin and ethnicity to determine survival. In the volatile but fragile life in the borderlands, it was difficult to determine from one year to the next who the Sudanese supported in the struggle for Chad. Very few town-Arabs in Darfur could accept Habre, the *zurqa*. Some Arabs in Darfur had originally supported FROLINAT and the Vulcan Force of al-Baghalani, but the more prominent Arab families in Darfur supported Goukouni Oueddei. They had respect for his close association with the French-educated Acheikh Ibn Oumar, who was the son of an Arab mother from eastern Chad and a father who was a Tuareg and *marabout* (holy man). They had, however, close ties of kin and commerce that linked them to the Fur, Kordofan, and the Nile. In history they had supported those whom they perceived could promote their best interests. The appearance of Hissene Habre and his FAN upset these traditional relationships, particularly when he continued to rearm his forces in preparation to return to Chad.

Mitterrand Assumes Command

In June 1981 the OAU Committee for Chad met at Nairobi to consider a peacekeeping force in Chad. The Francophone leaders from West Africa strongly supported the proposal in their anxiety to frustrate the Libyan occupation of Chad. They were also deeply concerned that the French no longer appeared willing to protect them. François Mitterrand, who had become president of France in May, had been an outspoken opponent of the French military presence in Chad during the Tombalbaye years. Having lost the election to Giscard d'Estaing in 1974, he was now the victorious candidate of a united left in May 1981. Mitterrand had a long familiarity with Chad, and his leadership of the Socialists in the National Assembly demonstrated that French policy in Chad would be his own. He neither terminated nor renegotiated the many secret military arrangements that had governed French activity in Africa since 1960, but he was quite prepared to reduce the French military presence in Africa in return for French financial assistance for an African peacekeeping force.[7] After his election the OAU Council of Ministers had urged both radical and conservative states to participate in the peacekeeping force. Only Zaire, Senegal, and Nigeria, however, agreed to send troops with funds provided by the United States, Great Britain, and above all France. Houphouët-Boigny, president of the Ivory Coast, Abdou Diouf, the successor to President Leopold Senghor in Senegal, and Mobutu Sese Seku from Zaire had all privately expressed their disenchantment with the new French policy for Chad.

Mitterrand, however, was not inclined to support Habre or antagonize Libya. He lifted the arms embargo Giscard had imposed upon Libya and approved the sale of Mirage jets, helicopters, and gunboats to Libya and requested the resignation of the director of SDECE, Count Alexandre de Marenches. The count was the director of the vaunted Service de Documentation Extérieur et de Contre Espionnage, which was hostile to Libya and particularly to Colonel Qaddafi. SDECE was reorganized as the Direction Générale de la Sécurité Extérieur (DGSE), whose new director, Pierre Marion, was favorable to Goukouni but was apparently not informed that Habre had been previously provided with arms and supplies "by an operation involving the old SDECE, the CIA, and the Egyptian intelligence service."[8] American officials were disturbed by this reorganization, which they disparaged with contempt as "self-managing socialism" in Francophone Africa. The hostility between Paris and Washington reached its nadir in August 1981 when Mitterrand recognized the guerrilla forces in El Salvador, calling them a "representative political force."[9] When Jean Pierre Cot, minister of cooperation and development, principal advisor to President Mitterrand on African affairs, arrived in Washington, he received a very cool reception not only because of El Salvador but also because his father had been a known Soviet agent.

The deepening distrust of Mitterrand and the French by the Reagan administration and its assistant secretary of state for Africa, Chester Crocker, produced the expansion of the close relations already established by the Carter administration with Egypt and the Sudan. The Americans began to provide surveillance for their allies in the Nile Valley and the deserts to the west during the summer of 1981 by United States AWACS reconnaissance aircraft.[10] Alarmed, Numayri reinforced his somnolent forces in Darfur to contain more than 22,000 refugees fleeing from violence in Chad and crowding into camps at Geneina during October.[11] The Sudanese division at El Fasher was brought up to strength to interdict the flow of refugees eastward into central Darfur and Kordofan, but the massif of Jabal Marra discouraged the Sudanese from any confrontation on the other side of the mountain where communications with El Fasher were always tenuous.

Habre on the Attack

Nothing is ever secret in Darfur. Goukouni and Qaddafi were soon aware that Habre was rebuilding his army and responded by moving reinforcements, including tanks and artillery, into Abeche. The appearance of this military power was manifestly unpopular with the border chiefs and religious leaders at this northern intrusion upon their independence. Numayri was, of course, alarmed by the Libyan military buildup in Wadai, but he was not about to commit himself to a forward course on the frontier. At the same time, he could not afford to be intimidated by Goukouni and his patron, so he continued to facilitate the rearming of the FAN. In June 1981 the FAN crossed the border and overran the

Libyans at Iriba, a strategic village some twenty-five miles inside Chad. In mid-July Habre's troops crossed the frontier in force and routed Libyan forces at Abeche and Oum Chalouba. The Libyans retreated toward Ndjamena to regroup and launch a massive counterattack, which the FAN eluded, disappearing once again into their Sudan sanctuary.

Despite his embarrassing defeat at Abeche, Goukouni boasted that "Hissene Habre exists perhaps in the Sudan or Egypt, but in terms of a force, he no longer exists."[12] His defiance was Gourane bravado by the president of Chad and the leader of an army disintegrating from the personal ambitions of his own GUNT commanders. When Abdoulaye Adoum Dana, leader of the small but troublesome Western Armed Forces (Forces Armées Occidentales, FAO, formerly known as the Third FROLINAT Army) sought to take charge of military operations, Goukouni promised Wadal Kamougue that his units "would form the core of the new national army."[13] Ahmat Acyl was not only foreign minister of Chad but also the commander of the Forces d'Action Communes (FAC), which was the most disciplined unit in GUNT. He had led the FROLINAT forces down the Wadi Bahr al-Ghazal toward Ndjamena in 1978 and now hoped to replace Goukouni as president. These endless tawdry intrigues manipulated by petty politicians masquerading as warlords, who could not even command the respect of their warriors, required Qaddafi to reinforce his Libyan troops to sustain his ambitions and his intervention. By September 1981 there were 15,000 Libyans and Islamic Legionnaires in Chad.

Anticipating a FAN assault from Darfur, Libyan aircraft began to strike border villages in both Chad and the Sudan on 10 September. For three weeks Kulbus and Tine in Dar Zaghawa were bombed. Guereda was strafed, and there were "forays over Geneina [the administrative headquarters of the Sudan in western Darfur] itself where two Libyan Jaguars were shot down by Habre's men," whose pilots were Sudanese "recruited in Libya."[14] These skirmishes came to a crisis when an Italian Marchetti of the Libyan air force was shot down after strafing a village near Adre.[15] Despite warnings from the governments of the Sudan and Egypt, Libya continued its air attacks all along the impoverished villages and desiccated cultivation on the frontier, all recorded by American AWACS. The Egyptian government denounced these air strikes and the Libyan military presence in Chad, while the Sudanese armed forces were put on an alert for a Libyan invasion into Darfur.[16]

These vehement protestations against Libyan aggression were not merely for domestic consumption on the Nile. President Numayri was well aware that his adversary was capable of bizarre and autocratic ambitions, one of which was the acquisition of Darfur. The Mirage jets and propeller planes could hardly do little damage either to the FAN or to the Sudan villages and cultivation decimated by drought. Qaddafi's preoccupation with the accumulation of worthless territory south of the Sahara challenged the sovereignty of the Sudan and its citizens, which could not be ignored. In Ndjamena, however, the goal of Qaddafi and his surrogate, Goukouni Oueddei, for the union of Chad and Libya proved more elusive when the troops of Wadal Kamougue mutinied in the capital. Not having received their pay for months, they looted and left for southern Chad. A lapsed Catholic consumed by greed and alcohol, Kamougue attempted to create a Republic of Logone in the south but lost control of his commanders, who degenerated into banditry. Qaddafi then proposed the formation of a Chad army of national integration designed to ensure the continuation of the Libyan presence in Chad. Ahmat Acyl, the Chad foreign minister, signed a provisional agreement for such on 17 August.[17]

During the twelfth anniversary celebrations of the Libyan Revolution on 1 September 1981, Qaddafi emphasized the organic unity of Libya and Chad. Before Yasser Arafat and the Libyan multitude he warned Goukouni, "My brother, you are now the last obstacle to a merger which the peoples of our countries demand. . . . We once more stress to the world that the security of Chad is linked with the security of Libya."[18] With his presidency in decline Goukouni sensibly decided to go to Paris in mid-September 1981 to mend fences. In meetings arranged by Jean Pierre Cot, Goukouni sought diplomatic support for his government and military aid. He received neither. Over a long and unsatisfying lunch, Mitterrand made it clear that France wanted diplomatic relations with Libya. During this lunch, Habre's FAN had perversely overwhelmed the Chad government garrison at Guereda, a village located on the Ennedi Plateau and defended by Libyan "volunteers" and forces loyal to Ahmat Acyl. The Toubou and Zaghawa in the FAN destroyed them.

After Paris Goukouni continued to Algiers, which had long been a sanctuary for supporters of FROLINAT. In his "desire to enlarge the foreign relations of Chad," Goukouni explained his policies to his former FROLINAT comrades-in-arms. Publicly, Goukouni admitted, "We have no problems inside the country, but we have difficulties on the border with Sudan, where the situation requires the Libyan presence." Goukouni sought to persuade his colleagues and the Algerians that it was only the threat from Habre that kept Libyan forces in Chad. An OAU peacekeeping force could replace them.[19] When Vice President Hosni Mubarak arrived in Washington in October, he brought an "urgent" letter for President Reagan from President Sadat concerning "the tense situation between Libyan and Sudanese forces" that had resulted from Libyan planes bombing "Sudanese towns along the border for nineteen days."[20] Sadat had exaggerated the damage to a frontier unknown to him by air strikes on drought-stricken lands and villages observed only by the AWACS. The United States was aware that Sadat had exaggerated the damage, but the United States sought to use this opportunity to assert its unilateral right to use force against states employing acts of international terrorism. In Cairo the Egyptian minister of defense had become convinced that the "Soviets and Libyans were going to do something" along the Chad-Sudan frontier. Egypt wanted U.S. protection from possible Soviet retaliation should Sudan and Egypt choose to initiate a preemptive strike on Libyan forces in Chad or even on Libya itself.[21] The United States, of course, would not consider any attack on Libya by Egypt or the Sudan, which might cause the Soviet Union to intervene to defend Qaddafi and lead to an unwanted international confrontation. On 6 October 1981 the world was stunned by the assassination of Egyptian President Anwar Sadat.

United States Secretary of State Alexander Haig and President Numayri of the Sudan attended the funeral of Anwar Sadat but few other Arab dignitaries attended. Qaddafi publicly praised the death of the "Pasha" and seized the opportunity to condemn Numayri as "dirty and depraved" for one whom Qaddafi had "saved his neck from the gallows in 1972."[22] His hostility toward Numayri was translated into a bizarre and futile assassination plot against the Sudanese president and more serious subversion on the western frontier.[23] Numayri closed all Libyan offices in the Sudan and ordered the arrest of known Libyan agents. He approved the establishment of the National Front for the Salvation of Libya (NFSL) by a group of Libyan exiles with resources from Egypt and close ties with Hissene Habre. The Sudan-Egypt-United States entente withstood the Sadat assassination, and in the months that followed the Reagan administration was more determined than ever to strengthen its alliance with Egypt and the Sudan. "Military advisors" from the Intelligence Support Agency (ISA) of the Department of Defense were sent to Khartoum in 1982 to "advise" Sudanese security on how best to protect the president.[24]

In October 1981 two carrier-based U.S. Navy F-14s shot down two Libyan SU-22s in the Libyan "security zone" over the Gulf of Sidra. Three days later at the OAU summit in Addis Ababa, Qaddafi "declared he was going to have President Reagan killed," and when rumors circulated about "assassination teams," the prospect of American assistance for Habre were considerably improved.[25] Despite his bravado, or perhaps because of it, the OAU accepted Qaddafi's invitation to hold the 1982 summit in Libya. Perhaps its members expected the responsibility would "make him more sensitive to African accusations that his behavior [in Chad] was in breach of the OAU charter" and that the departure of Libyan troops would be a foregone conclusion after this concession.[26]

In that same month François Mitterrand and Ronald Reagan met at the conference of world leaders at Cancun, Mexico, where they discussed the Chad-Sudan-Libya-triangle of entanglements. To the dismay of President Mitterrand, Reagan made no effort to hide his intention to support Habre. Although reluctant to endanger French relations with Libya over Chad, Mitterrand could not but regard any overt American intrusion into Francophone Africa as a breach of international etiquette by an ally in a recognized sphere of French influence. Reagan's strong statement in support of Habre was all the more troubling for President Mitterrand. When he learned that Israel was also providing military advice to Habre, his consular official in Kousseri, Pierre Richard, reported that Habre's FAN were now in a position to control the long and tenuous trans-Saharan line of communication between Libya and its troops in Ndjamena, Mitterrand had no choice.[27] The French would return to Chad.

Qaddafi was furious and ordered reinforcements to his beleaguered garrison in Ndjamena accompanied by his confidant, Major Abd al-Salam Jalloud. Jalloud arrived in the capital on 27 October to learn to his disbelief that the council of Chadian ministers of President Goukouni had unanimously demanded the immediate evacuation of all Libyan forces from Ndjamena and the Chari-Baguirmi prefectures. Jalloud was then told with bravado unrestrained by reality that all Libyan troops must leave Chad by 31 December 1981.[28] President Goukouni confirmed the decision of his council and in subsequent interviews implied that France would rearm the GUNT while Libyan troops were retiring to their "high mountain" sanctuaries in the Tibesti.[29] Clearly the Libyans were no longer welcome in Ndjamena, but none of the GUNT "chieftains," let alone Goukouni, were willing to seek an arrangement with Habre, whose army was marching on Ndjamena. They continued to bicker among themselves, while the French and the OAU peacekeepers were mobilizing on the horizon, presumably to contain a bizarre situation that no one could hope to understand.

Libyan Troops Depart Followed by the GUNT

November 2, 1981, was a busy day in Ndjamena. Before leaving for Paris and the annual Franco-African meeting of heads of state, Ahmat Acyl, the GUNT foreign minister, declared publicly his unequivocal support for the continued presence of Libyan troops around Ndjamena, in contradiction to the decision of the GUNT council of ministers demanding their immediate withdrawal. Qaddafi, not surprisingly, was infuriated with these conflicting statements and ambiguities by the petty chieftains of GUNT. His Libyan troops had suffered heavy casualties and the loss of a great deal of expensive materiel, the reward for which was a demand to withdraw from those whom he personally despised. In his mercurial fashion he dramatically ordered Colonel Radwan Salah Radwan, the commander of Libyan forces in Chad, to withdraw to Aozou. Colonel Radwan unfortunately received this preemptory order during an interview with foreign correspondents, which created as much consternation among them as it did a visibly shaken colonel. By the next day even the most skeptical of the inhabitants realized that the Libyans were leaving the capital, and during the following days Libyan and Islamic Legion troops were evacuated from bases in central Chad to Aozou and the Fezzan.[30] Qaddafi's family-owned transportation company, managed by his nephew Lt. Colonel Hassan Ishkal, and its fleet of Mercedes trucks were assiduously gathering everything moveable to carry north up the traditional trans-Sahara caravan routes to Libya.[31] The retreat was the end of a Libyan adventure that had cost 2,100 dead and many wounded and missing; no one in Tripoli had "figured out how to break the news" to their families.[32] Habre appeared as surprised as his GUNT rivals in Ndjamena at the precipitous retreat of the Libyans and, with as much grace as opportunism, declared a cease-fire to facilitate the Libyan departure.

The Libyan withdrawal coincided with the opening in Paris of the annual meeting of Francophone African states in October 1981, chaired by François Mitterrand. For over a decade Mitterrand had been an implacable critic of French policy in Africa, and he and his ministers were now anxious to demonstrate that cooperation, not coercion, would determine French activities south of the Sahara. Regrettably, this was easier said than done. Jean Pierre Cot, the minister of cooperation and development and Mitterrand's principal African advisor, failed in a major interview with *Le Matin* to distinguish the new French African policy of Mitterrand from the old of Giscard. It was not clear if Mitterrand had struck a deal with Qaddafi or Habre or if he was prepared to save Goukouni and the GUNT.[33] It was clear, however, that without French intervention Habre and his FAN would soon occupy Ndjamena. Ahmat Acyl publicly blamed Goukouni for the withdrawal, a "serious error of political judgment."[34]

The Libyan retreat created more difficulties for Mitterrand than he would admit. At Cancun, Mitterrand had considered financial, material, and logistical support for the GUNT, but these considerations were made irrelevant by Habre's rapid advance. Consequently, during the meeting of the Francophone states in Paris, the French, to avoid direct intervention to save an unreliable and contentious GUNT, advised Goukouni and his foreign minister to sign an OAU protocol that provided for the imposition of a neutral peacekeeping force in Chad. Jean Pierre Cot justified the French role as "an act within the framework of the OAU efforts [to] help the Africans take responsibility for their own security problems in Chad and elsewhere" and concluded sententiously, "This will always be our doctrine." Cot supported the "Nairobi resolution" and argued with more cynicism than reality that there existed in Ndjamena "a Chad government which seemed to be the authentic expression of all the component parts of Chadian unity."[35] As a gesture of French intentions, their ambassador returned to Ndjamena accompanied by eighteen tons of supplies for the "armée Nationale intègre," a new name for the ragtag followers of the GUNT chiefs. In Khartoum President Numayri was delighted by the retreat of the Libyan army to Aozou and Qaddafi's humiliation. He offered Sudanese troops for the OAU peacekeeping force, whose intervention would presumably be followed by a cease-fire and national elections.[36] Always aware of French sensibilities in Francophone Africa, the U.S. state department sought to smooth the ill-disguised irritation in Paris at President Reagan's support for Habre by authorizing $12 million to transport the OAU peacekeeping force to Chad. As part of the OAU operation a contingent of Zairean paratroopers arrived in Ndjamena on 15 November 1981. Soldiers soon followed from Senegal and Nigeria.[37] In December a 3,000 man force, only half that originally requested by the OAU, were deployed in Chad.

This latest peacekeeping effort by the OAU was more symbolic than real. On the one hand, the OAU had demonstrated its maturity by organizing an African response to an African problem. On the other, the more radical members of the OAU were deeply concerned that its creation was more a combination of French neo-imperialism and U.S. paternalism, which would compromise the neutrality of the OAU task force. These ideological considerations were irrelevant on the eastern frontier, where Habre and his FAN had occupied Adre, Guereda, Iriba, and Abeche. Here Habre seized a massive storehouse of Libyan arms and ammunition amid a populace who had been previously hostile to him and his Toubou. The lack of discipline among the GUNT and Libyan units was not surprising, but it did not instill confidence in the town patriarchs. They had been outraged by the damage to the commercial establishments in Abeche by the northern troops of Ahmat Acyl, who clashed with Kamougue's southern FAT in April 1981. Many civilians were killed in the indiscriminate cross fire of automatic weapons in the hands of those who did not how to use them. Libyans followed the Chadians and looted what was left. Perhaps it was the cynical acceptance by the inhabitants of Abeche of yet another change of rulers. Perhaps it was their fear of frontier bandits and the Vulcan Force of GUNT, or the arrogance of the Abeche patriarchs, or the damage to themselves and the merchants by the southern regulars of the Chad army that persuaded them to transform Habre and his FAN into liberators rather than bandits. He was given the customary salutations for the conqueror but not necessarily the admiration or loyalty of the citizens of Abeche and his new subjects in Wadai.

After the fall of Abeche, the FAN emerged much stronger than the combined forces of Habre's opponents, including Goukouni's FAP, Kamougue's FAT, and the FAC forces loyal to Ahmat Acyl. Despite the presence of the OAU peacekeepers, Habre continued his advance toward Ndjamena. The OAU peacekeeping force seemed paralyzed by indecision. Its units at Ati did not know whether to attack or defend. Habre wanted no confrontation with the OAU, and his offensive discreetly bypassed Ati. One column pressed on toward Ndjamena; another moved toward the B.E.T. and Faya. The small OAU force in Ndjamena was besieged; it chose to be a passive observer rather than an active participant as Habre's FAN drove to the outskirts of the capital.[38]

Habre Triumphant

Deprived of the Libyan presence and support, the GUNT government of President Goukouni collapsed. By 1982 Goukouni's "ghostly national government" had no authority outside of Ndjamena and little in the city. The national army, the armée nationale intègre, had become a paper proclamation.[39] In December 1981 the FAN overran Oum Hadjer and threatened the strategic center at Moussoro. In desperation Goukouni appealed to the OAU peacekeepers to attack the advancing FAN, only to be coldly informed that its purpose was to maintain the peace not to contribute to its destruction by the civil and petty rivalries among the factions of Chad. Enraged, Goukouni denounced the OAU peacekeepers as "tourists," and despite strong appeals from the West African leaders, he refused to negotiate with Habre.[40] Surrounded by his GUNT rivals in Ndjamena and studiously ignored by the OAU, Goukouni's influence in Chad came to an end after the FAN took Faya Largeau on 14 February 1982. Habre had avenged his defeat at his birthplace in November 1980, and from the Faya oasis the FAN could now prepare to take advantage of the extensive modernization of Chad's northern infrastructure, undertaken by Libya during its occupation, in preparation to move south to the capital.

Unable to stop Habre, the last vestiges of Goukouni's government began to crumble. The OAU ad hoc committee on Chad strongly objected when he refused a cease-fire and a referendum for the political future of Chad.[41] Confronted with Goukouni's obstinacy and the advance of Habre's victorious army, the OAU no longer saw any reason to provide funds for the peacekeeping force after 30 June 1982. Goukouni "stormed out" from a meeting of the OAU ad hoc committee on Chad, shouting "I am betrayed," crossed the Chari, and disappeared into Cameroon. Eight months after the departure of his Libyan patrons, Goukouni was a refugee, and the man he condemned as a "war criminal," Hissene Habre, entered Ndjamena on 7 June 1982. Here he was politely received by the commander of the OAU peacekeeping force, which had yet to fire a shot to ensure peace since its arrival in November 1981.[42] A few hours later the chairman of the OAU, Daniel Arap Moi, ordered the peacekeepers to leave Chad immediately.

The first effort by the OAU to deploy an all-African peacekeeping force had not been a great success. Although the Libyan occupation of Chad was sufficient reason for its condemnation, the OAU intervention violated one of its most sacred principles of "non-interference in the internal affairs of [the member] states." The OAU had not only ignored that prohibition but its implementation was anathema to its more radical members; its peacekeepers were Africans dependent upon resources, both financial and military, from the Western powers. Neither the mandate under which the OAU force operated nor its peacekeepers could achieve peace in Chad. The gallant intentions of the Africans and the concerns of the West for security in Chad were now confronted by an unpredictable and powerful Libya that could not overcome the fierce independence and the historic traditions of Africans, Arabs, and Toubou in their deserts, Sahel, and savannas to the south. They now possessed automatic weapons with destructive power far beyond anything they had known in the past. The traditional and almost insatiable passion for ethnic, religious, and territorial ambitions became even more intense and lethal. In Chad the impotent peacekeepers looked to Habre for a peace that they could not achieve.

When Habre's FAN entered Ndjamena in June 1982, the capital was in ruins. Essential services had been destroyed. Food was scarce. Fortunately, Ndjamena was the least populated of the capitals of Africa with only 200,000 inhabitants. The 3,000 members of the OAU peacekeeping force were quietly removed within a week. The triumphal entry of Habre and his FAN in Ndjamena was a contrast to his cautious reception in Abeche. Given President Reagan's past endorsement of Habre, it was not surprising that the United States pledged millions of dollars for economic assistance and began to spend very large sums on a secret military base northwest of Ndjamena that accommodated Libyan dissidents. With discretion, a senior Israeli military officer initiated a series of secret meetings with FAN officials. The result was a shipment of small arms and the arrival in Ndjamena of a group of advisors who consummated a secret alliance against Libya and particularly Qaddafi, an understanding that lasted for many years.[43]

The reclusive Habre, privately charismatic and publicly dour, showed little inclination to flaunt himself in Ndjamena, preferring to use his mauve-beret troops and his reformed intelligence service to project his power among the populace. He preferred the confines of the presidential palace and the company of a small circle of Toubou and Zaghawa friends, the most important of whom was Taher Guinassou, the faithful old follower of "the boss," who was made the interior minister in Habre's new government in Ndjamena.[44] Habre immediately imposed a military dictatorship directed by the National Armed Forces Command Council (CCFAN), a political bureau of thirty members, nearly all of whom were Gourane from central and northeast Chad. Hissene Habre had established his command council at Wadi Barid, near Iriba, before the FAN had begun its final advance on Ndjamena. Of its thirty members, only one was a southerner, the former chief of staff, Gouara Lassou. The Command Council (CCFAN) was responsible for government operations, but a National Consultative Council dominated by northerners and composed of leaders from the fourteen prefectures was given a symbolic role in local government. Despite these cosmetic trappings, Habre and his government made no presumption to be anything other than a military dictatorship. Half the deteriorating national budget of Chad was consigned to the military. Habre chose his allies carefully but conspicuously enlisted southerners and soldiers from other regions to reorganize the army, without diminishing the predominate presence of his Gourane and Toubou, who had marched with him for the past decade.

The United States and Habre

In the past the U.S. Department of Defense had been a silent partner in the support of Habre against Libya. Weapons were transferred through Egypt and the Sudan to the FAN. When Libya threatened to bomb Chad airports, the Pentagon approved the shipment of ground-to-air missiles for their defense accompanied by U.S. military advisors with strict instructions not to engage in combat. Meanwhile, American AWACS and U-2 reconnaissance planes maintained a constant vigilance of the GUNT, Libya, and the FAN in the B.E.T. and Chad. The Libyans were constructing a runway to accommodate wide-bodied jets near Tummo Wells. Tummo Wells was a vital oasis in Niger on the edge of the great sand sea of Ténéré (Tamasheq, Tuareg for desert) and a traditional site to water the camels and prepare for the hazardous journey northwest to the Garamantean Road to Tripoli and the Mediterranean.

When the president of Niger, Seyni Kountche, visited the United States in October 1981, he, not surprisingly, complained of this Libyan air base on his borders and the numerous incidents precipitated by Libya to undermine his government. The United States immediately approved $3 million to upgrade Niger's defense capacities, best measured in the past by camels, to defend a desert of sand in Niger to contain Qaddafi.[45] These financial resources for Niger were made more meaningful, visible, and persuasive by the presence of the Sixth Fleet in the Gulf of Sidra and $4 million from the United States Agency for International Development (USAID) to rebuild the infrastructure of Ndjamena.[46] A program of food for victims of drought was inaugurated by USAID, and modest efforts were also made to encourage American corporate investment in Chad, particularly to revive the moribund Shell-CONOCO oil exploration, which had been discontinued in 1980.

Qaddafi in Defeat and the
Beginning of Organized Terror

When Goukouni Oueddei arrived as a refugee in Tripoli in May 1982, Qaddafi refused to meet with him. The president of Libya was looking forward to chairing the OAU summit in Tripoli in August.[47] He had withdrawn his troops from Chad and paid obeisance to his enemies in the OAU in order to be the host of the seventeenth summit of the OAU, which would legitimize his emergence as a national leader. Unfortunately for Qaddafi, the summit was a diplomatic and personal disaster. Twenty-two of the fifty OAU members boycotted the meeting. Saudi Arabia, Egypt, and the United States had used their influence to ensure the failure of the meeting. The Sudan did not attend. Nigeria was there to argue against Qaddafi's "progressives" and in opposition to establishing a movement among the "moderates" to create a new OAU with membership restricted to African nations south of the Sahara. This dichotomy between north and south had been present in the organization since independence, but the members of the OAU regarded these quarrels as an internal matter for the states to settle without international intervention. When the OAU met in Tripoli, it did not have the sufficient members for a quorum necessary to elect Qaddafi or any new chairman, and the meeting adjourned to reconvene a few days later in Addis Ababa. Here the chiefs of state assembled at the OAU headquarters in Addis, where Qaddafi agreed to submit his claim to the waters of the Gulf of Sidra to the World Court for a decision, but he adamantly refused to renounce Libya's right to the Aozou Strip.[48]

In October 1982 Habre became president of Chad and attended the annual Franco-African summit held in Kinshasha. Some thirty-seven representatives of the African states were present, but Qaddafi refused to appear. Given Chad's relative stability, the United Nations invited a host of development agencies to Geneva in November 1982 to consider its problems and obtain pledges of economic assistance. The UN estimated that a minimum of $370 million was necessary to begin the rehabilitation and subsequent development of Chad, of which the Western nations pledged half.

After his crushing defeat, Goukouni sought to organize the opposition using Libyan assistance to create a base of operations at Bardai. Qaddafi inexplicably appeared willing to forget his past failures, and Goukouni was reconfirmed as leader of the Transitional Government of National Unity. GUNT issued daily pronouncements over the clandestine "Radio Bardai," a creation of Libyan intelligence. Ouchar Tourgoudi, the former Chadian minister of information and ambassador to Germany, claimed that "from the first meeting in Bardai" the Libyans sabotaged the GUNT leadership and "imposed" on it Ahmad Ibrahim, "an ideologist of the *Green Book.*" Tourgoudi claimed that Ibrahim "ridiculed our national emblem in order to impose a third theory. . . . The Libyans came to explain to us, the Chadians, what was good for Chad. I answered them with a Chadian proverb: 'You can never teach an orphan to cry.'"[49] The historic memories of the peoples of the Sahel are very long and the expedient ideologies and personal ambitions of the present are but a fragment in time. They are placed in perspective in the vast reaches of the Sahara, Sahel, and Sudan where the vagaries of nature in Aozou, Faya, and the sinkholes of Ndjamena shackle those who presume.

Ahmat Acyl was tragically decapitated when he reportedly backed into the moving propeller of a Libyan plane in Ndjamena. He was popular among the Hadjerai and the Arabs of east central Chad and very much the heir to a failed Goukouni, but there were other vultures quite prepared to take Acyl's place. Acheikh Ibn Oumar, the second in command to Acyl and presumed to be a "fellow tribesman," quickly replaced his leader. Acheikh had attended school in France and received a degree in mathematics from Orsay. Like Acyl, he had been known as a Marxist, Francophobe, a tool of Libyan policy, and like Acyl, he would soon be called "Libya's favorite." Acheikh was indeed disposed to follow Libyan orders, but he was not about to support an organization that had failed. He moved his headquarters to Sebha from where he established contacts with revolutionaries in Algeria, Congo, Benin, and Mozambique.

Meanwhile the remnants of the GUNT army had regrouped in Bardai, where Goukouni hoped to replace the heavy losses sustained in the defeat and retreat of his army. Personalities rather than policy dictated many of the decisions made on both sides in this conflict in the wastelands of the sands of time. Goukouni was dependent upon Qaddafi for arms and ammunition, but his survival appeared to be attributed more to the fact that Qaddafi personally despised Habre than any belief that he could achieve his unreal ambition in Chad. Goukouni continually belittled Habre for not being more Toubou, while Qaddafi denounced Habre for being too much the Toubou. Qaddafi explained that Libya sided with Goukouni Oueddei, for "he is a Muslim and he leads the revolution of the Muslims in Chad." As a Muslim, Habre had made the pilgrimage to Mecca and was now *al-haj*, but Qaddafi refused to acknowledge his commitment to Islam, publicly proclaiming him and his Daza Toubou as members of "a non-Muslim minority of the Muslim Chadian people." The civil war in Chad was a *jihad*, "an Islamic Revolution," against misguided Muslims.[50]

Qaddafi was obsessed by the vision of a greater Arab world in which the Toubou were the mercenaries armed by Libya to advance into Chad to complete his vision of a Pan-Arab world. This was the objective of his implementation of "strategic terrorism." The Anti-Imperialism Center (AIC) would support "liberation and revolutionary groups," including those operating in Chad and the Sudan. Under Musa Kusa, a confidant who was later promoted to Libyan deputy foreign minister, the AIC established a number of ideological and terrorist training camps and promoted "anti-Western conferences" in Tripoli. Its members were assigned to Libyan embassies throughout the world, and to "its own independent clandestine operations" separate from those of the Libyan government. The AIC absorbed the Libyan terrorist operations previously directed by Sa'id Rashid, who "began to direct attacks specifically against U.S. interests in late 1981, when he assumed overall operational responsibility" for terrorism against President Jaafar Numayri in the Sudan and Hissene Habre in Chad.[51] The introduction of organized clandestine subversion by terrorism convinced the Reagan administration, some of who had dismissed Chad as a worthless land of sand and rock, that "the Libyans attach more importance to Chad than to any other country." They now began to watch Rashid and his subordinates as they trained and equipped Sudanese terrorists "who attempted to bomb U.S. interests on several occasions using concealed bombs equipped with decade timers" and Semtex-H explosives.[52] The introduction of organized subversion changed the shooting war in Chad into a clandestine one by Libyan terrorists, who now sought to achieve the destruction of Habre and his allies that had not been accomplished on the field of battle.

Notes

1. *Al-Sharq Al-Awsat* (London), 31 December 1980; "Sudan's Leaking Frontiers," *New African* (August 1979): 55–56.

2. See P. Edward Haley, *Qaddafi and the United States Since 1969* (New York: Praeger, 1984), pp. 210–211.

3. Alex de Waal, *Famine That Kills: Darfur, Sudan, 1984–1985* (Khartoum: Save the Children Fund, 1986), p. 30.

4. Michael Asher, *A Desert Dies* (New York: St. Martin's Press, 1986), pp. 242–243.

5. "Cultivate Your Own Garden," *Economist*, 7 February 1981, pp. 36–38.

6. Numayri's secret police had infiltrated one of the cells of Zakariya's Revolutionary Committee but had failed to forestall an attempted Libyan coup against the president in 1983.

7. "La Visite á Paris du Président Goukouni Oueddeï: Declare M. Jean-Pierre Cot," *Le Monde*, 17 September 1981, p. 3.

8. Richard Deacon, *The French Secret Service* (London: Grafton Books, 1990), pp. 271–272. For the relationship between the Count de Marenches and the United States, see Robert Woodward, *Veil: The Secret Wars of the CIA, 1981–1987* (New York: Simon and Schuster, New York, 1987), pp. 39–41.

9. Raymond Bonner, *Weakness and Deceit* (New York: Times Books, 1984), pp. 287–288.

10. W. Scott Thompson, "U.S. Policy Toward Africa: At America's Service?" in *Africa in the Post-Decolonization Era*, ed. by Richard E. Bissell and Michael S. Radu (New Brunswick, N.J.: Transaction, 1984), pp. 123, 264.

11. *Al Ayyam* (Khartoum), 30 September and 4 October, 1981.

12. "Rebels Not a Threat, Chad President Says," *New York Times*, 19 September 1981.

13. "Chad: The Shaping of New Alignments," *Africa Confidential*, 15 June 1981, pp. 1–3.

14. Michael Asher, *In Search of the Forty Days Road* (Essex: Longman's), p. 1.

15. "Ex-Chad Official, in Sudan, Reported to Plan War," *New York Times*, 19 October 1981, p. A13.

16. MENA Radio in Arabic, Cairo, 2257 GMT, 17 September 1981.

17. The treaty was not made public until 7 October 1981. "Le Depart des troupes libyennes," *Afrique Contemporaine* 118 (November-December 1981): 18–19.

18. Reported by Radio Tripoli, Domestic Service, in Arabic, 1744 GMT, 1 September 1981, and AFP in English, 0920, GMT, Paris, 13 September 1981.

19. "Chad: The Shaping of New Alignments," *Africa Confidential*, 15 June 1981, pp. 1–3.

20. *Expresso* (Lisbon), International Supplement, 24 October 1981, p. 11.

21. P. Edward Haley, *Qaddafi and the United States Since 1969* (New York: Praeger, 1984), p. 282.

22. Radio JANA in Arabic, Tripoli, 1715 GMT, 10 October 1981.

23. Joseph C. Goulden, *The Death Merchant: The Rise and Fall of Edwin P. Wilson* (New York: Simon and Schuster, 1984), pp. 334–345.

24. The ISA "developed good contacts with top Sudanese authorities, which later proved helpful in collecting new intelligence." Steven Emerson, *Secret Warriors: Inside the Covert Military Operations of the Reagan Era* (New York: G. P. Putman's Sons, 1988), p. 186.

25. Woodward, *Veil*, p. 167.

26. *Times* (London), 1 November 1981.

27. Dan Raviv and Yossi Melman, *Every Spy a Prince* (Boston: Houghton Mifflin, 1990), pp. 273–275.

28. Radio AFP in French, Paris, 11345 GMT, 31 October 1981. Jalloud was incredulous and appears to have been unaware of the depth of anti-Libyan feeling in Ndjamena. He was publicly astounded that Goukouni would request the withdrawal of Libya troops.

29. Paris Radio Domestic Service in French, 1200 GMT, 1 November 1981.

30. Radio AFP In French, Paris, 1440 GMT, 3 November 1981.

31. *Al Inqadh*, in Arabic (Munich), April 1984, pp. 37–39.

32. "Chad Rebel Loses Backing of Sudan Leader," *Washington Post*, 20 November 1981.

33. "Western Europe," *FBIS*, 12 November 1981, pp. K2–5; *Le Matin*, 3 November 1981, p. 8.

34. There was considerable discussion in the international press over the fact that Habre and Acyl had a long-standing blood feud in the "northeast" (the Ennedi Plateau and Wadai), where both had kin who sought control. "Chad's Mosaic of Death," *Economist*, 12 December 1981; *Africa Institute of South Africa Bulletin* 6 (1982).

35. "Western Europe," *FBIS*, 12 November 1981, pp. K2–5; *Le Matin*, 3 November 1981, p. 8.

36. "North Africa," *FBIS*, 9 November 1981, p. Q6.

37. The financial pledge was made on 29 October 1981 by the U.S. House of Representatives Foreign Affairs subcommittee meeting on Chad.

38. Amadu Sesay, Olusola Ojo, and Orobola Fasehun, *The OAU After Twenty Years* (Boulder: Westview Press, 1984), pp. 40–46.

39. "Chad's Mosaic of Death," *Economist*, 12 December 1981.

40. AFP Radio in English, Paris, 0740 GMT, 19 January 1981.

41. *Africa Institute of South Africa Bulletin* 6 (1982).

42. "Western Africa: Chad," *Africa Report* (May–June 1982).

43. "All Change in Chad," *Middle East* (July 1982): 14; "Flashpoint Chad," *Middle East* (August 1983). See also Raviv and Melman, *Every Spy*, pp. 273–275; *West Africa* 17 (January 1983); for the FAN-FAT, see "Inside Habre's Chad," *Africa* (May 1983): 46–47; on the Israeli connection see Benyamin Beit-Hallahmi, "In and Out of Africa," in *The Israeli Connection: Who Israel Arms and Why?*, ed. Benyamin Beit-Hallahmi (New York: Pantheon Books, 1987), pp. 38–75.

44. *Jeune Afrique*, 29 February 1984, p. 31.

45. B. E. Arlinghaus, *Military Development in Africa: The Political and Economic Risks of Arms Transfers* (Boulder: Westview Press, 1984), pp. 68–69.

46. *PID/PP Review, Chad-Refugee Rehabilitation*, U.S. Agency for International Development, Washington, D.C., 5 August 1983.

47. "All Change in Chad," *Middle East* (July 1982).

48. "Descent into Immobility," *West Africa*, 23 May 1983, pp. 1225–1227. See also "Death Knell of the OAU," *Middle East* (September 1982): 2.

49. "GUNT," *Liberation* (Paris), 27 July 1984.

50. "North Africa," *FBIS*, 6 July 1983, p. Q1.

51. "Central Africa," *FBIS*, 6 July 1983, p. S3, from Radio Bardai in French, 1800 GMT, 4 July 1983.

52. Office of the Coordinator for Counterterrorism, Office of the Secretary of State, *Patterns of Global Terrorism, 1991*, Washington, D.C. , 30 April 1992.

8

The Libyan Counterattack

Hissene Habre may have been secure in Ndjamena, but his rival, Goukouni Oueddei, was busy reviving his shattered FAP forces of the GUNT at Bardai. The GUNT now consisted of eleven factions, the numbers of which were more facile than firm; they had little in common except their opposition to Habre. Goukouni spliced these rivals into a single command structure of a reconstituted GUNT army, the Popular Armed Forces (FAP), reinforced by Libyan units and Islamic Legionnaires, including hundreds of Sudanese dissidents "for the infiltration and destabilization of western Sudan."[1] In November 1982 the FAP, now rearmed, successfully defeated the FAN at Gouro in Borkou to occupy this strategic oasis. With Libyan support it turned back fierce counterattacks by the FAN in December 1982 and February 1983. Elated by their foothold in Borkou, the GUNT command council in Tripoli (CDR) proclaimed that the popular armed forces had inflicted "Habre's most important defeat since his return to Ndjamena."[2] In Wadai the FROLINAT First Army of FAP, now under the command of Mahamat Abba Said and in alliance with Goukouni, launched a campaign to isolate Abeche. His forces cut the Abeche-Dourbali road to Ndjamena, and Radio Bardai reported that in central Chad only a few Toubou and Zaghawa remained loyal to Habre.

The resurgence of Goukouni and his FAP, not surprisingly, alarmed France, the United States, the Sudan, and Egypt, who were aware that the FAP, strengthened by the Islamic Legion, had returned to challenge their ally in Chad. Habre redoubled his efforts to obtain arms and sent his men to recruit their kinsmen among the Toubou and Zaghawa of Chad and the Sudan. Having taken Gouro, Goukouni now threatened Faya Largeau from his Libyan bases in Aozou and Ma'tan as-Sarra. Faya, however, was a long distance from Borkou, and he could not launch a strike against Faya for another six months. He had serious internal dissension within GUNT, on the one hand, and the reservations of Qaddafi as to his competence to carry out Libyan ambitions in Chad, on the other. While his enemies plotted at Bardai and Sebha, Habre imposed discipline on the government bureaucracy in Ndjamena. He revived the tribal authorities among his more independent tribal followers to discuss policy in the expectation of a decision based on consensus. Failing this Bedouin custom of unanimous agreement, Habre's decisions were law. He would tolerate no political opposition, and he ruthlessly suppressed all political dissidents within FAN and any leaders whose kin and abilities might challenge his personal rule. His intelligence service was not only expanded but also made more efficient as was his bodyguard of Toubou. He was sufficiently prescient to temper his autocratic determination to rule by promising disaffected leaders in the north and the south a prominent role in his government and the military in return for their loyalty.

In February 1983 Habre reorganized his Northern Army Force (FAN) into a National Armed Forces of Chad (Forces Armées Nationales du Tchad), the FANT. The High Commission of FANT was chaired Idriss Deby, a talented twenty-eight-year-old Bedeiyat who had joined Habre in 1979 after having received flight training in France. Deby commanded the respect of the Bedeiyat and Zaghawa and earned the respect of the southerners after he had restored discipline to the Muslim units in the FAN who had brutalized Africans in the south. He had also sought to contain the FAT troops of Kamougue's southern units fleeing from Ndjamena in the summer of 1981. They had dissolved into commando groups, known as "Codos," who by 1983 had degenerated into bandit gangs that roamed "the Sara regions of Logone" and as far south as Ngambaye.[3] Most went over to the FANT, bribed by cash and a safe passage to Ndjamena. Here Habre combined his position and his power to convince the southerners to join his government and to change the political climate that had divided Arab and African and precluded the evolution of a strong central government.

The United States, Chad, and the Sudan

While the FANT regrouped at Faya, the United States carried out intensive aerial surveillance, which indicated that Libyan troops were moving south into the B.E.T. and beyond. The United States shared this information when Habre visited the United States in 1982. He met with Deputy Assistant Secretary for African Affairs James Bishop to request more assistance, both financial and military, which France had refused. Although the president was sympathetic to Habre, his concerns for Chad could not subsume United States diplomatic etiquette in Francophone Africa nor make a commitment to Habre that the more experienced French were not prepared to undertake. The United States response was not positive. Habre remarked, "I do not think the United States will give military aid to Chad."[4] Nevertheless, the Reagan administration prohibited American companies from purchasing Libyan oil. Qaddafi led its list of international enemies. Vice President Bush, William Casey, Director of the CIA, and Secretary of Defense Caspar Weinberger remained convinced that Libya sponsored terrorists.[5]

In 1981 the Reagan administration had implemented a new unified military command "to represent American interests in the Middle East and North Africa." In October the Middle East Rapid Deployment Force was expanded to include

Egypt and the Sudan, which evolved into USCENTCOM (United States Central Command), a unified military command with responsibility for North Africa and Chad. In February 1983 four E-3A AWACS were deployed to Cairo in response to "a Libyan-sponsored coup against Sudan." Military assistance and support for covert activity soon followed. James Bishop from the State Department and Noel Koch from the Defense Department arrived in Ndjamena in February 1983. Deputy Director Vernon Walters of the CIA appeared shortly thereafter. The U.S. political and military intervention that began with Operations Early Call in February 1993 and Arid Farmer in August 1993 and the AWACS reconnaissance, F-15 fighters, and RC-135 refueling planes, supported by Egyptian-based aircraft, "were able to forestall a Libyan attack" against the Numayri government.[6]

Walters proceeded to France to discuss the problem of Chad with President Mitterrand, who had no interest in providing military assistance for Habre. Indeed, Article 4 of the 7 March 1976 convention signed by the then prime minister, Jacques Chirac, and Malloum had presumably freed France from any legal commitment for military aid to Chad or for the defense of its government. These legalities, however, were often lost in the sand and the volatile internal affairs of Chad. The United States and particularly the Francophone states used their influence so that Mitterrand could not simply ignore Chad because of an agreement signed six years before by his political rivals. Habre, of course, was deeply suspicious of any French connection, but he had no reason to doubt that the obsession of the Americans with Qaddafi's ambitions and intrigues in the Aozou, the B.E.T., and the Sudan would result in military assistance for his FANT. Now that CENTCOM was actively providing support for Egypt, the Sudan, and Chad, Secretary of State George Schultz announced with his lugubrious zeal that Qaddafi had been put "back in his box, where he belongs."[7]

The Sudan had created as much, if not more, interest in Washington than Chad. No sooner had Qaddafi come to power in Tripoli in 1969 than he sought to advance his imperial and religious ambitions in the Sudan. The failure of his Sudanese allies to overthrow Jaafar Numayri in 1976 did not discourage him from further attempts to unseat a secular government in Khartoum that had accepted African autonomy in the Southern Sudan rather than carry the *jihad* for Islam and the Arabs up the Nile. A second coup d'état to overthrow Numayri was planned for 18 February 1983 to be carried out, as in 1976, by Sudanese expatriates flown in three Libyan TU-22s to Khartoum supported by Libyan army units at Kufra and Ma'tan as-Sarra. They were prepared, in whatever fashion, to cross the sands of the Northern Sudan to the capital at the confluence of the Nile. The attack was to be accompanied by MiG-23 and fighter-bombers based at Kufra to immobilize the military sites that surrounded the capital, particularly the headquarters of the Sudan tank corps south of Khartoum. The plot was bizarre. The prospect of Libyan fighter-bombers discovering and destroying the Sudan government's military establishments spread over the vast expanse of the Sudanic plain was almost as absurd as Libyan forces crossing seven hundred miles of desert to reach the Nile. The ill-conceived plot was easily discovered. Numayri rapidly rounded up Qaddafi's agents in Khartoum, and Egypt mobilized the reserves and deployed its F5 fighters to air bases near the Libyan border.[8] Mubarak immediately flew to Khartoum to denounce Libyan violations of Egyptian airspace near Jabal Uwaynat, where the boundaries of Libya, Egypt, and the Sudan meet, and to demonstrate Egyptian support for their Sudanese ally.[9]

In Washington the State Department was busy considering means to neutralize Qaddafi's public and clandestine advocacy for international terrorism. The discovery of the attempted coup in Khartoum had enabled the United States to demonstrate its support for Numayri. The gravity of the U.S. commitment to the Sudan was emphatically demonstrated by the arrival of the carrier *Nimitz* in the Gulf of Sidra and regular flights by AWACS reconnaissance planes to patrol the Libya-Sudan frontier and monitor Libyan planes flying from their bases at Kufra and Ma'tan as-Sarra. After his visit to Ndjamena in February, Bishop continued to Khartoum where he negotiated an agreement to permit the United States to stockpile military equipment and supplies at Port Sudan, the principal deepwater port on the Red Sea. Although Port Sudan had very limited anchorage and antiquated dock facilities, it was an important port of embarkation for any defense of western Arabia, the Yemen, and the Horn of Africa.

While the United States mobilized its resources to assist in the defense of the Nile Valley, Egypt and the Sudan were organizing arms for Habre. Large quantities of Egyptian weapons crossed the desert to the FANT forces in the Ennedi Plateau, while the Sudanese army sought to close the routes used by GUNT to move arms to Guera, eastern Chad, and the borderlands with the Central African Republic. In August 1983 the Sudanese army joined the "Bright Star" military exercises being held in the western desert by Egypt and the United States. As one American remarked, "Ever since Anwar Sadat indicated to the Carter administration that Sudan is the 'soft underbelly' of Egypt, our government has been seeking to guarantee the survival of Numayri's own government against external threats, particularly those perceived as originating from Libya." By 1984 the concern of the United States had evolved into a "close military and economic alliance with Africa's largest country."[10]

In 1983 the U.S. Department of State had publicly issued its study of Libyan foreign policy in which Qaddafi's ambition was "to expand his power beyond the limits of Libya by persuasion, force, or subversion in the name of his self-styled revolution," which included the incorporation of Chad. That report provided a detailed chronicle of Libyan acts of terrorism for more than a decade, which had begun by giving shelter and training to the terrorists who had attacked the Israeli Olympians at Munich in 1972. This assistance and use of terrorism was accompanied by the staggering growth of the regular Libyan armed forces from 22,000 in 1975 to 85,000 in 1983 and the purchase of more than $28 billion of the most sophisticated weapons, $20 billion of which had come from the Soviet bloc.[11]

Qaddafi on the Attack

Frustrated in the Sudan, Qaddafi ordered major reinforcements into the Aozou Strip accompanied by his public denials of any aggressive intentions. Despite making every effort to train its own pilots, Libya could not produce a sufficient number, given the rapid acquisition of aircraft. Libya, therefore, began recruiting Palestinians to fly cargo and passenger planes between Sebha and Libyan bases at Aozou and Bardai as well as more specialized reconnaissance missions. Chad's foreign minister, Idriss Miskine, ridiculed Qaddafi's denial of aggression by denouncing the daily flights of Libyan reconnaissance planes into Chadian airspace.[12] Idriss Miskine proved to be an exceptional spokesman in Ndjamena, and given Habre's reclusive lifestyle, the foreign minister soon became the most visible member of the government. He mingled easily with all the ethnic groups in Chad, including the Arab minority. He was a Hadjerai of the non-Muslim Kinga clan from Guera, the hilly country near Mongo where his people had close ties with the Daju to the north and the Arab clans to the south. The legends of eastern Chad recount that the Kinga were instrumental in the founding of the kingdom of Baguirmi and its capital at Massenya, southeast of Ndjamena on the Ergig River in the sixteenth century. Although influenced by their Muslim neighbors, the traditions of the *margai* cult were deeply rooted and widely observed. Both Habre and Qaddafi courted the Hadjerai and the Kinga among whom Miskine was greatly respected. Historically, the Hadjerai, like the Toubou, kept their distance from the Arabs of the center and east, although many Kinga had traditionally served in the armies of the Kingdom of Baguirmi and the Sultan of Wadai. The French had regularly recruited the Kinga for its colonial army.

Miskine, who always enjoyed a game of basketball in the United States embassy compound, and Orozi Fodeibou, who had joined Habre's central governing committee in 1982, were especially effective in obtaining modern weaponry from the Pentagon. Fodeibou was an engineer trained at the Pratt Institute in New York and became Habre's principal military advisor, largely responsible for the flow of arms from the United States, including M-40 grenade launchers, Stinger ground-to-air missiles, armored personnel carriers, and even the more classified TOW anti-tank weapon. Habre and his followers were welcomed in the United States by leading officials, and although some regarded them as a "rough crowd," there was never any doubt that the Forces Armées Nationales du Tchad (FANT) would use the arms they were given and use them effectively.

A *razzia* was conducted in the spring of 1983 by the Gourane and Arabs into the B.E.T. and eastern Chad. It was motivated more by the "guns equal virility . . . money to be made, sport to be had, manhood to be asserted" than ideology or policy.[13] Nevertheless, the government of Chad used the opportunity to place yet another complaint before the United Nations in March that Libya, by occupying Aozou, had violated Article 3 of the OAU Charter, which guaranteed the "respect for the sovereignty and territorial integrity of each State." Libya replied in a letter to the Security Council that the Aozou was "an inseparable part of Libyan territory and not subject to bargaining."[14] Chad then responded with yet another complaint in this endless and sterile debate requesting that Aozou be placed on the UN agenda of the OAU during its nineteenth session in June 1983 at Addis Ababa. These diplomatic maneuvers by Chad received unexpected support from the Africans when Qaddafi in March 1983 was "unable to attract a quorum of OAU states to Tripoli—a failure that resulted in large part from Libya's belligerent activity in northern and central Africa."[15]

Most African leaders could not distinguish between Qaddafi's territorial ambitions in Chad in the 1970s and those of Mussolini in the 1930s. They were particularly incensed by his blatant efforts to pit Arab against African, a tactic that the majority of the 800,000 Arabs in Chad found not only distasteful but not sensible. Moderate Arabs objected to "Qaddafi's radical credentials and revolutionary firebrand politics and worried about him becoming the spokesman for Africa." States like Niger that had suppressed a revolt assisted by Libya could simply not accept him.[16] Indeed, leaders in West Africa had not forgotten Qaddafi's boast that "Niger is next in line." Some statesmen expressed their objections in private, fearing that Qaddafi would use terror to support his territorial ambitions. Others, however, publicly rebuked Qaddafi and rescheduled the nineteenth OAU summit meeting, and transferring it from Tripoli to Addis Ababa where in June 1983 the OAU leadership passed from Qaddafi to Ethiopia's Mengistu Haile Mariam. It was a crushing personal defeat for Qaddafi by all of his African, Arab, and European enemies, real or imaginary, from whom he now sought revenge.[17]

Victories at Ounianga Kebir and Faya

After the occupation of Gouro in November 1982, a GUNT force commanded by General Negue Djogo, an able commander and former minister in Malloum's government who had gone over with Kamougue to GUNT, advanced 130 miles across the Sahel in March to capture the strategic crossroads of Ounianga Kebir. The FANT contingent was once again outgunned and outmanned by artillery and ground troops supported by Libyan air cover. GUNT had to depend upon superior firepower for "professionalism and motivation [were] not the strong suits" of the Islamic Legion and the GUNT regulars.[18] The victory at Ounianga Kebir had assuaged Qaddafi's humiliating diplomatic defeats at the OAU and emboldened his foreign minister, Abd al-Ati Ubaydi, to defend Libyan claims to the Aozou Strip. "Let me tell you, Sir, that Aozou is an integral part of Libyan territory. It is out of the question that we should negotiate on a Libyan region, either at the OAU or at the United Nations, much less with the Ndjamena puppet regime. . . . What is the basis for their claim to Aozou? The resolution on territories inherited from colonialism? Ridiculous! This resolution is based on an arbitrary partition made to suit colonial interests."[19] The West African leaders were appalled. Houphouët-Boigny in the Ivory Coast denounced the declaration. "Part of Chad has been annexed by another OAU member. We cannot accept that." Senegal's Abdou Diouf condemned Abd al-Ati's statement. "If this facile solution [Libyan incorporation of northern Chad] is adopted it marks the end of the territorial integrity of all African countries."[20]

Once again rebuffed and humiliated, Qaddafi responded with vengeance. All previous restraints on GUNT in Chad were now ignored. Additional Libyan reinforcements were sent to Aozou, and Goukouni's forces, numbering 5,000 men, were now given license to attack Faya. All of these military movements could not go unnoticed on the sands of the Sahara, and the AWACS provided a detailed reconnaissance, which Washington passed on to Mitterrand. During a state visit to Cameroon in June Mitterrand seized the opportunity to advise Qaddafi in a press interview that "Paris would not accept any action, which would signify that Chad was permanently open to foreign enterprises."[21] The warning was ignored. On 23 June Goukouni's forces advanced to within twenty-five miles of Faya to wait for the weather to clear so that Libyan fighter-bombers could support their attack on the oasis. In London, the Chad chargé d'affaires, Ahmad Allam-Mi, offered a hopeful but cryptic comment that the government forces holding at Faya could defeat any attack, for Chad had "received guarantees from friendly nations in case of massive intervention by Libya."[22] On 23 June General Djogo attacked Faya supported by an impressive array of Libyan firepower that included Soviet "Stalin organs," SAM-7 ground-to-air missiles, and rocket propelled grenades. Two FAP battalions launched the assault, one from Elbeye in the west, the other from Goey in the northeast. The FANT garrison of 3,000 men was overrun; the survivors melted into the desert.[23] Habre was reported to have participated in the battle for his birthplace and to have accompanied the retreating FANT south to Salal and Moussoro to make a stand. GUNT pressed its advantage to attack the FANT at Fada, the second largest settlement in northern Chad. Again confronted by overwhelming firepower, the FANT, commanded by the talented Hassan Djamous, retreated southwest to the wells at Oum Chalouba on the Faya-Abeche caravan route.

In the past, the invasions from the north into the African Sahel and savanna had always been accompanied by superior weaponry. This latest military expedition was no different except that the sophisticated military technology of the twentieth century was more devastating than that of the Romans, Arabs, Turks, or the Italians. The government of Chad requested French military assistance to balance the disparity of triumphant technology. For domestic reasons, the French government no longer perceived that it was in their national interest to become embroiled in yet another *Beau geste* war south of the Sahara. It referred Habre to the Chirac convention of 1976, whose terms specifically relieved France of any obligation to rescue the government of Chad. There was little sympathy for Habre in Paris and much petulance at the increased American involvement. Mitterrand remained noncommittal. Habre claimed that two of Mitterrand's closest confidantes, "roving ambassador Guy Penne and French envoy to Algeria Guy Georgy," formed part of "a pro-Libyan business lobby."[24] Reconnaissance by the United States, whose information was verified by similar French aircraft, confirmed that the Libyans were indeed invading Chad in large numbers despite the gratuitous comments from Claude Cheysson, the French foreign minister, that France "would not behave like the United States in Nicaragua or Honduras."[25] Oum Chalouba was captured after FANT units were again outgunned by an artillery barrage from self-propelled 105mm artillery commanded by East Germans. These defeats alarmed both Hosni Mubarak and Jaafar Numayri, who met in Cairo to "review the deteriorating situation in Chad" and to consider "necessary measures" to assist Habre to repel the FAP and the Libyans.[26] Despite these defeats in Chad, Mitterrand did nothing. On 7 July Mubarak held very unsatisfactory discussions in Cairo with Claude Cheysson, the French foreign minister. On 8 July the FAP captured Arada, the gateway to Biltine and Abeche. Mubarak immediately ordered a substantial increase in Egyptian arms shipments to Ndjamena.

Everywhere in Chad FANT was in retreat. Niger, the Central African Republic, and Cameroon strongly petitioned Mitterrand to come to the aid of Habre. Each of them feared the loss of Chad to the Libyans and their surrogates, which would be an open invitation for Islamic, Arab, and Libyan subversion throughout Francophone and even the Anglophile states of West Africa. In Washington the Chad ambassador, Mahamat Ali Adoum, appealed for support to his beleaguered government, while Mobutu sent a contingent of 2500 Zairean paratroopers to Ndjamena to defend the government of Chad, more a symbolic gesture for Habre than defiance against Qaddafi.[27] Despite furious African diplomatic activity to halt the Libyan invasion the State Department remained unsure of the French response and, still deferential to French susceptibilities, were "quietly praising" the vagaries of French warnings to the Libyans.[28] French government spokesmen emphasized that France had no security pact that obliged it to use troops in Chad. "There are no French soldiers in Chad and there will be none." Reports, however, trickled out of Ndjamena that French military personnel in mufti were quietly operating in Chad with strict orders "to stay out of the fighting."[29]

The Gourane Counterattack

The FANT were in retreat, and the GUNT were now mobilizing to advance on Abeche and then to proceed in triumph to Ndjamena. Unlike in 1980, however, in 1983 the Libyans were prepared to provide the arms but not to carry the brunt of the fighting. They would now remain in the rear to facilitate the formidable logistical problems of supply over great Saharan distances and vast wastelands. Perhaps more important was the presence of the Libyans to strengthen with words more powerful than arms the deliberations of the ruling council of GUNT in Tripoli, the Commandement Démocratique Révolutionnaire (CDR).

In consultation with the CDR, Libya agreed to supply General Djogo with the necessary weapons, military supplies, and air strikes for the Arab offensive into Chad. Discussions in the CDR, dominated by Acheikh Ibn Oumar, concluded that Goukouni and his Teda were no longer needed after Djogo's GUNT had defeated the FANT and occupied Abeche on July 9. Oum Chalouba and Faya were remote oases, crucial locations on the historic north-south trans-Saharan caravan routes but of little importance to the savanna plains of the *Bilad al-Sudan.* Abeche, however, was the nineteenth-century capital of the sultanate of Wadai and a strategic market emporium linking the eastern trans-Saharan trade with caravans traversing the Sahel from east to west. It was not surprising, therefore, that the powerful patriarch of West African politics, Houphouët-Boigny of the Ivory Coast, demanded that his West African colleagues rescue Habre and Chad from the North African, Arab, and Islamic designs of Qaddafi.

The GUNT occupation of Abeche was premature. The FANT counterattacked on 11 July and after a fierce firefight recovered Abeche. Zaire sent reinforcements from its peacekeepers in Ndjamena escorted by Zairean jet fighters. On 25 July United States cargo planes landed at Ndjamena with jeeps, combat clothing, and military supplies.[30] The reoccupation of Abeche placed the GUNT on the defensive and revitalized the FANT. They recaptured Oum Chalouba and Kalait and in a brilliant tactical maneuver crossed the nearly impassable Djourab erg to surprise Djogo's troops entrenched at Faya on 30 July. After heavy fighting and heavy casualties on both sides, but particularly in the Islamic Legion, Djogo's army fled in disarray to the Libyan strongholds in the Aozou. Defeated on the ground, the Libyans responded in the air with their MiGs to bomb and strafe Faya. Disgraced, General Negue Djogo was replaced by Libyan Colonel al-Khafi, the commander of Libya's Islamic Legion, whose troops had been badly mauled at Faya. In retreat they were now supported by Libyan jets from Kufra and Ma'tan as-Sarra and reinforced on their flank by Colonel Abd al-Hafiz Massaoud, the military governor of the Fezzan who had married Goukouni's niece in 1981. The Djogo's defeat and the failure of Massaoud to recover the initiative against Habre enraged Qaddafi. He personally assumed command in order to recover victory from defeat, presumably by his inspiration and panache, found wanting in his subordinates, especially "superseding temporarily the East German–trained Colonel al-Khafi."[31]

Qaddafi ordered ten days of bombing that did more damage to Faya's ancient and productive date groves than to the Chad government defenders. Nevertheless, the Hadjerai loyal to Idriss Miskine and a Gourane force commanded by Idriss Deby decided to abandon the devastated oasis to retire into the security of Dar Zaghawa. Having taken command, Qaddafi issued conflicting orders resulting in the crash of a Libyan bomber killing its crew. In southern Libya he ordered all personal vehicles to be commandeered to transport more reinforcements and supplies to the B.E.T. His few futile days as commander-in-chief soon convinced Qaddafi to return the details of warfare in the sands of the south to his unsuccessful commanders.

Operation Manta

Devastated by Libyan air power, the FANT retreated and the GUNT advanced. By early August GUNT had pushed 200 miles south of Faya, only 230 miles north of Ndjamena. "Mercenaries, particularly Sudanese immigrants who [had] been enticed into Libya in search of a better life" . . . were now reported doing "much of the fighting."[32] President Reagan immediately authorized $25 million for new military materiel to be sent to Habre. Mitterrand could not disregard this persistent and unwelcome Libyan invasion. More intolerable, the vigorous response from Washington in support of Habre now appeared to replace the long and heroic French connection. France now purchased much of its petroleum from Libya, yet it was impossible for Mitterrand to abandon *France-Afrique*, the mystique of General de Gaulle, and most important, the strong and enduring cultural ties between France and Africa. The leaders of Francophone Africa had been outspoken. Whatever his suspicions and skepticism as to the future of France in Africa, Mitterrand realized that he could not abandon Habre to Qaddafi, Arabs, and Islam, no matter how much he personally disliked him.

On 9 August French "instructors" arrived in Chad to implement Operation Manta. They were the outriders of a major expeditionary force to be followed by a light brigade comprising 2,700 men of the Force d'Intervention created by Charles de Gaulle and now comprised of the elite 11th Parachute Division. President Mitterrand invoked the terms of the 1976 Franco-Chad military accord to justify yet another French intervention. Operation Manta was commanded by Brigadier General Jean Poli, a tough soldier who had spent his military career of thirty years in Africa, including the post of military advisor to President Mobutu of Zaire in 1981–1982. Africa was not unfamiliar to the 11th Paratroopers. Their last encounter with Africa had been their successful punitive response in 1977–1978 for the government of Zaire in Shaba province.

Operation Manta was the first French operation in Africa since 1962 and the end of the Algerian war. More than 20,000 military personnel were involved, during which France tested a number of new weapons, including the AMX 10 RC personnel carrier, the new Rolls Royce of the desert. To support the ground units, Crotale anti-aircraft missiles were installed for combat. French Jaguar fighters were now flying over Chad from Bouar in the Central African Republic to be refueled in the air by French Air Force KC-135s so that they could strike as far north as Faya. French intelligence soon identified the locations of most of the GUNT, but Mitterrand had been very careful to define Operation Manta as a "preventive" action to protect Habre, not to provide him with a military advantage to confront Libya north of the fifteenth parallel.[33] His caution limited the French commitment, on the one hand, while not challenging Qaddafi, on the other. This may have satisfied the ambiguities of French policy, but once again France had, in effect, recognized the de facto division of Chad by leaving the

B.E.T. to Libya. French troops would not attack so long as the Libyan-supported rebels remained north of a "Red Line" that stretched from Salal in the Wadi Bahr al-Ghazal in the west to Arada between Oum Chalouba and Abeche. The French defense minister, Charles Hernu, used the term "Red Zone," an African *cordon sanitaire* between the 15th and 16th parallels where any concentration of GUNT forces would not be tolerated.[34] Once again the French had saved a Chad government, as they had with Operation Tacaud, while appearing to acquiesce in the Libyan occupation of the B.E.T.

The French Red Line protected Habre and his FANT from invasion, and to restrain any provocative activities north or south of its cartographic demarcation, a secret understanding was negotiated between "Qaddafi and Mitterrand's [personal] attorney, Roland Dumas, who made several trips to confer with Qadhafi in Tripoli."[35] If Habre's battalions attacked north of the Red Line, they would receive no support from France, who would regard this as an unprovoked *casus belli* and revoke the Chirac agreement of 1976 and relieve France of any military commitment to Chad. Habre would be left to fight his battles alone. Mitterrand and Qaddafi might recognize the need to restrain their more tempestuous surrogates on a volatile frontier. Habre, of course, would tolerate the presence of the French, who, as in the past, were the shield for the Chad government, but he refused to accept the Red Line as the northern frontier of Chad. For the moment, however, there was peace on the border insured for the moment by 3,000 troops of the French Rapid Reaction Force. With few news stories to report from the restored bucolic atmosphere amid the ruins of Ndjamena, the international press corps departed in search of more exhilarating stories in more comfortable accommodations.[36]

In Washington the return of the French to Chad was regarded as a responsible response to a crisis in their sphere of influence, to which President Reagan had authorized the airlift of $11 million of military supplies (mostly vehicles, recoilless rifles, and ammunition) to assist Habre.[37] Two AWACS were stationed in Khartoum, and additional U.S. fighters were sent to Egypt. Mitterrand was, of course, irritated by the United States meddling in a French sphere and characterized it as an ill-disguised attempt "to force France to respond militarily to the Chadian developments." He innocently asserted in public interviews that he only had learned of the AWACS reconnaissance from the newspapers. This petulance brought a stinging response from Secretary of Defense Caspar Weinberger that the AWACS had been deployed as part of the U.S.-Egypt joint exercise in the western desert, "Bright Star." They had been deployed not because of any request from the government of Chad but "because the French indicated they wanted them."[38] Despite this petty bickering, the 11th Parachute Brigade had achieved the objective of Operation Manta. Entrenched along the 15th parallel, General Poli's paratroopers armed, trained, and reorganized Habre's 4,000 men on the Red Line.[39]

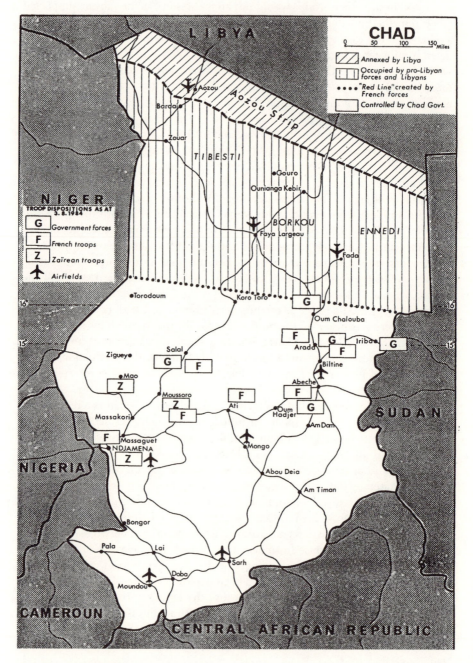

MAP 8.1   Chad, 1984

Stabilizing the Red Line

Despite the growing United States presence, Mitterrand made it clear that France had not relinquished its historic role in Chad. In August Charles Hernu arrived in Ndjamena to impress upon Habre that the French would not support any independent provocation by Chad. This was a bitter pill for Habre to swallow particularly when Mitterrand in an interview for *Le Monde* dismissed "any idea of partitioning Chad on the understanding that the Aozou Strip, on the Libyan border, should be treated as a separate case."[40] The return of the French had been a mixed blessing for Habre. They had prevented any offensive by the GUNT forces from Faya, Ounianga Kebir, and Ogri, but the French would not tolerate any strikes by the FANT across the Red Line.

Unwilling to accept the "gentlemen's agreement" between Mitterrand and Qaddafi to refrain from aggression in the "Red Zone," which appeared to deprive him of a victorious return to Ndjamena, Goukouni ordered a motorized column against the FANT at Oum Chalouba 65 miles north of the French paratroopers at Arada. Led by Idriss Deby and Ibrahim Muhammad Itno, the FANT repulsed the assault and counterattacked to send the GUNT in disarray back to Faya. The FANT at Oum Chalouba were all hardened veterans who could fight all day and disappear at night into the desert to reform to fight another day.

Idriss Deby was a Zaghawa whose people had roamed the grasslands and plateaus south of the Sahara for over a thousand years. The Zaghawa were the Toubou-speaking black, non-Arab nomads who had settled northeast of Lake Chad in the eighth century. They established a kingdom ruled by the legendary non-Muslim Dugawa dynasty but disappeared with the rise of the Saifawa dynasty of Kanem at the end of the eleventh century. Thereafter, they controlled the vast region in what now consists of northern Chad, southern Libya, the northwestern Sudan, and southwest Egypt. Renowned as warriors, they appeared in all the armies of the *Bilad-al-Sudan* as mercenaries as far west as the Niger and south to the edge of the savanna. In the latter decades of the twentieth century they had been severely dislocated by drought, which stimulated their predatory instincts, and the young men, like Idriss Deby, often sought their fortunes in the more modern world beyond the Sahel.

Ibrahim Itno came from this same tradition and expressed the attitude of the desert Bedouin warrior. "We don't accept the idea that Qaddafi should keep what he has taken through invasion and aggression. . . . [Chadians had died fighting Hitler.] Why wouldn't the French do the same against Qaddafi?"[41] Like Habre his captains were deeply suspicious that France would abandon them in return for a diplomatic solution to the problem of Chad rather than a resolution to its problem on the field of battle.

The battle at Oum Chalouba marked the end of fighting in the Sahel for nearly six months. It was a welcome respite for the adversaries in Chad and their international patrons. The United States was able to reduce its visibility in Ndjamena.

The French began a reconsideration of its military policies in Africa. The Force d'Intervention was reconstructed in 1984 into the Force d'Action Rapide—five divisions that Charles Hernu, minister of defense, claimed "would allow France to act (on her own volition) in defense of countries close to her." Mitterrand's reluctant commitment to the territorial integrity of Chad had been received with enthusiasm throughout Francophone Africa. The approbation by their African allies was much appreciated by the French, but it did not resolve Mitterrand's doubts or his dilemma. Having frustrated the Libyan invasion of Chad, he "could not withdraw his own forces until the Libyan threat was gone." As so often happens in international relations, the greater state becomes the hostage of the lesser, and in this paradox of power, Qaddafi "was permitted to become master of France's fate" in Chad.[42]

While France and the United States gave the appearance of allies working together to ensure the integrity of Chad, there were fundamental differences in regard to Libya. France sought to reduce Libyan influence in Chad. The United States sought to isolate Qaddafi within the OAU, the United Nations, and the Muslim world. President Reagan met with Mubarak in September 1983 and with Numayri in November to discuss Libyan aggression in Chad.[43] The French had established an important economic relationship with Libya, oil for the refineries at Marseilles, and their more historic interests in Africa and the Levant required that Qaddafi be treated firmly but not with overt hostility. Thus the United States might support Habre, but France would consider any option to escape their entrapment in Chad and a contentious civil war without end.[44] "The struggle for Chad" was not a remote battle to be ignored "either by the big powers or by the other states—African or Arab—in the region. . . . Its implications stretch[ed] east to the Horn of Africa, north to Libya and Egypt, and west to the Maghreb Sahara." France, the former colonial power, was "deeply involved and the two superpowers, though reluctant to be drawn in directly, cannot remain indifferent to the outcome."[45]

Although the struggle for Chad—a country so poor that in 1981 the gross national product barely exceeded $500 million—seemed absurd, the players valued the stakes much higher than the per capita income. It was difficult to understand French motives. French paratroopers had prevented the advance of GUNT; they did not bring a resolution to the civil war. The Red Line implied French acceptance of Libyan occupation of the B.E.T. There were numerous proposals to seek a resolution to the civil war, each of which required, however, the participants to surrender their publicly established objectives. Perhaps Tripoli would be willing to discard Goukouni if Habre would declare Chad an Arab Islamic Republic, accept Libyan annexation of the Aozou Strip, and sign a "strategic and military alliance" with Libya. These conditions were precisely those that Habre would never accept. He regarded the Red Line as a dangerous imperial cartographic aberration. It would divide Chad between the French, who would maintain their influence in a neocolonial Africa south of the Sahel, and the Arabs from Libya, who would control the north. While the Libyans were busy building airfields during the armistice produced by the presence of the French, Habre's FANT were not going to receive French air support. "What is the role of the French force? We have yet to receive a precise response."[46]

Habre was not encouraged by the "private agreement" arranged by Roland Dumas with Qaddafi to limit military activities north and south of the 15th parallel. Mitterrand, the socialist critic of French imperial policy in Africa, was more concerned with domestic problems than *France-Afrique*. He desperately wanted to rid himself and his government of the Chad imbroglio, but he received virtually no support from the Francophone states. They were determined to protect their own self-interests against Libyan Pan-Arab, Islamic imperialism. Chad had become the battleground of what the West African leaders perceived as a larger conflict. It was no surprise that they were adamant in their support for Chad in the UN Security Council in August 1983 despite the reluctance of the council to agree on the resolution condemning Libyan aggression.[47] The UN response was to encourage discussion, dialogue, and debate rather than war. Once again President Mengistu Haile Mariam, the new chairman of the OAU, was able to coax Mitterrand, Qaddafi, and a pugnacious Goukouni to yet another "round table" conference on Chad at Addis Ababa in December for "negotiations without formalities."[48]

The Vittel Conference

On 3 October 1983 President Mitterrand opened the tenth Franco-African summit at Vittel, France, with a "strong statement of support for the beleaguered President of Chad, Mr. Habre."[49] Despite his reservations, Mitterrand had to support the Francophone states, but he was very annoyed by the upstart Mengistu taking the initiative in these interminable negotiations over Chad. At Vittel the Africans wanted an assurance that the Red Line did not signify that Libya had acquired sovereignty over northern Chad. They received nothing, and the thirty-eight participants, including twenty-four African heads of state, came to no conclusion. They all expressed the pious hope that both France and the OAU would take a more active role in resolving the conflict in Chad. Habre refused to speak with Goukouni, defiantly demanding that the only meaningful negotiations were those with Libya, not its surrogates. Rebuffed at Vittel, Goukouni agreed to attend the "round table" conference of Chad belligerents that OAU Chairman Mengistu was about to convene at Addis Ababa in December. Habre was unimpressed. He hoped that the OAU would make a positive contribution to the peace process at the forthcoming Addis Ababa conference, but "we do not harbor [any] illusions."[50]

At the Addis Ababa summit meeting in June 1983 the OAU had officially recognized the FANT as the legitimate government of Chad, and Habre had made it abundantly clear that he would not attend any subsequent conference that did

not recognize him as chief of state. He consequently strongly objected to the maneuvers in Paris by the international secretariat of Mitterrand's Socialist Party to
give Goukouni equal status at the forthcoming conference at Addis Ababa. He
launched his own political offensive against the GUNT using propaganda to neutralize Goukouni and Acheikh. Idriss Miskine, the Chad foreign minister, was
warmly received at the Islamic foreign ministers' conference held in Bangladesh
in December. On his return through Paris he announced that the conflict in
Chad would also be on the agenda of the Islamic Conference Organization to be
held in Casablanca in January 1984. Meanwhile, the Chad minister of defense,
Rotouang Yoma, was in Zaire to confirm the support of President Mobutu. In
Ndjamena Habre was to lead a delegation of Chad government officials to the
nineteenth UDEAC (Customs and Economic Union of Central Africa) meeting
at Bangui in the Central African Republic where, after an absence of more than a
decade, Chad was prepared to rejoin the organization.

François Mitterrand did not appreciate these diplomatic initiatives by Hissene
Habre. Personally, neither cared for the other. The postcolonial history of Chad
has been characterized by two decades of an active French presence on the frontiers of Chad, with justifications for French intervention dominated more by personalities than by ideologies or territorial ambitions. President Mitterrand was
struggling to extricate France from a historic commitment surrounded by ethnic
determinism for limited resources constrained by a fragile environment, which
the French no longer wanted to protect or exploit. During his visit to Chad on 31
December 1983, Charles Hernu, the French defense minister, celebrated the New
Year with French paratroopers at Biltine to define, to their mystification, the Red
Line they were defending as the "Red Zone" between the 14th and 15th parallels.[51] Hernu dismissed Habre's contention that the FAT was preparing to attack
Iriba, a village in the heart of Dar Zaghawa 75 miles from the border with the
Sudan and north of the Red Line. Defended by 160 of his troops, Habre sought
confirmation that the French would not permit his eastern outpost to be overrun. Hernu was not prepared to give such a guarantee. The Red Line had been established at Gouro. Since Iriba was beyond the Red Line it was not the responsibility of the French "red berets" to protect it.

Besieged by the French and his supporters at the OAU, Habre agreed to attend
the latest round table conference at Addis Ababa on 11 January 1984, only to can-
cel his government's participation after the sudden death of his principal nego-
tiator and vice president, Idriss Miskine, on 7 January. Some thought Habre was
using a timely death to avoid negotiations. Others interpreted the cancellation as
a sign of internal discontent within Habre's government precipitated by Miskine's unexpected death.[52] In Ndjamena the death of Miskine was attributed to
malaria. Radio Bardai took this opportunity to comment on the numerous and
unusual deaths of Chad leaders. Baghalani, Brahim Youssuf, and Ahmat Acyl
had all "disappeared under obscure circumstances," and Radio Bardai attributed
their passing to personal hostility between Miskine and Habre and fundamental

disagreements over Chad foreign policy. Miskine had emerged as the "supporter of a peaceful solution to the Chad conflict" and had withdrawn to his Dhera constituency only to be called out of retirement to attend the Vittel conference. There were rumors of his attempted assassination and perhaps "regrettable consequences of the current Addis Ababa peace conference."[53] These internal intrigues within the government of Chad, combined with the refusal of Habre to accept Goukouni Oueddei as an equal at the negotiating table, effectively ended the joint French-OAU effort for a reconciliation conference at Addis Ababa.

Pacifying the South

Despite the stalemate in northern Chad, Habre's pacification of southern Chad had nearly succeeded until Libya revived the southern insurgency against the government in September 1983. Habre's opposition in the south was composed of small bands left over from Kamougue's defection that were now more mercenary than political. The FANT occupied most southern towns, Doba, Moundou, Sahr, and controlled the important Sahr-Maro road to the border with the Central African Republic. Pacification was smart policy. The people wanted peace without force. It was also good business for COTONTCHAD; it could operate without having to pay protection money to rebel leaders who had turned to extortion. Parts of the countryside and its villages remained under the control of "Codo" bands loyal to Colonel Abdelkader Kamougue, but their influence was dispersed and in decline. The only large force of Kamougue's followers operated from the Central African Republic, but when they tried to infiltrate into Chad through southern Darfur, they were intercepted by the FANT near Birao and destroyed.[54] Habre sought the assistance of General Kolingba, the president of the Central African Republic, who was only too delighted to rid himself of troublemakers, as were the French who wanted stability to ensure the security of their strategic air base at Bouar. Regular troops from the Central African Republic, accompanied by their French advisors, demolished the training camps of Kamougue's "Codo." Those who escaped disappeared into Brazzaville. Others managed to receive Libyan funds to travel north and enroll in GUNT only to be stationed on the Red Line. Those Codos who went over to Habre were integrated into the FANT but remained quietly among their kin to keep the peace for the government in the south.

In Washington, the House of Representatives Intelligence Committee met in February 1984 to hear testimony on Chad from a CIA witness whose information was leaked to the press. The committee was notorious for its lack of confidentiality, and the hearings on Chad were no exception. The United States had already supported covert operations in Chad and had supplied Habre $10 million in 1982. The critics of the CIA in Congress were astonished that a mere $10 million could oust Goukouni, the Libyan puppet. The United States had become, after France, the most important foreign donor in Chad despite the fact that Saudi

Arabia "pays the bills for the Chadian army."[55] The testimony of the CIA convinced the Congress that, like it or not, the United States had a commitment to Habre, not for any ideological purpose but because of the fact that he was the toughest, the most determined, and the most dependable of all the arrogant, vane, and unreliable chieftains in Chad.

Habre's UNIR, Qaddafi's CLN

While the FANT contained his enemies in southern Chad, Habre began in June 1983 to create a political party, the National Union for Independence and Revolution (UNIR), consisting of representatives from all the regions and ethnic groups of Chad. The platform, however, would be dominated by his own personality cult. The purpose of the National Union (UNIR) was to project the policies of Habre's government at Ndjamena into the far-flung regions of Chad that had been ignored by all the previous regimes. The UNIR was to have a much broader base than the governments of the past. Habre certainly wanted national recognition, which could best be obtained by national reconciliation. The National Armed Forces Command Council (CCFAN), composed of thirty members who controlled the government, was replaced by the UNIR Central Committee, composed of eighty members. The Central Committee included most of the FANT military leadership, particularly the Toubou chieftains Orozi Fodeibou and Taher Guinassou, the Zaghawa commander-in-chief of FANT, Idriss Deby, and the Bedeiyat chieftain Hassan Djamous. The committee invited those rebel leaders who came over to the government to join the UNIR. Symbolically, the UNIR seal was two crossed swords splayed on a sky-blue map of Chad and the Aozou Strip.

The successful counterattack by Idriss Deby at Oum Chalouba gave Habre the opportunity to restructure his government with the UNIR, but the FANT military victory and subsequent stalemate on the Red Line only confirmed Qaddafi's reservations about Goukouni's leadership in the command council (CDR) of GUNT. Qaddafi's disenchantment with Kamougue was due as much to ethnic and religious differences as dissatisfaction with his military performance and, therefore, more understandable than his frustration with Goukouni. He had insisted that Kamougue, as the vice-president of GUNT, represent the rebels from southern Chad in Tripoli, which exposed all his contradictions. At a meeting of southerners from Chad in Brazzaville in October 1983, Kamougue was vehemently denounced by Chadians of every political persuasion—former ministers in the Tombalbaye and Malloum governments—for having "sold out" to the Libyans. He contemptuously denied these allegations as an "insult," claiming that he had never endorsed the Libyan assimilation of the Aozou Strip.[56] This dramatic and doubtful assertion was later to complicate his life in Tripoli.

Habre was not the only one to restructure his government. After interminable squabbling amid the factions of GUNT, the Libyans intervened. In November 1983 the National Liberation Council (CLN) replaced the Commandement Démocratique Révolutionnaire (CDR) of GUNT. The CLN was born at Bardai by an unholy marriage of the factions within GUNT under Qaddafi's shotgun. The principal organizers for the revitalization of a moribund GUNT included the relatively unknown al-Haj Muhammad al-Fasayid, who represented the FROLINAT First Army/Vulcan Force, and Acheikh Ibn Oumar for the CDR. Goukouni Oueddei, the only surviving son of the *Derde*, could not be denied his leadership of the Popular Armed Forces (FAP). The National Liberation Council was not just another rearrangement of clans and kinsmen but the evolution of a movement that began with FROLINAT in 1958 and had undergone numerous permutations motivated by personal ambition, religious commitment, and political ideology. The original FROLINAT had disbanded under the stress of these conflicting objectives in a hostile environment that produced deep belief, implacable responsibilities to kith and kin, and fierce traditions of independence. The survivors of FROLINAT continued to follow Issa Abdallah Muhammad, its secretary general, in the pursuit of its "ultimate goal" of socialism in Chad.[57]

Colonel Wadal Kamougue, the former GUNT vice president and commander of the FAT forces in southern Chad, was conspicuously absent from the National Liberation Council. Colonel Kamougue had numerous personal interests and few ideologies except survival. He arrived in Paris in December 1983 to announce that "his faction" had created a new political organization, the Chadian People's Revolutionary Movement (MRP). Kamougue considered the CLN "a political organ superior to the GUNT" and one that would succeed in "wiping out the factions and resolving the contradictions in order to bring all Chadians under one banner on [a] progressive and socialist basis."[58] The French were amused. Those from Chad and Libya who knew Goukouni were not about to give him support in the National Liberation Council (CLN) to form a government.

Goukouni was given authority to lead the CLN for 14 months during which time he would be "answerable" to a council of fifteen members, including seven of eleven signatories to the 1979 Lagos Accords that had created the GUNT.[59] After four years of failure, it is not surprising that his patron and his followers would circumscribe the activities of the defeated Toubou chieftain and son of the *Derde*. The restrictions placed on Goukouni did not apply to his position in the CLN, which had no authority over the Libyan civilian and military personnel in Chad who were busy forming Popular Committees in anticipation of the founding of a B.E.T. Jamahiriya, the Republic of Borku, Ennedi, Tibesti.[60] Qaddafi had long ago concluded that Goukouni was not the militant missionary for his ambitions south of the Sahara and thus turned to Acheikh Ibn Oumar, "marked by a degree of racism," for "Tripoli has always preferred to rely on the Arab groups in Central Chad."[61]

More Strains Within the Rebel Leadership

The French had never displayed any confidence in Goukouni, and the passage of time appeared to justify their initial assessment. The French and Mitterrand turned to Acheikh as the "Third Man" who could replace Ahmat Acyl and become the intermediary between Goukouni and Habre for stability in Chad and the advantage of France. Giscard d'Estaing had been the first to propose enlisting Acheikh in an attempt to resolve the Chad problem. The strategy was later embraced by Mitterrand in a socialist inspiration for ethnic compatibility in a "Federation of Chad." A map had been "worked out in the Elysée . . . modeled more or less on the Nigerian system."[62] The irony of the French subscribing to British cartography in Nigeria was not lost on the officials at the Quai d'Orsay. Well aware of the disenchantment at home and abroad with Goukouni, Acheikh began discreet discussions with Idriss Miskine.

The talks ended abruptly when Miskine died of malaria in January 1984. There are no secrets in Chad, and when he learned of Acheikh's initiative, Goukouni denounced his activity as treason while gratuitously announcing in February 1984, "I have said several times, I am ready to step aside for another Chadian, on condition that Hissene Habre does likewise."[63] As in the past Goukouni displayed his rage at Habre's arrogance by ordering those troops still loyal to him to attack Ziguey, a government post forty miles north of Mao but *below* the Red Line. The FANT outpost was overrun and two Belgians from the renowned medical humanitarians Médecins sans frontières France, who had just arrived to give medical assistance to the victims of the drought, were captured.[64] Like *L'affaire Claustre* in 1976, the Toubou were now burdened with two European doctors who, like the Claustres, immediately proved to be an international embarrassment. Those invading Chad and their supporters wanted no international liabilities; those in the international community wanted no responsibility for rescuing or ransoming them.

Unhappy with the impasse in Chad and his foreign policy failures in Africa and the Arab world, Qaddafi approved in July 1984 the creation of a Libyan foreign policy review committee headed by Abd al Ati al-Ubaydi. This committee was instructed to coordinate their deliberations with the office of strategic studies, which reported directly to Qaddafi.[65] The central question in Chad was the role of the National Liberation Council (CLN),which had replaced GUNT in a flurry of yet more acronyms. To no one's surprise, the review demonstrated that the Chad leaders were a disappointing lot. Goukouni was neither statesman nor warrior, and Acheikh was a blatant opportunist. Worse, they were both autocratic and greedy. In August 1984 rumors circulated through the B.E.T. that the two had fallen out. Acheikh blustered that he would not tolerate interference "either by the President of GUNT or by the Libyan authorities in the internal affairs of our movement whose independence and integrity we intend to preserve."[66] These were defiant words, and Acheikh's demonstration of independence was too much for Muammar Qaddafi. Acheikh was summarily ousted as minister of defense in the National Liberation Council (CLN), arrested at Fada, and confined to the pleasures of the Achatil Hotel in Tripoli. A "safe" Libyan, Rakhis Manani, replaced him as minister of defense but only managed to aggravate the divisiveness in the National Liberation Council.

There were those who were Chadians first and Libyans second; there were those who perceived their future lay with an affluent Libya rather than an impoverished Chad. Acheikh's arrest symbolized this disunity within the CLN. Mahamat Abba Said, commander of the original FROLINAT (GUNT) First Army, demanded the release of Acheikh on the grounds that Goukouni's effort to reconstitute the GUNT without including Oumar violated both the NLC pact of 28 November 1983 and the Lagos Accord of 1979. Said's brief for Acheikh was based on the legal wording of political agreements designed by opportunists and was subsequently ignored by its signatories and thus appealed to no one. When Said presented yet another long list of unrealistic proposals to solve the Chad problem, he was gratuitously snubbed and in a petulant fit promptly defected to join Habre.

The fragmentation of GUNT continued. In November 1984 Yacoub Mohamat Ourada, the son of the former sultan of Wadai and a former member of the FROLINAT Council, founded the Union Populaire de Tchad from disenchanted followers of the old FROLINAT. Ourada was considered a Libyan puppet, and his defection from Goukouni's leadership was rumored to have been another desperate attempt by Qaddafi to find someone who might lead the fractious rebels. Ourada may have been just another instrument to bring control over a disintegrating insurgency, but he was a dangerous adversary for both Goukouni and Habre. As the son of the former sultan, he could depend on old loyalties from the chieftains in Wadai and Darfur for the sultanate. These influential but aging leaders had little use for the alien commoners, particularly Habre and even Goukouni, an errant son of the *Derde,* but Ourada was unable to exploit these historic and traditional ties, as Qaddafi soon learned, because of his own personal incompetence.

From Tripoli to Crete

Operation Manta may have momentarily contained Qaddafi's territorial ambitions, but it did not reduce his determination to advance them by his unlimited resources. During the annual independence day celebrations on 1 September 1984, Qaddafi, accompanied by that old survivor Goukouni on the reviewing platform, could contemplate his arsenal of 2,600 tanks, 2,000 armored personnel carriers, 1,000 heavy artillery pieces, and 450 planes, including ultramodern MiG-25 "Foxtrots." In 1983 he had purchased $822 million in arms, which by 1985 would be greater than that of France.[67] This massive infusion of sophisticated weaponry was accompanied by those who knew how to use it for the purpose of training those Libyans who did not. By 1984 there were 4,000 foreign military advisors—one for every twenty Libyan soldiers—2,000 of whom were from the Soviet Union.

Two weeks after this impressive array of military might passed in review, Claude Cheysson, the French foreign minister, arrived in Tripoli on 16 September.

After lengthy discussions with Qaddafi and shuffling between Tripoli and Paris, they issued a "joint decision."[68] The communiqué, parts of which have remained secret, recognized the "complete and concomitant evacuation from Chad of French armed forces and Libyan elements supporting GUNT." The simultaneous withdrawal of men and equipment would begin on 25 September. Cheysson in a press conference explained the agreement succinctly. "They leave, we leave. They stay, we stay. They return, we return."[69] The communiqué was issued simultaneously in Paris and Tripoli but remained silent about any consultations with the government of Chad, which precipitated sardonic commentary in the French press. *Le Point* summed up informed French opinion. "To believe that [Qaddafi] has walked away from Chad is naive." Qaddafi was so consumed by his determination for union with Chad that nothing would dissuade him from that policy.[70] The *New York Times* was more sanguine. Chad had become everyone's liability, and thus Qaddafi "was unlikely to renege" on his promise to withdraw his troops.[71]

On 12 October Cheysson announced in a press interview that French Mirage IV P/C1 reconnaissance planes had photographed Libyan troops leaving Chad. The power of high-altitude surveillance has long been established and confirmed by even more sophisticated satellite surveillance twenty years later. Its most enthusiastic advocates, however, will admit that it does not disclose everything that happens on the ground. Issa Koue, chief of the GUNT at Fada, spoke with the foreign press at Biltine to inform them that Libya was reinforcing its positions and that an estimated 3,000 GUNT troops backed by 5,000 Libyans were dug in north of the 16th parallel. The Libyan forces were being rotated and troops of *race blanche* were being exchanged for those of *couleur noire.*[72] At Wadi Doum the Libyans were also constructing a 4,000-meter runway and accompanying facilities to accommodate fighter-bombers to support the Libyan troops stationed east of Faya and GUNT forces in Wadai and Darfur.[73] The Chad foreign minister, Gouara Lassou, also presented a petition before the UN Security Council stating that Muammar Qaddafi had also sanctioned the assassination of his president, Hissene Habre.[74]

Although the French had honored their part of the Cheysson agreement by withdrawing the last French convoy from Ndjamena into Cameroon on 7 November, Libya had yet to leave the B.E.T., Faya, Ouninga, or Fada. It was an unpleasant reminder for President Mitterrand that very little ever goes smoothly in Chad, particularly when he was tired of providing an annual subsidy of $250 million a year in French military and economic aid. Thus, when Premier Andreas Papandreou of Greece, who had long proclaimed that Athens was the bridge between the Arab and Western worlds, offered to act as mediator to bring Qaddafi and Mitterrand together, his offer was accepted with alacrity. They all met with Papandreou in Crete in November 1984, where Mitterrand announced that Libyan troops had begun their withdrawal from Chad. In Ndjamena, Habre in a press interviews confirmed that Libyan reinforcements had, in fact, arrived at

Faya. The all-seeing eyes in the air of the AWACS substantiated on 16 November 1984 these more pedestrian observations; there were 5,500 Libyan troops in northern Chad. The official, laconic response was diplomatic and factual. "We share our information with the French, and we both know that most of the Libyan troops with their equipment are still in Chad."[75]

The meeting in Crete between Mitterrand and Qaddafi was not encouraging for Habre. "France had recognized Libya's rights to examine Chad's affairs," to which Habre responded that his government could not survive in a nation divided.[76] Papandreou's mediation was scorned in the international press. "The exposure of Libya's duplicity and of France's gullibility" was a matter "of no small embarrassment."[77] In Egypt President Mubarak needed no further confirmation of Qaddafi's deception when Libyan intelligence agents were arrested in an assassination attempt of a Libyan exile in Cairo. In France, *Le Monde* reported that the Libyan Army had not evacuated the B.E.T., where there were 2,000 Libyan troops and tanks, thirteen aircraft, and a dozen helicopters. United States intelligence then discovered four mechanized infantry battalions, tanks, rocket launchers, aircraft, and helicopters at Fada and Faya. On the roads leading south from the Fezzan, Libyan trucks were carrying supplies for an estimated 6,000 troops.

The endless African war in these worthless wastelands of Libya, Chad, and the Sudan was characterized by personal ambition, greed, and survival superimposed upon historic relationships of kin, trade, and state-building on a tumultuous frontier in the Sahara, the Sahel, and the Sudan. Their traditional institutions had been disrupted throughout history by incomers, imperial or religious. There were those who sought the profits from commerce, African gold, ivory, and above all slaves. Others sought empire for the exhilaration of conquest and the tribute of subjects. There were those who came to expand the faith. And there were those who reduced history to an irrelevant footnote in order to seek personal gain.

On 19 December 1984 Roland Dumas, the new French foreign minister who had replaced Claude Cheysson, paid his respects on behalf of President Mitterrand to those French who had fallen in support of governments of Chad. He specifically included Major Galopin who "was murdered under conditions known to you all, and by the person or persons whose cause you seem so eager to espouse." The headline in the *Quotidien de Paris* challenged his condemnation of Habre: "Dumas Calls Habre a Murderer."[78] Two days later *Le Monde* also severely criticized Dumas, saying his comments were false. Despite his personal dislike of Habre, the interests of France, and the new relationship with Francophone Africa established in Crete, President Mitterrand could not deny at the end of 1984 the continued presence of Libyan troops in Chad. His reservations were further complicated when Colonel Jalloud accused France of violating the Tripoli agreement. Aerial photography "au dessus du nord du Tchad" exposed the presence of French troops along the borders of Cameroon and the Central African Republic, and French officials admitted a possible return of French troops to Chad. Jalloud hoped that a mixed Greek-French-Libyan commission would soon "confirm the absence" of French and Libyan forces in Chad.[79] The actors were in their places in the theater of international politics; the charade was complete.

Notes

1. U.S. Department of State, Bureau of Public Affairs, *The Libyan Problem,* Special Report no. 111, October 1983.

2. "FROLINAT, First Army Claims Success," *West Africa,* 17 January 1983, p. 170; "Habre's Opponents Advance," *West Africa,* 21 March 1983, p. 749.

3. *Middle East International,* 4 March 1983, p. 4.

4. James F. Clarity, "Chad Keeps Anxious Watch on Libya," *Times* (London), 3 March 1983, p. 6.

5. J. E. Persico, *Casey: From OSS to the CIA* (New York: Viking Penguin, 1990), p. 298. See also William J. Casey, *Scouting the Future: The Public Speeches of William J. Casey* (Washington, D.C.: Regnery Gateway, 1989), p. 45.

6. They were followed by Operation Eagle Look, which had followed the bombing of Omdurman. See U.S. Department of Defense, *American Eagle in the Sand: The Story of the United States Central Command* (Washington, D.C., 1996).

7. U.S. Department of Defense, *American Eagle in the Sand.*

8. U.S. Department of State, Bureau of Public Affairs, *The Libyan Problem; Akhir Sa'ah,* in Arabic (Cairo), no. 2524, 9 March 1983, pp. 16-17.

9. *Middle East International,* 4 March 1983, p. 8.

10. J. E. Sutton, Jr., "Prepared Statement," *Sudan: Problems and Prospects,* U.S. House of Representatives, Committee on Foreign Affairs, 28 March 1984.

11. U.S. Department of State, Bureau of Public Affairs, *The Libyan Problem..*

12. "Mise au point tchadienne après la déclaration du Colonel Kadhafi," *Elima* (Kinshasa), 11 February 1983.

13. Clifford D. May, "Chadians Mop Up Around 2 Desert Outposts," *New York Times,* 4 September 1983, p. 13.

14. United Nations Security Council, document S/15884, New York, 22 July 1983; see also "M. Hissène Habré a subi un revers militaire dans l'extrême nord," *Le Monde,* 10 March 1983, p. 6.

15. "Wary Niger Wonders: Why Is Qaddafi Smiling?" *New York Times,* 15 March 1988.

16. Ibid. The United States had spent $18 million from 1982–1987 to help the air force of Niger counter Qaddafi's rapidly growing air power and in 1987 helped to construct the Dirkou base in order to observe Libyan activities in the Tibesti.

17. R. B. St. John, "Libya's 'New' Foreign Policy," *Congressional Review,* July 1983, pp. 15-18; *Wall Street Journal,* 11 March 1983.

18. François Soudan, "Kaddafi en position de force," *Jeune Afrique,* 1 February 1984, pp. 34–35.

19. Senne Andriamirado, "Le Tchad ou comment s'en débarrasser," *Jeune Afrique,* 5 October 1983, pp. 30–31; François Soudan, "Hissein Habré dit tout," *Jeune Afrique,* 5 October 1983, pp. 24–27.

20. P. Blackburn, "West Africa Worries About Qaddafi," *Christian Science Monitor,* 16 August 1983.

21. "Chad Is Invaded by Dissidents Backed by Libya," *Guardian,* 24 June 1983.

22. Ibid.

23. "North Falls to Goukhouni," *West Africa*, 4 July 1983, p. 1541.

24. George E. Moose, "French Military Policy in Africa," in *Arms and the African*, ed. William J. Foltz and Henry S. Bienen (New Haven: Yale University Press-Council on Foreign Relations Books, 1985), p. 76.

25. "East Germans Man Soviet Artillery in Chad," *Daily Telegraph*, 8 July 1983.

26. "Libyan Designs on Egypt, Sudan Feared," *Los Angeles Times*, 5 July 1983.

27. The Zaireans arrived in June and departed several months later without having fired a shot to the relief of the citizens of Ndjamena.

28. "Chad Is Invaded by Dissidents Backed by Libya," *Guardian*, 24 June 1983; "France and Libya Facing Off," *Christian Science Monitor*, 8 July 1983; "Libya's Potential Foothold in Chad Presents Dilemma for France," *Baltimore Sun*, 8 July 1983.

29. "Chadian Government Intensifies Drive Against Rebels in North," *Washington Post*, 18 July 1983.

30. "Rebels Lose Grip on Key Chad City," *Washington Times*, 18 July 1983; "Ivory Coast Calls on West to Save Chad," *Fraternité Matin*, 11–12 July 1983; "U.S. Military Aid Arrives in Chad," *New York Times*, 26 July 1983; "US Military Aid to Chad: A Warning to Qaddafi," *Christian Science Monitor*, 16 July 1983; For U.S. aid see "U.S. Military Assistance to Chad," *Bulletin* (Washington, D.C.: U.S. Department of State, 19 July 1983). The U.S. response occurred when U.S. jets intercepted two Libyan MiG–23s after they "came within 100 miles" of U.S. aircraft carrier *Eisenhower*. The Libyan planes retired, but the U.S. Sixth Fleet was placed on full alert. "Kaddafi Stirs Up More Trouble," *Newsweek*, 11 July 1983.

31. "Libya Tightening the Reins," *Africa Confidential*, 21 September 1983, pp. 6–7.

32. Ibid.

33. "Tchad: La Troisième Intervention française," *Afrique Contemporaine* (October-December 1983): 47–49.

34. "Central Africa," *FBIS*, January 1984, p. S1, 3.

35. Michael Goldsmith, "Chad Civil War Settles into an Uneasy Stalemate," *St. Louis Post-Dispatch*, 30 October 1983.

36. The best the bored journalists could report were comments about Qaddafi's obsession with Chad and "lebensraum" or that Goukouni would only disappear if Habre agreed to an Islamic Republic, a military alliance, and annexation of the Aozou Strip by Libya. See A. Cowell, "Qaddafi's Assault on Chad Causes Fear of More to Come," *New York Times*, 14 August 1983; "Le Monde," *Guardian Weekly*, 21 August 1983.

37. This authorization had been approved by Congress in Section 506a of the Foreign Assistance Act.

38. "Weinberger: French 'Indicated' They Needed AWACS for Chad," *Nation & Review* (Bangkok), 24 August 1983.

39. "French Bring Miniboom to Chad's Capital," *St. Louis Post-Dispatch*, 16 September 1983.

40. "Le Monde," *Guardian*, 4 September 1983.

41. "At the Chad Front," and "Chad Equation," *New York Times*, 14 and 20 September 1983, respectively; John Chipman, *French Power in Africa* (London: Basil Blackwell, 1989), pp. 137-141.

42. U.S. Department of State, *Bulletin* (Washington, D.C., December 1983 and January 1984), pp. 50–51 and 84–85, respectively. See *Weekly Compilation of Presidential Documents* (Washington, D.C., 30 September 1983 and 25 November 1983), pp. 1363–1365 and 1608–1609, respectively.

43. H. Boyd, "Chad: A Civil War Without End?" *Journal of African Studies* (Winter 1983): 119–125; *World Today* (October 1983): 361–364.

44. "Flashpoint Chad," *Middle East* (August 1983): 19.

45. François Soudan, "Hissein Habré dit tout," *Jeune Afrique*, 5 October 1983, pp. 24–27.

46. *United Nations Chronicle* (October 1983): 11–15.

47. *Marchés Tropicaux et Méditerranéens*, 2 December 1983, p. 2908.

48. *Guardian*, 4 October 1983.

49. "France Steps Up Its Diplomatic Efforts," *Christian Science Monitor*, 6 October 1983; Radio Paris, Domestic Service in French 0700 GMT, 6 October 1983.

50. Agence France Press, quoted in "Central Africa," *FBIS*, 1 March 1984, p. S1.

51. *Le Monde*, 3 January 1984, p. 30; *Marchés Tropicaux et Méditerranéens*, 13 January 1984, p. 89.

52. "Central Africa," *FBIS*, 11 January 1984, p. S1.

53. *Afrique Défense* (November 1983): 18.

54. François Soudan, "Le Système Habré," *Jeune Afrique*, 29 February 1984, p. 31.

55. François Soudan, "La Menace qui vient du Sud," *Jeune Afrique*, 26 October 1983, pp. 36–37.

56. "Interview with Issa Muhammad, Secretary General of FROLINAT," *West Africa*, 2 January 1984, pp. 16–18.

57. AFP Radio in French, 1019 GMT, 29 December 1983.

58. "L'Opposition forme un 'Conseil National Libération,'" *Le Monde*, 1 December 1983, p. 5.

59. U.S. Embassy, Ndjamena, Cable 1822, 25 March 1984.

60. *Libération Afrique-Caribe-Pacific* 19–20 (December 1983-March 1984): 22–25.

61. Ibid., p. 65.

62. Ibid., p. 70.

63. *Marchés Tropicaux et Méditerranéens*, 13 January 1984, p. 89; Béchir Ben Yahmed, "I suffit d'oser . . . ," *Jeune Afrique*, 15 February 1984, pp. 22–23; François Soudan, "Jours d'angoisse à N'Djaména," *Jeune Afrique*, 15 February 1984, pp. 27–28. Habre's enemies claimed that he killed Miskine, but Chadians close to both of them have told the authors that Miskine died of malaria.

64. *Afrique-Asie,* 13–26 February 1984, p. 24.

65. "The Libyan Terrorist Association in France" (translated from Arabic), *Al-Bayadir Al-Siyasi* (Jerusalem), 28 September 1985, p. 34.

66. François Soudan, "Le Retour des diplomates," *Jeune Afrique*, 30 January 1985, pp. 27–28; Mohamed Selhami, "Le Dossier de la crise du GUNT," *Jeune Afrique*, 30 January 1985, p. 34.

67. For Soviet purchases and equipment in Libya, see "2000 Sowjetberater in Libyen," *Die Welt* (Hamburg), 4 December 1984.

68. *Al-Hawadith* (London), 26 December 1984, p. 43.

69. "Tchad: Coup d'arrêt à Kadhafi," *L'Express* (Paris), 28 February 1986, p. 32.

70. "Kadhafi: L'Appel du meuzzin," *Le Point*, 24 September 1984.

71. "Chad Accord: French Call It a Diplomatic Success," *New York Times*, 19 September 1984.

72. *Marchés Tropicaux et Méditerranéens*, 19 December 1984, p. 2568.

73. "Der libysche Zugriff auf Nordtschad," *Neue Zuercher Zeitung*, 16–17 February 1986.

74. "Khadafy Accused of Murder Plot," *Oregonian* (Portland), 1 February 1985; "Kaddafi's Latest Adventure," *Newsweek*, 11 February 1985.

75. "Col. Qaddafi's Weekend," *Washington Post*, 19 November 1984; "France and Libya Meet on Chad Accord," *New York Times*, 16 November 1984.

76. "Central Africa," *FBIS*, 3 December 1984, p. S1–2.

77. "Col. Qaddafi's Weekend," *Washington Post*, 19 November 1984.

78. R. Buijtenhuijs, *Politique Africaine* (December 1985): 91–95; "Qaddafi Pursues Dual Strategy," *Christian Science Monitor*, 26 June 1985.

79. *Marchés Tropicaux et Méditerranéens*, 26 December 1984, p. 3218.

9

Famine in the B.E.T.:
Instability in Darfur

In 1975 the great African drought had come to an end with the return of the rains. Less than a decade later an even more remorseless drought returned to the African Sahel. Beginning in 1982 the drought spread inexorably from the Atlantic to the Red Sea, from Senegal to the Sudan. In November 1983 the Chad foreign minister, Gouara Lassou, met with representatives of the international foreign missions in Ndjamena to request food aid. Once again there was famine throughout the land. There were 12,000 desperately hungry Chadians at Ati and 30,000 more at Adre. In Kanem the drought was particularly severe, and even in the normally well-watered south, food shortages were widespread. The diplomatic community in Ndjamena reported that hundreds of people were streaming daily into the capital in search of food. The nation's reserves were exhausted. Once again Western donors and the United Nations provided assistance. The United States had already promised $52 million in economic aid, which began in October, and was now prepared to authorize more for food.

Ironically, the drought that brought massive suffering to the people of Chad was largely responsible for the dramatic decrease in warfare. When GUNT took Oum Chalouba in September 1983, the B.E.T. had become an empty wasteland as the farmers and nomads fled south of the Red Line or north to the oases of southern Libya in search of food. There was a skirmish at Ziguey in February 1984, but the enthusiasm for battle on both sides could not compete with the implacable drought, and the antagonists settled down astride the Red Line. Operation Manta and the imposition of the Red Line had stabilized the Sahel. Consequently, when the rains failed for the third consecutive year, in 1984, the international humanitarian agencies were able to plan a rational attack on famine conditions without the fear of petty frontier wars or a new invasion by the Libyan imperialists and their surrogates from the north. The drought had a dramatic and deleterious effect on the cattle economy of central Chad. "A scant 100 kilometers north of Ndjamena the millet looks scraggly. As you move northward along the rutted road to Mao, capital of Kanem, you notice that the stalks are more stunted."[1] In the south the Codo could no longer loot the farmers, who had no food for themselves, let alone the bandits. They joined the thousands in flight from southern Chad into the Central African Republic where the government was desperate to feed 50,000 Chadian refugees. Disruption from the drought in southern Chad, not surprisingly, produced an increase in banditry but in fact facilitated, not unlike conditions on the Red Line, the efforts of the government to establish its authority among those ethnic groups who were historically hostile to any administration controlled by northerners.

Famine and Western Relief

In September 1984 the League of Red Cross Societies launched the largest international appeal in its history to save the thousands who were dying in Chad. Parents had to "abandon their children because they had no food for them."[2] The situation for those Chadians who had sought refuge around the French bases became desperate when French troops began to leave Chad in September. The displaced persons who settled near the bases at Moussoro and Biltine had no food, on the one hand, and in their vulnerable condition feared reprisals from their enemies, on the other. The French had provided food for an estimated 120,000 displaced persons, including 50,000 in Ndjamena, but even with the assistance from international donors, they had been able to meet only a minor fraction of the need. Funds were urgently sought to assist 500,000 displaced persons in a hundred separate camps and the rapid movement of relief supplies through the Central African Republic, Cameroon, and Nigeria, which soon collapsed in the archaic infrastructure of Chad. As the drought deepened and the water disappeared in the wells and *hafirs,* the FAO predicted a shortfall of 300,000 tons of cereal grains in Chad. Beginning in the Sahel, drought penetrated into the savanna deeper than any time since 1935. Consternation, frustration, and pessimism immobilized those already accustomed to a harsh environment. Perhaps it was god's will, but two decades of warfare seemed to justify his wrath destroying the vulnerable agriculture and pastoral economy of Chad. Drought in the south, combined with the revival of local banditry, closed seventeen cotton mills, resulting in 5,000 wage earners returning to their villages, now dependent upon their kin for subsistence. Faced with a devastating famine, with all its economic and political consequences, Habre sought to attract foreign investment for the poorest nation on earth. He failed. While crops withered across the Sahel and famine relief could not reach the destitute because of inadequate facilities, the new Ndjamena airport terminal, destroyed in the fighting of 1980, was reopened in November 1984. With loans from the African Development Bank of the International Monetary Fund this modern structure was undoubtedly the most important addition to the infrastructure of Chad.

In 1984 the threat of famine in Darfur was even worse than in Chad. The Commissioner for Refugees of the Sudan government had reported that hundreds of Chadians were daily crossing the frontier into Darfur. By November, 94,000 people of every ethnic group, mostly Zaghawa and Toubou, were in Sudanese refugee camps, which now held 10 percent of the Chadian population.[3] The drought in Darfur created confusion in Chad. Whole villages were on the move, and displaced camps sprang up overnight as Western relief agencies sought to avoid a more massive loss of life in 1980 than in the 1970s.

Instability in the Sudan

As in Chad, the drought in the Sudan temporarily prevented any efforts by Libya to advance its interests in the Sudan. As famine began to decimate Darfur, drought appeared to have precluded any Libyan imperial adventures in the western Sudan. His ongoing efforts to gain respect in Khartoum suddenly received an unexpected opportunity. In 1983 President Numayri had renounced his secular ways to embrace Islam. Having alienated the traditional political and religious leaders of the Northern Sudan, he had become totally dependent upon the army. He, therefore, now sought to embrace Islam in order to consolidate his deteriorating political position among the Northern Sudanese. The practical manifestation of this conversion was his decree that the laws of Islam, the *Shari'a*, were now to be applied to all Sudanese, a third of whom—mostly Africans in the Southern Sudan—were not Muslims. He revoked the terms of the Addis Ababa agreement of 1972, which had established an autonomous administration in the Southern Sudan. The reaction among his African subjects in the south was to rebel against the northern Muslim government in Khartoum, the revival of the same rebellion that had paralyzed the Sudan for seventeen years from 1955 to 1972. In March 1983 the 5th Battalion was composed of former insurgents of the Anya Nya, who had been integrated into the Sudanese army as part of the Addis Ababa agreement of 1972. They were now garrisoned at Bor, unpaid and discontented with the unilateral dissolution of the autonomous Southern Regional Government by Numayri. They mutinied, defeated the government forces marching from Juba to restrain them, and disappeared into the bush to make their way east into the safety of Ethiopia. Here they were organized under the command of Colonel John de Garang, a Bor Dinka and a respected senior officer in the Sudan, into the Sudan People's Liberation Army (SPLA). The Southern Sudanese resumed their civil war against the government in Khartoum, which continues with ever greater intensity to the present day. Qaddafi of Libya and Mengistu of Ethiopia were quietly pleased by the revival of the Southern Sudanese civil war, which was for them more an insurrection against Numayri than a liberation movement of Africans against Arabs. Although the eclectic Muslim and the sunshine Marxist were strange bedfellows, both hated Numayri as much for personal reasons as any ideological or territorial concerns, and they made common cause to supply John de Garang and the SPLA with arms.[4]

In May 1983 Jaafar Numayri was reelected president of the Sudan. Although he received 99.6 percent of the vote, the electoral landslide deceived no one. His determination to impose the *Shari'a* as the law of the Sudan and an Islamist polity upon a nation of ethnic, cultural, and religious diversity was unpopular among many Sudanese, Muslim and non-Muslim. In September 1983 Numayri decreed that he would enforce the *Shari'a* throughout the Sudan. To implement the *Shari'a* he announced the repeal of the Sudan civil and penal codes introduced by the British at the beginning of the twentieth century, which had achieved wide acceptance from all members of Sudanese society. The decree was anathema to the Southern Sudanese, and it was regarded with dismay by many Sudanese Muslims who foresaw religious conflict in the future where little had existed in the past. The acceptance of the *Shari'a,* known in the Sudan as the September Laws, could only be made legitimate by its imposition. To assert the very doctrine of the revolution required the rigorous interpretation of Islamic law, which was unacceptable and intolerable to the mass of Sudanese.

Jaafar Numayri had never been a very popular leader. He did, however, manage to survive twenty attempts to overthrow his government during the fifteen years of his presidency. His authoritarian rule increased in proportion to the growth of discontent against him. In January 1985 he ordered the execution of Mahmoud Muhammad Taha for heresy and placed Sadiq al-Mahdi under house arrest. The execution of Mahmoud Taha produced revulsion throughout the Sudan. He was the leader of the Republican Brotherhood, an innocuous political group that advocated a liberal interpretation of the Quran for non-Muslims and women. His dramatic and very public execution was as unnecessary as it was repugnant. Sadiq was the leader of the *Ansar* and *Umma,* and his polite confinement was deeply resented by his supporters in the West, where Qaddafi's agents had been active. In November 1983 Major General Umar Muhammad al-Tayib, first vice president and head of state security, publicly criticized Libya for its "plan to detach the western Sudanese province of Darfur, declare a government there, and await aid from Libya."[5] Real or imagined, this bizarre operation dissolved when the Sudan reacted with swift military and diplomatic action "to neutralize the effort, and the problem had lessened with the departure of Libyan forces from Chad."[6] In fact, Umar Tayib's security agents were now more concerned about discontent among the fractious politicians from Darfur than Libyan agents. The leaders of Darfur—Fur, Arab, Zaghawa, and Bedeiyat—were all hostile to Numayri and his riverine Arabs. They were *Ansar* loyal to the religious revolution of the Muhammad Ahmad al-Mahdi and his great grandson, Sadiq al-Mahdi. They had little use for the military parvenus from Khartoum and still less for Qaddafi, who was a religious nonconformist and yet another North African in search of dubious ambitions south of the Sahara in the *Bilad al-Sudan.* These historic animosities were now exacerbated by the drought.

There was dismay and then anger in Darfur when Khartoum did little to relieve the famine. Indeed, there was little more that Libya needed to do to destabilize Darfur. The old Fur sultanate could no longer preserve the peace north of

Kutum where the Islamic Legion were independent from dry wells, their water now carried in Libyan vehicles that roamed the desert and Sahel with a freedom unknown by the camel nomads. Here amid the devastation of drought, they could prepare for invasion against the FANT from their Sudan sanctuary. The threat of Libyan subversion was now replaced by Libyan propaganda from Radio Tripoli and Bardai against the "traitor" Numayri, who was denounced as an agent of the CIA to let "the snake Habre loose among the Chadian people."[7]

By 1984 the United States was deeply concerned that the drought would endanger the security of Chad and the Sudan and the American presence in the region. A friendly Sudan was regarded as a buffer that separated its radical neighbors—Libya, Ethiopia, and South Yemen—from America's more conservative allies in Egypt and the Arabian peninsula. In March 1984 Noel Koch, Deputy Assistant Secretary of Defense for International Security Affairs, acknowledged that Qaddafi and Mengistu were using the SPLA "in an effort to eliminate" Numayri, but he hoped that "Libyan-financed arms and training inside Ethiopia" would not divert the Sudanese from any Libyan threat to Darfur.[8] By 1984, however, the influence of the United States in the Sudan had been seriously eroded by its continued support for Numayri, despite his religious conversion and chimerical political convictions. Every ruler in the Sudan in modern times has been dependent upon the Nile, which has required him to commit the resources of the state to defend its waters in the upper Nile Basin. The events of the last half of the twentieth century have not changed this principle. The great regions of the west were far removed from the river by language, culture, and great distances traversed by camel over harsh terrain and not the ease and luxury of the *dahabiya* for those going up the Nile to the regions beyond the *Sudd*. The West had always been expendable in times of trouble when the upper Nile was not. Numayri was prepared to commit his resources to secure the Nile waters. He was reluctant to dissipate his military in the marginal lands of Darfur on a frontier that had never had peace. Darfur was a province with a long and proud tradition of independence, secured in the past by its control of the trade routes traversing the Sahel from west to east and meeting those from the north and south in El Fasher and Abeche. The inhabitants had their own local and historic rivalries, but they feared and despised the merchants, intellectuals, soldiers, and holy men who came west from the river. Numayri was not about to expend his resources in the west to convert those who were not devout Muslims or to challenge their independence by imposing government from the Nile.

The Reagan administration justified the continuation of its military assistance to the Sudan because Numayri kept "the Soviets and Libyans out," ample reasons for Washington, Riyadh, and Cairo to provide economic and military aid to the Sudan.[9] Washington was, of course, prepared to increase military aid to any of Qaddafi's enemies, particularly when Libya continued to purchase large amounts of Soviet weapons that could never be needed for its defense, while Qaddafi publicly supported terrorist assaults in London and Ndjamena. His infamous erratic behavior was demonstrated by yet another bizarre incident. In March 1984 a lone Libyan fighter suddenly appeared out of the blue sky of the Sudan to bomb the Khartoum radio station. The pilot missed the target and crashed in the desert outside of Omdurman to become a great joke in the capital, but it was yet another example of the strange behavior of their neighbor.[10] This incident did not go unnoticed in Washington, and two AWACS were immediately sent to Cairo to begin the aerial surveillance of the Egyptian desert west for the Nile, the frontier, and the Libyan bases.

Qaddafi Continues to Meddle in Chad

While Habre was seeking to reconcile his ethnic enemies in the south, Libya continued to send reinforcements into Chad north of the 16th parallel. The Libyan airstrip at Wadi Doum was completed, and new air bases were under construction at Kichi-Kichi and Chicha. In March 1995 Charles Hernu, minister of defense, dismissed the presence of "less than 4,550" Libyan troops. He acknowledged, however, that there were "more than should be there," and they were in violation of the Tripoli Accord arranged by Roland Dumas in October 1983.[11] In Ndjamena the minister of information, Mahamat Soumaila, estimated that there were 5,000 Islamic Legionnaires in Chad, and to prove his assertion, he produced captives from the Islamic Legion, leading the press to add, "There are members [legionnaires] in jail in Ndjamena [from] Sudan, Benin, and Senegal."[12]

Habre was convinced that France had acquiesced in the partition of Chad to protect their economic interests in Libya. He likened French policy to that of a nation seeking to be rid of the task of gendarme, policeman, for that of the *pompier*, fireman.[13] The Libyan contingent in the B.E.T. was more than 7,000 men supported by heavy weapons, including the T-62 Soviet tank. *Le Monde* reported the confusion in French diplomacy. At one moment the government supported Habre's claim to the inviolability of Chad and its ownership of the Aozou. The next minute it did not. There appeared to be a contradiction within French intelligence. In early 1985 it had reported morale problems within the Libyan army. "Almost all of the Libyan soldiers stationed in Northern Chad were replaced." In fact, there were large Libyan contingents who remained at Fada and Faya.[14] The airstrip at Wadi Doum was being used to transport men and supplies into southern Chad where in 1985 a Libyan serving as the paymaster to the last of the Codos distributed a great deal of "Libyan money." When Habre ordered his FANT units, led by Zaghawa officers, to eliminate the Codo gangs, the "Green," the "Red," and the "Hope," his loyal southerners were furious at this northern invasion. Habre promptly replaced these tough northern Gourane commanders by southerners as prefects, subprefects, and canton chiefs, who were generally accepted by the African populace and were able to revive a semblance of local administration.

During this time of troubles in the south, 50,000 Chadians fled to the Central African Republic, and despite Habre's efforts to pacify the south, Mitterrand put personal pressure on him to permit France to send a team to southern Chad to investigate human rights violations. Habre refused but instead invited Amnesty International—who had previously prepared an unfavorable report on the human rights conditions in Chad and was no friend of Habre—to come and report. Before Amnesty International could complete its inquiry, large numbers of refugees began to return to Chad, and "a number of southerners were even ready to recognize" that Habre "had made commendable efforts to calm ethnic rivalries." These positive developments were soon accompanied by a more substantial victory for Habre when the "Red" Codo commanded by Alphonse Kotiga surrendered to join FANT and acknowledged Habre's authority. Other southern leaders soon followed. Rumors were circulating that Generals Djogo and Kamougue were ready to join Habre.[15]

Habre's success in the south encouraged West African leaders to seek once again a solution to the problem of Chad at the conference table. In March 1985 President Moussa Traoré of Mali invited Habre and Goukouni for discussions at Bamako, but when nothing came of this initiative, the OAU responded to the demands of more moderate West African leaders to hold a conference at Brazzaville to include all Chad factions. Like Bamako nothing came of this effort, for Qaddafi made it clear to the National Liberation Council (CLN) of GUNT that it was neither in their interests nor those of Libya for them to travel to Brazzaville.

Numayri Is Deposed

On 6 April 1885 President Jaafar Numayri of the Sudan was overthrown. His relentless imposition of the *Shari'a*, his abrogation of the Addis Ababa Agreement of 1972, his continuation of the state of emergency in the Sudan, the malevolent activities of the security services, spiraling inflation, the devaluation of the Sudanese pound, and the reduction in subsidies for food, his expulsion of the Muslim Brothers from the Sudan Socialist Union, his demoralized and discontented army, and finally, his inept handling of the great drought and famine of 1984–1985—each contributed in its own way to his downfall. Indeed, given the litany of his abuse and failures, the fact that he remained in power as long as he did is best explained by U.S. financial support and the stoic patience for which the Sudanese are famous. His fall came when he was on a state visit to the United States to mend political fences and to request an increase in foreign aid.

In his absence the union of engineers initiated a general strike on 3 April, and for three days students, professionals, and the discontented took control of Khartoum. When the army refused to intervene, Numayri was washed away by a tide of enemies demanding the return of civilian rule. This was not to be, for the army joined the popular revolution only in order to dominate it. Led by General Swar al-Dahab, Numayri's chief of staff, a Transitional Military Council (TMC) took control but could not ignore the popular will that had coalesced into the National Alliance for National Salvation in order to depose Numayri. It promised to rule for only one year, after which the country would be returned to an elected civilian government. The generals were, in fact, reluctant to pick up the pieces from the wreckage that Numayri had left behind.

The Transitional Military Council immediately began to seek more sophisticated weapons for the army, which was hard-pressed by the SPLA insurgency in the south and demoralized in the west by its inability to contain the refugees from drought and war on a turbulent frontier in Darfur. They sought weapons from Egypt, Saudi Arabia, and the United States. Sadiq was sent off on a special mission to the Soviet Union, but no one was inclined to provide arms to a transitional government led by a Swar al-Dahab, a known sympathizer if not supporter of the Muslim Brothers. His promise of national elections would, hopefully, result in a more representative and stable government than that of another military junta, but it did not produce guns from Saudi Arabia or the superpowers. Having failed to acquire weapons from the West and their allies, Swar al-Dahab turned to Libya. Qaddafi was only too pleased to supply arms to those who shared his belief and commitment to Islam and to the Arabs who were everywhere south of the Sahara confronted by non-Muslim Africans, whether in the Southern Sudan or in Chad. In return for weapons from Libya to strengthen a beleaguered Sudanese army in the Southern Sudan, Swar al-Dahab terminated the flow of arms to Hissene Habre, closed the frontier, and opened another chapter in the strange history of relations between Khartoum and Tripoli.

Qaddafi immediately ended his military assistance to the SPLA and offered to train Sudanese army units. He was generous in giving Sudanese workers in Libya permits and "privileged status." Libyan cargo planes arrived in Khartoum and Libyan ships docked at Port Sudan. Sophisticated weaponry and new aircraft, including the Soviet TU-22 jet fighters began to arrive in Khartoum.[16] The Libyan opposition in Khartoum and the Sudan was summarily expelled. Jalloud arrived in Khartoum escorted by 140 well-armed Libyan "diplomats" to protect Ambassador Abdallah Zakariya, who was actively recruiting Sudanese into a revolutionary committee with its headquarters in Omdurman, conspicuously painted green and the command post for some 4,000 recruits, mostly refugees from Darfur.

In June a Sudanese military delegation visited Tripoli to meet with Colonel Abu Bakr Younis. He was emphatic that Libya had "no intention of forming any strategic alliance with Sudan," a statement that no one believed, particularly Habre and Mubarak, whose skepticism was confirmed by the announcement in Tripoli of the Libya-Sudan military protocol "for mutual defence."[17] After the fall of Numayri, the Egypt-Sudan-United States entente came to an end. The United States Department of State expressed its "grave concern" and officially informed the TMC that any military relationship between the Sudan and Libya "could only impact adversely on U.S.-Sudanese ties."[18] In Cairo, Mubarak employed the cautious strategy of Nasser toward the Sudan, but he was powerless to block the

Libyan diplomatic and military influence, which soon stimulated the historic distrust of the Sudanese for Egyptians of any ethnicity. On the one hand, the Libyan presence aroused the Sudanese Islamic revolutionary tradition that had always been circumscribed in Egypt by the repression of the Muslim Brothers. On the other, Mubarak was not about to dismantle an alliance that had favored Egyptian interests for more than a decade. Egypt was not insensitive to its ambiguous relationship with the Sudanese and had consistently applied a policy of accommodation throughout the half century of the independent Sudan, which did not change with the demise of Numayri. Libya, however, was another matter. The stormy and hostile relations between Cairo and Tripoli since Qaddafi came to power in 1969 were now aggravated by the expulsion of 100,000 foreign workers, most of whom were Egyptian, after the fall in world oil prices in September 1985. Egypt was not prepared to instantly assimilate into its own fragile economy the sudden arrival of its citizens. Mubarak publicly rebuked Qaddafi for having squandered the wealth of Libya on terrorist adventures, military foolishness in Chad, and the irresponsible disregard of Egyptians workers.

In Washington the Libyan presence in the Sudan was regarded as a threat to the strategic objectives of the United States to drive the Soviet Union from the Red Sea and the Horn of Africa and to contain its surrogates in Ethiopia and the Yemen. The U.S. Department of Defense Central Command could now no longer count on Sudanese air bases or Sudanese troops participating in the joint military exercises with Egypt and the United States in the western desert. Nor could the State Department depend on diplomatic support from the TMC as it had in the past from Numayri. Swar al-Dahab publicly supported the Libyan claim to the Aozou Strip, opposed the U.S. policy in the Gulf of Sidra, and dismissed Qaddafi's assistance for terrorists. At the annual meeting of the foreign ministers of the OAU in July 185, he stated that "what affects Chad really affects Sudan," but this most certainly did not mean the revival of military support from the Nile for Hissene Habre.[19]

The Libyan Buildup

The fall of Numayri was a terrible blow for Hissene Habre. The Islamic Legion patrolled along the Chad-Sudan borderland from its base at Ma'tan as-Sarra, ignored by the Sudanese army's 7th Division at El Fasher. Libyan agents were everywhere active in the west, and within six months they had enlisted some 2,000 Sudanese ruffians into the Legion. Habre publicly predicted that Libyan recruitment in the Sudan would expand the problem of Chad into Darfur. Throughout the history of the Sudan, between the Nile and the Niger, Darfur was the reservoir of men and arms to strike west into the petty border sultanates of Dar Tima, Dar Sila, Dar Masalit, and then on to the kingdoms of Wadai and Kanem. By October 1985 U.S. aerial photography had verified an extensive military buildup by Libya from its bases in northern Chad, including 300 armored vehicles and petroleum depots north of the Red Line. At Wadi Doum, Colonel Rifi Ali Sharif, a Sebha boyhood friend of Qaddafi and Jalloud, first secretary general to the Revolutionary Command Council, and an officer with long experience in Chad, commanded the Libyans in northern Chad. These forces were dependent upon the logistical link between Faya and Fada and the three-mile runway at Wadi Doum being completed by East German engineers in order to airdrop supplies to the GUNT operating in the B.E.T.[20]

In the summer of 1985 the rains returned to the African Sahel. Heavy rains fed the tributaries to Lake Chad, and at Bagasola a Chadian official monitoring the lake reported that he had "never seen the lake expand so rapidly in the last 20 years."[21] In central and southern Chad life slowly returned to normal, and although Habre was confronted by serious economic problems, the stability of his government convinced many former enemies to join him. General Djogo decided to switch sides to become minister of justice and his Codos were integrated into the FANT. Wadal Kamougue, the last survivor of southern leaderships, owed much more to Qaddafi than General Djogo and refused Habre's invitation to return to Ndjamena. Politically isolated and surrounded by a dwindling number of followers, he formally resigned as GUNT vice president and moved to Abidjan where he began a bootless search for a "third way" to end the civil war in Chad.

The return of the rains and the Libyan reinforcements in northern Chad could not disguise the fact that GUNT was disintegrating. Rumors, but also more authoritative reports, circulated in Chad and among the international intelligence community in the autumn of 1985 that the Teda Toubou and the African Kanembou quartered at Faya were fighting among themselves. The Gourane had even turned on the Libyans in Faya precipitating a major shoot-out leaving a hundred dead and many wounded. When the National Liberation Council (CLN) in October 1985 demanded the release of Acheikh Ibn Oumar, three battalions of the Islamic Legion arrived at Chicha, an insignificant watering hole located between Faya and Koro Toro, to reinforce the hard-pressed Libyans.

Despite these internecine struggles north of the Red Line, Habre had assiduously warned the French throughout the autumn of 1985 that the Libyans were preparing for another offensive south of the Red Line. When he attended the twelfth Franco-African conference in Paris on 9 December 1985, Habre personally repeated his earlier warnings to Mitterrand.[22] Habre was bitter that his forces had not received the weapons that the French government had promised when Operation Manta left Chad and required the outgunned FANT to "make withdrawals" from Wadai "near Biltine."[23] Habre told the French that Libyan activities in Darfur were to become a third prong in the Libyan offensive. One task force would attack south from the Aozou Strip. A second would advance south from Ma'tan as-Sarra through Fada. A third would strike from Darfur along the trade route to take Abeche and Wadai and link up with the columns moving into central Chad in preparation to envelop Ndjamena.

Operation Épervier

In December 1985 Qaddafi invited himself to the OAU summit meeting in Senegal where he presented a new peace plan to Abdou Diouf, president of Senegal and chairman of the OAU. The plan was a rehash of old ideas, but his arrival was accompanied by his usual dramatic entrance with 400 bodyguards and his usual coterie of armed women in their designer jeans to the delight of the international press and the disapprobation of the African leaders. Qaddafi declared that he "was prepared to treat former president Goukouni and Chad's Hissene Habre as rivals on the same footing of equality."[24] This was an astonishing disclosure. To regard Habre as an equal to Goukouni could only mean that it was another bizarre inspiration or that the only surviving son of the *Derde* had been dismissed to the dustbin of history. This decision was soon confounded by the release of Acheikh Ibn Oumar from house arrest to appear at Fada as the minister of state for the National Liberation Council (CLN). Oumar could hardly replace Goukouni if he could not succeed where Goukouni had failed in the conquest of Chad.

No sooner was he freed than Acheikh made a clandestine journey to Paris in the expectation of obtaining French support. The French listened but were bemused to learn that he had replaced Goukouni as Qaddafi's favorite. They remained noncommittal, but this did not deter Acheikh from launching an offensive against Habre and Chad to achieve what Goukouni had not. On 10 February the GUNT advanced from Kichi-Kichi and Chicha down the caravan routes that led to the south from Chicha in the east to Fada in the west. The GUNT army numbered 8,000 troops supported by "roughly the same number" of Libyan regulars and Islamic Legionnaires; FANT troops numbered 20,000. The GUNT, however, had very superior firepower, and after passing over the Red Line at four historic crossings, they overran the FANT contingents at Kouba Oulanga and Kalait. Within hours they were in position to move against the FANT as far south as the 15th parallel.[25] At Oum Chalouba the GUNT army was "reinforced by Libyan soldiers equipped with heavy weapons," to decimate the FANT defenders who fought with tenacity for the palm grove that guarded the strategic defile commanding the route from Faya to Abeche. Once the road was lost to the GUNT, the way to Biltine and Abeche was open.[26]

The FANT were again everywhere in retreat, but the impending collapse of the Habre government could not be accepted with equanimity by the French despite the personal animosity of its leaders. Three days after the GUNT offensive, the French government warned Libya that if its troops and those of the GUNT did not return north of the Red Line, France would respond. *France-Afrique* of the heroic days of Chad when its citizens rallied to Le Clerc's dramatic charge across the desert in 1942 was now a fading memory. Nevertheless, the historic mission of France in Africa could not be denied. Mitterrand assured Qaddafi that France was "not at war with Libya," but under intense pressure from the United States and Egypt, he authorized Operation Épervier (Operation Sparrowhawk) to airlift 1,000 troops to Chad. Arriving at Ndjamena, French paratroopers of the Force d'Action Rapide swept into central and eastern Chad along the Red Line to protect Abeche. When the GUNT continued their attack, the French used their air power. On 16 February seven French Jaguar fighter-bombers and four Mirage F-1s from Bouar in the Central African Republic attacked Wadi Doum and immobilized the runway. In the United Nations France invoked Article 15 of the UN Charter for individual or collective self-defense to justify the raid as a response to an act of war.[27] Deprived of victory by the French intervention, Qaddafi once again misjudged Habre's determination to fight and the reluctant but historic French commitment to support Chad. In March 1986 the FANT counterattacked up the Wadi Bahr al-Ghazal and overran the GUNT unit that had taken Kalait. On 17 March it destroyed the GUNT forces at Chicha, killing more than 200 Islamic Legionnaires. Koro Toro fell the next day to be followed by Wadi Chili (Tchie). The GUNT army retreated toward Faya where Libyan reinforcements were arriving in substantial numbers in a desperate attempt to contain the FANT advance.

Despite the defeat and the retreat of the GUNT army and the arrival of the French, the Libyans, now reinforced, were not about to abandon Chad. To support the GUNT, now in retreat in central Chad, "up to 5,000" Islamic Legionnaires were ordered to advance from Darfur onto the Ennedi Plateau from Darfur to support an additional 5,000 men under Libyan command who had just arrived from the north.[28] Led by Libyan officers this task force moved easily through Fada to confront the FANT outpost at Ziguey. This assault could not have been launched from the Ennedi without the support of the Darfur contingent of GUNT who had been rearmed by covert support from Swar al-Dahab and his Transitional Military Council (TMC) in Khartoum. Habre understood that Operation Épervier could frustrate Libyan designs in central Chad along the Red Line. But, the French would be reluctant and hard-pressed to contain an unexpected assault on its flank from Darfur in the east.

While fighting raged in eastern Chad, the TMC's civilian prime minister, Gizzuli Dafallah, visited Tripoli in March and, ironically, praised Qaddafi as a statesman and a man of the desert who had every right to the territorial waters of the Gulf of Sidra. Gizzuli returned to Khartoum with an assurance that Libya would supply oil at Port Sudan for the impoverished economy of the Sudan, which was particularly crucial if the TMC was to carry on its Arab and Islamic *jihad* against the African Southern Sudanese. Qaddafi's price was a "military cooperation agreement" that permitted the Libyans a free hand in Darfur.[29]

Once the TMC agreed to accept Libyan arms, the influence of the United States in the Sudan was reduced to humanitarian assistance to neutralize devastating famine in Kordofan and Darfur. Food was more important than guns, and the distribution of what became known as Reagan sorghum by the United States Agency for International Development (AID) was more important to the Sudanese than Qaddafi or his Libyans. The TMC, beleaguered by the drought, welcomed the international aid agencies and nongovernmental organizations, and in July 1985 USAID-Sudan pledged $200 million for a Western Relief Operation. The humanitarian assistance from the United States continued to sustain the American presence in Khartoum when it could no longer be justified by its military commitment to a government that had overthrown its ally and sought assistance from its enemies. "Were it not for the famine and the obvious need for American help, the April coup could have been a real disaster for us." Food relief poured into Darfur and Kordofan and continued for months despite the State Department having to take "extraordinary security precautions" to protect U.S. personnel. "Following the infiltration of several hundred Libyan agents into the Sudanese capital [the TMC was] no longer able to keep track of all the Libyans and their Sudanese allies."[30] In fact, Khartoum was a remarkably open city after the fall of Numayri. The political inclinations of Swar al-Dahab were strongly sympathetic to the Muslim Brothers, but he was well aware of the determination of the Sudanese for a more open political climate. He himself had no personal ambitions, and if he had there could be no question of yet another military government in Khartoum after Numayri. He remembered the popular upwelling of Sudanese yearning to be free that had overthrown Papa Abboud in 1964. In 1985 there could be no alternative to a civilian government. By April 1986 there were some forty political parties ecstatic about yet another try at democracy.

The United States Attacks Qaddafi

In 1981 U.S. intelligence had warned that a certain Sa'id Rashid, a Libyan agent, had begun to seek U.S. individuals and their domiciles in Europe for a possible terrorist attack. During the winter of 1984–1985 he recruited several Palestinians to target U.S. facilities in Germany and directed the April 1986 bombing of the La Belle Discotheque in West Berlin that was "specifically intended to kill American service personnel and their dependents." An American army sergeant was killed and 200 customers were injured. The day after the bombing, "Rashid traveled to Khartoum," where he was reportedly involved with "oppositionists" to the Sudanese government. Although the opposition remains unknown, it was most likely, given Rashid's employer, the National Islamic Front whose leader was Hasan al-Turabi.[31] Equally troubling were intercepts by the National Security Agency that Libya had planned a terrorist attack on the U.S. consulate in Paris, and Libyan agents were observed in covert surveillance of "American facilities in ten countries."[32]

When U.S. intelligence agencies confirmed that Rashid and Libya were responsible for the Berlin bombing, President Reagan reacted with anger and determination to retaliate against Qaddafi. He denounced him in a presidential press conference as "the mad dog of the Middle East" and ordered air strikes against Libya. On the night of 14 April 1985 United States F-111s flying from Upper

Heyford air base in England attacked sites at Benghazi, the Benina airport, and Qaddafi's Revolutionary Command headquarters at the Bab al-Aziziya Barracks in Tripoli. President Mitterrand was neither pleased nor impressed by the U.S. response. "I don't believe that you stop terrorism by killing 150 Libyans who have done nothing," but the American public fully approved, and even the NATO allies were privately pleased at the president's decisive action. The European Community immediately increased their surveillance of Libyan embassies and facilities and established more rigorous restrictions at customs and immigration for Libyans coming into and out of Europe.[33] Qaddafi narrowly escaped the bombing of his headquarters at Bab al-Aziziya and uncharacteristically retired from public occasions for many months, leading to much speculation as to his health.[34] Some attribute his disappearance to the belligerent reaction by the United States. Others argue that it was his dismay at the tepid rhetorical support from both fellow Arabs and Moscow that convinced him to reaffirm his alliances with both. Jalloud was sent to Moscow on a curious mission to obtain a formal treaty of friendship that would allow Libya to join the Warsaw Pact. This bizarre project did not impress the Russians nor result in any additional arms sales (Libya had already spent $15 billion on arms purchased from Moscow).[35] The Soviet response was, in fact, an indication that Qaddafi had become more of a liability than an asset, particularly after 1985, Mikhail Gorbachev, *glasnost*, and the thaw in the cold war.

Sadiq Victorious

The day after the U.S. attack on Libya some 4.5 million Sudanese went to the polls. The Umma party led by Sadiq al-Mahdi won 99 of the 301 seats in the Constituent Assembly. Its traditional rival, the Democratic Unionist Party (DUP), led by the Mirghani family and supported by the Khatmiyya religious brotherhood *(tariqa)*, won 63 seats. These returns were expected. To everyone's surprise, the National Islamic Front (NIF), led by Hasan al-Turabi, won 51 seats and made a very strong showing in Khartoum where it received more than 40 percent of the vote. Sadiq's electoral victory was accompanied by anti-American demonstrations against the bombing of Libya during which a U.S. embassy employee was assaulted, resulting in the evacuation of all U.S. diplomatic personnel from Khartoum and 300 Americans from the Sudan.[36] On 15 May Sadiq formed a coalition government that included the DUP but neither the NIF, the Communists, nor the Muslim Brothers. After nearly twenty years Sadiq was once again returned by an election in "the only proper democracy in the Arab League, and one of the rare democratic regimes on the African continent."[37] Sadiq, "despite his impeccably Islamic background," had campaigned against the "Islamic excesses" of Jaafar Numayri and his failure to grant concessions to the SPLA in the Southern Sudan in an effort to project his image as a liberal leader from a conservative Islamic religious movement.[38]

Sadiq's relations with Libya had always been warm if not intimate since 1976 when Qaddafi had supported his *Ansar* in their abortive attempt to depose Numayri. There had never been any close relationship between Sadiq and the Egyptians against whom his great grandfather had rebelled to destroy the Turco-Egyptian colonial regime in the Sudan at the end of the nineteenth century. His relations with the United States were ambiguous. He was outraged by the U.S. air strike on Libya and had confirmed the TMC decision to recall the Sudanese ambassador to the United States for "consultations."[39] This hostility was reciprocated, and the U.S. embassy remained closed until Sadiq promised greater protection for U.S. personnel.

The United States would return to Khartoum, for it could not ignore the fact that the Sudan had eight separate land borders with neighboring states and the Red Sea coast. In 1986, however, the U.S. Department of State was preoccupied with Ethiopia and the Marxist government of Mengistu Haile Mariam to the neglect of the deteriorating situation in Darfur. As long as Qaddafi remained quiescent after the bombing, there was little interest in the events in Wadai and Darfur. In fact, the National Islamic Front (NIF) was very active in the west working with Qaddafi's Arab, Islamic agents to drive a wedge between Sadiq and his loyal Baggara. The Baggara had been the vanguard of Sadiq's great grandfather's revolutionary army in the last century and now were his political stalwarts. In the drought they were the principal predators of the non-Arabs in the west and the defenders of Islam against them and the Africans of the Southern Sudan. In 1986 the National Islamic Front organized political conferences in Kordofan and Darfur. The Baggara chiefs were given license to create a "human belt" of Islamists that would traverse the Sudan from Geissan and Um Dafog on the Chad-Sudan frontier in the west to the Nuba Mountains in the east. Within that belt the Baggara would be expected to "defend the cultural and religious purity of the [Arab] North."[40]

The appeal for Arab purity immediately aroused the historic hostility of the non-Arabs—the Fur, the Berti, the Zaghawa, the Bedeiyat, and the Gourane—who for centuries had defended their homelands against Arab invaders. This deep ethnic rivalry had been the foundation of violence or accommodation on the frontier since time immemorial. These relationships were regulated by the ferocious demands of nature in a marginal land, on the one hand, and their leaders who competed for power, territory, and the control of trade, on the other. The cement that prevented the dissolution of these societies into a Hobbesian state of nature had nothing to do with the cold war or the sophisticated ideologies of the West. These societies maintained their independence and their cohesion by principles clearly understood but never fully articulated. First, the needs of the nomads of the pasture were symbiotic with those cultivating the land. Second, there was the understanding that no one on the frontier could ever be permitted to dominate to the destruction of his neighbor. Third, these two principles were bound together by intermarriage and a sense of restraint as to the limits of violence.

Sadiq and Darfur

In the west the return of the rains in 1986 continued throughout the season. At last fortune had smiled and "heavenly rain" had let Sudan and Chad "live again."[41] The displaced left their camps, and there was the promise of a fine harvest in Darfur and Wadai. As the land revived, so did Qaddafi's spirits. Everywhere on the frontier, however, the farmers were attacked by a new plague. They were bandits and Islamic Legionnaires supported by the Libyan military to spread insecurity throughout the frontier from Dar Zaghawa in the north to the Central African Republic in the south, which could not be contained by the tradition means to settle disputes. The Islamic Legion had opened a truck route from Kufra oasis through Ounianga Kebir, Fada, and on to Kutum in Darfur. Another desert route began at Ma'tan as-Sarra then skirted east of the Erdi Plateau to continue south to the Meidob Hills in Kordofan. As the Islamic Legion prepared to attack Habre's forces in eastern Chad, hundreds of Libyan trucks appeared in El Fasher, and Libyan military officers were no longer harassed but were now received in the officers' mess of the Sudanese army.

Libyan agents had less success in recruiting Islamic Legionnaires from among the impoverished Zaghawa, Bedeiyat, and Sudanese *abbala,* the non-Arabs of the Sahel who supported Habre, Deby, and Djamous, their fellow Gourane. They had much better success among the Arab Baggara, who were attracted more by the prospect of loot than any ideological appeals to Pan-Arabism. Islamic Legionnaires in Libyan battle dress were now openly proselytizing in Darfur and ignored by the Sudanese army. Twenty years after the Sudan had first allowed FROLINAT to use Darfur to attack the Tombalbaye government, the Sudanese army, which had contained Libyan activities during the Numayri years, was now ordered to once again serve the interest of Sadiq and Qaddafi.

Although the United States had been President Numayri's staunch ally, his demise did not mean that Washington was prepared to abandon the Sudan. Indeed, the United States had every reason to continue its support. To be sure, the Americans were conscious of northern and Muslim domination of the Transitional Military Council, but Swar al-Dahab had been Numayri's chief of staff. He tactfully disguised his close relationship with the Muslim Brothers and had promised and delivered elections. Sadiq may have had long if ambiguous relations with Qaddafi from whom he and his *Ansar* had received financial and military assistance. Yet Sadiq had been democratically elected prime minister, and he was very soon concerned about the subversive activities of Libyan agents and Islamic Legionnaires in the very heartland, Darfur and Kordofan, of his historic constituents. The problem of Chad and the continuation of conflict on his western frontier were most certainly not in the interests of Sadiq. Stability on the frontier was to the advantage of those on the periphery, whether in Khartoum, Ndjamena, or Washington. The U.S. offered to expand its reconnaissance capability west of the Nile with more logistic military assistance for the Sudanese to patrol its long and volatile frontier with the Central African Republic, Chad, and Libya. The Pentagon immediately authorized C-130 cargo planes, sophisticated HUM-V land reconnaissance vehicles, and logistic delivery systems to strengthen the Sudan's air defense capability in the west. Much of this material was, not surprisingly, later transferred by the Sudanese government to recover from its defeats in the civil war in the Southern Sudan. The delivery of this military equipment was welcomed, but it did little to restrict the subversive operations in Darfur.

Ever the politician and rarely the statesman, Sadiq would devote his enormous energy to rebuilding the Umma party in both the Sudanese core and its periphery. Although his *Ansar* remained the most powerful political, if not military, element in Darfur, he paid little attention to the security of the frontier, like every Sudanese ruler, once he had reached the waters of the Nile. His political enemies feared that the Libya-Sudan partnership would flourish under Sadiq, especially since the prime minister had publicly reaffirmed a secret agreement that allowed Libya to station troops in Darfur.[42] These activities were not unknown to the populace of the frontier where reality was always embellished by rumor. The Fur, in particular and perhaps because of their deep loyalty to the *Ansar*, were deeply disturbed by the barter and sale of large numbers of automatic weapons by Islamic Legionnaires and Libyan agents to their ethnic enemies in the west.

Notes

1. *Liberation* (Paris), 2 December 1983, pp. 24–25.

2. "Red Cross Launches Drive to Aid Victims of Drought in Chad," *Baltimore Sun*, 9 September 1984.

3. Hiram Ruiz, *When Refugees Won't Go Home: The Dilemma of Chadians in Sudan* (Washington, D.C., U. S. Committee on Refugees, June 1987). See also "French Bases in Chad Are Magnets for Poor," *Washington Post*, 29 September 1984; "Is It Too Late for Chad?" *West Africa*, 3 December 1984.

4. Robin B. Wright, *Sacred Rage: The Wrath of Militant Islam* (New York: Simon and Schuster, 1986), p. 201.

5. Ibrahim M. Zein, "Religion, Legality, and the State," doctoral dissertation, Temple University, Philadelphia, 1989.

6. Joseph C. Goulden, *The Death Merchant* (New York: Simon and Schuster, 1984), pp. 334–345.

7. Radio Bardai, B.E.T., Chad, 1815 GMT, 23 May 1983. For the Islamic Legion see "Traum von der arabishen Nation," *Frankfurter Allegemeine Zeitung*, 20 October 1985; "Fuhrer der Revolution," *Der Spiegel*, 5 May 1986. Qaddafi began to recruit for the Islamic Legion in 1974. By 1986 the legion had enlisted some 12,000 foreign mercenaries trained and paid for by Libya to support the 73,000 Libyans of the regular army.

8. U.S. House, *Sudan: Problems and Prospects,* 98th Cong., 2d sess., 28 March 1984, p. 7.

9. U.S. General Accounting Office, *Sudan: Conditions on U.S. Economic Aid,* Memorandum B–211263, Washington, D.C., 2 June 1986.

10. "U.S. Sends Two AWACS to Egypt," *Wall Street Journal,* 20 March 1984, p. 2.

11. "Ghadafis Vertragsverletzung in Tchad," *Neue Zuercher Zeitung,* 30 March 1985. Hernu had previously admitted the presence of Libyan forces in Chad but claimed that there were only two or three battalions, numbering no more than 1,200 men.

12. *Africa Now* (February 1985): 21.

13. "Qaddafi Pursues Dual Strategy in Effort to Expand Libyan Influence in Chad," *Christian Science Monitor,* 26 June 1985.

14. Laurent Zecchini, "La Libye renforce sa présence dans le nord du Tchad," *Le Monde,* 16 April 1985, p. 7.

15. Laurent Zecchini, "Tchad," *Le Monde,* 27 October 1984, p. 6; François Soudan, "Le Retour des diplomates," *Jeune Afrique,* 30 January 1985, pp. 27–28; Mohamed Selhami, "Le Dossier de la crise du GUNT," *Jeune Afrique,* 30 January 1985, p. 34; "Chad Toward Peace," *Africa Confidential,* 10 April 1985; "Arab Africa" (Chad subsector), *FBIS,* 8 June 1985; "Codos Threaten Habre's Lifeline," *New African* (June 1985). An eyewitness account of a visit to Codo forces loyal to Kamougue in April-June 1985 appears in *Afrique-Asie,* 9 September 1985, pp. 34–35. On Chadian refugees see United States Committee for Refugees, *World Refugee Survey: 1988 in Review* (Washington D.C., 1989), p. 39.

16. *Al Majallah* (London), 2 September 1985, p. 14.

17. "Country Profile: Sudan," *Economic Intelligence Unit* (June 1986): 9; "Government Statements on Military Pacts," *Sudan Times,* 11 June 1989, p. 1.

18. U.S. Department of State, *American Foreign Policy: Current Documents, 1985* (Washington, D.C., 1986), pp. 897–898.

19. "North Africa," *FBIS,* 23 July 1985, p. Q3.

20. "Der libysche Zugriff auf Nordtschad," *Neue Zuercher Zeitung,* 16/17 February 1986; "Back in the Chadian Quicksands," *Middle East* (April 1986).

21. *New Nigerian* (Kaduna), 19 August 1985, p. 1; *Triumph* (Kano), 15 October 1985.

22. "Tchad: Coup d'arrêt à Kadahfi," *L'Express,* 28 February 1986.

23. "Der libysche Zugriff auf Nordtschad."

24. "Qaddafi, Diouf Hold Hushed Talks on Chad," *Washington Times,* 5 December; "Qaddafi Eases Chad Position," *Washington Times,* 6 December 1985.

25. "Chad: The Latest Round of Civil War," *Jane's Defense Weekly,* 8 March 1986.

26. "Fièvre sur la ligne rouge," *Le Point,* 17 February 1986.

27. "Épervier fait son nid," *Le Point,* 24 February 1986.

28. "Central Africa," *FBIS,* 28 April 1986, p. S1; Hugo Sada, "Kaddafi recrute . . . ," *Jeune Afrique,* 19 March 1986, p. 49.

29. "Middle East and South Asia," *FBIS,* 17 March 1986, p. S2.

30. "U.S. Takes Steps to Protect Envoys," *Washington Post,* 4 July 1985.

31. Office of the Coordinator for Counterterrorism, Office of the Secretary of State, *Patterns of Global Terrorism* (Washington, D. C., 30 April 1992).

32. C. Dobson and R. Payne, *The Never Ending War: Terrorism in the 80s* (New York: Facts on File, 1987), pp. 69–87.

33. *Corriera della Sera,* 27 and 28 January 1986, p. 7 and p. 2, respectively; *Avanti!* (Rome), 29 January 1986, pp. 1, 12; "Italy Takes Over Base Libya Targeted," *Chicago Tribune,* 2 June 1986.

34. "Trail of Mideast Terror," *New York Times*, 5 January 1986. On 4 April 1986, Undersecretary of State Michael Armacost made a statement on the USAID Worldnet program that Washington was working with its European allies to impose "real costs" on Qaddafi. The influential Congressman Lee Hamilton supported this view. See *Foreign Affairs Newsletter* 6, no. 5 (Washington, D.C.: Rayburn House Office Building, May 1986); "La guerra de Reagan," *Hoya* (Santiago, Chile), 21–27 April 1986; Lou Cannon, *President Reagan: The Role of a Lifetime* (New York: Simon & Schuster, 1991), p. 634.

35. "How Moscow Embraced Gadafy at Arm's Length," *Guardian*, 23 April 1986; "Jalloud und Kaddam in Moskau," *Neue Zuercher Zeitung*, 30 May 1986; "Qu'est que Kaddafi peut attendre de Moscou?" *Jeune Afrique*, 11 June 1986; "Gadahfi Skips Appearance," *Washington Post*, 12 June 1986; Cord Meyer, "Libyan Raid Eroded Qaddafi's Position," *Washington Times*, 22 August 1986.

36. "Centrist Leads Vote Returns," *New York Times*, 21 April 1986.

37. "Fragile Democracy in Sudan," *New York Times*, 10 May 1986.

38. "Sudanese Parties Reach Agreement," *Washington Post*, 11 May 1986.

39. "Sudanese Leader Seeks Good Ties with Libya," *Washington Post*, 24 April 1986; Robert D. Kaplan, "A Microcosm of Africa's Ills," *Atlantic* (April 1987).

40. Fund for Peace, *Living on the Margin: The Struggle of Women and Minorities for Human Rights in Sudan* (New York: Fund for Peace, July 1995), pp. 18–19.

41. "Heavenly Rain Lets Sudan Live Again," *Times* (London), 26 November 1986.

42. This agreement was reported in "Le Soudan à l'épreuve de la rebellion sudiste," *Le Monde Diplomatique* (Paris), June 1989, p. 11. Bona Malwal, editor of the *Sudan Times,* frequently made reference to this secret agreement but did not give details or citations.

10

Habre Victorious

After the U.S. F-111s had carried out their retaliatory raid against Libya on 14 April, Qaddafi retired into seclusion for several months during which he threatened to replace the Libyan army with a people's militia while reshuffling his army command. Even Colonel Abd al-Hafiz Massaoud, who had been in charge of operations in Chad, was publicly rebuked. When his confidence returned, Qaddafi appeared to be more cautious, disguising his support for terrorist groups by using commercial companies and surrogates to conceal any Libyan involvement. Libyan diplomats were instructed to avoid any direct association with terrorists, although Libya was implicated in an attack in April 1986 in Khartoum, which injured a U.S. embassy official, and a bombing of the World Vision office in Mondou, Chad, in October 1987. At the meeting of the nonaligned nations in Harare, Zimbabwe, Qaddafi gave a rambling speech that denounced his hosts for appeasing the United States and especially the representatives of the Francophone states for maintaining a "special relationship" with France and even Great Britain. He remained surprisingly silent when the Chad foreign minister, Gouara Lassou, condemned Qaddafi for the Chad crisis.[1]

Unknown to Lassou, the Libyans had already begun to reassess their Chad policy. In the volatile life of Libya, where personalities were more important than policy, Goukouni, the Toubou chieftain disgraced by defeat, reappeared in Tripoli after the Aziziya bombing to attend a GUNT conference opened at Sebha in early summer where this extraordinary survivor could not be ignored.[2] In a petulant fit, Kamougue resigned from the GUNT in June and departed hurling epithets against Habre, Goukouni, and even Qaddafi. Qaddafi returned to Sebha to restore peace among his surrogates with his usual energetic declamations that he would no longer tolerate the lack of discipline that characterized the GUNT.[3] Colonel Massaoud, in disgrace for defeats in Chad and obviously transmitting Qaddafi's wishes, announced the formation of a triumvirate—Goukouni, Acheikh, and Kamougue—that would now prosecute the war against Habre on three fronts, each of which would be separately commanded. Goukouni was once again reduced to a battalion commander, rather than the surviving son of the

Derde, to lead the GUNT insurgency south from the Tibesti. To the east, Acheikh Ibn Oumar and his troops were to create an "autonomous front" at Fada.[4] As for Kamougue, his tantrums apparently forgiven, he was expected to open a third front against Habre from southern Chad.

Six commanders were discreet but forceful at Sebha in their objections to Qaddafi's unilateral reorganization of GUNT. As field commanders they were appalled by the failure of Goukouni and Kamougue and were bewildered by Qaddafi's motives, for his reorganization appeared to be designed more for military disaster than victory by those who had already proven themselves incompetent. They reconvened in September in the customary medium of the Toubou to resolve differences by consensus in a hostile environment. The conference brought together many old players. There were Acheikh's politicians from the CDR in Tripoli and the chieftains from the First Army of Mahamat Abba Said, the People's Armed Forces of Mahamat Issa Idriss, the Western Armed Forces of Moussa Medela Yacine's original FROLINAT, the Fundamental Chadian National Liberation Front of Hadjaro Sanussi. They all agreed that something had to be done to resolve their differences, but neither Acheikh, Goukouni, nor Qaddafi could bring unity to these fiercely independent and headstrong chieftains of the desert and Sahel for whom panache and amour propre were more important than ideology. While these eternal disputations were being debated in northern Chad, Habre had united the resources of the government of Chad in the center and the south, albeit under the Gourane leadership.

While the rebel leaders dithered, Libya used the pause in the fighting to augment its forces in Darfur. Habre responded to these transparent maneuvers with a diplomatic offensive. The Chad foreign minister, Gouara Lassou, attended the twenty-second OAU summit meeting at Addis Ababa in July 1986 where he remonstrated once again that Libya was planning another invasion of Chad. The OAU was urged to approve a resolution demanding that Libya remove its forces from Chad, and the OAU chairman, President Sassou-Nguesso of the Congo Republic, was only too pleased to allow a full debate on the problem of Chad. He had been personally offended when Goukouni had tactlessly spurned the chairman's personal invitation to attend his proposed OAU reconciliation conference in March. The Libyan representative asserted that "it was the French troops who were to withdraw from Chadian territory," but the Libyan argument was overwhelmingly rejected. Most of the OAU members found the presence of Libyan troops in Chad "intolerable," and Nigeria expressed the sentiment of many members when its representative urged all "non-Chadian" forces to leave the country.[5] The moribund OAU ad hoc committee on Chad-Libya—the same founded at the 1977 Libreville Conference—was revived and soon afterward, a decade later in 1986, received the approval of the Conference of Non-Aligned Nations (the NAM), which now "gave its full support" to national reconciliation in Chad. Cotton prices, which had produced 80 percent of Chad's export revenues in the past, had drastically declined to produce a $100 million trade deficit in 1986. Chad's economy may have been dependent on Western charity, but NAM "urged the international community to contribute to the national reconstruction of Chad."[6]

Acheikh and the CDR Revolt

During the convoluted manipulations by the rebel leaders for the control of GUNT, Goukouni publicly protested his demotion and refused to follow orders from the Libyan military command or Qaddafi. He was summarily arrested and sent to Tripoli. When he declined to "recognize Acheikh Ibn Oumar's government," he was placed under house arrest "to ensure his safety."[7] It was the final insult for the son of the *Derde* and a symbol of the split in the GUNT between Arab and Toubou.

In August four hundred armed followers of Acheikh Ibn Oumar, representing the Commandement Démocratique Révolutionnaire, the CDR of the GUNT, arrived at Erdi to carry out the orders of Colonel Massaoud to reduce the GUNT presence in Ennedi by ordering the Toubou to retire to the Tibesti. Their place was to be taken by the CDR in anticipation of Acheikh opening a second front against Habre. The CDR tried to disarm Goukouni's Popular Armed Forces (FAP). The two opponents were about evenly matched, and when the Islamic Legion refused to intervene in what they regarded as a tribal dispute, the Toubou of Goukouni and the Arabs of the CDR of Acheikh slaughtered one another with enthusiasm. After heavy casualties on both sides, the FAP withdrew, regrouped, and encircled Erdi. They demanded that the CDR surrender, but when Acheikh's troops refused, the Toubou launched a devastating assault on 5 October. When the CDR defenders were about to be overrun, Colonel Khalifa, commander of the Libyan expeditionary forces in Chad, ordered his air force to strafe the Toubou to save Acheikh who had just arrived to take command of an embarrassing defeat. The FAP succeeded in shooting down one Libyan plane but now outgunned, they retired from Erdi into their sanctuaries in the Tibesti. During its retreat the FAP destroyed a large Libyan convoy guarded by T-62 tanks and covered by Sukhoi jets between Faya and Aozou to capture a huge amount of arms and 135 Libyan troops to exchange for Goukouni Oueddei, under house arrest in Tripoli.

The battle for Erdi and the Toubou retreat was a Pyrrhic victory, which compromised Qaddafi's expectations of a quick and decisive offensive to conquer Chad. He sought the assistance of Sadiq al-Mahdi and his influence to obtain a diplomatic cease-fire in the real war that he had been losing in the B.E.T. Sadiq could not deny his Libyan supplier. A Sudanese delegation, including Governor Yusuf Bakheit of Darfur, was sent to Ndjamena where it was received with civility. The Sudanese had little to offer except propaganda from the government media in Khartoum, and when Habre refused their proposals, the talks collapsed and the Sudanese went home empty-handed.

Acheikh had suffered heavy casualties, and without the Libyans the CDR was not a serious fighting force. The Islamic Legion was not much better, for Goukouni's

Toubou were regrouping in the Tibesti, while Habre's FAP harassed the Libyans stationed at Gouro, Gourma, and Kika inflicting heavy losses. Throughout these weeks of desultory fighting, Goukouni, under house arrest in Tripoli, remained in telephonic contact with Adoum Togoi and his beleaguered forces in the B.E.T. until October 1986 when his phone was mysteriously disconnected. Although now isolated from his followers, Adoum Togoi, the Fada-born GUNT foreign minister and strong supporter of Goukouni who had become the FAN's first military commander after Goukouni had been arrested, now began to send peace feelers to Habre's representatives in the Tibesti. Togoi's defection was neither ideological nor religious but the recognition of the rules of relationships in a marginal environment with traditions forged over centuries of survival. While these discussions were proceeding in the time-honored ways of the desert and the Sahel, a column of 3,000 FANT Toubou moved southeast from the Tibesti to the Red Line to bivouac at Koinimina, just north of Oum Chalouba.[8]

Habre took pleasure in Goukouni's predicament, but he also knew that Acheikh and the Libyans would reinforce Fada before his FANT were sufficiently armed to take the offensive. In November 1986 Libyan jets flew innumerable sorties against the Toubou, Zaghawa, and Bedeiyat villages in the B.E.T. Thousands fled to seek sanctuary in caves or crossed into the refugee camps in Darfur.[9] The government of Chad denounced these air strikes as genocide against a people accustomed to armed raiders from the land not the sky. Chad pursued the case in the UN Security Council, which responded with all diplomatic speed by innocuous statements on this highly controversial subject. As before, the UN urged the parties to seek a peaceful settlement to their dispute. Unmoved, Habre prepared a counterattack to recapture the Ennedi.

Goukouni the Captive

Goukouni's demotion and house arrest once again caused extraordinary problems in Chad and thwarted Qaddafi's ambitions south of the Sahara. Qaddafi's relations with Goukouni were clearly ambivalent. On the one hand, Goukouni was the son of the *Derde,* the leader of the Toubou. On the other, he had failed as the hereditary leader to rally the Toubou, and worse, he had demonstrated his incompetence as a commander, disgraced by defeat on the field of battle. Qaddafi publicly criticized Goukouni's Toubou animosity toward Acheikh because he was an Arab and "not from their region." Whether Goukouni would ever again appear on the platform with Qaddafi was now as questionable as whether Qaddafi could return to conquer Chad. Jacques Chirac presented the official opinion of the French government by chastising Libya for its "occupation" and "open military aggression" in Chad. Qaddafi's response was uncharacteristically tepid if not conciliatory.[10] He seemed preoccupied by the subversive activities within Libya of a nascent Hizbollah movement, whose Islamist leaders were beginning to protest the government's policies, particularly those they regarded, to Qaddafi's consternation, as contrary to Islam.[11] These internal concerns were more immediate than the sun setting over Qaddafi's Arab, Islamic, and imperial ambitions south of the Sahara. On the night of 18 October Libyan security forces opened fire on Goukouni's residence. During the ensuing exchange of automatic weapon fire with the resident bodyguards, Goukouni was wounded in the stomach.[12] Reports swept through Tripoli that Libyan agents had sought to assassinate Goukouni. True or not, Goukouni was hospitalized and survived, but in the aftermath fifty-five officials of GUNT were placed under arrest. After a short hospitalization Goukouni was returned to his amiable house arrest and his convalescence. Qaddafi continued to call Goukouni his "friend." Acheikh, however, who had been visiting Brazzaville at the time of the shooting, returned to Tripoli and responded to the press with solemn equanimity that this lamentable incident was the appropriate punishment for Goukouni's "adventurist initiative," which had led to the battle, the defeat, and the humiliation at Fada.[13]

In his predictably mercurial fashion, Qaddafi abruptly revised his Chad policy in December 1986 when he expressed his lack of confidence in Acheikh by requesting Colonel Kamougue to reorganize GUNT. This bizarre game of musical chairs should have surprised no one, least of all Kamougue, who was in Lagos at the time, looking after his own interest. Kamougue suggested that the remodeled GUNT should be "the establishment of a very small organization whose mission would be to negotiate" with Ndjamena.[14] It was, as Kamougue knew, a proposition that Qaddafi would never forget nor forgive. In response, Qaddafi at once organized a meeting of his followers from southern Chad to be held in Benin in November 1986. At the same time, Goukouni's loyal commanders were outraged at this gratuitous seduction of Kamougue, and from their sanctuaries in the B.E.T., they too opened secret talks with Hissene Habre. Qaddafi's containment of Goukouni and his conspicuous attempt to conscript Kamougue did not impress Moussa Medela Yacine, Mahamat Abba Said, or Abdelkader Sanussi of the original FROLINAT, who would never accept Acheikh. The GUNT was shattered beyond repair, and Goukouni's army, including the surviving FROLINAT units, were no longer a threat to Habre.

Habre Conquers All

Habre was convinced that the meeting in Benin was nothing more than a transparent attempt by Qaddafi to recruit "mercenaries of all nationalities for the Islamic Legion." He publicly denounced his enemies and their support for Acheikh.[15] Shortly afterward at the twelfth Franco-African summit held at Lomé, *Le Monde* reported that Habre was "the star" of the meeting, and that he "was just as self-effacing as ever—to the extent of seeming distant—and . . . literally obsessed by the conviction that Chad exists because he is creating it."[16] At the meeting his former antagonist François Mitterrand described the problem of Chad as one that had progressed from civil war to international conflict, forcing France to send military assistance. In his speech, Prime Minister Jacques Chirac sternly announced that French foreign policy was "not liable to change. . . . It was conceived by General De Gaulle. It was he who set the main principles of it, drew up the foundations particularly through his personal and individual relations with the states. . . . He was respected and loved by everyone. Based on all this, the policy has continued under various presidents of the republic."[17]

After twenty years the problem of Chad at the twelfth Franco-African meeting had now become an apostrophe in the history of France in Chad. After two decades of independent French Africa, nothing had changed. Jacques Amalric argued in *Le Monde* that Mitterrand had now given Habre "the go-ahead to carry out a number of lightning raids well beyond the 16th parallel [and] to establish contact with [Goukouni] Oueddei's supporters."[18] *Le Nouvel Observateur* was dismayed that in Lebanon and Chad, France was "bearing the burden of its former colonialism," and thus, "its capitulation [in Chad] would mean resignation to pure violence and, above all, the definite renunciation of the universal characteristics of its culture." Habre was certainly no fool. He was well aware of the ambiguous character of French support. Allies, like armies, were "those which are victorious"; this was the Napoleonic maxim of the Reagan administration. The battle for Chad had as little subtlety as its deserts. It was the difference between sand and sky, between footprints in the wadi and the rock outcrops on the horizon. It was the relationship of those who had come throughout the centuries south of the Sahara and those who were there before them, the "invaders and the invaded."[19] The Egyptians were even more forthcoming than Mitterrand was. Egyptian foreign minister Boutros Boutros-Ghali arrived to deliver a letter to Habre from President Hosni Mubarak promising his continued support to share Egyptian information on the Sudan, particularly the activities of Sadiq al-Mahdi, who had just been elected prime minister, and on Libyan subversion in the western Sudan.

This twelfth meeting of the leaders from France and Francophone Africa demonstrated, if nothing else, the ambiguity of French policy in Chad, torn between history and economic expediency, on the one hand, and the disarray and credibility of the Chad rebels and their unpredictable supporter on the other. In these decades of dismay, Habre in 1986 had not only survived but had overcome most of the rebel pack that had begun their revolutionary careers in opposition to Ngartha Tombalbaye. Despite being a Muslim and having demonstrated his devotion during the pilgrimage to Mecca, Habre had received the support of many non-Muslim African leaders as long as his FANT succeeded in keeping the Libyans at bay. Habre had a talent for governing that demanded no dissent. By 1986 even his Arab enemies had to admit he had outlasted the FROLINAT and destroyed the Libyans who depended upon the Chad insurgents—Acheikh's force in Borkou and Ennedi, Goukouni's Toubou in the Tibesti, and the Codo rebels active in southern Chad and presumably those loyal to Kamougue. Libyan arms went to support Acheikh's Arab-dominated forces from the CDR in eastern

Chad, those Toubou who had become the mercenaries of the Libyans and had begun to understand that they were "just a Kleenex for Qaddafi."[20]

The dissension within GUNT was its destruction. Habre knew this well, and it was now time for him to exploit the principal weakness of his enemies. Before his entourage left Lomé at the conclusion of the Franco-African meeting, they had "whispered to journalists" that the FANT would soon begin the reconquest of Ennedi.[21] Although the Red Line remained calm, the 6,000 Libyan and Islamic Legion troops in Darfur were daily receiving reinforcements. Their presence, moreover, had become so flagrant that Sid Ahmad al-Hussein, the minister of the interior in Khartoum, accused Libya of "spying in Western Sudan." The Libyan military was using "the cover of humanitarian missions" to roam freely throughout the vast expanse of northern Darfur beyond Kutum where Islamic Legion units were being prepared to reinforce Acheikh's contingent at Fada. It was time for Habre to launch a preemptive strike.[22]

Libya Attacks Goukouni

Despite the military and personal defeats he had suffered in 1986, Qaddafi was still determined to pursue his Pan-Arab, Islamic, and imperial adventures south of the Sahara. He had now conceived of a new strategy to promote his designs and end the months of "armed peace." He was tired of responding to Chirac, who had argued at Lomé that Libya had sought to destabilize Chad through "open military aggression." As far as Qaddafi was concerned, it was France that had to withdraw its troops from Chad. It was France that had destabilized much of Francophone Africa. It was France that had organized coups in the Central African Republic, Chad, Congo, Guinea, and Niger. Qaddafi warned that if the French were to return to Chad, Libya would match force with force. If France were to fight in Chad, Libya would fight. As Chad's neighbor to the north, Libya should be permitted "to guarantee Chad's peace and stability." He was adamant that the Habre regime in Ndjamena was "illegal."[23] After the failure throughout the past two decades of maneuver and manipulation of surrogates and his own mercenaries to achieve his ambitions in Chad, the time had now come for the big battalions. The Libyan offensive was now to be under the direction of Musa Kusa, the thirty-six-year-old director of the International Center for Revolution in Tripoli. Musa was, not surprisingly, a very influential member of the Libyan ruling hierarchy. He had been expelled from Britain in 1980 for his clandestine activities, remarkable for their incompetence. After he was asked to leave England, he soon surfaced in northern Darfur where he was seen at Kutum and El Fasher.[24]

The French with their long experience and intimate sources of information were predicting that Libya was about to advance beyond the Red Line. American intelligence did not agree, expecting that Libya was about to attack the remnants of Goukouni's Toubou north of the 16th parallel. Everyone appeared to agree that the FANT could not sustain any attack north of the Red Line. Nevertheless,

Habre was convinced that his best interests were to strike before his enemies had prepared a massive offensive, which his troops could not forestall. He had the support of the Reagan administration and "with the blessings of the Americans," he would attack. At Lomé Mitterrand had accepted the fact that the survival of Hissene Habre was "the justification of [French] policy undertaken since 1983."[25] This did not mean that Mitterrand approved of any FANT offensive. He had long regarded Chad as a peripheral interest to France. He desperately wanted to be rid of the legacy of Charles de Gaulle, and the riffraff of chieftains, for whom he had nothing but contempt. This intractable problem of Chad, in which the American robust enthusiasm for desert warfare was no consolation, was a difficulty best sent to the UN Security Council to be buried in its bureaucracy and where debate would work to the advantage of France and its president.

Before any such debate could even occur, however, Musa Kusa and Colonel Rifi Ali Sharif, commander of Islamic Legion and Libyan forces in Chad and the senior Libyan officer in the Fezzan, launched a surprise assault on Goukouni's strongholds at Zouar and Bardai. Their mission was to drive the Toubou from the B.E.T., who would be replaced by Arab Libyans with Acheikh Ibn Oumar as governor of a new province incorporated into Libya.[26] On 11 December 1986 the promise by Muammar Qaddafi made ten years before and repeated during the past decade of a Toubou Protectorate in the B.E.T. was consigned to the dustbin of history. Two columns of heavily armed Libyan troops from Sebha merged with a third from Aozou to advance through the Korizo Pass and attack Zouar. Surrounded, Goukouni's Toubou defenders requested supplies from Habre who, in turn, asked the French to respond despite the fact that Zouar was north of the Red Line. Within forty-eight hours two French transports dropped arms, ammunition, and food at Zouar and Wour, which were "threatened by famine and [Libyan] reprisals." In Tripoli the Libyan foreign minister officially warned the French ambassador that the French action in Chad would be regarded as "a serious threat to the security and integrity of Libya."[27] On 19 December more than 8,000 Libyan troops attacked at Zouar. The United States immediately sent $15 million in emergency assistance to Ndjamena, and on 29 December a C5-A cargo plane landed at Ndjamena carrying military vehicles, weapons, and ammunition. Secretary of State George Schultz, on his first trip to West Africa for discussions with West African leaders, had placed the problem of Chad at the top of his agenda.

It appears that the French sought to restrain Habre by warning him that their aircraft would not provide cover if he sent his troops north to aid the beleaguered Toubou in Zouar. Habre was not about to be intimidated by French caution and by the New Year unilaterally ordered his troops to advance across the Red Line. The FANT needed no encouragement, and moving with great speed in their armed Toyotas, bypassed Faya to link up with Goukouni's Toubou. The joint force counterattacked, and with all the enthusiasm of the traditional Toubou *razzia*, the warriors of the desert now well equipped, overwhelmed the Libyans and recaptured Zouar. The Libyans suffered heavy casualties and lost all their military supplies, particularly armored vehicles and light weapons. Within hours of this dramatic Toubou victory, the FANT attacked Fada with equal éclat to overwhelm the Libyan garrison there after a fierce firefight and the most costly battle in the Chad wars. On 2 January 1987 the FANT took Fada, demolishing scores of Soviet T-55 tanks and killing more than half the 1,000 Libyan regulars and mercenaries from the Islamic Legion. It was not a cheap victory for the FANT. They lost more than four hundred of their most seasoned veterans.

After the victories at Zouar and Fada the FANT integrated thousands of disillusioned Toubou from Goukouni's GUNT in an ethnic agreement characteristic of the Sahelian frontier, where blood flows deeper than water. Adoum Togoi, one of Goukouni's captains, was now quite prepared to rally in victory with his distant kinsman Mahamat Nouri, Habre's minister of the interior, and the FANT commander, Ibrahim Muhammad Itno. Having neutralized the Toubou opposition north of the Red Line, the FANT advanced against Faya from the northwest and southeast. The latter column was commanded by Hassan Djamous, a Zaghawa born at Fada, who sent a diversionary column against Faya before advancing in strength against the giant Libyan air base at Wadi Doum.[28] Although Radio Ndjamena broadcast its tiresome martial music interrupted by declarations that the "Libyan slave traders" would soon be driven from Chad, these slave traders, now possessed massive firepower. Libyan jets strafed FANT positions north of the Red Line with impunity, but when four MIG-23s bombed Arada and Biltine south of the Red Line, the French retaliated. On 7 January ten French jets attacked Wadi Doum with "runway destruction bombs" to inflict extensive damage. This was not just a demonstration of French air power or an exercise in French resolve to protect a client state. Mitterrand's instincts, as in the past, might urge caution, but Prime Minister Chirac was delighted to embarrass Qaddafi by supporting Habre and his government at Ndjamena. Mitterrand continued to insist that French troops would not support any advance above the 16th parallel yet French planes continued to drop food, munitions, and fuel to FANT units operating north of the Red Line. Irrespective of the policies and positions of the adversaries, the problem of Chad continued to produce a vigorous arms race as the practical manifestation of determined and powerful patrons to secure a personal advantage over a wasteland controlled by feudal barons and their intrepid followers. In Washington the Pentagon was debating whether to send more aid to Habre. In Ndjamena Habre met with the French chief-of-staff, General Jean Saulnier, to appeal for more weapons. In Moscow Qaddafi's envoy to the Soviet Union requested more arms. Weapons were needed to counter the resurgence of a neocolonialist France, which sought to maintain its stranglehold on Chad, the Central African Republic, Cameroon, and Niger.

Qaddafi Attacks "Ibri"

On 12 January 1986 Qaddafi addressed the West African *fuqura,* the holy men, and those from the Islamic *Dawa'a,* the Islamic charitable organization, who had gathered in Tripoli. Ironically, his presentation coincided with the time that his forces in Chad were in desperate retreat from defeat. In another rambling discourse the Chad "revolution" was condemned as the product of a Christian minority "controlling the Islamic majority in Chad." Extolling the Islamic virtues of the savanna grasslands south of the 16th parallel, Qaddafi denounced Habre who had "split from his Muslim brothers and joined the Christians." Qaddafi then declared that Habre was an "Ibri," a Hebrew, and that the Toubou were reared by "Hebrews." Habre was the kept man of Israel, France, and Washington. Qaddafi had created the specter of an "America [that] wants to move against Sudan so that it reaches the Red Sea, wants to work against Libya so that it reaches the Mediterranean, and against Nigeria so that it reaches the Atlantic."[29]

There was nothing new in this declamation to those dedicated civil servants of the international intelligence community who listen to the aberrations of the world's leaders. The rhetoric of Qaddafi attributing the success of Habre to a Hebraic past and his more recent intervention only confirmed the bizarre frustrations of a world leader with more money than responsibility. Qaddafi's *jihad* against Israel is well known. More important was Qaddafi's eternal quest to seek justification for his Pan-Arab, Islamic, and imperial ambitions south of the Sahara, which were more reminiscent of Mussolini than Muhammad. This was no different than the dilemma of Muhammid al-Amin ibn Muhammad Ninga, more commonly known today in Chad as Shaykh al-Kanami. Al-Kanami was born in the Fezzan of those who later sired the *Derde* and his sons. In the first decades of the nineteenth century Al-Kanami dominated the central Sahel from the steppes of Bornu in the west to Kanem in central Chad, but he never reestablished the ancient kingdom over the eastern state of Wadai. He died in 1835, but there are few who will not remember his determination to sustain the unity of Chad, then known as Kanem-Bornu, against the predators north of the Sahara.

The Libyan troops attacked Yebbi Bou in the Tibesti and Kalait in Ennedi. They were routed with many casualties while the flanking column of the Islamic Legion advancing through Niger toward Zouar was trapped and destroyed. In less than two months the Libyan army had lost 2,000 men and mountains of arms and ammunition. The Libyan treasury had been plundered for weapons, and its oil wealth squandered to satisfy Qaddafi's military dreams at great cost to the Toubou Gourane guerrillas and their Toyota Chariots, which had destroyed his "modern" army.[30]

Although the Qaddafa were desert Arabs, their past included the intermixture of conquerors from time forgotten—Greeks, Romans, Berbers, Kanuri, Turks, and Italians—who had occupied Libya. Muammar Qaddafi had always expressed his fascination for the long and ancient history of the Maghrib, Northern Africa, and its interior. To the Greeks who dominated commerce and empire in the Mediterranean, the coast west of Egypt was known as *Libye*. The Roman emperor Diocletian referred to his granary and principal supply of olive oil in Cyrenaica as *Libya*. Qaddafi's Libya did not officially exist until the end of the Italian conquest and the proclamation of the colony of *Libia* in 1934. His ignorance of Chad was matched only by his ignorance of the Africans south of the Sahel, and he would have been well advised to heed the advice of Herodotus in 460 B.C. One does not intrude into treacherous territory inhabited by those who wish to defend it with determination and the knowledge of the landscape to protect their way of life. Indeed, the war for Chad had plunged the Libyan people "into an unprecedented tragedy," in which "the butcher's bill has been so steep that the relatives of a Libyan soldier killed in Chad are not now informed even of the bare fact of his death. And a final disengagement is not in sight."[31] There were now reports that Libya's radical Islamists—"previously discounted as a serious threat"—had revived and that a clandestine "Party of God," like the Hizbollah in Lebanon, had become active. Qaddafi moved quickly to crush this Islamic dissent closing "48 Islamic institutions" and exercising strict control over the mosques and Friday prayers.[32]

When the critics of the regime denounced the secular authority in the sermons from the sanctuary of the *minbar* (pulpit) of the mosque, Qaddafi's reactions increased in fury proportional to the defeat of his armed forces and were ever more irresponsible. Increasingly concerned about Qaddafi's behavior, President Mitterrand reluctantly recalled Jacques Foccart from retirement to meet at Cotonou with Qaddafi's confidant, Ali al-Turayki, the former foreign minister and now the Libyan representative at the United Nations. Turayki was emphatic that Qaddafi, in defeat, wanted no confrontation with France, but both Foccart and Turayki knew that Qaddafi would not negotiate with Habre.[33] This volatile situation continued until February 1987 when there was another flurry of diplomatic and political activity. When the OAU secretary general arrived in Tripoli, he offered to mediate the Chad-Libya dispute. He soon gave up. Sadiq al-Mahdi then appeared but, not surprisingly, contributed nothing. Next, Acheikh Ibn Oumar tried unsuccessfully to gather the various Chad factions together at Brazzaville. Finally, when the fighting continued throughout February the French prime minister, Jacques Chirac, met privately with the OAU chairman Denis Sassou-Nguessou, president of the Congo, in Brazzaville, who also offered a peace plan that found no takers in Tripoli, Ndjamena, or Paris.[34]

Despite his apparent disgrace, or perhaps because of it, Goukouni Oueddei suddenly appeared in public to urge a cease-fire. He then immediately dashed off to Algiers where a few hours later he publicly appealed to the African nations to recognize the Habre government. He was careful to condition this extraordinary volte-face by refusing to join Habre's government, for his family was being held hostage in Tripoli. Dumbstruck, an astonished Qaddafi asserted that there had to be "some misunderstanding." He acknowledged Goukouni "as chief of Tibesti," and despite what Goukouni may have said in Tripoli or Algiers, the Teda would "never allow Hissene Habre in that region."[35] Goukouni's betrayal was not lost on Wadal Abdelkader Kamougue, in exile in Libreville, who promptly bid adieu to his Gabonese hosts, explaining "today, it is my turn to return home." On arriving in Ndjamena this quintessential opportunist, now much chastened, discreetly condemned his former fellow rebels. "I regret that certain leaders do not understand the need to make a sort of brave men's peace, because in the end the greatest victim is the Chadian people and I regret that some fellow countrymen have been exploiting these Chadians." He joined the Action Coordination Committee (CAC) of the Chad governing body, the CDR, and the Chadian Democratic Front (FDT), the political party of former southern rebels who had just committed themselves to Habre. Hoping to be given an important post in the government, he claimed that his return to Ndjamena would help forge "territorial unity" and allow the government "to regain its sovereignty throughout its territory."[36]

Libyan Forces in Darfur

While the Chadian deck was being reshuffled, Libya increased its force in the B.E.T. to 11,000 men and a reserve of another 8,000 men at Ma'tan as-Sarra and Kufra in anticipation of a FANT offensive. The Libyan air force flew daily sorties to bomb the FANT headquarters at Zouar. In mid-February skirmishing increased around Bardai and Zouar, and a Libyan convoy arrived in El Fasher carrying food and medical supplies for the Islamic Legion mobilizing on the Sudan frontier. As the Libyan army regrouped and prepared to launch its own offensive, Qaddafi had not been inactive. He sought to break his diplomatic isolation in January 1987 by concluding a bilateral agreement with the Sudan involving cooperation in economic, trade, and cultural matters. The economic agreement, which included substantial amounts of financial assistance to the Sudan, was very ephemeral, for Libya's oil revenues had fallen "by three-quarters since 1980," and Libyan arms purchases had left the Libyan treasury with little cash reserves.[37] Qaddafi was determined to persevere in his ambitions, however, and in February 1987 proposed the economic integration of Kufra and Darfur "as a first step toward the establishment of the unity between the two fraternal countries."[38] While the Libyan press extolled the virtues of "brother" Sadiq al-Mahdi, this piece of divine inspiration simply confirmed the deep distrust of Qaddafi by the Khartoum press. In Khartoum, there was no interest, and indeed hostility, for such a bizarre idea, which was regarded as a gratuitous prospect from an arrogant and irresponsible troublemaker at a time when insecurity in Darfur had become more provocative with every passing day.

Qaddafi, however, used Sadiq to buy time, and in early February the Sudan foreign minister, Taj al-Din, visited Ndjamena where he urged Habre to send a Chadian representative to Khartoum for a "secret" meeting with Libyan representatives.[39] Habre agreed, and the talks were convened in Khartoum in March only to fail when the Libyans refused to discuss Chad-Libyan differences, demanding instead that Habre accept a reconciliation conference involving all Chadian factions. The negotiations collapsed, but their confidentiality was quickly violated in order for Tripoli to assert that Libya had made a good faith effort to "settle the Chadian issue" by reconciling "all the conflicting Chadian factions."[40]

The Chad government responded to Libya's description of these "secret" talks by insisting that the negotiations had failed because of the Libyan demand that its troops remain in the B.E.T., the sovereign territory of Chad. The Chad government angrily belittled Sadiq's claim that the talks had resulted in a cease-fire and argued that Libyans in Darfur, the heartland of Sadiq's political power, were, in fact, a real threat to Sadiq and his government. In response Libya asserted, "We in Libya do not allow anyone to speak of the presence of Libyan forces in Sudan because that would mean changing the facts. The forces there are GUNT forces and it is of no concern to us whether they withdraw or not," for they were only there "trying to liberate their country, Chad."[41]

Although Sadiq had denied that there were foreign troops in Sudan, travelers reported the presence of some 400 trucks carrying Libyan troops "in the areas of Al-Junaynah [Kutub], Al-Tinah [Tine], Kalabsh, and Wad Hura," who were bivouacked in Darfur 100 miles east of the Chad-Sudan boundary. The Libyan government disingenuously claimed that these troops were needed to guard relief convoys in regions infamous for banditry, and Libyan agents continued to recruit in Dar Zaghawa. The Sudanese were promised generous employment in Libya— Qaddafi bragged that "we will bring cheap workers from all over the world" to build the domestic economy—only to be coerced into the Islamic Legion. When the Libyan press printed a series of articles in February asserting that the Sudanese army had "launched an operation to purge" Darfur of Chadian troops, the Islamic Legion had crossed into Chad in two columns of 1, 000 men each to Wadi Doum and Fada.[42] Ironically, the Libyan presence in Darfur had long been acknowledged over Radio Bardai, the GUNT clandestine radio. It also reported that Acheikh's National Liberation Army (ANL) had attacked Adre, the strategic Chad border town on the El Fasher-Abeche road, where it destroyed "the military camp, the customs and excise office, and several vehicles." The Islamic Legion had also established a stronghold at Tine, a Zaghawa village that straddled the Chad-Sudan boundary, from which it sallied forth "dozens of times in less than a year" to attack the FANT positions in Chad.[43]

As both sides prepared for a new round of fighting, Radio Tripoli began a campaign of disinformation to demoralize the FANT and its troops. One of the great revolutions in the lives of those who roamed the desert and the Sahel was the transistor radio carried next to the water skins and listened to with a concentration usually reserved for the discussions in the councils during the long, cold Saharan nights. By the 1970s every nomad and cultivator possessed these inexpensive purveyors of lascivious music, soccer scores, and political commentary, which introduced them to a world that they and their elders had not previously known. Radio Tripoli saturated the airways with reports that Idriss Deby, the FANT commander and an important member of Habre's executive bureau, had defected to the GUNT. Deby, like Hassan Djamous, was a FANT commander of great talent. He was equally at home in Dar Zaghawa and Darfur where he had received his early education. He had returned to Ndjamena in December 1986 after spending eighteen months at the Paris Higher Inter-Service School

(War College) and thereafter was often seen with Habre. He denied with good humor, not expected from a Bedouin warrior from Chad, that he was contemplating going over to the GUNT, for it was a Libyan creation.[44]

Despite these denials, there appeared something amiss within the FANT, for Ndjamena radio continued to announce unconfirmed government victories to disguise the fact that the war had also cost the lives of many of Habre's best soldiers. The firefights of the past may have produced many Libyan body bags, but it was at great cost to the FANT who had lost many of their very best in victory. There were other problems. The drought and war during these years had escalated a historic tradition of banditry that could no longer be romanticized by the *Riffs* of the desert, made more formidable by devastating need and the impersonal destruction of automatic weapons. These arms of indiscriminate killing and wanton looting were inimical to all the traditions of the frontier peoples. There were now widespread depredations, no longer the old-style *razzia*, in Dar Zaghawa and northern Darfur, including the theft of Zaghawa and Bedeiyat camels and other livestock.[45] Nevertheless, the FANT was active across a broad front in the B.E.T. Habre confirmed his confidence in Deby by naming him the chief of a mission that arrived in Washington in March 1987 in search of arms.

Meanwhile, to frustrate any Libyan offensive from Darfur along the frontier from Geneina to Dar Zaghawa, the French strengthened their forces in Wadai and in March 1987 redeployed units of Operation Épervier in eastern Chad. In a display of strength the French increased the Force d'Action Rapide to 2,400 men equipped with Crotal and Stinger missiles and 200mm cannon at Biltine and Abeche. The runway at Abeche, a paved airstrip 132 miles south of the Red Line that had been badly damaged in 1979 and 1981, was repaired and the dirt strip at Biltine, 80 miles south of the Red Line, was improved and a military depot hastily constructed. Radar was installed at Abeche to track Libyan planes, and the French extended their patrols to the Sudan border. These decisions were the result of the intervention of Michel Aurillac, the new French minister for cooperation. After the 1986 legislative elections, which had brought Jacques Chirac to power, Aurillac was appointed to revive the moribund ministry that had languished under Jean Pierre Cot and Christian Nucci. The ministry was now to advise the government on African affairs, a role that had previously been the prerogative of the special advisor to the president, Jacques Foccart and Guy Penne. Aurillac had first been to Chad in 1959 and justified his decisions as necessary to "close the Sudanese frontier," to provide needed "air cover," and to demonstrate French determination "to aid Chad on a long-term basis." Resurfacing the Biltine runway would "provide a new platform for French warplanes if Habre needed air support in the north or for transport planes to help keep supplies moving to his troops."[46] French deployment of its formidable forces not only extended their presence in Wadai but also brought stability, a halt the sporadic advance of Acheikh's eastern army, the old Vulcan Force, and the return of Chad refugees from their sanctuaries in Darfur.

Qaddafi and Khartoum

In a rambling speech during a meeting of the Sebha General People's Congress on 2 March, Qaddafi's meandering soliloquies created confusion among his listeners, and some began to question his leadership, which appeared to be the result of revelation rather than reason. He no longer had any "conflict with Chad" nor with Habre, who in a miraculous metamorphosis "had never been on the side of those who are against us." Qaddafi reminded the assembled that "Habre was one of the FROLINAT leaders—alongside Goukouni, Muhammad ibn Said, Al Bughalani, Acyl." In a flight of fancy he described Habre as not only "one of the FROLINAT leaders" but one who "was brought up in Libya; he studied in Libya. After the revolution he was part of the FROLINAT's leadership that was set up in Libya. He could not be hostile to us and Libya could not be hostile to someone who has a history like that."[47] This may have been his usual bizarre bravado, but Qaddafi left no doubt at the end of his speech that he still supported Acheikh and the GUNT. These words appear to have confused his listeners, but Major Abd al-Salam Jalloud was more explicit when it came turn for his contribution. He was emphatic that there could be no solution to the problem of Chad until the French withdrew. "Chad is on our border . . . and if France has one reason for intervention there . . . we have one thousand reasons." Jalloud warned that Libya had been on the verge of an "African solution" but French forces had "spoiled everything."[48] At Sebha Qaddafi may have appeared confused or conciliatory, but Jalloud was determined and implacable. Libya continued its air attacks on the Ennedi throughout March. Habre warned Sadiq that the Libyans were mobilizing at Tine to renew their three-pronged offensive. As before, one column was expected to attack from Aozou to take the Tibesti. A second would advance from Ma'tan as-Sarra to attack Fada. A third, the eastern army, would march from Darfur against Fada and threaten Abeche. Habre was ready.

Victory at Wadi Doum, Darfur, and Ounianga

In early March 1987 the FANT took the initiative before the heat of summer to attack the Libyans in a series of battles near Zouar. The Libyans, of course, responded with ever more sorties from their aircraft against Fada and ordered Acheikh and his eastern army in Darfur to advance into Chad. His column proceeded, as have thousands before them, along the historic frontier through which have passed the feudatory followers of the border chieftains, the merchants, and the pilgrims from Darfur and Wadai and beyond to Wadi Doum and Fada. It should have been no surprise that they would be ambushed at Bir Sora. The FANT, equipped with a fleet of heavily armed but extremely mobile pick-up trucks, the famous Toyota Brigade, trapped the column in the defile at Bir Sora and destroyed it. The only innovation in this reconstruction of the Battle of Thermopylae in a similar defile between Sparta and the Persians in 480 B.C. was neither courage nor determination but the effective use by the FANT of Toyota technology, which made them victorious. A thousand men of the Islamic Legion were rushed forward only to fall into the same trap in the same defile to the disbelief of the FANT commanders. Like those of Acheikh's eastern army who had preceded them, they suffered heavy casualties before the survivors fled to safety in the north. The jubilant FANT pursued the remnants of Acheikh's eastern army and the legionnaires, moving more swiftly if not more dependably in their Toyotas than by camel. On 22 March a strike force composed of hundreds of Toyota trucks surrounded the huge Libyan airstrip at Wadi Doum.

The Libyan air base at Wadi Doum had been built by the East Germans in order for Libyan aircraft to overfly not only the Ennedi but also southern Chad. Operation Épervier had bombed its runways, but the damage was soon repaired. It was an inviting target, a symbol of how air power might conquer a vast and hostile environment that no one in the long history of the Sahara and Sahel had ever conquered or ruled for long. *Le Monde* had predicted that Habre would attack Wadi Doum with arms supplied by the United States.[49] Wadi Doum was considered impregnable. Ahmad Goura, a thirty-one-year-old Faya-born Toubou, commander of Habre's presidential guard and a graduate of the United States infantry school at Fort Benning, Georgia, conducted a thorough reconnaissance and thought otherwise. He advised Habre to attack.

The FANT accomplished one of the great victories in the history of desert warfare. Avoiding a ring of minefields, the FANT armada of Toyota pick-up trucks firing French "Milan" missiles drove through the entrance of the base to overwhelm the GUNT and Islamic Legionnaires. Libyan armored vehicles were demolished and a hundred Libyan tanks were captured or destroyed. Twenty planes were burnt in their revetments or along the runway and the two-mile strip was severely damaged. A Soviet missile radar installation under construction since 1985 by the East Germans was destroyed. In four days of fighting 1,200 Libyan soldiers were killed, and the facilities for the Libyan and Islamic Legion garrison of 4,500 were leveled. Three hundred FANT were killed. Gouara Lassou and Hassan Djamous were among the hundreds wounded.[50] The war materiel captured—batteries of Sam-6 missiles, fifteen L-39 light aircraft, two Tu-22 bombers, a MIG-21 fighter—had cost half a billion dollars. Today $500 million appears a manageable sum, but in Libya in 1986 it represented a massive debt when the oil revenues to pay for it had precipitously dropped from $20 billion in 1980 to $4 billion in 1986. In Libya Qaddafi could hardly be satisfied with the execrable performance of his troops and with the unexpected determination and military competence of those whom he had called "a handful of barefoot Africans." The Gourane were exuberant in their stunning victory, but Gouara Lassou urged vigilance for "a wounded fool is always dangerous."[51] Djamous was evacuated to Val-de-Grâce hospital in Paris, with a head wound.

This astonishing victory took the West completely by surprise. In one single stroke Libya had lost a seemingly impregnable fortification and its most important base south of the Aozou Strip. Not content with victory at Wadi Doum, however, the FANT struck across the frontier into Darfur where it clashed with Libyans and Islamic Legionnaires at Abu Suruj, Abu Qamari, Kutum, Kalas, and along the Wadi Howar. In the Sudan Sadiq al-Mahdi sought to make the best of an embarrassing situation during his speech before the Sudanese parliament, insisting that Libyan troops who had launched attacks against Chad from Darfur had done so only after they had been told to leave the Sudan. No one believed him, least of all his *Ansar* from the West.

With the loss of Wadi Doum, the GUNT base at Faya was outflanked. Fearing they would be isolated, the Libyans retired on 27 March leaving behind 3,000 Chad civilians to welcome the FANT.[52] Faya, the strategic oasis and former French headquarters, Faya Largeau, for the B.E.T., had a population before the Libyan occupation of 25,000 inhabitants. After they had protested the execution of "three senior leaders of the Goukouni faction," who had been accused of assisting the opposition to the Libyan occupation, the Gourane of Faya had been systematically persecuted. The Libyans retired to their base at Ounianga Kebir, itself an important junction at the head of the Borkou Valley some sixty miles south of the Aozou Strip and the gateway through which Libyan convoys traveled from the Aozou to Fada. Once again the FANT struck with lightning speed on 30 March to overwhelm the Libyan garrison at Ounianga and win yet another dramatic victory. Their reward was another huge cache of Libyan war materiel. Two days later the FANT took Gouro from which the Libyans retreated with their surrogates to end, for the moment, Libyan imperialism in Borkou and Ennedi. The Fezzan remained secure, but the Sahel and northern Chad had been lost.

In defeat that could not be denied, Qaddafi immediately ordered the reorganization of his army and air force in a display of desperation, "presumably to decrease the risk of a conspiracy" involving disaffected officers.[53] Exhilarated by Habre's victories the United States promised an additional $10 million in military assistance, and overnight Ndjamena became a preferred stop on the itinerary of American diplomats. In April Ambassador to Chad, John Blane, who himself had been involved in Chadian affairs for a decade, welcomed Assistant Secretary of Defense Richard Armitage for talks with Habre and other Chad officials. The United States, which had already promised $32 million in military assistance—including some sophisticated ground-to-air missiles—offered funds to "strengthen the development ministries of Chad." The State Department then urged Habre to use his stunning victories to "devote desperately needed attention to the country's economic development."[54]

The Fezzan Threatened and the Hadjerai Revolt

After the whirlwind of the FANT assault and the storm of battle had settled into the sands, the losses to Libya were staggering, considering the land, the number of combatants, and the equipment available to them. In just a few months, 9,000 of the 71,000 soldiers of the Libyan army were killed. Qaddafi was in "a very bad situation," and even French intelligence, as well as the Europeans and the United States, began to speculate how long the Libyans could sustain such heavy losses, which had affected so many Libyan families.[55] The FANT now began to pursue the Libyan retreat along the ancient caravan route northward to the Fezzan in the sovereign territory of Libya itself. Qaddafi instinctively turned to his perpetual supplier of weapons, the Soviet Union, but now without the abundant cash reserves of the past. He "threatened to join the Warsaw Pact," another bizarre idea that even astonished those who had become accustomed to his whims and wild notions. The Soviet foreign ministry "refused even to acknowledge that the Libyan leader had uttered the offer," and the Soviet leadership "confidentially contacted U.S. officials," expressing concern that the Chad war could escalate. The United States responded that Libya was a Soviet "client state . . . [and Moscow] "should exercise more responsibility in restraining its aggressive behavior."[56] Rebuffed by Moscow, Qaddafi reacted by firing rhetorical thunderbolts at Presidents Reagan and François Mitterrand and vowed that a reign of terror would strike Europe. It appeared that a reign of terror of a different kind was about to attack him in southern Libya. With the Libyan forces everywhere in retreat, the Red Line was irrelevant, and when Libya continued its bombing of northern Chad, the French defense minister, André Giraud, implied that French forces would no longer feel restrained by that artificial barrier.[57] When the bombing continued, the French Force d'Action Rapide of Operation Épervier moved across the Red Line into Faya where they began to clear the minefields and provide humanitarian and logistic assistance. As momentary calm descended on the B.E.T., Libya still retained control of the Aozou Strip. Goukouni reappeared after his brief apostasy in Tripoli. Acheikh Ibn Oumar's forces were rearmed, and despite a myriad of diplomatic efforts by the OAU to impose a cease-fire, Qaddafi was not about to come to the conference table as long as French troops remained in Chad and Libya held the Aozou.[58]

Ironically, Habre's triumph was almost compromised by the Hadjerai revolt in eastern Chad. The Hadjerai leadership had mistrusted Habre ever since the mysterious death of Idriss Miskene. Miskene had been the brilliant, educated member of the Kinja clan of the Hadjerai. His sudden death at a young age had aroused suspicion of foul play amongst his kin. These doubts lingered despite the indisputable proof that Miskene had died of natural causes. In April 1987, in the full flush of victory over the GUNT and Libya, the ghost of Miskene returned after an encounter involving two young Gourane and a Hadjerai maiden in Ndjamena in April 1987. Reports of the incident escalated, resulting in protests by the Hadjerai community to which Habre responded with uncharacteristic haste and invective, dismissing his Hadjerai member of cabinet, Gody Haroun. Haroun fled to Guera where, among his kin he denounced Habre in April and immediately began to organize yet another rebel army to oppose Habre. In Guera, Haroun was supported by the prominent Hadjerai politician, Maldoum Abbas, who was hostile to Habre and who had mobilized his opposition with the founding of the Mouvement Patriotique du Salut (MPS). Haroun could now appear in Tripoli claiming that he was leading an army of 2,000 Hadjerai rebels against the government of Chad.[59] Supported by Libyan arms the MPS soon emerged as a dangerous fighting force in Batha and Guera. Government troops were sent to restore order, and the rebellion in Guera was infiltrated by Habre's secret police. Jails began to fill. "Enemies" disappeared. The government gave no cognizance to the OAU African Charter of Human Rights, which it had ratified in June 1986.

In May the OAU ad hoc subcommittee on the Chad-Libya boundary dispute convened in Libreville but soon adjourned when Libya refused to attend the session. Chaired by President Omar Bongo of Gabon, it had sought to use the decisive victories by the government of Chad in the B.E.T. to resolve the Aozou dispute. The committee prepared a report for the July 1987 OAU summit meeting. The Sudanese had been active attempting to arrange a Chad-Libya-Sudan meeting, which was abandoned when Libya refused to attend. Next Mitterrand and the Algerian President Chadli Benjedid sought to bring about reconciliation between Habre and Goukouni without success. During a visit to Paris in July Habre was urged to consider using the International Court of Justice as a means to resolve the Aozou impasse. Habre had considered this option, but within days the diplomatic offensive occurring in Africa and Europe was overtaken by the war in the B.E.T.

The FANT Invades Libya

On 8 August 1987 the FANT launched at attack on the Aozou oasis, which had been occupied by Libya since 1973. Planned by Hassan Djamous and Ahmad Goura, their forces easily overran the Libyan garrison for another stunning victory, a triumph for Habre and more humiliation for Qaddafi, which continued the deflation of his prestige at home and abroad. Libyan troops and the Islamic Legion were rushed to the Tanoa air base on the border between Libya and the Aozou Strip from which Libyan planes were flying daily bombing raids. In consultations with their Soviet advisors, the Libyan commanders launched the first of three counterattacks on 19 August. They failed to retake the oasis, bur when the extensive aerial bombardment and the extensive use of napalm continued, the FANT could no longer hold Aozou. They vanished like their forebears into the unlimited sand sea and the canyons of the desert, with their wadis and deep wells known to those who live on the land and not to those who sweep out of the sky.

The FANT offensive appeared to have been stopped at Aozou. The State Department praised "Mr. Habre [for he] has done a very effective job of nation-building under very difficult circumstances. . . . There is no parallel in Africa to his ability to co-opt his opposition."[60] The American officials involved in African affairs respected Habre for his candor in contrast to the dissimulation from the

French concerning the problem of Chad. The Americans could not condone Habre's indifference to human rights but understood and had supported his determination to retain his authority in Ndjamena as the president of a state where in the past its leaders had been characterized more by personal despotism and greed than the welfare of their subjects. Having retired from Aozou, the FANT reformed to cross the Libyan border in September. The objective of this strike to the northeast was the mammoth Libyan air base at Ma'tan as-Sarra. Once again the Libyans were taken totally by surprise. For those who lived and fought in the desert, this was not unusual; and now the hostile differences of terrain, hitherto traversed by camels, were even more efficiently crossed by the Toyota, aided by sophisticated reconnaissance from above. The Libyans at Ma'tan as-Sarra were not of the desert nor did their expensive aircraft provide information of the coming invasion by Chad. The raw recruits of the Libyan army were equipped with a technology they did not know how to use and were no match for those who could smell the water from a sand-covered well. The FANT attack came over the dunes to destroy thirty jet fighters on the ground and hundreds of Libyan soldiers. The FANT retired like the legendary *Riffs* of the desert, but with a billion dollars worth of sophisticated military equipment instead of women and gold.

The FANT had dealt Qaddafi another defeat. In less than a year more than 7,000 Libyan troops had been killed and billions of dollars of equipment either destroyed or captured by Qaddafi's adversary. Indeed, the victories at Wadi Doum and Ma'tan as-Sarra seemed a turning point in the long civil war, and in France the government pointed out that the Libyan defeats stripped bare the pretense that what was occurring inside Chad was a civil war. Acheikh's troops from Darfur had been almost totally destroyed. The Libyan army had retreated to the safety of Kufra, while the FANT slipped back into the B.E.T., transporting as much Libyan military weapons and equipment as they could carry. In Tripoli the French ambassador to Libya was summoned and given the usual warning that France had "direct responsibility for Chad's aggression."[61] In Ndjamena the people celebrated the Libyan defeat. It was the first time in their memory that an African army had defeated the Muslim Arabs from the north.

The OAU again called for a cease-fire, which the battered Libyans and the exhausted fugitives from the GUNT were only too happy to accept on 11 September. The OAU ad hoc subcommittee on the problem of Chad was revived. Despite the large number of Libyan casualties, the destruction of Libyan arms, and Libyans captured and imprisoned, Qaddafi refused to negotiate with the OAU peacekeepers. The government of Chad never seemed more secure than at any time in the past twenty years. Habre reorganized his government, giving cabinet posts to Kotiga (the former "Red" Codo) and Kamougue. The Teda Toubou, who presumably owed allegiance to Goukouni but had fought with tenacity against him, were promoted to command the highest ranks in Habre's military command.[62] The Libyan defeat marked a turning point in Qaddafi's relation with France. In Paris, Minister of Interior Charles Pasqua had dealt firmly with Islamic terrorism, and French threats to attack terrorism at its source, combined with defeats in Chad, caused Tripoli to undertake a serious reevaluation of Libya's policy toward France. Qaddafi was as determined as ever to strike at the United States and Chad, but he soon displayed a willingness to bide his time and to forgive and forget his past differences with France.

Notes

1. "Central Africa," *FBIS*, 9 September 1986, p. S1.

2. "Goukouni Weddeye s'incline devant Habré," *Jeune Afrique*, 29 October 1986, p. 20. Goukouni appeared on Tripoli Television Service, 1941 GMT, 23 April 1986.

3. See François Soudan, "Tchad: La Nouvelle Guerre du Nord," *Jeune Afrique*, 10 December 1986, pp. 26–29.

4. SUNA Radio, Khartoum, 1442 GMT, 31 March 1987.

5. "Inter-African Affairs," *FBIS*, 31 July 1986, p. 1, and "Chad," p. S1. Qaddafi was interviewed on 27 April by *Sunday Today* (London) and then was not seen in public for many months.

6. "Habre Strengthens Position," *Arab News*, 7 June 1986; "Middle East and Africa," *FBIS*, 12 September 1986, p. L4.

7. "North Africa, *FBIS*, " 8 January 1987, p. Q1.

8. "Goukouni Weddeye est bien fini," *Jeune Afrique*, 12 November 1986, p. 28.

9. "L'Ancien Président Goukouni Oueddei aurait été 'grievement blessé' par des militaires libyens," *Le Monde*, 4 November 1986, p. 4.

10. "North Africa," *FBIS*, 11 August 1986, p. Q2; "North Africa," *FBIS*, 8 January 1987, p. Q1; *Paris Match*, 17 October 1986, pp. 38–39.

11. In late 1986 Libyan security arrested these Libyan "Islamists," who were tried for crimes against the state and disappeared, presumably executed. See Laurent Zecchini, "Les Forces tchadiennes contiennent l'offensive des libyens," *Le Monde*, 29 December 1986, pp. 1, 3.

12. "Un succès pour M. Hissène Habré, " *Le Monde*, 20 October 1986, p. 1. This incident is graphically described in François Soudan, "Comment Goukouni Weddeye a été blessé et ses gardes du corps tués à Tripoli," *Jeune Afrique*, 3 December 1986, p. 23.

13. "North Africa," *FBIS*, 3 November 1986, p. S1.

14. François Soudan, Le Kaddafi nouveau arrive," *Jeune Afrique*, 24–31 December 1986, pp. 34–36.

15. "Central Africa," *FBIS*, 1 December 1986, p. S2.

16. Jacques Amalric, "De la 'guerre des chefs' à la 'guerre de libération'?" *Le Monde*, 16–17 November 1986, pp. 1, 4; "Inter-African Affairs," *FBIS*, 20 November 1986, p. Sl.

17. "Inter-African Affairs," *FBIS*, 18 November 1986, p. S5.

18. Amalric, "De la 'guerre des chefs' à la 'guerre de libération'?"

19. J. Juillard, "La Guerre des nerfs," *Nouvelle Observateur*, 12–18 September 1986; "France Will Give Chad Weapons," *Washington Times*, 17 November 1986.

20. "Chad Finds Unity in War with Libya," *New York Times*, 28 December 1986.

21. "Hissène Habré monte en ligne," *Le Point*, 24 November 1986.

22. "Sudan, l'écran humanitaire," *Le Point*, 2 February 1987. On Hussein, see "Sudan's Foreign Minister," *Foreign Report*, Economist Publications (London), 6 April 1989; "Tripoli Decamps to Find Oasis," *Sunday Times*, 11 January 1987.

23. François Soudan, "La Nouvelle Guerre du Nord," *Jeune Afrique*, 10 December 1986, 47–49. D. Blundy and A. Lycett, *Qaddafi and the Libyan Revolution* (Boston: Little, Brown, 1987), pp. 163–164.

24. Private information to J. Millard Burr in April 1989.

25. "Un Succès pour M. Hissène Habré," *Le Monde*, 20 October 1986, p. 1; "Hissène Habré monte en ligne," *Le Point*, 24 November 1986.

26. "France Parachutes Food and Supplies in Chad," *New York Times*, 18 January 1987.

27. "U.S. Sending Emergency Military Aid to Chad," *Washington Post*, 19 December 1986; "Muslim Tribesmen Tip Balance," *Times*, 14 January 1987.

28. "Chad Storms Libyan Bastion," *Buenos Aires Herald*, 3 January 1987; "Chad Claims Napalm Used by Libyans," *Washington Post*, 4 January 1987; "Libyans Said to Bomb Chad," *New York Times*, 5 January 1987; "A Message for Kaddafi," *Newsweek*, 5 January 1987; "Colonel Bogey," *Times*, 5 January 1987; "Chirac's Dilemma," *Middle East International*, 9 January 1987.

29. "North Africa," *FBIS*, 13 January 1987, p. Q1–3; Radio SUNA in Arabic, Khartoum, 1434 GMT, 13 January 1987; *FBIS* Report JN 131643/19987.

30. Muhammad Yusif al-Magariaf, former Libyan ambassador to Egypt and leader of the opposition to Qaddafi, estimated that between 1975 and 1985 60 percent of Libya's income was spent on the purchase of arms. "Chad Poses the Problem," *Oregonian*, Portland, 19 January 1987.

31. Excellent reports were send from Ndjamena in February 1987 by Christian Millet of the Agence France Press; see "Paris-Tripoli: L'Épreuve de forces," *Le Point*, 16 February 1987; *Le Monde*, 12 February 1987, p. 6; "Central Africa," *FBIS*, 25 March 1987, p. S1; "Libya Suffers Blow in Chad," *Washington Post*, 24 March 1987.

32. "Chad Adventure Puts Qaddafi in a Vise," *Washington Times*, 5 February 1987.

33. "Exclusif: Rencontre secrète à Cotonou," *Jeune Afrique*, 4 February 1987, p. 42.

34. "Chad: Chirac, OAU Chief Pessimistic," *Buenos Aires Herald*, 11 February 1987.

35. Alain Franchon, "Je donne le conseil à la France de se retirer du Tchad," *Le Monde*, 6 February 1987, pp. 1, 3.

36. "North Africa," *FBIS*, 4 February 1987, pp. S1–2.

37. "Qaddafi's Search for Proselytes Creates New Foes," *Independent*, 9 April 1987.

38. "Chad Shows Off Retaken Base," *Washington Post*, 13 January 1987.

39. "Chad, Libya Hold Secret Peace Talks," *Buenos Aires Herald*, 10 March 1987.

40. "North Africa," *FBIS*, 10 March 1987, p. Q1.

41. "North Africa," *FBIS*, 13 April 1987, p. Q2; see "Crowds Hail a Chadian Victory," *Times*, 24 March 1987.

42. "North Africa," *FBIS*, 13 February 1987, p. Q1.59; see "L'Événement," *Fraternité Matin* (Abidjan), 26 February 1987, p. 24; "Sudan, l'écran humanitaire," *Le Point*, 2 March 1987; MENA Radio in Arabic, 1610 GMT, 14 March 1987; *FBIS* Report NC141845/1987; "Libyan Industrial Base in Decline, Says Qaddafi," *Arab News*, 25 May 1987.

43. "Libya Suffers Blow in Chad," *Washington Post*, 24 March 1987; see "North Africa," *FBIS*, 26 March 1987, p. Q4; and "Central Africa," *FBIS*, 31 March 1987, p. S1. On the Libyan buildup in Darfur, see *Le Quotidien de Paris*, 27 February 1987, p. 15; *FBIS*, NES–87–199, 15 October 1987, p. 10.

44. "Central Africa," *FBIS*, 19 February 1987, p. S1.

45. The split between Habre and Idriss Deby is often explained by the former's unwillingness to punish the Toubou theft of livestock and weapons or halt the constant incursions onto grazing land claimed by the Zaghawa of Chad and Darfur.

46. "Tribalism and Transition," *Christian Science Monitor*, 24 June 1992.

47. "North Africa," *FBIS*, 3 March 1987, p. Q3.

48. "Libya Demands French Removal of Chad Troops," *Buenos Aires Herald*, 10 February 1987, p. 1.

49. Alain Franchon, "Je donne le conseil à la France de se retirer du Tchad," *Le Monde*, 6 February 1987, pp. 1, 3.

50. "Chadian War Goes Sour on Gaddafi," *Financial Times*, 24 March 1987; "Libya Suffers Blow in Chad," *Washington Post*, 24 March 1987; and "Libyan Retreat Reported in Chad," *Washington Post*, 26 March 1987; "Desert Cunning Brought Victory to Chadians," 2 April 1987; "Desert Tactics of Chadians," *New York Times*, 5 April 1987; "Corpses, Tanks, and Planes Litter Site of Libyan Defeat," *Daily Telegraph*, 13 April 1987.

51. "Muammar's Mortification," *Newsweek*, 6 April 1987. Commentary on this victory was extensive. See "Crowd Hails a Chadian Victory," *Times*, 14 March 1987; "Chadian War Goes Sour on Gaddafi," *Financial Times*, 24 March 1987; "Gaddafi Checked," *Daily Telegraph*, 31 March 1987; "Oudi Doum," *Le Nouvel Observateur*, 27 March–2 April 1987.

52. "Gaddafi's Crews Quit Tanks To Flee," *Daily Telegraph*, 14 April 1987.

53. "Libya's Anxious Anniversary," *Times*, 18 April 1987.

54. USAID-Chad to AID-Washington, Cable, "Post Goals and Workplans for FY–1988," September 1987.

55. "Bogged Down in the Desert," *Newsweek*, 21 September 1987.

56. Cord Meyer, "Is Qaddafi Running Out of Lives?" *Washington Times*, 3 April 1987.

57. *L'Express*, 3 April 1987; "Down and Out in Faya-Largeau," *Time*, 6 April 1987.

58. "Denial on French Role in Chad Fighting," *Manchester Guardian Weekly*, Le Monde English Section, 12 April 1987; on the African leaders, see "Sauver l'honneur de Kaddafi," *Jeune Afrique*, 29 April 1987, pp. 16–17; "Tchad: La Paix en danger," *Le Point*, 17 August 1987.

59. "Kadhafi vise Habré au coeur," *Le Point*, 11 April 1988.

60. Cord Meyer, "The Humiliation of Qaddafi," *Washington Times*, 28 August 1987; "Chad Plans Push Against Libya, Officials Say," *Miami Herald* (International Edition), 28 August 1987, p. 5A.

61. "Qaddafi's Designs Crumble in Chad," *Insight*, 28 September 1987; AFP Radio in French, 1722 GMT, 11 May 1987; see "Chad Says Troops Are Razing Base," *New York Times*, 5 September 1987; "Bogged Down in the Desert," *Newsweek*, 21 September 1987.

62. "Focus on Africa," *BBC World Service Report*, 1515 GMT, 2 April 1987.

11

Conflict in Darfur

By 1987 Sadiq al-Mahdi had greater influence on the civil war in Chad than Muammar Qaddafi ever had on the civil war in the Sudan. Sadiq professed, perhaps too much, that he was neutral in the problem of Chad, yet he had made no effort to circumscribe the freedom of Libyan troops or the Islamic Legion to establish encampments, trade freely in arms, or recruit among the Sudanese of Darfur.[1] He was deeply in debt to Qaddafi from whom he had received "massive support from Libya during his years in opposition to Numayri." In his elliptical way, Sadiq may have encouraged Qaddafi in his pursuit of Pan-Arabism by alluding to "political unity [with the Sudan] if he [Sadiq] ever attained power."[2]

There were, however, deep ambiguities in this relationship. Both derived their political strength from the periphery of power in their respective countries. Both had an irresistible desire to interfere in the affairs of their neighbors. Both were contemptuous of their African citizens, whether they be Toubou or Nilotes. Neither had ever established a warm relationship with any African leader south of the Sahara. Both were devout Muslims but were regarded by the more orthodox *ulama* as representatives of religious radicalism. Sadiq al-Mahdi could not abandon the *Ratib* of the teachings by his great grandfather, Muhammad Ahmad al-Mahdi, the nineteenth-century Islamic reformer whose mission had been to cleanse the Sudan of the corruption of Islam by the Turks and the Egyptians. The *Green Book* of Qaddafi was equally heterodox to the orthodox Sunni Muslims. Perhaps the most important bond was their mutual hostility to the Sanusiyya. Founded in the mid-nineteenth century by Muhammad ibn Ali al-Sanusi, the Sanusiyya dominated Cyrenaica, the B.E.T., and Wadai, from which the Sanusi began to seek converts in the Sudan in peaceful competition with the teachings of Muhammad Ahmad al-Mahdi. Darfur and Kordofan were the two western provinces of the Egyptian Sudan from which the Mahdi derived his most enthusiastic followers, the *Ansar,* who became the vanguard of his *jihad,* which swept away the Muslim heretics in the Nile Valley. The Mahdist state in the Sudan was destroyed in 1898 by the British to ensure the security of their empire at Suez by the control of the

Nile waters. The authority of the Sanusiyya was similarly circumscribed by the Italians in Libya, the French in Chad, principally in the B.E.T., and by the British in Darfur. Fiercely independent, the Grand Sanusi had spurned an offer by Muhammad Ahmad al-Mahdi in 1883 to become one of his khalifas, and thereafter there has been theological and political rivalry between the two brotherhoods on the western frontier. In 1969 Muammar Qaddafi overthrew the King of Libya, Idris al-Sayyid Muhammad al-Sanusi and leader of the Sanusiyya, whose *tariqa*, brotherhood, Qaddafi relentlessly suppressed to the satisfaction of the Mahdists, whose spiritual heartland remained in the western Sudan.

In August 1986 it had become apparent that Sadiq was quite prepared to assist Qaddafi. *Al-Hadaf,* the Sudanese Arab Socialist (Baath) Party newspaper, reported that Libyan troops were massing on the frontier. Another 1,000 Libyans, ostensibly administering drought relief, were encamped near the El Fasher airport. Sadiq and his foreign minister, Abidin al-Hamdi, denied their presence, but Major General Fawzi Ahmad al-Fadl, the commander-in-chief of the Sudanese army, admitted that Libyan troops had been active "for several months" in western Darfur.[3]

Sadiq and the Libyans

During 1986 a group of Sudanese officials arrived in Tripoli and returned to Khartoum with exciting prospects of financial assistance for education in Darfur and Kordofan and an exchange of students and teachers.[4] There were discussions in Tripoli about free trade zones, roads, and the diversion of the Nile waters to Libya. In the meantime, the Islamic Legion continued to recruit Sudanese from northern Darfur. These activities—commercial, religious, or subversive—were soon overwhelmed by the internecine warfare between Goukouni and Acheikh Ibn Oumar at Fada in October 1986. Libyan units had rushed to Fada from Darfur at the outbreak of hostilities but refused to intervene. When the FANT offensive was launched into the B.E.T. in January 1987, Sadiq demonstrated his ambiguous support for Qaddafi by signing an innocuous agreement for cooperation in trade, culture, and the media. To the *ulama* patricians in Khartoum, this was full payment for Sadiq's debts to Qaddafi without any future commitment. Sadiq failed to convince Qaddafi to agree to a cease-fire. When Habre later pressed him to explain his acquiescence to Libyan troops and the Islamic Legion in Darfur, Sadiq attributed their presence as "a relief convoy" that would soon return home. He appeared to be under the illusion that his bumbling intervention in Tripoli had been a success.[5] No one else was deceived, least of all the French who reinforced its Sparrowhawk contingent in Wadai to observe the Libyans in Darfur.[6] In Khartoum *Al-Hadaf* reported that French Jaguar jets were flying support for the FANT Toyota Brigades that had crossed the border to defeat the Libyans and their Islamic Legionnaires at Abu Suruj and Tendelti. Seizing the initiative the FANT continued to harass the enemy at Abu Qamari, Kutum, Kalas, and along the Wadi Howar until they were forced to withdraw in late April 1987 from lack of ammunition and petrol.[7]

After their defeat in the Ennedi, the Libyans and Acheikh's troops retreated into the Sudan pursued by the FANT. The FANT had fought hard and had suffered many casualties. They were also exhausted and consequently consolidated their forces at a fortified encampment ninety miles north of El Fasher at Wakhaim whence they could observe the movements of Acheikh along a tenuous line of communications. In defeat Acheikh Ibn Oumar distributed 1,500 automatic weapons to his Arab allies in Chad and "across the international boundary in Darfur."[8] Within two months this dramatic supply of firepower revived the desperate fortunes of the Islamic Legionnaires, who were now more active than ever in Darfur. After receiving instructions from Khartoum, the Sudanese army released four trucks they had detained with weapons for the Islamic Legionnaires.

Peace in the B.E.T.

The Libyan withdrawal from the B.E.T. and their defeat at Ma'tan as-Sarra gave Mitterrand an opportunity to reduce the French Épervier force to 1,400 men. Habre considered this decision premature. The French considered his criticism presumptuous.[9] The French had been annoyed by Habre's visit to the United States in June and disturbed when the United States agreed to supply more sophisticated weapons than the French. Habre had also received encouragement from Egypt. After a week of secret discussions held in mid-August, Egypt urged the Sudan not to allow Libya the use of its territory for any attack on Chad. Egypt's foreign affairs minister Boutros Boutros-Ghali "announced Egyptian support for Chad against any threat from the north."[10]

Pestered by the OAU ad hoc committee on Chad to reopen peace talks and by growing economic problems at home, Qaddafi dramatically announced in September 1987 a cease-fire in Chad. On 19 September Radio Tripoli broadcast that the war in Chad was over and "following the expulsion of the mercenaries from the Libyan lands," Libya would close its border with Chad "for good" and leave "Chad to the Chadians."[11] This decision surprised Khartoum, delighted Paris and Washington, and was disbelieved in Ndjamena. Qaddafi conceded that the Libyan involvement in Chad had been a "mistake," the internecine struggles for power were "endless," and "today Goukouni and Habre fight, tomorrow Goukouni and Sheikh Ibn Oumar will fight, and the day after, Sheikh Ibn Oumar and I do not know who [else] will fight." This unexpected revelation was just what the OAU wanted to hear. Its ad hoc committee on the Chad-Libya conflict was immediately revived and a meeting was scheduled for September, which Qaddafi abruptly canceled. Libyan planes continued to fly over the FANT positions in the B.E.T., and the commander of the Libyan armed forces was officially received at the administrative headquarters of the Sudanese government in El Fasher.

Meanwhile, Habre sent an official warning to the Western embassies in Ndja-mena that he expected the invasion of Chad before the New Year. The Sudan could no longer disguise its compliance with Libya and the fact that there were heavily armed Libyan contingents in Darfur. Habre sent his usual rhetorical warning that Sadiq would be held "solely responsible for whatever happens [in Chad] since he is completely under the control of and in the tentacles of al-Qaddafi."[12]

In November the Islamic Legion crossed the border near Kulbus 60 miles north of Adre. Once again Habre sought to convince Sadiq not to assist Qaddafi "to open a new front east of Chad."[13] In an interview with Egyptian journalists, Habre was emphatic that he could no longer tolerate the occupation of Tine, an oasis on the border virtually unknown to Egyptian journalists, but strategically situated to launch a *razzia* against Habre's forces in the Ennedi Plateau.[14] In his New Year's Eve message of 1988 Habre warned all Chadians that Libya was "concentrating men and equipment in Darfur." Their opportunity to recover from defeat and to mobilize for a new offensive against Chad could not have been achieved without "the complicity of the Sudanese authorities."[15]

1988 in Ndjamena, Tripoli, and El Fasher

In Chad 1988 began quietly. There were those who were encouraged that peace might come to Chad and that Qaddafi would implement the unilateral cease-fire he had announced in September 1987. The contentious and emotional issue over the ownership of the Aozou Strip, this wasteland of sand and acrid wells, might finally be resolved through adjudication rather than war. Lawlessness in the Chad-Sudan borderlands was troublesome, but it was generally quiet in Biltine and Wadai despite the poor rainfall in 1987. Cultivators and herders were praying for rain, and perhaps more indicative of the battle fatigue of Chad, the Had-jerai rebels were quiescent. Habre was still concerned by the presence of Libyan forces in Darfur, for the Libyans and their surrogates, by distributing automatic weapons and recruiting disgruntled westerners, had exacerbated old frontier rivalries that had nothing to do with Pan-Arabism or Arab socialism and little to do with the inspired zeal of the great nineteenth-century reformers of Islam, the Grand Sanusi and Muhammad Ahmad al-Mahdi. Their legacy had disappeared into the sands, and neither the *Ratib* of the Mahdi nor the *Green Book* of Qaddafi could revive the religious fervor of the past. The Libyans now represented the purveyors of arms, the dispensers of wealth, while contributing to the decimation of a population already ravaged by drought. They contributed not food but civil disorder to exacerbate the agonies of famine. In times of dearth it requires little talent for those with objectives to exploit the volatile and historic rivalries to their advantage.[16]

When the Sudanese government failed to exert its authority throughout Darfur and especially on the frontier, a contingent of a 1,000 Islamic Legionnaires crossed the border unopposed and "at will, often bringing relief supplies but often under escort by Libyan Army vehicles."[17] In southern Darfur the rump of the old FROLINAT were still active, more as bandits than rebels, and when confronted by their *razzias,* the FANT would ignore the few and indistinct border cairns and cross the frontier in hot pursuit for hundreds of miles. These forays across the border produced innumerable skirmishes that contributed to the ravages of drought and the disintegration of civil administration and security. In March Mahamat Ali Adoum, the Chad ambassador to the United States, made an official visit to the State Department to protest that Libya still had "several thousand troops operating in the Western Sudan," who were being reinforced with men and supplies in preparation for a major offensive.[18]

Perhaps the Libyan mobilization in Darfur was to deceive Habre rather than to challenge him; a deception to divert his limited resources to the eastern frontier to reduce any prospect of a FANT attack on Libyan bases in the Aozou Strip. In April 1988 André Giraud, French minister of defense, speculated that an unregenerate Qaddafi would continue "to reorganize the Chadian opposition so that it strikes at the heart of Chad . . . to destabilize President Habre's government from within."[19] In the history of Africa's thirty years war, no one trusted anyone. Consequently, everyone was astonished when Qaddafi suddenly announced during the anniversary celebrations of the OAU on 25 May with his usual flair, if not bizarre sense of theater, that Libya would recognize the government of Hissene Habre. The mercurial Qaddafi even invited Habre to meet with Goukouni in Libya. He publicly admitted that he had misjudged the situation in Chad. He offered financial assistance to rebuild those regions that had suffered from the war, but he remained studiously silent as to the future of the Aozou Strip. Habre was cautious, but he could not reject the magnanimous offer.

Before making his dramatic gesture Qaddafi had consulted neither the GUNT of Goukouni Oueddei nor the neo-GUNT of Acheikh Ibn Oumar. Both were furious and both denounced this preposterous proposal. After fifteen years of seeking to acquire power in Chad, these two old incompetent warlords suddenly were abandoned. If indeed Qaddafi were to recognize the government of Chad, the war would be over and so would the ill-starred careers of Goukouni Oueddei and Acheikh Ibn Oumar. Betrayed by Qaddafi, Acheikh resorted to the means of survival that had become a characteristic of everyone involved in the thirty years war. Ideology, principle, and even honor were no substitute for self-preservation by the chieftains of the Sahara, the Sahel, and the savanna; they were accustomed to adapting to changing circumstances in order to endure. Seeing the *habub* descending from the north, Acheikh and his followers immediately decamped from southern Libya to appear in Geneina. Here he placed himself and his troops under the protection of the Sudanese government and its startled border officials. From Geneina, Acheikh immediately contacted Habre in Ndjamena with a view to open discussions as to their future relationship.

During his customary speech on the anniversary of the nineteenth celebration of the 1 September Revolution in 1988, Qaddafi again admitted that his policies toward Chad had been a mistake. The reason for this admission of candor, from one who was internationally famous for his lack of it, remains unclear. Perhaps, he had finally begun to realize that the Libyan economy could no longer afford the Chad adventure. The national debt was now $7 billion, and oil revenues had shrunk from $23 million in 1980 to $4.5 billion in 1987 and were expected to be no more than $3.5 billion in 1988. Libya's standard of living was in decline after a decade of euphoric growth. The people were grumbling about the bloated bureaucracy and a privileged elite living beyond their means, while those in the urban slums and on the margins of subsistence in the arid lands and oases to the south remained in poverty. It was simply no longer possible for Qaddafi to purchase arms whimsically or to maintain a large standing army. He appears to have understood the malaise that had overcome the Libyans, especially those who had lost loved ones in the sands of the south for no perceptible reason. He perceived that there was a need to recharge the revolutionary fervor of twenty years ago. The General People's Congress, acting on his orders, dissolved the army and police and incorporated them into the People's Guards of the Jamahiriya. Ostensibly, Abu Bakr Younis al-Jabir, the chief of staff of the army, was retired "with a bouquet of flowers and a golden sword," but the army itself survived intact and continued to send troops and supplies to Aozou and Darfur.[20]

Libya used the vast Sahelian steppes of northern Darfur to quarter and hide its Islamic Legionnaires. From their encampments it was a simple matter to follow the historic caravan routes, now motorized, deep into the interior of Darfur to destabilize and challenge the fragile Sudan administration, which had endured in El Fasher despite drought, the Libyans, and the Islamic Legion. There was a steady flow of Libyan arms from Ma'tan as-Sarra through central Darfur to the south, known as the Western Bahr al-Ghazal, the borderlands of the Central African Republic and the Sudan, where no government throughout history has ever imposed its authority. Here the Hadjerai rebels had denounced Habre's government and were roaming throughout the frontier with some 2,000 men armed with automatic weapons from Libya.[21]

More disturbing to the Sudanese, however, was the Libyan enthusiasm to provide automatic weapons for the tribes in the heartland of Darfur—the Gourane from northern Darfur and the Arab Rizayqat from the south—presumably to secure Libyan clients. Libya had a surfeit of automatic weapons that it was more than willing to distribute in return for services rendered in the advancement of the Chadian war. This vast supply of arms and, equally important, ammunition, could not be distributed for the purpose of Libyan territorial aggrandizement without the agreement and assistance of the frontier chieftains, the *shaykhs*. They could not have been more delighted to be the purveyors of firepower beyond their wildest fantasies. Fiercely independent, their historic responsibility was to maintain their personal authority as the representatives of their people in the predatory life of the border. This was a fundamental prerequisite; the legitimacy of their authority could not always be confirmed by personality, physical prowess, or the bonds of kin and clan. The success and indeed survival of any chieftain, *shaykh,* was normally assured by his ability to contain or defeat hostile neighbors not only for self-protection but also for pillage.

The massive influx of rapid-firing guns, not unlike the famous Maxim guns of the European imperialists a century before, enabled the chieftains to demonstrate, as they were expected to do, that they were Big Men among their people. As a Big Man, however, the temptation to use sophisticated weaponry for the *razzia* in a land devastated by drought and nominally administered by the overlords in Khartoum spread disorder and the disintegration of government in Darfur. The influx of arms into Darfur was the most criminal act by Qaddafi in the thirty years war for Chad. The 1983–1985 drought was the third in three decades. It was a natural phenomenon, but now that the people were heavily armed, their need to survive replaced former predatory inclinations, the *razzia,* to produce the disintegration of the fragile civil administration of the Sudan government, which became the principal cause for the famine.

The Fur chieftains and *shaykhs* were vulnerable, exasperated, and to defend their people formed their own militia. The Fur, who were devout Muslims but emphatically not Arabs, were despised by the Libyans, ignored by Khartoum, and surrounded by traditional enemies. The Fur leadership readily approved the creation of a potential rival to their authority, but one that would defend the Fur. The Federal Army of Darfur was founded by a small circle of clandestine *Jakab* (struggle) fighters, most of whom were related in the bonds of kin and clan of the western frontiersman of the *Bilad al-Sudan. Jakab* cells were established in a score of Fur villages, and by May 1988 the Fur had 6,000 armed militiamen and training centers in southwestern Darfur in the no man's land of the Western Bahr al-Ghazal on the border with the Central African Republic. The traditional Fur leaders used their historic relations and the prestige of the sultanate to obtain funds to purchase arms, which were smuggled up through southeastern Chad, the Central African Republic, and across the border to El Fasher, the Fur capital in the west.

When the Arabs of Darfur learned that the Fur were arming, the Baggara requested weapons from their patron, Sadiq al-Mahdi, and his minister of defense, the influential *Ansar* and Baggara leader, General Burma Nasr. They soon began to receive additional arms through Libyan agents operating from northern Darfur, with the indifference of the Sudanese authorities, through the commercial routes to El Fasher and then south into the Baggara country. Now that each ethnic group, tribe, had its own popular militia armed to the teeth, Darfur exploded in the autumn of 1988. Arab and non-Arabs, cultivators and pastoralists, rival chieftains and *shaykhs* turned against one another in the bloody "War of the Tribes." Every ancient insult, any remembered dispute, any trivial grudge over land or love was now rationalized by personal or political ideologies to escalate into savage attacks made more thorough in their killing by the automatic weapons. Outgunned by the Baggara, the Fur suffered heavy casualties that *Al-Ayyam* described as "genocide," to which the Sudanese prime minister, Sadiq al-Mahdi, remained indifferent.

The warfare in Darfur did not receive much coverage in the international press. Darfur was an isolated region whose severe problems of drought and war the government in Khartoum had been reluctant to acknowledge. Its attention was completely absorbed by the civil war in the Southern Sudan, which was longer that the thirty years war within Chad. Since the resumption of this civil conflict in the Southern Sudan in 1983, the fighting between the government forces and the insurgents of the Sudan People's Liberation Army (SPLA) had resulted in very heavy casualties for the government, the substantial capture of military equipment, and no victories. The hostilities in Darfur could be disguised as tribal rivalries, but the conflict in the Southern Sudan was civil war. Tired of incessant conflict the Sudanese elite in Khartoum, particularly the senior army officers, demanded that Sadiq honor his campaign promise to open negotiations with the SPLA. Sadiq could not fail to respond and agreed in March 1988 to negotiations with the SPLA just as the frustrations of the Arabs and the Fur erupted in bloody fighting throughout the frontier from the Wadi Salih to Jabal Marra and Garcila.

Deby and the Zaghawa Defy Habre

The fierce tribal fighting in Darfur in March 1989 had resulted in hundreds of Fur fleeing their villages in the Wadi Salih, which were soon occupied by "soldiers" coming over the border from Chad. Who these invaders were and what they wanted was not immediately clear. The UN High Commissioner for Refugees had previously reported that nearly all the Chadians who had sought refuge in the Sudan during the 1983–1985 drought and during the 1987 warfare had returned home. Chad seemed at peace, and the government had just announced a record 1988 cereal harvest of 825,000 metric tons.[22] Those who came to occupy the vacant Fur villages in the Wadi Salih were indeed soldiers. They were under the command of the advisor to the president of Chad for national defense affairs, Idriss Deby, and the commander-in-chief of the Chad army, Hassan Djamous, and the minister of the interior, Ibrahim Muhammad Itno. They were all Zaghawa and Bedeiyat members of Habre's government who had denounced him as a tyrant and were now determined to overthrow him.

This triumvirate represented Habre's most important ministers, all in positions of command and responsibility in the government of Chad. Habre discovered their plan for a coup d'état, and on 1 April 1889 he ordered their arrests. This command precipitated an immediate attack on the presidential palace organized by Djamous and Deby and their Zaghawa dissidents, who were dispersed with considerable loss by Habre's Toubou palace guard. Djamous and Deby were old friends of Habre and proven commanders in the FANT. Itno was Habre's most successful politician. Ironically, this coup demonstrated the depth of dissent among the Zaghawa at a time when Habre's political fortunes appeared to be on the ascendancy, particularly after Qaddafi's extraordinary offer for reconciliation. To be sure, Habre, in his efforts to broaden the base of his government, had caused widespread discontent among the Gourane. His old allies were furious when he incorporated into his government and appointed to important positions the followers from Acheikh's CDR and Kamougue's FAP, who had once been his most determined enemies. The United States embassy was surprised by the abortive coup, but the French were conspiratorially silent. They dismissed the shoot-out at the palace as just another incident in the War of the Chiefs. Itno was arrested in Ndjamena. Djamous was seriously wounded but escaped with Idriss Deby and his Zaghawa to Darfur with Habre's loyal FANT in hot pursuit. Adoum Haggar, commander of the Mao military district in Kanem on the frontier with Niger and Nigeria, and Mahamat Deleo, commander of the Mongo military district in central Chad, joined Deby in the flight to Darfur. They all crossed through the ephemeral border to Sudanese sovereignty in the sanctuary of Darfur with 2,000 FANT veterans who had decided to defect with their commanders rather than remain in Chad to defend Habre. During their retreat the Zaghawa and the FANT skirmished all the way to the Sudan frontier. Djamous died twenty-five miles from the border. In Ndjamena there were again heavy casualties among the Toubou and Zaghawa guards who had defended the capital with great tenacity. In the firefight Habre lost three kinsmen and Deby even more, the deaths of which would have to be paid by revenge or restitution. The attempted coup and the escape were, ironically, reminiscent of those dark days for Deby and Habre that had followed the departure of their troops from Ndjamena to sanctuary in the Sudan in December 1980.

The rebels from Chad arrived in Geneina to be officially detained by the Sudanese authorities and greeted with enthusiasm by the Libyans. In Khartoum Sadiq peremptorily rejected Habre's demand to return the rebels to Chad and then flew to El Fasher to visit the refugees and organize the flight by Sudan Air of Deby to Tripoli where he immediately became absorbed in talks with Qaddafi. The Islamic Legion was reorganized. Deby was provided with Libyan resources, dispersed by Qaddafi's paymaster, Hassan Fadul, in order to return to Darfur to command his loyal Zaghawa and the discontented from the FANT into the 1 April Movement. Their numbers were soon augmented by the ragtag remnants of the CDR under Dr. Moctar Moussa and Adoum Togoi and an equally unsavory bunch from the followers of Maldoum Abba Abbas. Libyan money reinvigorated those who were now determined to end the government of Hissene Habre. Unlimited funds from Qaddafi and an inexhaustible supply of the most modern weapons proved irresistible to the hundreds of Zaghawa mercenaries wandering through western Darfur. They swarmed into the camps of their kinsmen who would lead them, as in the past, to the south, to Ndjamena.

Hassan Djamous had been one of the ministers that had brought stability to the government of Hissene Habre. Deby, the military hero, was a political novice. He had always maintained close relationships within the French military. American officials were impressed by him particularly those who met him during his official trips to Washington in March and October 1987. After the failure of his coup d état, the prospect of his marching all the way from Darfur to drive Habre from Ndjamena appeared to be an aberration motivated more by traditional ethnic tensions than any political ideology. The three dissident leaders were all Zaghawa. All were from Biltine. All had objected to Habre's exclusive use of Toubou in the presidential guard. All had protested the demotion of the Zaghawa unit commanders. Habre's troubles, in fact, began in 1987 after his failure to contain the Hadjerai. He had used his presidential guard of 3,000 elite Toubou, commanded by his Toubou friend Ahmad Goura, to suppress the Hadjerai dissidents. Goura, who had fought the Libyans in the Aozou with tactical skill and panache, had employed the same tactics in Ndjamena against the heavily armed Hadjerai to overwhelm them. The Hadjerai, however, were not Libyans. The subsequent incarceration, torture, and assassination of Hadjerai politicians, soldiers, and businessmen left a bitter and unnecessary legacy. It festered and infected those who now began to question whether Habre was sincerely committed to an ethnically diverse Chad and to sharing power with its chieftains.

Habre, like his predecessors, had been increasingly concerned about the loyalty of the Zaghawa and, quite sensibly, sought to ensure their fidelity by granting generous privileges and the official restoration of the authority of their *shaykhs* in the Ennedi. This imperial solution to administration on the periphery, where the central government of any persuasion had limited authority, appeared to be a reasonable solution. It was greeted with enthusiasm by the chieftains, the elders, and the *shaykhs,* who were only too pleased to have their legitimate authority not only appreciated but also reaffirmed by the central government at Ndjamena. Habre's decision was bitterly opposed by the young and energetic commanders of the FANT. Siddick Fadul, whose credentials are at best unconfirmed, was reported to be the principal financier and supplier of arms to the Zaghawa loyal to Djamous. Fadul's brother, Hassan, was related to Djamous by marriage, which did not inhibit their profitable arrangements with the minister of the interior, Ibrahim Itno, in return for appointments of Zaghawa in the intelligence service.[23] Habre had his personal intelligence sources keep a close watch on Deby and Djamous, who were thought to be involved the inexplicable movement of weapons between Ounianga Kebir and Darfur. These arms were, in fact, destined for Zaghawa villages in Darfur and beyond to the Hadjerai rebels in southeastern Chad and the Western Bahr al-Ghazal for the purpose of overthrowing Hissene Habre.

In 1989, however, the influence of the Zaghawa in Chad and its government was being systematically dismantled after the unexpected return of Acheikh Ibn Oumar and his followers to Ndjamena. When Acheikh and his Arabs were rewarded with important positions in the government, the Zaghawa were outraged. Despite the fact that Ibrahim Muhammad Itno, the Bedeiyat, had sought to forge a government from a melange of competing military leaders and regional politicians in the government, the Gourane of Habre no longer ruled Chad. Deby and Djamous had been instrumental in the success of the 1982 military campaign that had returned Habre to power in Ndjamena. They had led the campaign in 1986 and 1987 that had defeated and humbled the Libyan army. Habre's acceptance and his recognition of Acheikh Ibn Oumar and his Arabs was now perceived as a gross betrayal of their loyal service against the Libyans and confirmed their reservations and growing hostility toward Habre and his government. Habre and his Toubou were never numerous. They had suffered heavy losses over the years, which had made them vulnerable. Habre had needed all the youth he could recruit from the riffraff in the slums of Tripoli, the expendable youth from the oases of southern Libya, or the delinquents from the alleys of Abeche. Habre had sent Deby to the École Supérieure de Guerre in Paris to make the young warrior "a true military man."[24] This may have been his greatest mistake.

The Collapse of the Chad-Libya Rapprochement

Having alienated the Zaghawa and uncomfortable with both Africans and Arabs, Habre had become ever more isolated in the spring of 1989. His usual solitude became an obsession imposed by his preference for privacy with a few close friends. The defection of Deby and Djamous were followed by his disengagement from democracy, which had begun at the UNIR conference in November 1988. The promulgation of the new constitution that guaranteed freedom of speech and freedom of assembly was quietly abandoned. The violation of human rights for the security of Chad had now become of interest to the international community.[25] The rapprochement with Libya came to an end when Qaddafi would not abandon Deby, despite the restoration of diplomatic relations in October 1988. When the Sudan was prepared to give Deby and his Zaghawa sanctuary in Darfur, relations with Chad suddenly melted in the heat of the Sahel; the exchange of ambassadors proposed in the more halcyon days during the autumn of 1988 was never consummated. No longer having any mission after their failure to achieve reconciliation, the OAU ad hoc committee on Chad ceased to meet.

The coup d'état that failed in April 1989 also ended the tenuous peace on the Chad-Sudan frontier. Habre rejected the legal interpretation by Sid Ahmad al-Hussein, the Sudanese minister of foreign affairs, which stated that Deby and his men were refugees and were disarmed and moved to a "safe area" in the east where they would be held in protective custody.[26] Habre had never trusted the Sudanese and did not trust them now. Deby's forces had indeed been moved—not to the eastern frontier—but north of Geneina, where they fraternized with the Libyan officers and Islamic Legionnaires and behaved more as conquerors than guests among the inhabitants, whose complaints were studiously ignored by the Sudanese authorities. Officials from the international aid agencies concerned with famine relief, journalists, and even the odd tourist were refused permits to enter the frontier and were confined to El Fasher. UN personnel seconded to Darfur were not allowed west of Malha or in Dar Zaghawa to investigate the infestations of locusts that historically bred and swarmed on the frontier whence they migrated eastward to decimate the agriculture of the Sudan, Northeast Africa, and Arabia.

In Khartoum the opposition in the General Assembly criticized Sadiq for the failure of the government and its military forces to defend the sovereign territory of the Sudan, saying he had permitted the creation of an "Independent Republic of Darfur."[27] *Al-Ayyam* and *Al-Siyassa,* which normally supported the government, blamed not Libya, the Islamic Legion, or the rebels for the insecurity in Darfur but Habre for providing weapons to the Fur. In June *Al-Sudani* reported that the FANT had crossed the border in a search and destroy mission that had penetrated deep into the interior.[28] This incursion into Darfur was accompanied by a Chad delegation to Khartoum, which failed to convince Sadiq to repatriate Deby and his warriors and returned to Ndjamena to prepare an appeal to the United Nations. In June an Islamic Legion contingent arrived in Darfur from Kufra to provide additional reinforcements presumably for another invasion of Chad. Alarmed, the French immediately canceled the phased withdrawal of their troops. The French embassy in Ndjamena in an unusual public statement reaffirmed its support for the government.

Tribal Tensions in Darfur

After meeting with Qaddafi in Tripoli, the arrival of Idriss Deby in Darfur precipitated a new round of ethnic warfare. In Jabal Marra "a common sight [was] scorched vegetation—a Fur security measure, designed to stop herders grazing their animals."[29] Sudanese government officials admitted that in May 1989 "3,000 murders" had taken place in the region southwest and west of Nyala. Around Jabal Marra the Beni Halba and Salamat militias, "accompanied by some armed Chadian elements," had attacked villages, "presumably for water and grazing rights" and killed 1,500 Fur. Another serious firefight between the Fur and the Baggara Arabs supplied with automatic weapons by the Islamic Legion took place at Kass. Sadiq held Habre responsible, "both morally and physically," for the escalation of tribal conflict on the frontier in which Sadiq's *Ansar* and the Baggara had been able to demonstrate their superiority by the firepower of Libyan weapons.[30]

The Fur justifiably blamed Sadiq for their troubles and were hardly reassured when Mubarak al-Fadl al-Mahdi, Sadiq's confidant and minister of the interior, accompanied by Brigadier al-Dab of Sudanese intelligence, visited Libya in late April. Talks were held in Tripoli and Sebha with Colonel Abu Bakr Yunis, minister of defense, and Colonel Abd al-Hafiz Massaoud, the coordinator for the Islamic Legion in Darfur. The Sudanese were promised "$4 million to prepare for the invasion" of Chad, and Qaddafi had approved improvements for the Saq al-Na'am Sudanese base in the Kabkabiya district of northern Darfur. By May 1989 tribal conflict had spread far beyond the homeland of the Fur around Jabal Marra "to the area southwest up to the border with Chad."[31] When Libyans continued to distribute arms to the Bedeiyat and Zaghawa refugees, who had just arrived from Chad, the Fur found themselves invariably outgunned in the innumerable skirmishes that usually accompanied attempts to settle ancient disputes for the more immediate objective of controlling animals and the land.

After a week of fierce fighting from 13 to 18 May between the Baggara Arabs and the Fur, the exhausted combatants agreed to a tribal conference in El Fasher on 24 May. Such meetings were an honored and ancient institution recognized by the chieftains and *shaykhs* of all ethnicities for resolving disputes that could escalate beyond the propriety of frontier conflict. In an astonishing disregard for these established customs, the Baggara chiefs boycotted the conference. No other gesture could have been a greater insult. No other symbol could convey the arrogance of those convinced of their superiority by the power of their weaponry over the Fur whom they regarded as defeated. Within days the fighting resumed with uncontrolled ferocity. Scores of people were killed in the battle between Arab and Fur on 22 June. Over 50,000 Fur sought refuge in Nyala. In Khartoum the little-known Sudan Rural Solidarity Group issued a statement calling for the Sudanese tribes—Arab, Fur, Zaghawa, and Masalit—to end their tribal feuds and for the government to suppress the tribal militias, for Darfur seemed "ripe for foreign annexation."[32] Sudanese officials, however, were powerless, if not unwilling, to contain the ethnic slaughter, for "foreign elements" were everywhere in the province. It was no longer clear "what the people were fighting one another for." The Sudanese Supreme State Council deplored the "serious situation in Darfur" and criticized the activity of "several" foreign elements "entangled in this bloody struggle."[33] The comments and explanations were the same as those from Ndjamena during the years after Habre had broken with Goukouni.

During the conflagration in Darfur the only encouragement from the Sudanese authorities was the ironic declaration by the governor that any advance by the army of Chad across the border would be considered a "hostile act."[34] This, of course, was precisely what Habre was preparing to do. In late June, he ordered the FANT to strike. They crossed the border to penetrate more than 100 miles into northern Darfur but failed, for reasons that are still obscure, to find and engage Deby's forces or the Islamic Legion.

Revolution in the Sudan

On 30 June 1989 a small circle of unknown Sudanese army Officers led by Brigadier Umar Hasan Ahmad al-Bashir succeeded in overthrowing the civilian government of Prime Minister Sadiq al-Mahdi. The Sudanese officers who seized control of the Sudanese government on 30 June were determined to construct a new Sudan. The state would now be governed by Islamic principles and the laws of the Quran, interpreted and regulated by the doctrines of the National Islamic Front (NIF) and promulgated in Arabic, the language of the Quran. Upon these twin pillars would reside the lintel of a defined and homogeneous Sudanese society.

Not all the fifteen officers of the Revolutionary Command Council (RCC), who carried out the 30 June coup d'état, nor all the members of the amorphous Council of Forty, who advised it, could pass this legal and literary test of citizenship. They soon disappeared from positions of authority as members of the National Islamic Front ascended to power.

In order to produce the new Sudan, the Islamists introduced a complete ideology encompassing all aspects of life in the Sudan. Its purpose was to indoctrinate, shape, and thereby control the Sudanese without any dissent. The army was purged, the officers and ranks were replaced by a Muslim militia; the police and the civil service were systematically dismissed and their positions filled with the politically correct members of the NIF, who were given preference more for religious orthodoxy than ability. The foreign service, judiciary, and the hitherto untouchable trade unions were now to be organized along Islamic principles. The most insidious of these new cadres was the Popular Defence Force (PDF) consisting of existing Arab militias. Ironically, these militias were established by Sadiq al-Mahdi in 1987 to become the infamous *murahiliin* in Kordofan and the Bahr al-Ghazal. In the northern Sudan the PDF consisted of students and professional "volunteers," who rushed to the call of the *jihad,* and adults dragooned into six weeks of compulsory military training, the curriculum of which was absorbed by calisthenics and religious indoctrination. These civilian soldiers of God were not a great success, judged by their heavy casualties on the field of battle in the Southern Sudan. More efficient was the elaborate state security apparatus that Bashir had inherited from President Numayri, which had lingered on during the brief liberal days of democracy between 1985 and 1989. In order to secure the revolution, however, Bashir introduced the Revolutionary Security Guards, whose subsequent accomplishments include torture behind the walls of the "ghost houses" in the new Sudan.

It was widely believed that the coup d'état of 30 June and the subsequent Government of National Salvation would not last six months, but this prediction was not fulfilled. The determination of the Islamists for the revolution, on the one hand, and the divisions between the northern and southern opposition, on the other, have prolonged its life for more than a decade. Those in the Northern Sudan hostile to the regime remain an impotent opposition in government. The National Democratic Alliance (NDA) originated in 1985 when all unions and political parties except the NIF signed the "Charter of the National Alliance" and the "Charter to Protect Democracy" in order to galvanize civil disobedience against any future coups as in the days of generals Abboud and Numayri. After the overthrow of the elected government of Sadiq al-Mahdi by the coup d'état of 30 June 1989, the National Democratic Alliance was revived. Sadiq's nephew and confidant, Mubarak al-Fadl al-Mahdi signed a provisional charter of cooperation with the Sudan People's Liberation Movement/Army (SPLM/SPLA) on 31 October to overturn the Revolutionary Command Council (RCC) that had seized power under Umar Hasan Ahmad al-Bashir and to return democratic government to Sudan.

The RCC denounced Mubarak. As Sadiq's minister of the interior, he had ordered the police to break up the demonstrations of the National Islamic Front (NIF), the political supporters of the RCC, protesting the peace process that Sadiq had initiated with the SPLM/SPLA.[35] Sadiq was imprisoned but later placed under house arrest. Mubarak, however, continued to pursue his tortuous but successful negotiations with the SPLM/SPLA, which in February 1990 resulted in an agreement on "the basic challenges and problems" facing the Sudan. A formal charter of unity was signed in Cairo in March by the SPLM/SPLA, "opposition political forces," unions, and professional organizations creating the National Democratic Forces Forum, known by its old name, the National Democratic Alliance, the NDA.

Libya-Sudan Brotherhood

At Ndjamena Habre watched and waited. He had never really trusted Sadiq al-Mahdi, and his policies in Darfur, as elsewhere, were so aimless that Habre dismissed Sadiq's ethereal pronouncements and reserved his hostility for the more pragmatic designs of Qaddafi and his Islamic Legion. To be sure, Sadiq owed much to Qaddafi for his support during the failed coup d'état of 1976 and the financial and economic support for his government in 1986. These obligations were acceptable, but his tepid response to the Libyan occupation of northern Darfur was so confused that he was no longer taken seriously in Tripoli, Ndjamena, or Khartoum. Sadiq and Qaddafi had never been compatible. Sadiq was the scion of a revered religious revolutionary in the Sudan. Qaddafi was a wealthy parvenu with territorial and religious ambitions that could only be achieved at the expense of his remittance men in Khartoum.

If Sadiq had been incapable of decisions in his political constituency, Bashir and the RCC were determined to control events in Darfur to achieve their religious and political objectives and to demonstrate that, indeed, they were the *hukuma,* the government. They had, like the British, the imperial need to return law and order to the frontier in preparation for the advancement of Arabic and Islam. To accomplish these objectives in an impoverished Sudan the RCC had no choice but to pay the only Pied Piper who would play the tune. Bashir was now prepared to support the Libyans on the western frontier and his unreliable surrogate Idriss Deby in return for containing and then controlling the endemic ethnic warfare that had devastated the frontier. These two objectives were, of course, contradictory. Bashir could not establish the authority of his revolutionary government in Khartoum on the Nile among the *Awlad al-Balad,* the people of the river, in the west, Kordofan, Darfur, and the frontier, by the support from those who were the hated and historic enemy from the north.

Habre, of course, realized very soon that the threat from any alliance between Libya and the Sudan was a greater danger than any he had previously encountered in the twenty years of defending the independence of Chad from northern and now eastern imperialism. His serious concerns were immediately confirmed. To obtain its objectives in the west, the Revolutionary Command Council in Khartoum within thirty days was avidly seeking the friendship of Qaddafi in Tripoli. A Libyan-Sudan Joint Ministerial Committee was established as the first step to regional integration. To obtain political support, financial assistance, and weapons, Bashir had resurrected the seductive vision of a Pan-Arab union, which Qaddafi had first proposed in 1969. Twenty years later Bashir was now eager to accept what Jaafar Numayri had rejected. Ironically, the only Libyans who had ever thought to bind together the economy of the Darfur with that of North Africa were the proscribed Sanusiyya. Qaddafi had no interest in a vanishing trans-Saharan trade. Political and religious imperialism drove him. Thereafter, Libyan delegations flew into Khartoum, and Sudanese landed with regularity in Tripoli.

In Khartoum Brigadier al-Tijani al-Tahir, Major General Zubeir, and Major Ibrahim Shams al-Din of the Revolutionary Command Council were frequent guests of the Libyan embassy in Khartoum.[36] Tahir, a devout Muslim born near Kutum in northern Darfur and an able but little-known logistics officer, was named political supervisor for Darfur. There was no secret, however, about his intimate association with the Libyans, so cozy, in fact, that the United States embassy assumed he was in their pay. Certainly, Tahir and his extended family members, including former ministers in the governments of Numayri and Sadiq, were considered opportunists, and although he was a Fur, he was not inclined to prefer them in favor of his own personal interests. As the political supervisor for Darfur, he became a regular commuter to Tripoli, visiting the capital on at least five occasions in his official capacity, presumably to solicit arms but also, in fact, to negotiate financial and political terms to his advantage in Darfur. One was a military agreement signed in July 1989, which was a revision of a previous draft agreement negotiated by Sadiq al-Mahdi in 1988 that was never ratified by the General Assembly in Khartoum. In September Tahir was back in Libya to request more oil and arms. He returned in November as the head of a large and official Sudanese delegation. In January 1990 he accompanied Bashir to Darfur, and shortly thereafter, he arrived in Tripoli to discuss events on the western frontier. Whenever asked about Darfur, Tahir's response was always the same. The troubles and its violence were the result of historic ethnic violence on a volatile frontier. Being a Fur from the frontier Tahir appears to have understood the truth of this statement and its reality even if his masters in Khartoum and Omdurman did not.

The new government in Khartoum could hardly forget Chad while negotiating with the Libyans. Immediately after his coup d'état, Bashir blamed Sadiq al-Mahdi for the violence and chaos on the frontier and denied that there were Libyan troops in Darfur.[37] There was a great deal of truth in this accusation. Bashir had promised Chad that his government would be more responsive to the problems of the west than Sadiq, but Habre, of course, dismissed Bashir's disclaimer with disdain. Tahir was immediately sent off to Ndjamena in August 1989 to review relations between Chad and the Sudan and to reassure the government of Chad that "any relief assistance given by Sudan to Chadian elements was solely for humanitarian reasons."[38]

Despite Tahir's soothing words and Bashir's public statements that the Sudanese government had disarmed the Chadian dissidents in Darfur, Habre understood that the Libyan presence in the west was the greatest threat to his government. This was the heartland of the Islamic revolutionary tradition. It was the land of those who were determined in modern times to assert and to follow Islam in the path of the Prophet and his Mahdi. He could not ignore, as had Numayri and Sadiq, the drought, but more important was the intrusion of the Libyans and their independent surrogates.[39] The FANT had defeated and driven the Libyans in retreat to the north from which there was no immediate threat, despite the unresolved and perpetual claims to the sovereignty of the Aozou Strip. Habre was quite aware that any Libya-Sudan alliance meant trouble. He flew to Bamako in a futile effort to revive the interest of the OAU in the interminable problem of Aozou. He then paid a personal visit to Bashir to express his concern about violence on the frontier and the ill-disguised activities in Darfur by those who were hostile to his government. Having been in power for less than six months, Bashir and his Revolutionary Command Council appeared anxious to normalize relations, exchange ambassadors, and "restore the problems created between the two neighboring countries during the past regime in Sudan." This temporizing dissimulation fooled no one, least of all Habre, who "described the four-hour talks as far-fetched."[40] Neither Tahir, the Fur political supervisor of Darfur who hated the Toubou, nor his colleagues on the RCC had any intention of reducing their support for those in Darfur prepared to reestablish the historic traditions of those who ruled the *Bilad al-Sudan.*

The Algiers Agreement and the Aozou

In Ndjamena the pessimism that had accompanied the change of government in Khartoum and the possibility of a more formal alliance between Libya and the Sudan were momentarily dissipated on 31 August. In Algiers the representatives of Chad and Libya met to sign an agreement for the peaceful resolution of their dispute over the Aozou Strip. The Algiers Agreement was a dramatic transformation, a feature of Qaddafi diplomacy, for sovereignty over a wasteland whose value consisted of uncertain uranium deposits. After a generation of killing for the Aozou, the apparent determination of Libya to settle ownership for this worthless yet symbolic territory appeared to be confirmed when their representatives in Algiers also negotiated a Treaty of Brotherhood and Good Neighborliness and a Treaty for Financial and Economic Cooperation. These symbols of reconciliation were to be consummated with the appropriate ceremonies in Ndjamena on 20 October 1989. In Khartoum the RCC welcomed this surprising turn of events for an agreement to the Aozou controversy. Bashir eagerly promised Habre's foreign minister, the ubiquitous Acheikh Ibn Oumar, that henceforth Chadian exiles would be treated as refugees and consequently not legally permitted to practice political or armed activities that could jeopardize relations with Ndjamena.[41]

The Algiers Agreement may very well have symbolized the aspirations of Qaddafi and Habre, but it ignored the fact that the Zaghawa were at that very moment preparing to strike into Chad from northern Darfur. The mobilization of the Zaghawa, the Bedeiyat, and the Islamic Legion did not go unnoticed across the border in Chad. Here the FANT began to harass with brutality the Zaghawa and their sympathizers in Wadai and Biltine, destroying scores of villages and precipitating thousands of Chadians, and not just Zaghawa, to flee for safety into Darfur. The UN High Commissioner for Refugees reported the arrival of more than 22,000 refugees at the vacant camps near Geneina. As in the long history of ethnic relations on the frontier, violence soon erupted between the unwanted refugees and those on the land in a region that extended from Geneina all the way around Jabal Marra to El Fasher. In Khartoum the killing was attributed to the proclivity for banditry by the inhabitants of the border now caused by an "alien infiltration" into the frontier.[42]

Acheikh Ibn Oumar arrived in Khartoum in late September to discuss with Bashir and Ali Shumo, the Sudanese foreign minister, the concentration of the Zaghawa under the command of Idriss Deby. In Khartoum, Acheikh immediately consulted with "his spiritual father," Hasan al-Turabi, the ideological and practical patron of Bashir, seeking his intervention to stabilize the border conflicts in the interest of Chad, if not the Sudan.[43] The talks failed to convince Habre that if the Arab and Islamic leader, Acheikh Ibn Oumar, now his foreign minister, could not persuade Bashir to intervene to prevent the invasion of Chad from Darfur, there could be no accommodation with Khartoum. A month later, October 1989, the Sudanese government officially restricted travel to Darfur but did not impede the Zaghawa from crossing the border to continue their *razzias* in Chad. The FANT, led by Habre's personal bodyguard, retaliated by roaming and ravaging through western Darfur in a futile attempt to confront and destroy the elusive Zaghawa.

Habre and Deby Struggle for Darfur

On 16 October Chad launched a major offensive over the border that ultimately penetrated as far as Kutum, 120 miles east of the frontier, which was justified as "a counterattack against Libya's Islamic Legion on the Chad-Sudan border" threatening FANT bases from Ourba to Adre.[44] The frontier war came to a climax in a fierce battle for Innosoro between the FANT and the forces calling themselves the 1 April Movement, commanded by Idriss Deby and Moldom Bada. Both sides suffered very heavy casualties. Two of Deby's chief commanders,

Adoum Haggar and Mahamat Deleo, were killed, and the FANT commander-in-chief Allafouza Koni Wori-mi was severely wounded.[45] The Battle of Innosoro was followed on 30 October by a FANT attack at Bamissi (Bamshi), a former French fort set in the rocky outcrops of the Umm Sidr that had been fortified with heavy weapons and Islamic Legionnaires. The FANT had to launch a frontal assault up the Wadi Bamissi and through a narrow cul-de-sac to storm the citadel at great cost and heavy casualties sustained by the finest combat veterans of the Toubou. They took Bamissi despite their losses and pressed on to overwhelm the Libyan garrison at Al-Bay.[46]

While the FANT consolidated their positions at Bamissi and Al-Bay, on 2 November the Sudanese ambassador to Chad delivered his credentials to Habre. Ironically, on the same day the media in Ndjamena denounced "the omnipresence" in Darfur, with the complicity of the Sudanese government, of "several Libyan intelligence officers charged with supervising aggressive maneuvers against Chad." Undeterred, the FANT continued its offensive, sacking villages in the Fata Bornu Rural Council and causing thousands to flee to Kutum. Once again the FANT were victorious. Some 235 Islamic Legionnaires were killed, and the wounded and defeated fled to Libyan bases at Aponu and Maarten Bishalla.[47] By November the FANT offensive was spent, its troops exhausted, and over a thousand were reported killed. With more bravado than sincerity Ndjamena Radio announced that 1,000 rebels and Islamic Legionnaires had been killed. There appeared to be no question that Habre had frustrated the designs of his enemies to invade Chad and march to Ndjamena, but his FANT had failed to destroy them.

The victorious FANT returned to Biltine and Wadai, but Habre was too astute not to know that his costly victories in Darfur had not resolved the problem of Chad nor had they contained the historically fissiparous rebels in Darfur. He was convinced that the "massive and compulsory enlistment of thousands of Chadian and Sudanese workers in Libya," would eventually be used as "cannon fodder" in attacks that would surely be forthcoming.[48] A Chad government film taken after the Battle of Innosoro and widely distributed throughout Africa and Europe displayed their Sudanese prisoners with Libyan arms, money, and unflattering stories of their recruitment. Habre complained bitterly about the activities of the Islamic Legion in the Sudan, particularly Darfur, and blamed the Bashir government for allowing Deby and his rebels to invade Chad. The Sudanese government could do little but deny their complicity to assist Deby's 1 April Group in Darfur. Bashir even denied that Libya had extended assistance to the Chadian opposition in the Sudan. After the battles of Bamissi and Innosoro, Habre had no illusions for any rapprochement between Chad and Libya or Chad and the Sudan. Libyan willingness to resolve the Aozou dispute had dissolved. The Algiers Agreement had become, like so many in the past, yet another rhetorical statement, a document of dissimulation for personal rather than public purposes.

Relations between Chad and the Sudan reached their nadir in December 1989 when Acheikh Ibn Oumar, during an informal evening with the diplomatic community in Ndjamena, announced that Deby's 1 April Force was rearming in Darfur "with the complicity of certain Sudanese authorities."[49] In the cool of a December evening in Ndjamena he failed to disclose the disturbing report that the FANT had been forced to abandon the villages of Tine, Am Zoer, and Guereda in Dar Zaghawa.[50]

Notes

1. "Central Africa," *FBIS,* 2 September 1986, p. S1.

2. *Sudan Democratic Gazette,* October 1990, p. 4.

3. "North Africa," *FBIS,* 30 September and 26 November 1986, respectively.

4. SUNA Radio (in English), 0925 GMT, Khartoum, 18 January 1987.

5. SUNA Radio (in Arabic), Khartoum, 1420 GMT, 9 March and 1020 GMT, 31 March 1987; Paris International Service (in French), 1245 GMT, 31 March 1987.

6. SUNA Radio (in Arabic), Khartoum, 1415 GMT, 24 January 1987.

7. SUNA Radio (in Arabic), Khartoum, 1442 GMT, 31 March 1987.

8. "Soudan, l'écran humanitaire," *Le Point,* 2 February 1987; "Sudan Looks at Secession for Rebels," *Washington Post,* 29 April 1987; Africa Watch, *Denying 'The Honor of Living': Sudan, A Human Rights Disaster* (Washington, D.C., March 1990).

9. *Al-Ittihad* (Abu Dhabi), 16 July 1987, p. 8; JANA Radio, 1425 GMT, Tripoli, 8 September 1987.

10. *Al-Wafd* (Cairo), 17 August 1987, p. 12.

11. "Arab Africa," *FBIS,* 21 September 1987, p. 12.

12. "Arab Africa," *FBIS,* "Arab Africa," 21 September 1987, p. ll.

13. "Arab Africa," *FBIS,* 22 October 1987, p. 5; "Chad Drives Back Libyan Troops," *Buenos Aires Herald,* 26 November 1987; *FBIS,* 4 January 1988, p. 8.

14. "Arab Africa," *FBIS,* 15 and 22 October, 1987, pp. 5 and 10, respectively, and 4 November 1987, p. 7.

15. "Habre on Military, Economic Situation in 1988," *FBIS,* 4 January 1988.

16. "Country Profile: Sudan," *Economist Intelligence Unit,* (London, June 1986), p. 9; "Government Statements on Military Pacts," *Sudan Times,* 11 June 1989, p. 1.

17. "Sudan Turns to Gadhafi For Weapons," *Washington Post,* 27 February 1988.

18. "Libyan Border Activity Sends Mixed Messages to Chad, West," Christian *Science Monitor,* 8 March 1988.

19. "Sudan Turns to Gadhafi for Weapons," *Washington Post,* 27 February 1988; "Libyan Border Activity Sends Mixed Messages to Chad, West," *Christian Science Monitor,* 8 March 1988; "Kadhafi vise Habré au coeur," *Le Point,* 11 April 1988.

20. "Relaxing of the Political Climate in Libya" (English translation), and "Die Libyshe Revolution in der Korrektur," *Neue Zuercher Zeitung,* 27 July 1988 and 4/5 September 1988, respectively; "In Libya, Marketplace Is Making a Comeback," *Washington Post,* 11 September 1988.

21. "Habré on French Visit," *Buenos Aires Herald,* 13 July 1987, p. 5; "Kadhafi vise Habre en coeur," *Le Point,* 11 April 1988.

22. U.S. Embassy, Ndjamena, Cable 1215, 6 March 1989; see also the U.S. Committee for Refugees, *World Refugee Survey* (Washington, D.C.: U.S. Committee for Refugees, 1988).

23. "Chad: Habre at the Turning Point," *Africa Confidential,* 28 April 1989; and "Chad: Factional Facts," *Africa Confidential,* 9 June 1989.

24. Hugo Sada, "Tchad: Habré lâche par les siens," *Jeune Afrique* 19 April 1989, pp. 10–13.

25. *Amnesty International Report,* (New York: Amnesty International, 1989), pp. 42–44.

26. "Sudan and Chad Trade Accusations," *Sudan Times,* 17 April 1989; "Premier Accuses Chad," *Sudan Times,* 18 April 1989; "Chad Wants Rebel Force Handed Back," *Sudan Times,* 19 April 1989; "Sudan Refutes Chadian Charges," *Sudan Times,* 6 June 1989.

27. "Sudan: Sense of Unreality," *Middle East International,* 7 December 1990, pp. 17–18.

28. *Al-Sudani,* 27, 28 June 1989; *Al-Meidan* translated into English and published in *Sudan Times,* 18 May 1989, p.2.

29. "Sudan: War and Peace," *Africa Confidential,* 13 May 1989.

30. R. Libby, "Sudan: South Relief Project Trip Report and Field Notes," USAID, Khartoum, June 1989; "460 Die in Tribal Clashes," *International Herald Tribune,* 24 May 1989; "Situation in Darfur Remains Serious," *Sudan Times,* 22 May 1989, p. 1; "Role of Chad in Darfur," 24 May 1989, p. 1, "Full-Scale Tribal Warfare Erupts in Darfur," *Guiding Star* (Khartoum), 25 May 1989; see also *Al-Qwat Al-Musalaha* (Khartoum), 6 July 1989.

31. "Sudan Refutes Chadian Charges," *Washington Times,* 6 June 1989, pp. 1, 4. There were unsubstantiated reports by Sudanese exiles that the Sudanese base at Saq al-Na'am was financed by Libya This base is triangulated at 12.07N & 25.07E.

32. There were many reports from Darfur about the fear of foreign occupation, but the inhabitants appear to have been more concerned about imperialism from Libya than Europe. "Sudan Rural Solidarity on Darfur Problem," *Sudan Times,* 18 June 1989, p. 1; T. O'Neill, Sudanese Red Crescent, "Water Distribution Program, Monthly Report" (Khartoum), 30 June 1989; P. Curtis to USAID-Sudan/GDO, "Relief Allocations Committee Meeting" (Khartoum), 7 June 1989; League of Red Cross Societies, "Monthly Report" (Khartoum), June 1989; Agricultural Planning Unit, "Food and Agricultural Bulletin," no. 2/89 (El Fasher), 10 June 1989; "Tribal Conflict," *Sudanow* (Khartoum), August 1989, p. 7;

33. "Minister of Interior Lays Emphasis on Role of Chad in Darfur," *Sudan Times,* 24 May 1989; *Al-Ayyam,* 3 June 1989; *Al-Meidan,* 7 June 1989; *Al-Sudani,* 8 June 1989; "Sudan Rural Solidarity on Darfur Problem," *Sudan Times,* 20 June 1989; "Chad Slowly Rebuilding," *Reuters Library Report,* 10 July 1989.

34. "Sudan Relations with Chad," *Sudan Times,* 18 June 1989; *Al-Siyassa,* 16 June 1989.

35. Mubarak was characterized by the RCC as "the prominent symbol of corruption and subversion during the hateful partisan era." Omdurman Domestic Service (in Arabic), 1320 GMT, 22 December 1989.

36. "Sudan Commander Leads Coup of 'National Salvation,'" *United Press International,* 1 July 1989.

37. "Daily Bulletin," *SUNA,* 7 July 1989, p. 10.

38. SUNA Radio (in English), Khartoum, 0935 GMT, 25 August 1989.

39. BBC World Service, 1709 GMT, 25 July; AFP Radio (in French), 1239 GMT, 26 October, 1989.

40. "Daily Bulletin," *SUNA,* 23 August 1989, p. 13.

41. SUNA Radio (in Arabic), 1050 GMT, Khartoum, 1 September 1989; "Daily Bulletin," *SUNA*, 6 September 1989, p. 13. PANA Radio (in French), 1433 GMT, Dakar, 24 September 1989.

42. *Al-Sudan Al-Hadith* (Khartoum), 19 September 1989; "Armed Men Kill Eight Soldiers in Western Sudan," *Xinhua General Overseas Service,* 19 September 1989; "Daily Bulletin," *SUNA*, 20 September, 1989, p. 13.

43. "Chad: Operation Rezzou," *Africa Confidential,* 4 May 1990.

44. AFP Radio, 1739 GMT, 27 October 1989; AFP Radio, 1923 GMT, 7 November 1989.

45. The usually reliable *Africa Confidential* reported on 3 November that Wori-mi had in fact been kidnapped in late August by Deby's MPS during a surprise raid on Abeche.

46. Radio Ndjamena, 1900 GMT, 5 November 1989.

47. AFP Radio, 1334 GMT, 2 November 1989; "Daily Bulletin-Foreign News," *SUNA*, 16 November 1989, p. 1; AFP Radio, 1239 GMT, 26 November 1989.

48. Libreville Africa No. l Radio, 1830 GMT, 10 November 1989; AFP Radio, 1544 GMT, 13 November, 1989.

49. Radio Ndjamena (in French), 2130 GMT, 1 December 1989.

50. AFP Radio, 1923 GMT, 1 November 1989; Paris International Service, 1230 GMT, 21 November 1989.

12

Deby Victorious

The first meeting of the Joint Libya-Sudan Ministerial Committee was convened in Tripoli in November 1989 where their respective foreign ministers reviewed those common institutions between the two countries that could be most easily integrated—agricultural investments, commercial exchanges, and military cooperation.[1] Before the New Year the committee had met three times to discuss innocuous matters of commonality—agriculture and seismic exploration—to which both parties could readily agree. The only resolution of any importance was an understanding that Libya would finance the construction of an all-weather road from Kufra to Atbara, 150 miles north of Khartoum. Atbara was not only the confluence of the river by the same name with the Nile but the headquarters of the facilities that controlled all rail transportation throughout the Sudan and the strategic junction for the road east to Port Sudan. Like Cecil Rhodes and his imperial vision of a Cape-to-Cairo route to bind Africa, Qaddafi now contemplated not railroads but roads across the sands to open the interior of the southern regions of his republic isolated on the North African littoral.

He also wanted to pave the ancient and deteriorating caravan route from Kufra to El Fasher with an all-weather road to bind Libya and the western frontier to Tripoli rather than to Khartoum, a project in which Brigadier al-Tijani al-Tahir proved an accommodating and influential advocate. In October 1989 there were 7,000 insurgents from Chad loyal to Deby in the Sudan.[2] These were non-Arabs from the frontier whose deep and parochial loyalties were not always accepted but certainly understood by the Fur. What alarmed the Fur leaders were not their Arab enemies in the south, the Baggara, who were newcomers to the frontier in the eighteenth century, but the arrival in Darfur at the end of the twentieth of Arabs from Libya. Not only were they unwanted, but their presence was protected by the riverine Arabs in Khartoum whose new pasha, Umar Hasan Ahmad al-Bashir, had promised an "integrated region" of Darfur in the Sudan and Kufra in Libya.[3]

The Libya-Sudan Integration Charter

When the Sudanese delegation arrived in Tripoli on 28 February to attend the annual Libyan People's General Congress, Abd al-Salam Jalloud and Colonel Yunis Jabir personally met Bashir and his entourage.[4] Qaddafi opened the congress. He declared, to the astonishment of Bashir and his Sudanese, that 1990 would "witness the formation" of a General People's Congress in the Sudan. The "Sudanese Jamahiriya" would assume "full authority" to complete the "unionist project between Libya and Sudan," which would "lead to unity in four years." This "comprehensive unity" was "at the heart of the Islamic creed . . . to ward off the onslaught of the imperialists, Zionists, and crusaders who support each other in attacks against our beliefs and our right to a free and decent life." Libya and the Sudan working together through unified laws "on the basis of Islamic *sharia*" would spread Islamic values "across the world" as the Arab language and culture were "bolstered and disseminated."[5] They agreed to coordinate the "activities of their security organs," cooperate in military training, and conclude "military pacts for supply and common defense," and Bashir had accepted "on behalf of the people of the Sudan" a "form of unity" with Libya.[6]

Despite these preemptory appeals, if not orders, for unity, negotiations continued at Tripoli for an integration of the two countries. Such proposals for Arab solidarity were not new for Qaddafi. They had been a cornerstone of his foreign policy since his coup d'état in 1969. Here was another astonishing opportunity to forward the course of empire to fulfill the destiny of Pan-Arabism and Pan-Islam throughout the Sahel, the savanna, and the forests of Africa. Bashir had many aspirations similar to Qaddafi's, although he knew that his neighbor was totally unreliable. He and his officers in the Revolutionary Command Council had come to power with little enthusiasm from the Sudanese. A third of his citizens were not Muslims and refused to be judged by Islamic law. The RCC needed Libyan cash, resources, and arms to bring the civil war in the south to a successful conclusion. There was the ancient and troublesome dissent in Darfur, the stronghold of Sadiq al-Mahdi, whom Bashir had overthrown. The west was a volatile frontier that Khartoum had never controlled. The inhabitants were Muslims, but Bashir, like all his predecessors, Turks, Egyptians, and British, had to exert his authority hundreds of miles from the Nile at Khartoum. The recognition of Libyan influence in the west was the price Bashir was prepared to pay as long as the pact of unity would produce Libyan oil to fuel the Sudanese economy and Libyan arms to resurrect his army, which was disintegrating from weak leadership.

The Libya-Sudan Integration Charter was ratified 25 March 1990 by the General People's Congress in Tripoli and on 11 April by the Revolutionary Command Council in Khartoum. Ramadan Ali Bashir, the secretary of the Libyan Brotherhood Office, grandly envisaged, not surprisingly, that the integration of the Sudan and Libya would be a positive force in Arab-African relations, for it would now facilitate the "strategic penetration" of Africa by the new consolidated Arab state. Tahir, now a major-general, continued his campaign of vilification against Habre, to which he responded in kind by denouncing the RCC for plotting with Deby in preparation for an offensive against Chad.[7]

Deby Takes the Offensive

When Lieutenant General Idriss Deby returned to his headquarters in Kutum in northern Darfur from Tripoli in January, he was determined to reorganize his scattered forces with the new and substantial resources from Qaddafi. His goal was to drive the government forces from the B.E.T. and Wadai. By March he had consolidated his followers and persuaded exiles from Chad in the Maghrib and West Africa to return to support Operation Rezzou. No one disputed his leadership, an astonishing confirmation of his ability, or the fatigue of frontier warfare made uncivil by violent weaponry. He reorganized the opposition in Darfur as the Mouvement Patriotique du Salut, the MPS, who were soon to be strengthened by a "750-strong Libyan force backed with four tanks and 10 armored vehicles."[8] Beyond Chad the exile communities in the Maghrib and West Africa were exhilarated by the prospect of a leader.

On 25 March 1990, the day the Libya-Sudan Integration Charter was published in Khartoum, Deby launched his assault across the border from their bases at Innosoro, Tougan, and Bamissi to attack the Chad army in the Biltine. Habre had been fully aware of an imminent attack, and, in fact, the presence of the MPS poised on the frontier north of Geneina with the compliance of the Sudanese government had been broadcast from Ndjamena Radio for many weeks. It remains unknown why the FANT were taken by surprise on the 25th other than the presence of a great *habub* that enabled the MPS to advance unobserved in the sandstorm.[9] The objective of the MPS was to overrun the FANT positions at Guereda, Iriba, Bahai, and Ourouba.[10] The confrontation on Chad's eastern frontier was now a reality, and Habre requested support from the French for his hard-pressed garrisons. The Épervier force consisted of 1,300 troops who were being withdrawn according to an established policy of rotation from which the French were not about to deviate.[11] Habre had become dependent on his former Arab and Sara enemies in his attempt to achieve a broader base of support for his government among the ethnic diversity of Chad. He needed their recruits for an army that could no longer find the necessary reinforcements from the Gourane or the Toubou to replace the heavy losses during the years of conflict. Three hundred FANT officers had been trained in France since 1984, but few returned committed to the struggle of their fathers.

In Ndjamena 5,000 students demonstrated in support of Habre. Amid cries of "down with Libya, down with Kaddafi, down with Al-Bashir," he departed for the front dispensing a flurry of statements that Chad had been deceived and that the RCC was just another corrupt regime from Khartoum. Manufactured demonstrations in Ndjamena could be ignored. The official Chad complaint at the OAU of Libyan aggression and Sudan complicity could not be so easily dismissed despite the long history of such presentations, which had never elicited much enthusiasm at the OAU. In response the OAU revived the former Chad-Libya commission, which was customarily noncommittal, by immediately arranging another conference to hear the detailed accusations from the government of Chad. Libya, of course, denounced the Chad protest. It argued that the fighting in Biltine and Wadai was strictly an "internal" matter that did not involve Libya.

The support for Habre in Ndjamena, whether contrived or real, could not disguise the fact that he had miscalculated the determination of Qaddafi to supply whatever weaponry was required for Deby to defeat those who had twice humiliated him. The MPS assault overwhelmed the FANT at Iriba, and Deby's Zaghawa were steadily eroding the defensive perimeters of the FANT at Biltine. There were heavy casualties on both sides, and a thousand prisoners were taken, accompanied by pronouncements on both sides proclaiming victory. Despite their surprise attack across the frontier, their victory at Iriba, and their fierce assault against the FANT defenses, the Zaghawa still failed to take Guereda. Habre immediately ordered a counteroffensive and on 7 April the FANT forces attacked along a front of a hundred miles from Silea to Tine with its best elite troops crossing the Sudan frontier at the strategic border town of Tine. Having regained the initiative, the FANT swarmed through the frontier in their ubiquitous and mobile pick-up trucks. This offensive was designed as a surprise in Bedouin tradition, which Habre had ironically divulged when he inexplicably informed Bashir in Khartoum of the impending attack. Bashir immediately warned Deby who, in turn, withdrew his overextended and battered forces into the vastness of the Sudan.

By mid-April Habre had 4,200 well-equipped troops roaming through western Darfur in their Toyotas and driving the MPS eastward in search of a sanctuary. Deby and his MPS were in disarray, and as in past encounters, now thirty years old, Libyan reinforcements were, once again, sent from Kufra and Ma'tan as-Sarra accompanied by SU-22 fighter-bombers. On 20 April the Sudanese foreign minister, Ali Sahloul, arrived in Ndjamena to meet with his counterpart, Acheikh Ibn Oumar, to demand that Chad withdraw forthwith from the Sudan, which they had invaded. This was certainly an understandable but unrealistic appreciation of the history of the western frontier to which Acheikh, of all people, protested that the crossing of the frontier by Chad forces was the legitimate response to the malevolent neutrality of the Sudan. No sooner had Sahloul left Ndjamena than the FANT announced another victory. Two "Sudanese Islamic Forces" in their camps on the border had been overrun to capture large amounts of weapons, ammunition, food, and medicine.

Beyond the border forty-one villages were razed, most inhabited by Fur and some Zaghawa in Fata Bornu southwest Kutum. War had now eliminated the traditional means to deal with drought. Thousands of Sudanese fled from the violence produced by the massive destruction from automatic weapons that now pervaded security, life, and water east of the Jabal Marra massif. The offensive into Darfur by Habre's FANT in reaction to the *razzia* by the MPS was a tragic demonstration of triumphant technology now measured by the elusive Toyota and proven by the destructive authority of automatic weapons to confirm the famine. Drought in the Sahel has been recorded by tradition and in the chronicles for the past two millennia but only measured in the past century. Modern meteorological analyses have yet to anticipate the vagaries of nature, the consequences of which are of great antiquity and have involved migration, shared resources, kinship, and the concern for the human condition. Once the traditional relationships of those who live on marginal land disintegrate, there is an inevitable escalation of conflict for the remaining resources. The competition for the land is now made more terrible by the increasing efficiency of the power of the gun and the perplexity of those who do not understand why the old ways no longer work to ensure survival.

The Arabs from Zalengei took advantage of the FANT invasion to resume their "long-standing feud" with the Fur. Bashir's officials incarcerated the non-Arab dissidents, Fur, Masalit, Meidob. More than a hundred Fur leaders were arrested, including former politicians of the DUP and Umma, the two major political parties in the Sudan, to be dumped in the execrable Shalla Prison south of El Fasher to rot.[12] In June 1990 Amnesty International reported the arrest of another thirty "prominent" Fur members, and human rights activists reported that Sudanese government troops had "recently begun to intervene on the side of Arab militia," the Baggara, the traditional enemies of the Fur.[13] The Fur and the Dinka of the Southern Sudan had been "targeted by General Bashir's junta for extinction . . . for they are both non-Arab and large enough groups to be considered a threat to reactionaries like Bashir to what he would consider 'his people'—fundamentalist Moslem Arabs."[14] In Darfur, Ali Shimal, a prominent member of the NIF and a committed Muslim Brother, founded the People's Committees and a People's Defense Force from which the Fur were excluded.

After the impetuous Operation Rezzou had failed and the FANT counteroffensive had driven the MPS into their sanctuaries in the heart of Darfur, the victors were, in fact, the riverine Arabs, the *Awlad al-Balad,* of which Umar Hasan Ahmad al-Bashir was the president. They cared little—intellectually, socially, or economically—for those from the west. Their contempt for the country folk was confirmed by the enthusiasm of the rural Sudanese for Sufism, Islamic mysticism, the way to God for millions of Muslims who cannot find spiritual succor in the more legal interpretations of the Word of God by the urban sophisticated orthodox on the Nile. The Muslims of the west had been prepared to die for the reformer of the Faith, Muhammad Ahmad al-Mahdi, which had now become anathema to the Islamists who had placed his great grandson and leader of the *Ansar* from Darfur and Kordofan under house arrest. The non-Arab Muslims of the west, as in the past, were convinced that they had been betrayed by the new riverine Arabs in Khartoum. They had no illusions about those bringing gifts from the Nile and regarded those bearing arms from the Mediterranean as allies, if only on their terms. In the dying decades of the twentieth century, agents of Mediterranean or Nile imperialism were represented by surrogates, suspect at best, distrusted at worst. As in the past, the diverse peoples of the frontier were not about to abandon their control of the land to enjoy the exploitation of the latest warlord with the latest arms.

Idriss Deby may have masqueraded as the defender of Darfur. Those on the frontier, however, had no doubt that Deby had received weapons from and was supported by the Libyans, who were regarded as the traditional arms merchants now hawking more efficient merchandise. The depth of hostility by the western-ers was reserved for the Sudanese government, which had incarcerated their spir-itual leader, ignored the drought and famine that had produced such hardship, and appeared disinterested in preserving law and order or even mediating the vi-olent disputes between the Baggara and themselves. By 1990 Bashir had lost the sympathy, the allegiance, and religious fervor of the westerners and has not to this day recovered it.

Having been once again defeated on the frontier, Idriss Deby fled before Habre's Toyotas from his headquarters at Kutum to El Fasher. Here a Libyan C-130 spirited him away to Tripoli and safety. In the retreat from Kutum, Ismail Bashira, a Sudanese Zaghawa and one of Deby's best commanders, was captured along with a large supply of Libyan arms, ammunition, fuel, food, and prestige. During this stunning defeat of the MPS, the 6th Division of the Sudanese army remained quiescent in their barracks in El Fasher, where they were left undis-turbed by both the FANT and the MPS, relieved to carry on their frontier war untrammeled by indifferent and incompetent interference.

Reaction in Darfur

In May 1990 the FANT expeditionary force returned from Darfur. Their *razzia* had been triumphant in the tradition of past victories in the north—Bardai, Faya, and Aozou—but at great cost. It was a Pyrrhic victory. Habre had sought but had failed to obtain more sophisticated weapons. France sent fifteen combat aircraft to Ndjamena but only to defend the capital. "Additional troops" were to be sent to reinforce the one hundred and fifty currently defending their national interests in Abeche. This "implicit warning" to Qaddafi was of no help to the forces of the government of Chad on the frontier.[15] Having received no reassur-ance, weapons, or supplies from the French, Habre should not have been sur-prised that they would not intervene on his behalf with Qaddafi.[16] When the FANT intercepted ten Libyan trucks loaded with arms on the frontier, the gov-ernment of Chad launched its usual rhetorical condemnation of Qaddafi, Libya, and the Islamic Legion.[17] Ali Sahloul, the Sudanese foreign minister, accused Chad of having kidnapped Sudanese and Libyan nationals during their invasion of the sovereign territory of the Sudan resulting in 10,000 people fleeing from Chad "as a result of the conflict there."[18] The Libyan representative was more dramatic. He declared that Chad would have to "choose between peace and annihilation."[19]

Drought in Darfur

War creates famine. Drought escalates the misery. In July 1990 the indigenous and reliable cereal crop of Africa, sorghum *(dura)*, planted throughout northern Kordofan and Darfur, had not received the normal rainfall, and the rains of August were accompanied by searing heat. The cycle of war, drought, and famine was about to return. "We may be seeing the initial stages of a major, nation-wide food crisis of 1984 proportions in Sudan."[20] The Islamist regime of General Umar Hasan Ahmad al-Bashir and his Revolutionary Command Council had displayed little concern about famine in the west.[21] Their "strategic reserve" was a fantasy that was not of any great concern to the government on the Nile for the non-Arab western rustics at a time when the security of the revolution required greater international support. The invasion of Kuwait by Iraq in the summer of 1990 immediately produced new problems for a beleaguered revolutionary government in Khartoum. When the RCC refused to join the international coalition organized by the United States to condemn and then to mobilize an expeditionary force to drive Iraq from Kuwait, the Arab states, including Libya, requested the Western governments to drastically reduce their embassy staffs to a symbolic number. The West African states severed diplomatic relations.

While the world was completely absorbed by these diplomatic and military operations in the Persian Gulf, a UN/FAO field survey predicted that without foreign food aid as many as six million Sudanese could starve in 1991. This alarming report resulted in the U.S. Agency for International Development (AID) offering to provide the United Nations with "up to one-third (not to exceed 100,000 metric tons)" of all emergency food aid.[22] The United States and the international donors were prepared to support another Western Relief Operation as they had in 1982, but the RCC, like Numayri in 1982, dismissed any talk of drought as antigovernment rumor. Satellite data and harvest assessments were ignored. The minister of agriculture, Ahmad Ali , and the minister of finance, Abd al-Rahim Hamdi, announced that the harvest was normal and did not require the government to request assistance as "antagonistic Zionist circles claimed." In November President Bashir personally denied the possibility of famine in the Sudan and accused the West of using food to damage the Sudan's image, particularly since its government had decided to support Iraq.[23] Chad, of course, had not escaped the famine. War, drought, and famine did not respect frontiers, particularly those as porous as in the west. Habre immediately authorized a Sahelian drought relief program and requested Western assistance. Some $312 million in food relief was allocated from Western sources for those in need in the B.E.T. and south along the frontier. By October 1990 40,000 tons of food were allocated and on the move for famine relief on the frontier in eastern Chad.[24]

Deby Counterattacks Again

President Bashir and the RCC soon demonstrated that they were more interested in rearming Idriss Deby and his insurgents than in providing food for Darfur. The combination of famine and discontent among the FANT provided Deby with an abundant supply of recruits, while the RCC provided an abundant supply of Libyan weapons. The Libya-Sudan Integration Charter gave an official imprimatur for the Sudanese officials in Darfur to cooperate with Deby and his Libyan advisors. The governor of Darfur, Major General Abu al-Qasim Ibrahim, represented this policy. He tactlessly boasted that relations between the Sudan and Libya had "witnessed a remarkable improvement," now that Darfur had been "twinned" with Libya's Tahadi province [southeastern Fezzan] to integrate trade.[25] Habre, as in the past, took the offensive rather than waiting until his enemies had regained strength in their Sudanese sanctuaries.

On 1 September the FANT struck across the border against the "Sudanese and Libyan Islamic Legion" near Geneina, Kutum, and Zalengei. For the second time in six months the inhabitants of northern Darfur fled for safety to El Fasher, and once again the Sudanese army remained in their barracks.[26] Supported by the calculated inactivity of the 6th Sudanese Division at El Fasher, Deby, the Islamic Legion, and the MPS continued to refit and rearm. Unable for a second time to entrap Deby, the lines of communication for the FANT were now stretched beyond their ability to supply the fuel for their Toyotas, and troops began to precipitate a hasty retreat to their defensive positions on the Chad frontier. Here they rearmed in anticipation for the counterattack that would be launched by those who had eluded them and who were now, in the frontier tradition, to exact revenge for the humiliation of retreat and safety in the sanctuaries of those they despised.

During the autumn of 1990 the Persian Gulf War absorbed the attention of the international media and enabled Idriss Deby to rebuild his forces in Darfur without any conspicuous coverage. By November he now appeared confident that his MPS was sufficiently strong to confront the FANT in their defenses along the border. In early November 2,000 troops crossed the border to launch an offensive on a broad front from the 14th to the 16th parallel. There was fierce fighting all along the line and, consequently, ambiguous reports as to the success of the attacks and counterattacks, but all reports confirmed heavy casualties. The MPS quickly overran Tine, Guereda, and Koulbous. Despite desperate firefights and unprecedented losses, the RCC denied over Khartoum Radio and Television any responsibility for the conflict and accused Habre for the resumption of traditional "tribal conflict and civil war."[27]

The French wanted no part of this latest outbreak of an endemic conflict from which they had been trying, with considerable ambiguity and indecisiveness, to extricate themselves for thirty years. They refused Habre's request to intervene by sending only 150 troops to Abeche to protect French military installations.[28] Acheikh Ibn Oumar, the foreign minister with a dubious history of defending the integrity of Chad, insisted that French inaction had encouraged Libya to press Deby to undertake yet another offensive along the frontier. Unable to secure a French military commitment to save his government, Habre turned in desperation to President Mobutu of Zaire for assistance. It was too late to expect any serious military support from that fragile and unreliable ally. The thirty-year struggle for Chad was about to reach a conclusion. A generation of endless Libyan imperial warfare had decimated the Toubou warriors, who for nearly twenty years had followed Habre from the Tibesti to Ndjamena. The survivors were exhausted. Deby now employed the successful tactics against the FANT that he had devised to defeat the Libyans. With his own flotilla of Toyota pick-ups equipped with mounted machine guns and cannon, Soviet AT-3 and AT-4 anti-tank missiles, and an inexhaustible supply of ammunition, he destroyed the FANT border defenses. There was, in fact, little difference between the swift, mobile Toyotas at the end of the twentieth century and the camels and horses of Dunama Dabalemi ibn Salwa, the *Mai* of Kanem in the thirteenth, except more efficient firepower. Having surrounded and overwhelmed the Chad defensive positions along an indefensible frontier, Abeche soon fell and with its occupation by the MPS, the road to Ndjamena was now an open road.

The advancing columns of the MPS raced 600 miles across the Sahel and the savanna to the outskirts of Ndjamena in two days. Hundreds of expatriates fled by car and on the few remaining flights. In 1980 Habre had retired across the Chari to Cameroon and safety. Now twenty years later he and his entourage crossed the Chari once again into the sanctuary of Cameroon. His eight-year rule was over. The FANT disintegrated, and after a night of pillaging by civilians and army deserters, Deby entered Ndjamena on 2 December in a black Mercedes-Benz flanked by his Zaghawa warriors packed into their Toyota chariots. At the same hour an irony of history, if not a symbol of a dying imperial past, occurred out of the blue skies of Chad when three companies of French paratroopers arrived at the Ndjamena airport. The new government of Chad consisted of Zaghawa and Arabs. The Africans from southern Chad were nowhere to be seen, despite Deby's declaration that the new Chad was a "democratic, pluralist" nation and that "the moment has come to lay down our arms."[29] The next day Colonel Abd al-Hafiz Massaoud, the Libyan director of operations in Chad for more than a decade, arrived with a delegation of forty Libyan advisors. On the same day 650 Libyan dissidents opposed to Qaddafi in training at the Dougia air base north of Ndjamena were flown to safety in Nigeria and Zaire.[30]

In the United States, President Bush, obviously preoccupied by more pressing matters in the Persian Gulf, was astonished to learn of the rapid collapse and disintegration of the Chad army. Nothing could be done to retrieve Habre's defeat, but the $34.5 million in military aid to Chad since 1983 to keep him in power was considered money well spent.[31] For a decade Habre had adamantly opposed Qaddafi. He had defeated the Libyan army, reduced its effectiveness, and destroyed much of its vast inventory of Soviet arms. Habre, as much as anyone, had been responsible for Qaddafi's diminished status both in Africa and the Arab world. Still, the Bush administration had been appalled by the human rights violations during the latter years of the Habre regime.[32] In the end it was best to regard Habre as a loser for the moment, who once again could play a major role in Chad. Washington had no immediate plans to finance his survival, but after thirty years of war in Chad, its tortuous relations with Libya and the Sudan, and the deep distrust in Washington for the French, no one could be quite certain as to what the future would have to offer.

The French could hardly disguise their delight that the Americans had lost a client. The French defense minister, Jean-Pierre Chevenement, personally instructed the French air force not to attack Deby's columns advancing on Ndjamena, which was commensurate with his policy of benign neutrality. French neutrality gave no satisfaction to Habre, but he had never been a French favorite and could not expect direct intervention in another lost cause in Africa, which would antagonize more important interests in North Africa. The French were well aware that Libya had provided Deby with 40 percent of his arms.[33] Their military attaché in Khartoum was actively assisting Deby and his lieutenants in planning his invasion of Chad to curry favor with Qaddafi and Turabi, whose Francophile sympathies were no secret. The military advice for Deby and the subsequent French accommodation with the Islamists in Khartoum were both cynical and a continuity with the past. French interest in Sudanese oil was a future prospect almost as much as the their determination to resume the construction of the Jonglei Canal. These, however, were trivial twentieth-century manifestations of an older French tradition of reconciling the ideals of the Revolution with those of Islam, which Napoleon had fervently sought and failed to achieve during his dialogue with the *ulama* of Cairo after his conquest of Egypt in 1789.

After nearly a decade France had simply tired of Habre's incessant demands for more economic and military assistance. With Deby in Ndjamena, Mitterrand was now in a position to strike a deal with Qaddafi that would improve the French insatiable thirst for oil and the Libyan need for more amicable relations with a major European power. Despite the reduction of their troops in Chad, there was no illusion that the French could not respond from their bases in the Central African Republic in sufficient force at any time to impose their unwanted authority in Chad. This was manifestly unnecessary if Idriss Deby would protect their interests in a way that Habre appeared less inclined to do. The French foreign minister, Roland Dumas, asserted superciliously that "the times have passed when France would pick governments or would change governments and would maintain others when it so wished," but no one believed him. A few days later

France extended a credit of ninety million francs to the government, and Deby was invited to Paris.[34] In Paris, Deby, like Habre before him, declared an end to anarchy. "This country must become a pluralist democracy." Like Habre before him, he appointed six former ministers to his government. All had been Habre's trusted advisers. After thirty years of independence there was still a shortage of capable administrators, and that quintessential survivor, Acheikh Ibn Oumar, was appointed Special Counselor to President Deby.

The More Things Change . . .

In reality the revolution of Idriss Deby did not seem so different from that of Hissene Habre, nor did it change the pattern of leadership in Ndjamena that had characterized the thirty years war. The Zaghawa replaced the Toubou, the Hadjerai the Zaghawa, and the Arabs and the Africans remained sullenly discontented in a government not of their own choosing. Human rights violations were just as prevalent, the intelligence service just as ubiquitous, and the French secret service just as active in the internal affairs of Chad. Dissidents denounced Deby for practicing "tribalism." but they were immediately silenced or disappeared.

There was no significant change by the central government in its relations with the distant, arid, and independent borderlands. Historically, no government from Tripoli, Khartoum, or Ndjamena had ever exerted its authority on the frontier throughout the millennia. The Romans could not in the Fezzan. Neither Mamluks nor Turks from the Nile could control the western frontier in Darfur. The French, British, and Italians all presumed to assert their authority upon their respective frontiers. Their vaunted imperial power, however, amounted to little more than a few beleaguered officials whose superior weaponry enabled them to demand peace in the B.E.T. and on the Chad-Darfur frontier in collusion with the traditional rulers. The containment of the *razzia* by the traditional authorities was a small price to pay for convivial relations with the imperialists whose gratitude for not having to call upon expensive punitive expeditions was returned by the demand for symbolic taxation. The border chiefs were only too happy to restrain their impetuous youth to fill the imperial coffers with trinkets.

The departure of the MPS from the Sudan did not commit the Sudanese junta to respond to the growing famine in Darfur. In 1991 the shortage of food had become so severe that thousands of Sudanese began to cross into Biltine and Wadai to the distress of the inhabitants, the traditional authorities, and the new government, which could not meet the demands of their own people on their side of the frontier. The RCC in Khartoum expressed little interest in the suffering of the rustics from the west, just another example of the continuity of disproportionate cultural animosity between those of the river and those of the *Bilad al-Sudan*. Neither the ideologies of the twentieth century nor the triumph of technology could dissolve the ancient and cherished cultural traditions of kinship in a productive land that the invaders, whatever religion or ethnicity, were prepared to destroy by neglect or by force of arms. Darfur was now ruled by Arab officials and by an Arab bureaucracy beholden to the central government during whose governance the non-Arab majority of Darfur had witnessed the disappearance of their patrimony by drought and the riverine imperialism from Khartoum, now supported by the Arabs from Libya. The Masalit, the Fur, the Zaghawa, the Meidob, and the Bedeiyat, and the other antique peoples of the border did not associate their latest calamity with Mussolini's grand design for a New Rome. They did not bother with Nasser's vision of Pan-Arab socialism or, as good Muslims, Qaddafi's interpretations of Islam in the *Green Book*. They were concerned about food in a drought that could no longer be accommodated amid the warfare for the political aspirations and personal greed of the few for the many in a generation of conflict, death, and despair.

Upon his arrival in Ndjamena, Deby revoked the 1989 constitution, dissolved the National Assembly, and disbanded Habre's infamous security service, the Document and Security Directorate (DDS). Hundreds of political prisoners were set free. All of these changes did not mean any dramatic disruption from the past, for Deby immediately requested that France continue to maintain the elite troops of Operation Épervier in Chad and to provide military and economic assistance.[35] It was Qaddafi, that mercurial, bizarre, but determined leader, who had persevered for thirty tumultuous years of history to establish North African rule and Libyan imperialism south of the Sahara. In 1990 he could take satisfaction in the results of his mission. He himself best summed up his triumph in Ndjamena and Chad on 12 December 1990. "We tell every African state that we will create a new Idriss Deby to wreck the capital of any African state which acts in collusion with imperialism against the revolution."[36]

Notes

1. *Al-Qwat Al-Musalaha* (Khartoum), 6 February 1991.

2. "Daily Bulletin," *SUNA* (Khartoum), 4 January 1990, p. 7; Khartoum communiqué reported by AFP Paris (in French), 1145 GMT, 24 October 1989 (*FBIS* translation, AB2410123089k, 24 October 1989).

3. *FBIS,* Report JN2602113690, 26 February 1990, translated from *Al-Ahram* (Cairo).

4. *Al-Inqaz Al-Watani* (Khartoum), 28 February 1990; Radio SUNA (in English), 0924 GMT, 28 February 1990; Radio Omdurman (in Arabic), 1930 GMT, 1 March 1990; "Daily Bulletin," *SUNA* (Khartoum), 2 March 1990, p. l; *Al-Sudan al-Hadith* (Khartoum), 8 March 1990; Radio SPLA (in English), 1300 GMT, 6 March 1990.

5. The details and quotations are in "Sudan Seeks Arab Help as Investors," *Saudi Gazette,* 14 March 1990, and were given extensive coverage by Tripoli Television Service (in Arabic), 1202 GMT, 2 March 1990.

6. JANA Radio (in English), Tripoli, 1819 GMT, 3 March 1990; "Daily Bulletin," *SUNA* (Khartoum), 5 March 1990, pp. 4, 11–14; Radio SPLA (in English), 1300 GMT, 6 March 1990.

7. Radio Ndjamena Domestic Service (in French), 2130 GMT, 1 December 1989.

8. "Network Africa," BBC World Service, 0730 GMT, 2 March 1990.

9. "Chad Says Libyan Forces Attacking Its Positions from Sudan," *Reuters Library Report,* 2 April 1990.

10. BBC World Service, 0730 GMT, 2 March 1990; "Chad: Operation Rezzou," *Africa Confidential*, 4 May 1990.

11. The French garrison at Abeche had been reduced to a hundred men; "Tchad: Combats dans le Nord-Est," *Marchés Tropicaux et Méditerranéens*, 6 April 1990, p. 955.

12. "Notes from Meetings on the Darfur Conflict," confidential report prepared in Darfur in May 1990, in the authors' possession.

13. "Junta Steps Up Repressive Measures," *Sudan Democratic Gazette*, July 1990, p. 7.

14. "Genocide and the Horn of Africa," *Washington Post*, 1 July 1990, p. B7.

15. "French Combat Buildup in Chad 'Implicit Warning' to Libya," *United Press International* (Paris), 31 March 1990.

16. "Libya Intervening in African Strife Again—U.S. Official," *Reuters*, 11 May 1990.

17. Ibid.

18. "Sudan Says Chad Abducted Sudanese, Libyans," *UPI*, 13 May; Radio Agence France Press (in English), 1812 GMT, 13 March; SUNA Radio (in French), Khartoum, 0915 GMT, 14 March 1990.

19. "Sudan Says Chad Burned Its Villages," 15 May 1990; "Chad Condemns Sudan's Complicity with Libya," *Xinhua Government News Service*, 16 May 1990; BBC, *Summary of World Broadcasts*, ME/o766/ii, 17 May 1990.

20. *FEWS Bulletin*, no. 8, U.S. Agency for International Development, Washington, D.C., 31 August 1990.

21. "Dying by the Thousands; Darkness in the Sudan," *New York Times*, 8 June 1990, p. 30.

22. See J. Millard Burr and Robert O. Collins, *Requiem for the Sudan: War, Drought & Disaster Relief on the Nile* (Boulder: Westview Press, 1994), Ch. 9.

23. *Al-Sudan Al-Hadith* (Khartoum), 27 October 1990; *Le Monde*, 5 November 1990.

24. "Harvest Assessment of Cereal Production," *FEWS Bulletin*, U.S. Agency for International Development, Washington, D.C., January 1991, p. 33.

25. *Sudan Update* (London), 25 September 1990, p. 1; *Sudan Update* (London), 5 November 1990, p. 3; *Sudan Democratic Gazette* (London), 1 November 1990.

26. "Chad Claims It Routed Attackers from Sudan," *Washington Times*, 12 November 1990, p. A2.

27. Ibid.

28. "France Sends Troops Near Chad-Sudan Frontier," *UPI*, 16 November 1990.

29. "Usurper Promises Elections in Chad," *Washington Times*, 3 December 1990, p. A7.

30. "Libya Irked at Move of Guerrillas," *Washington Times*, 11 December 1990, p. A7; *Washington Report on Middle East Affairs*, February 1991, p. 62.

31. Raymond W. Copson, *Africa's Wars and Prospects for Peace* (London: M. E. Sharpe, 1994), p. 127.

32. *Amnesty International Report* 33 (1990); *Le Figaro*, 5 December 1990.

33. "Central Africa: Chad," *FBIS*, 3 December 1990, p. 4.

34. "How a Rebel Victory Was So Easily Won in Chad," *New York Times*, 16 December 1990; "Sudan: Sense of Unreality," *Middle East International*, 7 December 1990; Sennen Andriamirado, "Le Multipartisme, demain . . . peut-être," *Jeune Afrique*, 5 February 1991, pp. 20–21. For the Deby visit to Paris see "Le Président Déby a demandé le soutien de la France," *Le Monde*, 14 February 1991, p. 9.

35. "Trafic d'influence," *Africa International*, February 1991, p. 30

36. "Horn of Africa: One Down, Two to Go," *Colin Legum's Third World Reports* (London), 30 January 1991.

13

The End of an Epic

By 1991 Africa's thirty years war had come full circle. The generation of struggle for its political unification was at an end not because of the inspiration by its new leader, Idriss Deby, but because the people of Chad were exhausted. Northerners prayed for rain; southerners prayed for peace. The drought in the Sahel, which had been present through many of the years of the independent Republic of Chad, was beginning its fourth decade. Another Gourane had seized power, and he was almost as taciturn as his predecessor and like him was surrounded by a humorless circle of friends and a Praetorian Guard of Zaghawa and Bedeiyat that represented a very small proportion of the people of Chad.

Idriss Deby had many problems. The B.E.T. was ungovernable. The Arabs in the heartland of Chad and Ndjamena despised both Gourane and southern politicians. The African south would prefer to secede than to be ruled by the Zaghawa, the Arabs, or the Muslim north. Nevertheless, Deby made appointments to his government from a wide spectrum of Chadians, which included Habre's former supporters. Not surprisingly, the Zaghawa, Bedeiyat, and Hadjerai replaced Habre's Daza in the Republican Guard. Deby, however, sought to incorporate the tribal leaders and their men from the defeated FANT to expand the army of Chad from 35,000 men in December 1990 to 50,000 under French instructors recruited in January 1991 to reorganize the Chad army. In southern Wadai some Hadjerai refused to accept Deby, but the disaffected seemed more interested in bush banditry and selling arms than in challenging the new government in Ndjamena. In the west, Habre had rallied his loyalists, who had followed him to Nigeria, but their members were small and they had no appetite for war.

Qaddafi, who had devoted his political life to backing losers in Chad, was astonished by Deby's dramatic victory. After three decades of frustration south of the Fezzan, he was much older if not wiser. He now had his man in Ndjamena, who acknowledged that Chad and Libya were "linked by history."[1] Deby appeared willing to open negotiations with Qaddafi and Bashir for a more unified political relationship with those on whom he had been dependent for the arms that had made possible his success. Deby was a Zaghawa, the traditional enemies of the Arabs, but he now openly spoke of "Arab unity" much to the discomfort of his Zaghawa followers, who had become the beneficiaries of the success made possible by the Arabs. As the months passed, Deby continued to consolidate his political ties with Libya and the Sudan. The Aozou was quiet, and in June 1991, the Libyans were withdrawing in the heat from their bases in northern Darfur. Their retirement from Chad and the Sudan appeared to resolve the problem of Chad. This calm was soon to be shattered, however, by Idriss Deby himself. Having received massive military support from Qaddafi and the sanctuary in Darfur from Bashir, he could not be as intractable as Habre, but he had to demonstrate to his enlarged non-Arab constituency that he was more a Chadian nationalist than Qaddafi would have supposed.

In February 1991 President Deby arrived in Tripoli to a grand reception, which was somewhat spoiled when he announced in his public address that Chad would press its claim to the Aozou Strip at the International Court of Justice. From Tripoli he traveled to Paris, where the confrontation between Habre and Deby was regarded with stoic ennui as yet another battle in the *guerre des chefs*, another *Tchado-Tchadien* struggle amongst the chieftains of the desert in which Mitterrand proceeded as though nothing new had happened in Chad. Deby extracted additional funds for development and the continued presence in Chad of Operation Épervier. Deby, like Habre, then exerted his independence by dismissing any integration of Chad and Libya. By 1992 Qaddafi's neighbors, regardless of ethnicity, ideology, or nationality, were now exhausted and contemptuous of the puerile pleas for political integration by those who had been cultural, economic, and territorial enemies for centuries.

Regional Realignment

Few mourned the passing of Hissene Habre—certainly not the French—and there were no illusions in the United States Department of State that Habre would reduce or end the intolerable human rights violations that had characterized the last years of his rule. His defeat, however, was not welcomed in Washington. The prospect of any entente between Chad and Libya was regarded as hostile to the interests of the United States. There was little reason for the government of the United States to agonize over the fate of a large and impoverished country. Chad was located somewhere in the heart of Africa inhabited by camels, irresponsible leaders, and a small population with a history of political disarray led by chieftains of dubious ability and proven duplicity. The Berlin Wall was falling, the Soviet Union was in collapse, and Iraq was invading Kuwait. A new world order was arising, like a Phoenix, from the ashes of the dying fires of the cold war in which Qaddafi confirmed the importance of Chad for the United States more than its African inhabitants south of the Sahara. The United States recognized the new government of Chad and agreed to provide, in cooperation with the European Economic Community, 40,000 tons of grain to ameliorate the devastating impact of the drought and famine in northern Chad.[2] This humanitarian offer was enthusiastically received by Deby, for his close association with Libya had raised questions in the United States Department of State about the recognition of his government at a time when his Zaghawa were seeking food and shelter for 8,000 "widows and orphans."[3]

Unlike the years of the Reagan administration, those of Bush were not consumed by the relationship between Chad and Libya or that between Deby and Qaddafi. During the decades of the thirty years war Qaddafi had been systematically isolated. His own advocacy of terrorism had produced a hostile reaction from the international community, the overt air strikes of the United States, the condemnations in the United Nations, and the rhetoric of exasperated African leaders at the OAU. After two Libyan intelligence agents were indicted in Great Britain and the United States for the demolition of Pan American Airways Flight 103 in December 1988 that exploded over Lockerbie, Scotland, the UN imposed economic sanctions against Libya that confirmed Qaddafi's isolation. Confronted by these international condemnations, he appears to have restricted but not abandoned his support for the terrorist organizations that had operated from Libya.[4]

In the Sudan drought and famine raged throughout Darfur in 1991 to the indifference of President Bashir, who celebrated the second anniversary of his Government of National Salvation on 30 June to a very sparse audience whose only dignitaries were Qaddafi and Idriss Deby. The laconic turnout for the Islamists "sums up the extent of success achieved by the [Bashir government] in two years—just Qaddafi and Deby. . . . the West had largely given up on the junta, and Khartoum has given up trying to win friends there."[5] In Ndjamena and in Khartoum, Qaddafi had became a middle-aged Nasserite who represented a threadbare political ideology unredeemed by an acceptable religious theology by either Sufi or Sunni. He had never been a *talibe* of the nineteenth-century Islamic reformers from the western Sudan and the Nile, or of the Grand Sanusi, whose homeland was in Libya and whose followers Qaddafi ruthlessly suppressed. Qaddafi, unlike Hasan al-Turabi in the Sudan, was intellectually unprepared or incapable to play any significant political or intellectual role in shaping the destiny of Islam at the end of the twentieth century.

During the thirty years war, the relations between Qaddafi and the leaders of Chad had been defined by ethnicity, personalities, greed, and the imperial dream for the control of land that had no relevance to its value. These motivations were no different from those of past invaders of the Sahara, Sahel, and the savanna of Chad. Soon after Idriss Deby and his Toyotas entered Ndjamena, he offended his patron in Tripoli and asserted the independence of Chadians from Libyan imperialism. The years of political and military defeats in Chad and the cumulative recriminations had taken their toll on Qaddafi, who was growing old. If Chad was tired of war, so was Qaddafi. In his mature and more moderate years, Muammar Qaddafi could derive the imperial satisfaction that as "emperor" he had survived

Tombalbaye, Malloum, Goukouni, and Habre. He now began to behave like a father figure.

In January 1991 Qaddafi warned President Bashir in Khartoum that his Islamist advisors led by Hasan al-Turabi were taking the Sudan down a dark and dangerous path. Qaddafi had published his heterodox views of Islam in the *Green Book,* which was unacceptable to the *ulama* and disturbing to Turabi. Now in 1991 Qaddafi was alarmed for political as well as religious reasons. He had become deeply concerned about "the conspicuous influx" of Iranians and *Mujahidiin* into Libya, many of whom had been "working in Islamist military training camps" in the Sudan.[6] Radical "Arab-Afghans" who were veterans of the fierce fighting in Afghanistan and had defeated the Soviet army were now using Turabi and his People's Arab and Islamic Conference, founded in Khartoum in April 1991 as a sanctuary and staging area to destabilize the governments of Algeria and Tunisia. In Khartoum the Revolutionary Command Council was "systematically dismantling the modern state of Sudan . . . in a dictatorship without a dictator" to build a theocratic state espoused by Hasan al-Turabi as a "new Islamic Model."[7] The state was to be directed by Umar Hasan Ahmad al-Bashir to consolidate the religious revolution through a pervasive security force and a relentless intelligence service dominated by the ideology and personnel of the National Islamic Front, the NIF. Bashir imposed the most implacable authoritarian government in the history of the Sudan, ancient or modern, to the astonishment, if not disbelief, of the Sudanese. "We have never known a situation like this in our history. . . . Today you are afraid to ask your brother if he is in [Turabi's] NIF."[8]

Once Deby had firmly entrenched himself in Ndjamena, Bashir and the RCC were finally free to crush the opposition in Darfur, whether traditional, ethnic, or religious. In August 1991 the infamous Colonel Al-Tayib Ibrahim Muhammad Kheir of the Revolutionary Command Council was appointed governor of Darfur with orders to reduce the insecurity of the rulers from Khartoum that had characterized the governance of the west for a generation. A former dentist and firm believer in the mission of the National Islamic Front, Muhammad Kheir was known as *Al-Sikha,* the Iron Bar, named for the one he carried and applied with enthusiasm to quell street riots in Khartoum. Kheir was the Chief of Islamic Security in the Bashir government and essential to its survival. He carried out his duties in Darfur with the same vigor that he had employed in the capital and Omdurman. Those Fur who resisted the Arab administration of Darfur, Kordofan, and Khartoum were resolutely suppressed, and those Zaghawa who had opposed Deby were forcibly disarmed in the Sudan. Kheir and his security forces collected a mountain of arms, and even the free-spirited Zaghawa realized that the *razzia* would have to be suspended. As long as Bashir was in Khartoum and Deby was in Ndjamena, the fractious Zaghawa no longer had a sanctuary in Darfur or Wadai.[9] Deprived of their weapons, the Zaghawa from Chad now had little choice but to join the 12,000 refugees being repatriated by the UNHCR to Chad in February 1992.[10] In addition thousands of Hadjerai who had sought asylum in southern Darfur were told by Kheir's officials that they would either have to return to Chad or be surrendered to Deby's officials. Few of them returned to Chad preferring to follow the traditional routes of the slave traders into the Central African Republic where they participated in rural banditry.

The demise of the Soviet Union produced a realignment of self-interest in Libya, Chad, and the Sudan as in central Asia. Qaddafi began to seek a rapprochement with Egypt at a time when the Sudan appeared determined to assume the leadership of the more fundamental Islamist movements in the Middle East. Qaddafi's overtures to Egypt ironically coincided with the transfer of terrorist training camps from Libya to the Sudan, where the recruits began to conspire to overthrow him. These reports elicited surprising commentary in the United States. "What do the U.S. and Libya have in common? . . . They share a growing concern over the rise of Islamic fundamentalism in Sudan."[11] Not surprisingly, the Libya-Sudan Integration Charter disintegrated. Qaddafi denounced Hasan al-Turabi's "public complaints" about "Tripoli's improving ties with Egypt" as an intolerable intrusion into Libyan affairs. He halted all oil shipments to the Sudan in November 1991 and demanded at least a symbolic repayment in return for the large loans he had given to the Bashir government.

In Ndjamena Deby understood that any tripartite alliance of Libya, Chad, and the Sudan was as dead as the Libya-Sudan Integration Charter. Despite his growing skepticism about Bashir and the RCC, which was reinforced by reports that the National Islamic Front was seeking "to infiltrate" his government, Deby continued to be received in Khartoum with the ebullient hospitality for which the Sudanese are famous.[12] Perhaps this was NIF dissimulation disguising more ambitious designs in Chad for the Islamic revolution of Hasan al-Turabi, in emulation of the nineteenth-century reformers Al-Hajj Umar, Muhammad Ahmad al-Mahdi, and the Grand Sanusi.[13]

Chad in Political Change

Upon his arrival in Ndjamena Idriss Deby had, like his predecessors, promised a New Chad in which all ethnic and political parties could participate, but unlike former presidents, he demonstrated an unexpected talent for reducing ethnic and regional tensions. At first his revolution appeared no different from those of the past and particularly that of Hissene Habre, except for the changing of the guard from Gourane to Zaghawa. After thirty years of war, famine, and greed, Chad was an exhausted country of arbitrary boundaries and inhabitants who were now prepared to ignore the rhetoric of the latest conqueror in return for the reality of stability upon which any return to a secure livelihood and economic prosperity was dependent. There had always been a lack of capable administrators in Chad so that President Deby, like Habre, was not going to deny the request of former leaders to return to Chad so long as they pledged loyalty to his government.

When Acheikh Ibn Omar, that quintessential survivor who had served every side in the thirty years war, decided to return, he was welcomed and made a special counselor to Deby. In May 1991 the old rogue, Goukouni Oueddei, returned to Ndjamena for the first time in nine years. Disclaiming any political ambition, which no one believed, he remained a few days to demand preferential treatment for his loyal followers before returning to Tripoli and obscurity.[14] Of course, Wadal Abdelkader Kamougue, another survivor, returned with many southerners who had fled to West Africa, among whom was the son of Ngartha Tombalbaye seeking to resurrect his father's political legacy.

The return of the old political warriors was more symbolic than real. Deby had to accept their presence as former politicians and warlords for they all had residual constituencies, and their ephemeral political parties with forgotten acronyms could not be ignored. Deby was aware, however, that they represented trouble not so much by their political past or the followers they could mobilize but by their proven incompetence, which would lead them into marginal disruption to the distraction of his government and his own ill-defined political objectives. In October 1991 the interior minister, vice president, and the resident Hadjerai revolutionary, Maldoum Bada Abbas, precipitated the first unsuccessful coup against Deby. It was dismissed as yet another demonstration of ethnic petulance, caused by the thirty years war, but this time against his Zaghawa.[15] Under Deby human rights violations were just as prevalent but perhaps more subdued. Nevertheless, his intelligence service was just as ubiquitous as that of Hissene Habre, and the French secret service (SDECE) continued to demonstrate its proficiency in the internal affairs of Chad under the command of the flamboyant Colonel Paul Fontbonne, whose displays of bravado were even too flagrant for his government. He was recalled in January 1992.

After the failure of the attempted coup d'état in October 1991, Deby dissolved Habre's nascent National Consultative Council, which had been elected in July and convened in October 1990. He abrogated the constitution that the council had approved and promulgated. The National Union for the Independence and Revolution (UNIR), the party of Hissene Habre, was dissolved. Deby's MPS quickly assumed its place as the only recognized political party in Chad, and in March 1991 he issued a national charter that promised a new constitution and an ambitious program for democracy. To fulfill this promise Deby announced in October 1991 that political parties were legally free to organize and campaign as long as they prohibited any tribal, regional, or religious discrimination for national elections in 1993. He also guaranteed elections for the High Transitional Council and the prefectures by April 1994. He appointed a Provisional Council of the Republic of thirty members, which would serve as the legislature until the national elections could be held. All of these affirmations were more reminiscent of the past than the future. The endless rhetoric, the appeals to democracy, and the creation of intricate institutions of government had little or no relevance to the traditional cultural, political, or religious manifestations of life in Chad.

On the one hand, Deby had promised democracy for Chad, which presupposed the authoritarian dissolution of Habre's ubiquitous security apparatus. On the other, he was determined to govern. Like Habre, he was a son of the Sahara and Sahel, and like Habre, he too turned to the same means to rule a hostile population in a harsh environment. These were the continuities of the past that Deby could not deny or ignore in the present. He re-created another demonic intelligence organization that was the equal to that of Tombalbaye and his Sara or Habre and his Gourane. To justify his own apparatus for authoritarian rule, the Deby media asserted that Habre had executed 40,000 political enemies and that the new government must exert vigilance against those who would use such brutal methods to return to power. At the same time he resuscitated Habre's dreaded Document and Security Directorate (DDS) to which was added a new agency, the Research Center for Intelligence Coordination, Centre des Recherches et de Coordination de Renseignements (CRCR), the principal objective of which appears to be the refinement of interrogation. The Public Security Directorate was expanded and its domestic investigations placed under the direct control of the president. Deby had been accepted in the expectation of better things to come. This optimism, that eternal hope for peace and prosperity, had never completely been extinguished throughout the three decades of the thirty years war. These hopes were now once again replaced by the fears of the past, the agonizing realization that the bad old days were a historic continuity rather than a thirty-year aberration. There was, of course, opposition to the return of tyranny. But Deby, like his predecessors, was able to repel a coup planned by his ministers, a mutiny in the army, and a general strike that followed the assassination of the human rights advocate Joseph Bihidi.

Habre, Hail and Farewell

Habre was determined to return by a last desperate roll of the dice. In January 1992 he rallied his supporters, who had congregated in eastern Nigeria in anticipation of a triumphal march to Ndjamena. His once formidable following had now, however, been reduced to a rabble in arms consisting of the sunshine warriors from the Movement for Democracy and Development (Mouvement pour Démocratie et Développement), the MDD, and the FAO. The MDD were the devoted supporters of Habre from the FANT under a new name. The FAO, the Western Armed Forces, the Forces Armées Occidentales, represented an insignificant rebel organization, which was more a nuisance than a threat on the Chad-Nigerian frontier despite their claim to have been the warriors of the Third FROLINAT Army in more heady days. Both of these groups now combined to restore Habre to power in Ndjamena, but they were publicly denounced by the governments of Niger and Nigeria who wished to disassociate themselves from their activities, which were characterized more by banditry than the restoration of Habre in Chad.

Led by Goukouni Guet, Habre's warriors were at first successful, capturing the towns of Liwa and Bol. But as they continued on to Lake Chad they were soundly defeated by the Chad army under the Zaghawa commander Mahamat Ali Abdallah, who was supported by 1,500 Zaghawa of the Republican Guard. Having suffered very heavy casualties, the survivors retreated in disarray to Nigeria leaving behind hundreds of dead and wounded. The government of Nigeria detained the defeated and refused to support Habre. He was, finally, a loser who would not involve Nigeria once again in the problem of Chad. The rebels were repatriated to Chad but not before most had fled to Niger where they continued to plot the overthrow of Deby and his government. His invasion of Chad in January 1992 was the last adventure of Hissene Habre.

Although Habre no longer was a danger to Deby, the Hadjerai continued to challenge him. In the councils of government in Ndjamena there was a rapid deterioration between the Zaghawa of Deby and the Hadjerai of Maldoum Abbas. There were inveterate disputes and interminable disagreements, which led to the purge of the Hadjerai representatives in the government and the arrest of their leader, Maldoum. Rhetoric and verbal diatribe soon deteriorated into physical violence. In October 1991 more than two hundred Hadjerai and Toubou were executed and hundreds more fled the capital. Hadjerai protesters were attacked in Guera.[16] Those who escaped to Darfur were attacked and harassed by the Sudanese army determined to eliminate armed Chadians on the frontier. They and their fellow rebels remaining in Wadai went into hiding.[17] The Hadjerai were contained, but Hadjerai banditry soon appeared in the south, presumably as much for profit as protest.

The people of Chad—whether in the north, center, or south—were very tired of thirty years of war. They had suffered enough. They had drunk very deep from the flagons of nationalism, regionalism, ethnicity, egocentrism, religion, and sectarianism. All the former personalities—young and old, near and far—had returned to Chad. Like old times, almost everyone devoted their energies to founding a political party, which Deby allowed rather than encouraged among the populace. For the first time in the history of independent Chad there appeared an opportunity to influence the government through the ballot box rather than the automatic rifle. In March Deby approved the creation of the Rally for Democracy and Progress. This was a coalition of insignificant and self-proclaimed political parties led by Lol Mahamat Choua, the mayor of Ndjamena, former president of Chad in 1979 and a loyal minister of transportation in the Habre government, and the self-styled politician Elie Romba. Four other parties were shortly recognized in March and April to begin a flood of repressed political activity; forty political parties were registered in the unrestrained freedom of association unknown in the past.[18] When Deby formed his new cabinet in May, it was representative of this expanded political participation if not the plethora of parties.

When President Deby celebrated the second anniversary of his entry into Ndjamena on 1 December 1992, his critics claimed that little had changed in Chad.

After thirty years of war and a new government promising peace and prosperity, Chad was still one of the poorest countries. The per capita income was less than $200 per year and the life expectancy only forty-seven years. Habre's "torturers and murderers" were "still walking around" Ndjamena, and a committee from the ministry of justice had reported the names of 1,075 individuals guilty of definable human rights violations, none of whom had ever been tried in a court of law by any government of Chad. "Under Habre people were killed in prisons, under Deby they're killed in the street. That is the only difference."[19] That was perhaps a much too bleak appraisal, for some things had indeed changed. In September 1992 the government signed peace agreements with several rebel organizations. The defeated rebel units of the FAO surrendered their arms to Sudanese officials after their defeat and organized themselves into a civilian political party under Mahmoud Ali Mahmoud, which participated in the Sovereign National Conference at Ndjamena in January 1993 attended by some 750 delegates. It was a surprising and strange end to FROLINAT.

This was not an easy or willing march to democracy. Tribal warfare and ethnic struggles did not disappear.[20] The great number of petty parties made political cooperation, coalitions, or cohesion quite impossible. Five parties were registered in the first week of June 1992. Another seventeen were "awaiting registration," but this incoherent number of organizations ironically provided Deby with the opportunity to assert his ascendancy as the leader of the one disciplined party that commanded the loyalty of the presidential guard and the army. In 1993 a Sovereign National Conference confirmed Deby as the chief of state of a Transitional Government and conducted the election of fifty-seven counselors to a Legislative Higher Transitional Council (CST) to govern under a transitional charter as a constitution.

Stability and governance in Chad remained a chimera when the presidency was transitional, the Higher Council of government was transitional, and the charter of their legitimacy was as transitory as its authors. Although Deby had agreed to submit his authority to national elections, by the time they would be held there was no doubt that he, like his predecessors and the most prominent warlords, would remain in office. In April 1993 Amnesty International published a scathing report denouncing the Chad security forces as "judge, jury, and executioner" in the massacre of civilians living in southern Chad.[21] After two years in power the government of Idriss Deby appeared as repressive as that of Hissene Habre, but he could not ignore the publication and international condemnation of the human rights violations of his regime, particularly in southern Chad. He closed the Research Center for Intelligence Coordination, the embarrassing symbol of his regime's repression and torture of political enemies.

Embracing democracy, on the one hand, and curtailing the excesses of his security forces, on the other, were not to characterize the future of Chad. After thirty years of war, Chad had been reduced to a state of poverty, an outpost in the global economy. The army and the bureaucracy still consumed in salaries alone half the state budget, and despite a good price for cotton and substantial financial assistance from the UN, Europe, and the United States, the government was virtually bankrupt. Deby opposed the attempts of his own African financial advisors and the French to restrict the printing of worthless money to pay the military and the civil servants.[22] Unfortunately for the government, the pillage of the public purse was not about to be restored by nature. After two good years of harvest, the drought returned to devastate Chad. More than half a million people were seeking food from government stocks that had all but disappeared.[23] By 1993 the economy of Chad had become totally dependent upon foreign assistance. The primary source of foreign exchange for Chad was cotton, which had received a favorable price in 1990s in the international market, but the government of Idriss Deby survived not through cotton revenues but the financial assistance of the Europeans, the United States, and the United Nations. The government presses continued to print currency with enthusiasm, which those in the corrupt and enfeebled government could not distribute with sufficient speed to pay its servants or the debts owed to domestic merchants. After thirty years of war the original disciplined and dedicated warriors of Chad were either dead or dying of old age. There were now, however, 40,000 men in the army of Chad, but these unpaid and ill-disciplined warriors of the popular defense force were neither mercenaries nor a militia. They presented no threat to the well-armed, disciplined, and ethnic presidential guard of President Deby and therefore constituted no threat to his government.

France, Deby, and Oil

The French were not about to support the intrigues of Hissene Habre to return to Ndjamena. Aside from their personal animosity for Habre, the French were convinced that he would fail. Their commitment to Deby was less than enthusiastic but demonstrated by the very public presence of French military advisors in the capital. They were now more conspicuous than at any time in the recent past, and French aircraft used the Ndjamena airport to provide Khartoum with aerial photographs of the Upper Nile and the activities of Southern Sudanese insurgents, the SPLA, under John de Garang. French commercial interests had revived, and the cotton market was flourishing in a mercantile atmosphere more free than had existed under Habre. When his ragtag forces actually invaded Chad from eastern Nigeria, the French sent 450 paratroopers to reinforce Deby's 1,200 troops around Ndjamena and placed its air force in Africa on alert. The French historic infatuation with Chad, however, was not an unrestricted mandate to support Idriss Deby. After thirty years of war that had frequently been a humiliating embarrassment to France and that had compromised the French government on more than one occasion, they were prepared to keep Habre out of Ndjamena but were cautious in embracing the new Zaghawa. Indeed, they began to distance themselves from the Deby government, particularly after another attempted coup in June of 1992 made the fragility of his rule all the more visible. The French were equally alarmed by Deby's gestures toward democracy, particularly his proposal for a national conference of all political factions in Chad. Indeed, "French officials believed that Deby's regime [would be] too weak to survive the ensuing debate."[24]

Despite their serious reservations about the stability and tenure of the Deby government, the discovery of oil dramatically changed the French attitude and policy toward his struggling regime. It was real petroleum and not the mythical uranium deposits of the Aozou Strip that would extract Deby from the economic sands of Chad by providing the economic resources none of his predecessors had enjoyed. An Exxon-Shell consortium had assumed the CONOCO concession after their unsuccessful explorations to discover significant reserves of high viscosity crude in four sedimentary basins in southern Chad with an estimated of one billion barrels. Exxon-Shell were well aware that the development of their field could not be realized in this French sphere of influence, whether colonial or neocolonial, without French participation, which was made abundantly clear by the French government. It was, therefore, diplomatic and expedient for the success of their investment to cede in 1991 20 percent of their concession to Elf, the principal French company involved in overseas oil exploration.[25] The Exxon-Shell-Elf consortium proposed to construct a 650-mile pipeline from the Chari Basin in southern Chad to the Atlantic coast of the Cameroon. The prospect of an infusion of oil revenues into the poverty of Chad encouraged the World Bank to reexamine the requests from Chad for financial assistance. Hitherto, the bank had avoided any commitments to Chad. Thirty years of war and political instability had discouraged both foreign and domestic investment; any resources that Chad might have possessed had been consumed by war, not devoted to the advancement of civil society. The prospect of developing resources, particularly petroleum, could no longer ignored by the World Bank in a country so desperately in need of assistance. The bank agreed to help finance a small refinery at Ndjamena that could provide fuel to generate electric power in Chad, where more than 98 percent of its people are without it. The refinery, to be completed in the year 2000, is the first positive project for economic growth in Chad in thirty years; it also lends stability and prosperity to the commercial and political elite controlling the government of Chad.[26]

The Aozou Solution

The historic stability of Chad did not, however, rest on the future promise of oil but on the resolution of the ownership of that wasteland known as the Aozou Strip. Many had died, governments had fallen, and the strategic forces of the Western world had been mobilized against Libyan imperialism and terrorism, symbolized by the Aozou, to deny Qaddafi's determination to ensure his sovereignty over this insignificant region of the Sahara consisting of nothing but sand and rock and wind. If Qaddafi had presumed that Idriss Deby would repay his generous support by accepting the Libyan assimilation of Aozou, he was soon disabused, if not disillusioned. After his triumphal entry to Ndjamena one of the first proclamations by the new ruler of Chad was to assure its inhabitants that he, Idriss Deby, had "never given a verbal or written pledge to Tripoli, and I have never gambled with Chadian territory."[27] In February 1991 he renewed the case for the sovereignty of Chad over the Aozou Strip, an issue that Habre had pressed before the World Court at the Hague since 1988. In February 1994 the International Court of Justice ruled 16 to 1 that the Aozou Strip belonged to Chad and that all the military and political officials from Libya should be withdrawn by 31 May 1994. With that decision a page in the book of the history of Africa was closed to bring an end to thirty years of violent conflict in which so many had died for so little. The epitaph was recorded in a very small article at the bottom of page A6 in the *New York Times* of 4 February 1994.[28]

The war for Chad was over. An older, more mature, and chastened Qaddafi accepted the decision of the International Court of Justice without rancor or protest. Libya immediately began to withdraw its forces to their bases in the Fezzan. On 25 May 1994 the Libyans abandoned Omchi in the heart of Aozou. Five days later the Libyan flag was lowered at Bardai. The ceremony was amicable and attended by the representatives of Libya, France, and Chad. For twenty years Aozou had been the outpost of Qaddafi imperialism whose forces had fought for thirty years on the frontier to carry the banner of the Arabs and Islam across the ancient routes of the Sahara to Africa. Like those who had preceded them during two millennia, they had failed. The French were there to represent their imperial past and the insatiable quest for remote and romantic lands by those seeking adventure, relief from boredom, or patriotism that never dies. The French at Bardai returned to command the eight hundred men of Force Épervier, which would remain as if nothing had changed in the history of Chad, not in thirty years nor a hundred. The French *mission civilitrice* had survived the Third International Theory and the Great Socialist People's Libyan Jamahiriyah of Muammar Qaddafi. After Bardai, Idriss Deby met with Qaddafi in Tripoli. Unlike the past there was no fanfare, no ceremony, and no rhetoric when the two of them signed a Chad-Libya "Treaty of Friendship" to end Africa's thirty years war. It was peace described as friendship, no more, no less.[29]

On that same day one of the great *habubs*, the great dust storms of the Sahara, surged across the B.E.T. and northern Darfur to cover the land mines of the western frontier, and in the way of nature, to return the land to its original condition. Beneath the blanket of sand a million mines remain as the detritus of a nasty little war to kill and maim those in the future who stray from the ancient routes whose remains will continue to remind their descendants of the folly and the terror of Africa's thirty years war.

Notes

1. "Trafic d'influence," *Africa International* (February 1991): 30–31.

2. U.S. Embassy, Ndjamena, Cable 1578, 1991; Ndjamena FAX No. FL. 037, F. Lee to FEWS/Washington, D.C., 8 April 1991.

3. *FEWS Bulletin*, U.S. Agency for International Development, Washington, D.C., 8 March 1991. See extensive data on the population, food production, and consumption in Chad during 1983–1993 in *FEWS Harvest Assessment*, U.S. Agency for International Development, Washington, D.C., February 1993.

4. Tripoli, JANA Radio (in Arabic), 1115 GMT, 3 January 1993; *FBIS*, Report LD0301154293.

5. "Africa Teeters on Famine's Edge," *Christian Science Monitor*, 25 June 1991, p. 4.

6. "Soudan: Le Sabre et Le Coran," *Jeune Afrique*, 4 January–10 February 1993, p. 4.

7. "Under Islamic Siege," *Africa Report* (September-October 1993): 26.

8. "Under Islamic Siege," p. 4; see also *Al-Hayah* (London), 10, 11 November 1993, p. 5.

9. "Sudan: Pacification of Darfur," *New African* (January 1992): 19.

10. UNHCR reports differ significantly from that of "Repatriation of Refugees to Chad," *Horn of Africa Bulletin* (February 1992): 12–13, which reported there were 157,000 refugees from Chad in the Sudan of which 30,000 lived in camps.

11. *Wall Street Journal*, 16 March 1992, p. 10.

12. Report in French on human rights violations in the Sudan prepared by Bernard Georgeot, Pax-Christi-France, 1995, in the authors' possession.

13. R. Buijtenhuijs, *La Conference nationale souveraine du Tchad* (Paris: Karthala, 1993), p. 128; John Chipman, *French Power in Africa* (London: Basil Blackwell, 1989), p. 161.

14. "Chad: The Return of Goukouni," *Africa Confidential*, 31 May 1991.

15. "France Sends Troops to Reinforce Chad," *New York Times*, 4 January 1992; Radio France International, 1230 GMT, Paris, 9 January 1992; Assane Diop, "Plus Ça Change," *Africa Report* (March-April 1992): 25–27.

16. "Histoire de Miracule," *Africa International* (December 1991): 23; "Central Africa," *FBIS*, 14 January 1992, p. 1.

17. "Zaghawa Under Threat," *Sudan Update* (London), January 1994; "Chad: Challenge on Four Flanks," *Africa Confidential*, 15 February 1994.

18. "Capitale de la Terreur," *Africa International* (March-April 1992): 39; "Triple Diagnostic: Lol Mahamat Choua," *Africa International* (January 1993): 36–37; "Plus Ça Change," *Africa Report* (March-April 1992): 25–27.

19. Statement by N. Yarongar of the Action Front for Democracy and Justice in "Habre's Henchmen Alive and Well in Chad," *Middle East Times* (Cairo), 21–27 July 1992, p. 5.

20. "Tribalism and Transition," *Christian Science Monitor*, 24 June 1992, p. 10.

21. "Amnesty Blasts Chad for Letting Troops Kill Civilians," *Washington Times*, 21 April 1993, p. A11.

22. "Les Raisons d'une brouille," *Jeune Afrique*, 23 August–29 September 1993, p. 25.

23. "Sahel Update," *FEWS Bulletin*, USAID, Washington, D.C., June 20-August 20, 1994.

24. *Chad Human Rights Practices, 1994*, U.S. Department of State, Washington, D.C., February 1995.

25. Claude Wauthier, "Une sourde concurrence sur le continent Africain," *Le Monde Diplomatique* (October 1994): 10.

26. "Chad: Oil Production Could Soon Begin," *African Business* (June 1993): 15; *Chad*, Energy Information Administration, U.S. Department of Energy, Washington, D.C., 14 February 1997.

27. "Central Africa: Chad," *FBIS*, 20 December 1990, p. 1.

28. "World Court Rules for Chad in Territorial Dispute with Libya," *New York Times*, 4 February 1994, p. A6.

29. In January 1995 Deby reacted with indignation to and rejected as "baseless fantasy" a Tunisian newspaper report that Chad would soon unite with Libya and the Sudan. "Chad Rejects Talk of Merger with Libya and Sudan," *Reuter* (Ndjamena), 11 January 1995.

Bibliography

Agostini, Col. Enrico de. 1922–1923. *Le popolozioni della Cirenaica e Tripolitania*. Benghazi and Tripoli: Azienda tipolitografica della Scuola d'artie Mestieri.

Agostino, Gaibi. 1934. *Storia delle Colonie Italiano*. Torino: Bramante.

Alawar, Mohamed A., ed. 1983. *A Concise Bibliography of Northern Chad and Fezzan in Southern Libya*. Outwell: Arab Crescent Press.

Allan, J. A., ed. 1982. *Libya Since Independence: Economic and Political Development*. Beckenham: Croom Helm.

Amnesty International. 1983. *Sudan, the Ravages of War: Political Killings and Humanitarian Disaster*. New York: Amnesty International.

Anderson, Lisa. 1986. *The State and Social Transformation in Tunisia and Libya, 1830–1980*. Princeton: Princeton University Press.

Asher, Michael. 1984. *In Search of the Forty Days Road*. Essex: Longmans.

_____. 1988. *Impossible Journey: Two Against the Sahara*. New York: Viking Penguin.

Baier, Stephan. 1980. *An Economic History of Central Niger*. Oxford: Clarendon Press.

Barclay, Sir Thomas. 1912. *The Turco-Italian War and Its Problems*. London: Constable.

Barth, Heinrich. 1965. *Travels and Discoveries in North and Central Africa, 1849–1855*. Vol. 2. London: Frank Cass.

Beer, G. L. 1923. *African Questions at the Peace Conference*. New York: MacMillan.

Beshir, Mohamed Omer. 1975. *The Southern Sudan: From Conflict to Peace*. Khartoum: Khartoum Bookshop.

Bjørkelø, Anders J. 1976. *State and Society in Three Central Sudanic Kingdoms: Kanem-Bornu, Bagirmi, and Wadai*. Bergen, Norway: University of Bergen Press.

Blundy, David, and Andrew Lycett. 1987. *Qaddafi and the Libyan Revolution*. Boston: Little Brown.

Boahen, A. Adu. 1964. *Britain, the Sahara, and the Western Sudan, 1788–1861*. Oxford: Clarendon Press.

Bouquet, Christian. 1982. *Tchad, genèse d'un conflit*. Paris: Éditions L'Harmattan.

Bovill, E. W. 1995. *The Golden Trade of the Moors*. Rev. ed. Princeton: Markus Wiener.

Brenner, Louis. 1973. *The Shehus of Kukawa*. Oxford: Clarendon Press.

Briggs, Lloyd Cabot. 1960. *Tribes of the Sahara*. Cambridge: Harvard University Press.

Brownlie, Ian. 1979. *African Boundaries: A Legal and Diplomatic Encyclopedia*. Berkeley: University of California Press.

Bruel, Georges. 1930. *La France équatoriale africaine*. Paris: Larose.

Buijtenhuijs, Robert. 1978. *Le Frolinat et les revoltes populaires du Tchad, 1965–1976*. The Hague: Mouton.

_____. 1993. *La Conference nationale souveraine du Tchad*. Paris: Karthala.

Burr, J. Millard, and Robert O. Collins. 1994. *Requiem for the Sudan*. Boulder: Westview Press.

Carbou, Henri. 1912. *La Region du Tchad et du Oudai*. 2 vols. Paris: Ernest Leroux.

Casey, William J. 1989. *Scouting the Future: The Public Speeches of William J. Casey*. Washington D.C.: Regnery Gateway.

Chambre de Commerce, d'Agriculture, et d'Industrie du Tchad. 1962. *Tchad 1962*. Monaco: Éditions Paul Bory.

Chapelle, Jean. 1980. *Le Peuple Tchadien: Ses racines et sa vie quotidienne*. Paris: L'Harmattan.

———. 1982. *Nomades noirs du Sahara*. Paris: L'Harmattan.

Chevalier, Auguste. 1907. *L'Afrique centrale française: Récit du voyage de la mission*. Paris: A. Challamel.

Chipman, John. 1989. *French Power in Africa*. Oxford: Basil Blackwell.

Clark, John F., and David E. Gardinier. 1997. *Political Reform in Francophone Africa*. Boulder: Westview Press.

Cohen, Ronald. 1971. "From Empire to Colony: Bornu in the Nineteenth and Twentieth Centuries." In *Colonialism and Africa, 1870–1960*, Vol. 3., edited by V. Turner. Cambridge: Cambridge University Press.

Cohen, Samy. 1980. *Les Conseillers du président de Charles de Gaulle à Valéry Giscard d'Estaing*. Paris: Presses Universitaires de France.

Collelo, Thomas, ed. 1990. *Chad: A Country Study*. Washington, D.C.: U.S. Government Printing Office.

Collins, Robert O. 1962. *The Southern Sudan, 1883–1898: A Struggle for Control*. New Haven: Yale University Press.

———. 1971. *Land Beyond the Rivers: The Southern Sudan, 1898–1918*. New Haven: Yale University Press.

———. 1984. *Shadows in the Grass: Britain in the Southern Sudan, 1918–1956*. New Haven: Yale University Press.

———. 1975. *The Southern Sudan in Historical Perspective*. Tel Aviv: Tel Aviv University Press.

———. 1990. *The Waters of the Nile: Hydropolitics and the Jonglei Canal, 1900–1988*. Oxford: Clarendon Press; Princeton: Markus Wiener.

Cordell, Dennis D. 1985. *Dar al-Kuti and the Last Years of the Trans-Saharan Trade*. Madison: University of Wisconsin Press.

Daly, M. W. 1991. *Imperial Sudan: The Anglo-Egyptian Condominium, 1934–1956*. Cambridge: Cambridge University Press.

Deacon, Richard. 1990. *The French Secret Service*. London: Grafton.

Decalo, Samuel. 1987. *Historical Dictionary of Chad*. 2nd ed. Metuchen, New Jersey: Scarecrow Press.

Deng, Francis Mading, and Prosser Gifford. 1987. *The Search for Peace and Unity in the Sudan*. Washington, D.C.: Wilson Press Center.

De Waal, Alexander. 1986. *Famine That Kills: Darfur, Sudan, 1984–1985*. Khartoum: Save the Children Fund.

Dobson, Christopher, and Ronald Payne. 1987. *The Never Ending War: Terrorism in the 80s*. New York: Facts on File.

Efendi, Abd al-Wahab Al-. 1991. *Turabi's Revolution: Islam and Power in the Sudan*. London: Grey Seal.

El Warfally, Mahmoud G. 1988. *Imagery and Ideology in U.S. Policy Toward Libya*. Pittsburgh: University of Pittsburgh Press.

Evans-Pritchard, Sir E. E. 1949. *The Sanusi of Cyrenaica*. Oxford: Clarendon Press.

Federal Research Division, Library of Congress. 1989. *Libya: A Country Study*. Washington, D.C.: U.S. Government Printing Office.

Furniss, Edgar Stephenson. 1960. *Troubled Ally: De Gaulle's Heritage and Prospects*. New York: Praeger.

Gali Ngothe Gatta. 1985. *Tchad: Guerre civile et désagrégation de l'état*. Paris: Présence Africaine.

Gautier, E.-F. 1937. *Le Passé de l'Afrique du Nord: Les Siècles obscurs*. Paris: Payot.

_____. 1950. *Le Sahara*. Paris: Payot.

Gentil, Emile. 1902. *La Chute de l'empire de Rabah*. Paris: Hachette.

_____. 1971. *La Conquête du Tchad, 1894–1916: Service historique de l'armée*. 2 vols. Paris: Payot.

Gera, Gershon. 1980. "Libya and the United States: A Relationship of Self-Fulfilling Expectations?" In Haim Shaked and Itimar Rabinovich, eds., *The Middle East and the United States: Perceptions and Policies*. New Brunswick, New Jersey: Transaction Books.

Giglio, Carlo. 1932, *La confraternita Senussita dalle sue origins a oggi*. Padua: CEDAM.

Graziani, Rudolfo. 1932. *Cirenaica Pacificata*. Milan: A. Mondadori.

Gurdon, Charles. 1984. *Sudan at the Crossroads*. London: Middle East and North African Press.

_____. 1986. *Sudan in Transition: A Political Risk Analysis*. London: Economist Intelligence Unit.

Habre, Hissene. 1984. *Pensées et citations*. Ndjamena: Direction de la Presse Présidentielle.

Hahn, Lorna. 1981. *Historical Dictionary of Libya*. Metuchen, New Jersey: Scarecrow Press.

Haley, P. Edward. 1984. *Qaddafi and the United States Since 1969*. New York: Praeger.

Hallam, W.K.R. 1977. *The Life and Times of Rabih Fadl Allah*. Ilfracombe: Arthur H. Stockwell.

Hamilton, J. A. de C. 1935. *The Anglo-Egyptian Sudan from Within*. London: Faber and Faber.

Hassanein, Ahmed Mohammed. 1925. *The Lost Oases*. London: Thornton Butterworth.

Hertslet, Sir Edward. 1967. *The Map of Africa by Treaty*. 3 vols. 3rd ed. London: Frank Cass.

Hill, Richard Leslie. 1939. *A Bibliography of the Anglo-Egyptian Sudan: From the Earliest Times to 1937*. London: Oxford University Press.

_____. 1951. *Biographical Dictionary of the Anglo-Egyptian Sudan*. Oxford: Clarendon Press.

_____. 1959. *Egypt in the Sudan*. London: Oxford University Press.

_____. 1959. *Slatin Pasha*. London: Oxford University Press.

Holt, P. M., and M. W. Daly. l988. *A History of the Sudan, From the Coming of Islam to the Present Day*. New York: Longmans.

Hugot, Pierre. 1955. *Le Tchad*. Vichy: Imprimerie Wallon.

Jansen, G. H. 1979. *Militant Islam*. New York: Harper & Row.

Jaulin, Robert. 1967. *La Mort Sara: L'Ordre de la vie ou la pensée de la mort au Tchad*. Paris: Librairie Plon.

Joffe, E., and K. S. McLachlan, eds. 1982. *Social and Economic Development of Libya*. Wisbech: Menas Press.

Kapteijns, Lidwien. 1985. *Mahdist Faith and Sudanic Tradition: The History of the Masalit Sultanate, 1870–1930*. London: KPI.

Kapteijns, Lidwien, and Jay Spaulding. 1988. *After the Millenium: Diplomatic Correspondence from Wadai and Dar Fur on the Eve of Colonial Conquest, 1885–1916.* East Lansing: Michigan State university Press.

_____. 1994. *An Islamic Alliance: 'Ali Dinar and the Sanussiya, 1906–1916.* Evanston, Illinois: Northwestern University Press.

Khadduri, Majid. 1963. *Modern Libya: A Study in Political Development.* Baltimore: Johns Hopkins University Press.

Kirkpatrick, Ivone. 1964. *Mussolini: A Study in Power.* New York: Hawthorn Books.

Korn, D. A. 1993. *Assassination in Khartoum.* Bloomington: Indiana University Press.

Langer, William L. 1968. *The Diplomacy of Imperialism, 1890–1902.* 2nd ed. New York: Alfred A. Knopf.

Lanne, Bernard. 1982. *Tchad-Libye: La Querelle des frontières.* Paris: Éditions Karthala.

_____. 1983. *Liste des chefs des unites administrative du Tchad, 1906–1983.* Paris: École des Hautes Études en Sciences Sociales.

Laqueur, Walter. 1974. *Confrontation: The Middle East and World Politics.* New York: Bantam Books.

Law, Robin. 1980. *The Horse in West African History: The Role of the Horse in the Society of Pre-Colonial Africa.* London: Oxford University Press

Le Cornec, Jacques. 1963. *Histoire politique du Tchad de 1900 à 1962.* Paris: Librairie Générale de Droit et de Jurisprudence.

Lemarchand, René. 1990. *Qaddafi's African Policies.* Bloomington: Indiana University Press.

Livingstone, N. C., and D. Halvey. 1990. *Inside the PLO.* New York: William Morrow.

Lunt, James. 1989. *Hussein of Jordan.* New York: William Morrow.

Macaluso, Giuseppe. 1930. *Turchi, Senussi, e Italiani in Libia.* Benghazi: Vitalie Colonie.

Mahdi, Sadiq al-. 1978. "The Concept of an Islamic State." In *The Challenge of Islam,* edited by Altaf Gauhar. London: Islamic Council of Europe.

Mann, M. J. 1962. *Fish Production and Marketing from the Nigerian Shores of Lake Chad.* Lagos: Government of Nigeria, Ministry of Economic Development.

Massey, W. T. 1918. *The Desert Campaigns.* London: Constable.

Merari, A., and S. Elad. 1986. *The International Dimensions of Palestinian Terrorism.* Boulder: Westview Press.

Metz, Helen Chapin, ed. 1989. *Libya: A Country Study.* Washington, D.C.: U.S. Government Printing Office.

Mezzetti, Ottorino. 1933. *Guerra in Libia.* Rome: Cremonese.

Miège, J. L. 1976. *L'Imperialismo coloniale italiano dal 1870 ai giorni nostri.* Milan: Rizzoli.

Mitchell, R. P. 1969. *The Society of Muslim Brothers.* London: Oxford University Press.

Muller, M. 1982. "Frontiers, an Imported Concept: An Historical Review of the Creation and Consequences of Libya's Frontiers." In *Libya Since Independence: Economic and Political Development,* edited by J. A. Allan. Beckenham: Croom Helm.

Nachtigal, Gustav. 1974–1980. *Sahara and Sudan.* 4 vols. London: C. Hurst.

Neuberger, Benyamin. 1982. *Involvement, Invasion, and Withdrawal: Qadhdhafi's Libya and Chad, 1969–1981.* Tel Aviv: Tel Aviv University Occasional Papers, No. 83, May.

N'Gangbet, Michel. 1984. *Peut-on encore sauver le Tchad?* Paris: Éditions Karthala.

O'Fahey, R. S. 1990. *Enigmatic Saint: Ahmad Ibn Idris and the Idrisi Tradition.* London: C. Hurst

_____. 1980. *State and Society in Dar Fur.* London: C. Hurst.

Palmer, H. R. 1936. *The Bornu, Sahara, and Sudan.* London: J. Murray.

Pelt, Adrian. 1970. *Libyan Independence and the United Nations: A Case of Planned Decolonization*. New Haven: Yale University Press.

Persico, Joseph E. 1990. *Casey: From the OSS to the CIA*. New York: Viking Penguin.

Piccioli, Angelo. 1934. *La Nuova Italia d'Oltremare: L'Opera del Fascismo nelle Colonie Italiane*. Vol. I. Milan: A. Mondadori.

Porch, Douglas. 1984. *The Conquest of the Sahara*. New York: Random House.

Qaddafi, Muammar. 1969. *New Views on Strategy, Mobilization, and the Principles of War*. Benghazi: National Press.

Republic of France, Service de Statistique. 1966. *Enquête démographique au Chad, 1964*. 2 vols. Paris.

Reyna, S. P. 1990. *Wars Without End: The Political Economy of a Precolonial State*. Hanover, New Hampshire: University Press of New England.

Rodd, Lord Rennell of. 1948. *British Military Administration of Occupied Territories in Africa*. London: His Majesty's Stationery Office.

Rossi, Ettore. 1968. *Storia di Tripoli e della Tripolitania delle conquista araba al 1911*. Rome: Instituto par l'Oriente.

Ruiz, Hiram. 1987. *When Refugees Won't Go Home: The Dilemma of Chadians in Sudan*. Washington, D.C.: U.S. Committee for Refugees.

Sadat, Jehan. 1987. *A Woman of Egypt*. New York: Simon and Schuster.

Santandrea, P. Stefano. 1964. *A Tribal History of the Western Bahr el Ghazal*. Bologna: Verona Fathers.

Santarelli, Enzo, Giorgio Rochat, Romain Rainero, Luigi Goglia. 1986. *Omar al-Muktar: The Italian Reconquest of Libya*, trans. John Gilbert. London: Darf Publishers.

Schulter, Hans. 1979. *Index Libycus: Bibliography of Libya, 1970–1975*. 2 vols. Boston: G. K. Hall.

Segrè, Claudio G. 1974. *The Fourth Shore: The Italian Colonization of Libya*. Chicago: University of Chicago Press.

_____. 1978. *L'Italia in Libia: Dell'eta giolittiana a Gheddafi*. Milano: Feltrinell.

_____. 1987. *Italo Balbo: A Fascist Life*. Berkeley: University of California Press.

Sesay, Amadu, Olusola Ojo, and Orobola Fasehun. 1984. *The OAU After Twenty Years*. Boulder: Westview Press.

Teruzzi, Attilio. 1931. *Cirenaica verde: Due anni di governo*. Milan: A. Mondadori.

Theobald, Alan Buchan. 1965. *'Ali Dinar: The Last Sultan of Darfur, 1899–1916*. London: Longmans Green.

Thompson, Virginia M., and Adloff Richard. 1981. *Conflict in Chad*. Berkeley: Institute of International Studies.

Tilho. 1919. *Documents scientifique de la mission Tilho, 1906–1909*. 2 vols. Paris.

Tombalbaye, F. 1963. *Rapport moral du Président François Tombalbaye*. Congrès Nacional. *Fort Archambeau, January 15–20, 1963*. Fort Lamy.

Triaud, Jean-Louis. 1987. *Tchad, 1900–1920: Une guerre franco-libyenne oubliée?* Paris: L'Harmattan.

United Kingdom Naval Intelligence Division Geographical Handbook Series. 1942. *French Equatorial Africa and Cameroons*. London.

United Nations Educational, Scientific, and Cultural Organization. 1963. *Nomades et nomadisme au Sahara*. Paris.

United Nations Food and Agriculture Organization. 1978. *Report on the 1970 World Census of Agriculture*. Rome: Census Bulletin, No. 21.

United States Congress, House of Representatives, Subcommittee on Africa. 1970. *Report of Special Study Mission to West and Central Africa, March 29 to April 27, 1970*. Washington, D.C.: U.S. Government Printing Office, August.

Urvoy, Yves. 1949. *Histoire de l'empire du Bornou*. Paris: Larose.

Vernhes, Monique, and Jean Bloch. 1972. *Guerre coloniale au Tchad*. Lausanne: Éditions La Cité.

Wallach, Janet, and John Wallach. 1990. *Arafat: In the Eyes of the Beholder*. New York: Lyle Stewart.

Warburg, Gabriel. 1978. *Islam, Nationalism, and Communism in a Traditional Society: The Case of the Sudan*. London: Frank Cass.

Weissman, S. R. 1974. *American Foreign Policy in the Congo, 1960–1964*. Ithaca: Cornell University Press.

Wingate, F. R. 1968. *Mahdism and the Egyptian Sudan*. Rpt. London: Frank Cass.

Woodward, Robert. 1987. *Veil: The Secret Wars of the CIA, 1981–1987*. New York: Simon and Schuster.

Wright, John. 1969. *Libya*. New York: Praeger.

_____. 1982. *Libya: A Modern History*. Baltimore: Johns Hopkins University Press.

_____. 1989. *Libya, Chad, and the Central Sahara*. London: Hurst.

Wright, Robin. 1986. *Sacred Rage: The Wrath of Militant Islam*. New York: Touchstone Books.

Zartman, L. W., and A. G. Kluge. 1984. "Heroic Politics: The Foreign Policy of Libya." In *The Foreign Policy of Arab States*, edited by Bahgat Korany and Ali El Hillal Dessouki. Boulder: Westview Press.

Zein, Ibrahim M. 1989. *Religion, Legality, and the State* (Doctoral Dissertation). Philadelphia: Temple University.

Zeltner, Jean Claude. 1980. *Payes d'histoire du Kamen*. Paris: L'Harmattan.

Index

NOTE: Organizations are listed under their full names. A list of acronyms can be found on pages xii–xiv.

Abatcha, Ibrahim, 37, 41, 43
Abbas, Maldoum Abba, 226–227, 240
Abboud, Ibrahim, 55–57, 68, 71
Abdallah Abd al-Sanusi, 49, 84, 129
Abeche, 16, 19, 27, 33, 35, 171, 222
    battles for, 150, 155, 262
Abu al-Qasim Ibrahim, 261
Abu Jummayza (Muhammad Zayn), 18
Acheikh Ibn Oumar, 148, 159, 219, 257
    arrest and release, 182–183, 199, 200
    and CDR, 171, 211
    in Deby government, 272
    defection to Habre, 236, 241
    and Goukouni, 182, 213, 233
    and GUNT, 159, 181, 209–210
    Libyan support, 214–215
    military commands/battles, 200–201, 211, 223–224,
        226, 228, 234, 249, 251
    views, 236, 262
    See also Armée Nationale de Libération
Acyl, Adam, 13, 115
Acyl, Ahmat, 119–120, 123, 125, 128–129, 133,
    150–151, 154, 159, 161(n17), 162(n34), 178
Adoum Dana, Abdoulaye, 75, 123–125, 129, 150
Adoum, Mahamat Ali, 170, 236
Africans. See Arab-African conflict; specific tribes and
    peoples
Agreement on Friendship and Cooperation (Chad-
    Libya), 93–94
Ahmad Abdallah, 86
Algiers, 38, 41, 151
Algiers Agreement, 248–250
Ali Dinar Zakariya Muhammad al-Fadl, 18–21
Allam-Mi, Ahmad, 169
Amalric, Jacques, 214
Amdagachi, battle of, 90
Amnesty International reports, 196, 258, 275
Anglo-Egyptian Agreement (1953), 56
Anglo-Egyptian Condominium, 55, 65, 67, 111
Anglo-French Declaration (1899), 14
Ansar, 18, 60, 69, 71–72, 81, 137, 146,
    193, 232. See also Mahdism; Mahdi, the
Anti-Imperialism Center (AIC), 160
Anya Nya, 83, 192

Aozou, 45–46, 227
Aozou Strip
    Algiers Agreement, 248–250
    Chad's diplomatic efforts to retain, 91, 115–116,
        124, 167–168, 268
    claimed by Libya/Qaddafi, 15, 86, 87(figure),
        106–108, 111, 158, 167–169, 248, 278
    dispute resolved, 278
    history, 15, 85–86, 91, 100(n30)
    Libyan occupation of, 6, 91–92, 96, 107–110,
        113–116, 153, 167–169, 175, 226–227, 278
    See also Red Line/Red Zone
Arab-African conflict, 55, 57, 65, 67, 93, 168, 204. See
        also Chadian civil war; Sudan, civil war; specific
        tribes and peoples
Arabs. See Pan-Arabism; specific tribes and peoples
Arab Socialist Union (Libya), 75
Armée Nationale de Libération (ANL), 221
Assad, Hafez al-, 76
Ata, Hashim al-, 81
Auffray, Brig. Gen., 106
Aurillac, Michel, 222
Awlad al-Balad, 61, 258
Awlad al-Sulayman, 12, 95
Azhari, Ismail al-, 56

Baggara Arabs, 10–11, 18, 27, 57, 61, 71, 92, 145–147,
        204–205, 238, 243–244, 258
    See also Missiriya Baggara
Baghalani, Muhammad Al-, 39, 41, 96, 110–111, 178
Baguirmi, Kingdom of, 16–17, 167
Bamissi, battle for, 250
Bani Sulayman, 9, 11
Bardai, 33–34, 97–98, 115, 159–160, 163. See also Radio
        Bardai
Barrani, Sidi Muhammad al-, 10
Bashira, Ismail, 259
Bashir-Sow, 84
Bashir, Umar Hasan Ahmad al-
    Deby supported by, 246, 257, 261
    drought/famine disregarded, 260–261, 264, 269
    Islamization of Sudan, 244–245, 255, 270
    Libya-Sudan alliance, 246–248, 254
    opposition suppressed, 258, 270–271

relations with Habre, 247–248, 250
Sadiq overthrown, 244–246
Bedeiyat, 35, 65–66, 137, 145–146, 204, 212
Bedouins, 11, 35–36, 75
Benghazi Declaration, 76
Berlin discotheque bombing, 202
Bilad al-Sudan (defined), 3, 21(n1)
Biltine, 42, 222, 249
Bir Sora, battle of, 223–224
Bishop, James, 165, 166
Black September terrorist group, 4, 73(n5), 104
Bongo, Omar, 116, 120, 142(n20), 227
Borkou, 163
Borkou-Ennedi-Tibesti Prefecture (B.E.T.)
    drought, 35–37, 64–66, 92–93, 190
    ethnic groups, 7, 32–33, 36, 84
    FAN in, 97–98, 109–110
    FAP victories, 163
    French presence, 25, 28, 32–33, 46
    FROLINAT in, 44–45, 50
    history, 15, 23, 32–33
    Libyan invasions/occupations, 164, 172–176,
        183–186, 195, 201, 212, 216–218, 220
    oil, 50
    population, 32
    rebellion in, 27, 28, 33–36, 44–48, 50–51
    travel restricted to, 34–35
    See also Aozou Strip; *specific towns and regions*
Boundaries, 13
    Chad-Libyan border, 82–88. *See also* Aozou Strip
    Chad-Sudan border, 44, 61–62
    enshrined by OAU constitution, 86, 91
    European delineation of, 3, 13–15, 26–27, 44,
        61–62, 86, 91, 111, 116
    See also Frontiers
Boutros-Ghali, Boutros, 214, 234
Bredeche, Raoul, 126
Bush, George, 164, 262–263

Cameroon, 22, 30, 116, 128, 135, 145, 156, 170, 262
Caravan routes, 3, 5–8, 16–17, 30, 34, 111, 114. *See also*
    specific roads
Casey, William J., 138, 164
Central African Republic (CAR), 22, 25, 30, 44,
    142(n20), 170, 179, 191, 271
Central Intelligence Agency (CIA), 83, 137–139, 149,
    179–180
Chad
    Aozou Strip dispute. *See* Aozou Strip
    Arab-African conflict, 55. *See also* Chadian civil
        war
    armed forces, 25, 48, 64, 94–95, 105, 118, 127, 157,
        267, 275–276. *See also* Forces Armées
        Nationales Tchadiennes
    boundaries. *See* Boundaries; Frontiers
    Choua government, 129
    civil war. *See* Chadian civil war
    constitution, 105, 265, 272

cotton production/export. *See* Cotton
Deby government. *See* Deby, Idriss
development projects, 116, 277
drought, 33–37, 92–93, 126, 190–191, 276
economy, 26, 31, 48–50, 93–94, 112, 126, 190–191,
    199, 210–211, 275–277
economic assistance, 26, 31, 94, 103–104, 121(n11),
    127–128, 157–158, 179–180, 190–191, 276
education, 23
ethnic groups, 12–13, 27–28, 32, 127. *See also*
    specific tribes and peoples
ethnic groups/rivalries, 274
famine/famine relief, 92–93, 104, 190–191,
    260–261, 268–269
and France. *See* France; French Equatorial Africa
frontier states. *See* Wadai
Goukouni government. *See* Goukouni Oueddi
Habre government. *See* Habre, Hissene
human rights violations, 227, 264, 272, 275
at independence, 22–25
intelligence service, 43, 94, 98, 106, 272–273
labor movement, 45
Libyan invasions/occupations. *See under*
    Aozou Strip; Borkou-Ennedi-Tibesti
    Prefecture; Libya
Malloum government. *See* Malloum, Felix
Muslims massacred, 125
National Assembly, 27–29, 47, 64, 96–97
1969 elections, 48
oil/natural resources, 50, 112, 127, 158, 277
police/security forces, 32, 94, 97, 129, 275
political parties, 23, 26–27, 265, 274. *See also*
    specific parties
refugees in/from, 145, 149, 192, 196, 264, 279(n10)
relations with the United States, 30–31
taxation, 29, 33, 36–37, 42–43, 48–50, 98
Tombalbaye government. *See* Tombalbaye, Ngartha
transportation, 23, 49
and the United Nations, 120, 126, 159, 212,
    260–261
well-drilling programs, 66
See also Borkou-Ennedi-Tibesti Prefecture; French
    Equatorial Africa; Wadai
Chadian civil war, 24
    battle for Ndjamena, 128, 131–132, 133
    beginning of revolt, 33–37
    dissidents in Cairo, 58–59
    Fort Lamy tax revolt (1966), 42–43
    French military intervention. *See under* France
    Libyan support for rebels. *See* Libya; Qaddafi,
        Muammar
    Nigerian peacekeeping force, 128–130
    1960s campaign, 41–45, 59–60, 63–64
    1970s–90s campaigns. *See specific organizations and*
        leaders
    OAU peacekeeping force, 154–157, 187(n27)
    rebel propaganda, 45, 48, 120
    Siddiq chosen to lead revolutionary armies, 89

Sudanese support for rebels. *See* Numayri, Jaafar
  Muhammad al-; Sudan
Tombalbaye's attempts to contain. *See* Tombalbaye,
  Ngartha
See also specific organizations and leaders
Chad, Islamic Republic of (in exile), 38, 57
Chad-Libya Development Bank, 104
Chahai, Siddi, 47
Chevenement, Jean-Pierre, 263
Cheysson, Claude, 131, 170, 183–184
Chirac convention (1976), 113
Chirac, Jacques, 109, 212, 214–215, 219
  Chirac convention (1976), 113, 165, 169, 173
Choua, Mahomat Lol, 129
Christians, 102
Claustre, Françoise and Pierre, 97–98, 106, 112. *See
  also L'affaire Claustre*
Codos, 164, 179, 191, 195, 196, 199
Combe, Marc, 97. *See also L'affaire Claustre*
Compagnies Tchadiennes de Sécurité, 94, 97, 105, 108
Congo, 27, 30, 31
Conseil de Commandement des Forces Armées du
  Nord (CCFAN), 157, 180
Conseil de Libération Nationale (CLN), 180–183, 199
Conseil Démocratique Révolutionnaire (CDR),
    119–120, 123, 138, 163, 170, 211, 214–215, 220,
    240. *See also* Forces Armées Populaires
Coon, Carleton S., 34
Cooperative des Transportateurs Tchadiens (CTT),
    92–93
Cortedellas, Édouard, 51, 94
Corvée, 13, 33
Cot, Jean Pierre, 134, 149, 154
COTONFRAN, 12
COTONTCHAD, 26, 31, 38, 179
Cotton, 12–13, 22–24, 26, 31, 50, 210, 276. *See also*
  COTONTCHAD

Dafallah, Gizzuli, 201
Daoud, Ali Arabi, 63
Darb al-Arbain (Forty Days Road), 6–7, 8, 16, 114
Darfur
  Chadian rebels in, 61, 65, 145, 148. *See also* Sudan,
    Chadian rebellion supported by
  Deby's forces in, 239–240, 242–243, 248–251, 254,
    256–259
  drought and famine, 35, 65–66, 93, 145, 192–194,
    201–202, 257–258, 264–265, 269
  ethnic groups/rivalries, 10–11, 39–40, 60, 145–147,
    204, 238–239, 243–244, 247, 265
  FANT incursions, 244, 249–251, 257–259, 261
  government impotence in, 146, 264
  history of, 7, 15–21, 198, 232–233
  instability in, 72–73, 137, 193–194, 205–206,
    237–239, 242–244
  Kheir's suppression of, 270–271
  Libyan presence in, 147–148, 194, 198, 201, 205,
    215, 221, 233–239, 243, 249–250, 254, 261

  refugees in, 145, 192, 197, 212, 242, 249
  See also Frontiers, Chad-Sudan frontier
Da'wa Islamiya (Islamic Call Society), 113
Daza Toubou, 33–34, 89, 109–110, 160. *See also* Forces
  Armées du Nord
Debré, Michel, 46
Deby, Idriss
  attempted coups against, 272, 273
  background and personality, 175, 221–222, 240,
    242
  and Bashir/RCC, 246, 271
  conflict with Habre, 239–242, 249–251, 256–259,
    262–265
  forces in Darfur, 248–251, 254, 256–259
  foreign relations, 263–265, 268–269
  government, 264–268, 271–275
  and Habre, 222, 230(n45)
  military commands/battles, 164, 171, 175
  MPS formed, 256. *See also* Mouvement Patriotique
    du Salut
  and Qaddafi, 221–222, 240, 242, 256–257, 259,
    267–268
  UNIR Central Committee membership, 180
de Garang, John, 192
de Gaulle, Charles, 22, 24–27, 31, 34–35, 46–48
Deleo, Mahamat, 240, 250
de Marenches, Count Alexandre, 142(n26), 149
Democratic Unionionist Party (DUP, Sudan), 57, 203
Department of Defense (United States), 138, 152, 198
Derde, the, 33–34, 41, 83, 86, 90, 106, 108–109, 112
Din, Taj al-, 220
Diori, Hamani, 62, 64, 102–103
Diouf, Abdou, 148, 169, 200
Djalabo, Abubakr, 38–40
Djamous, Hassan, 169, 180, 224, 227, 239–242
Djimé, Mamari Ngakinar, 94
Djogo, Negue, 34, 129, 168, 169, 171, 196, 199
Drought
  exacerbated by war, 5, 235–236, 257–258, 260
  in the 1960s, 35–37, 46, 64–66
  in the 1970s, 92–93, 126, 145, 158
  in the 1980s, 190–194, 199
  in the 1990s, 257–258, 260–261, 269, 276
  See also Famine
Dumas, Roland, 173, 177, 185, 263

Egypt
  alarmed by Goukouni's resurgence, 163
  Anglo-Egyptian Condominium, 55, 65, 67, 111
  and the Chadian rebellion, 38, 43, 58, 61
  Egyptian Revolution (1952), 56
  FAN/FANT supplied by, 138, 145, 147, 149, 166
  Federation of Arab Republics negotiations, 76
  FROLINAT supported, 61
  and Habre, 214, 234
  Italian-Egyptian Treaty (1925), 14
  and Libya/Qaddafi, 76, 79, 81–82, 114, 116, 118,
    150, 166, 185, 198, 271

and Libya's King Idris, 41
Mukhabarat (military intelligence), 56, 59
Muslim Brotherhood in, 67
and the OAU, 115, 158
peace with Israel, 114
and Sadiq, 204
Soviet retaliation feared for possible strikes against
    Libya, 151–152
and Sudan, 43, 53(n27), 55–57, 81, 114, 165–166,
    194–195, 197–198
and Tombalbaye, 59
and the United States, 118, 149, 151–152, 166, 176
See also Mubarak, Hosni; Nasser, Gamal Abd al-;
    Sadat, Anwar
Egypt's Liberation: The Philosophy of the Revolution
    (Nasser), 75
Elisende, Pierre, 59, 60
Elizabeth II, 70–71
Ennedi Plateau, 35–36, 93, 95. *See also* Borkou-Ennedi-
    Tibest Prefecture
Erdi, battle for, 211
Eritrea, 61, 68
European Community, 127–128, 203, 268
Evian Agreements (1962), 24

Fada, 35, 169, 217
Fadl, Fawzi Ahmad al-, 233
Fadul, Hassan, 240, 241
Famine, 5, 104, 190–194, 201–202, 260–261, 264–265,
    268–269. *See also* Drought
Faya (Faya Largeau), 33, 35, 109, 119, 169, 171, 199,
    217, 225–226
Federation of Arab Republics, 76
First Liberation Army, 89–90, 96, 119
    See also Front de Libération Nationale du Tchad;
    Siddiq, Abba
Foccart, Jacques, 24–25, 27, 29–30, 47, 51, 52(n4),
    90–91, 93, 95–96, 103, 219
Fodeibou, Orozi, 167, 180
Fontbonne, Paul, 272
Force d'Action Rapide, 175, 201, 222, 226
Force d'Intervention Interarmées, 25, 48, 90, 119, 124,
    131, 172, 175. *See also* Force d'Action Rapide
Forces Armées du Nord (FAN)
    arms and supplies, 138, 145, 147, 149, 155, 157
    battle for Ndjamena, 131–133
    battles with GUNT/FAP forces, 155–157, 163
    in the B.E.T., 97–98, 109–110
    Command Council (CCFAN), 125, 157, 180
    in Darfur, 145–146, 148
    ethnic groups, 146
    FROLINAT deserters recruited, 127
    and Habre-Malloum alliance, 125
    with Kamogue's forces, 129–130
    and *L'affaire Claustre*, 97–98, 109–110
    leadership, 95. *See also* Habre, Hissene
    and the Libyan invasion/occupation, 108–109, 130,
        133–135, 149–151

occupation of Bardai, 97–98
troop strength, 118
US support, 157–158
Forces Armées Nationales Tchadiennes (FANT)
    after Habre's defeat, 267, 273–274
    arms and supplies, 166–167, 171–173
    battles with GUNT/FAP, 168–171, 175, 200–201
    battles with Libyan forces, 170, 216–217, 223–228
    conflict with Deby's forces, 239–240, 249–251,
        256–259, 261–262
    FAN reorganized into, 164
    French military support, 172–173, 177, 233. *See
        also* France, military intervention in Chad;
        Operation Épervier
    incursions into Darfur, 236, 243–244, 249–251,
        257–259, 261
    joined by former enemies, 164, 196, 199, 217
    leadership, 164, 180. *See also* Deby, Idriss; Habre,
        Hissene; Union Nationale pour l'Indépendence
        et la Révolution
    1987 campaign, 216–217, 222–228, 233–234
    pacification of southern Chad, 179
Forces Armées Occidentales (FAO), 123, 150,
    273–275
Forces Armées Populaires (FAP), 119, 123, 128,
    131–133, 163, 169–171, 175, 182, 211
Forces d'Action Communes (FAC), 150
Foreign Legion (French Foreign Legion), 28, 49–52
Forest, Louis, 126
Fort Lamy, 22–23, 27, 29, 31, 42–43, 95. *See also*
    Ndjamena
France
    and Acheikh, 181–182, 200
    aerial surveillance, 184
    African policies, 22, 24–27, 116, 215. *See also*
        Franco-African summit conferences;
        specific French presidents
    alarmed by Goukouni's resurgence, 163
    arms sales to Libya, 78, 136, 149
    Chirac convention (1976), 113, 165, 169, 173
    colonial era, 10, 12–15, 17, 19–20, 26–27, 44, 86,
        111, 116. *See also* French Equatorial Africa
    and Deby's victory, 263–264
    delineation of African boundaries, 14–15, 26–27,
        44, 86, 91, 111, 116
    diplomatic efforts to achieve cease-fire (1987), 219
    economic assistance to Chad, 26, 47, 96, 106,
        121(n11)
    famine relief, 92–93, 191
    financial aid for African peacekeeping force, 148
    and Habre, 118, 138, 169–170, 172–173, 175, 185,
        195, 199, 234, 256, 259, 262–263, 276
    intelligence service, 25, 40, 43, 124, 142(n26), 195,
        272
    internal opposition to military involvement, 49–50,
        126. *See also* Mitterand, François
    and *L'affaire Claustre*, 97–98, 106, 108–110

and Libyan invasions of Chad, 134, 135, 142(n26).
    See also subhead military intervention in Chad
and Malloum, 106, 109, 112–113, 118–119,
    123–124, 126–127, 165
mediation between Qaddafi and Tombalbaye,
    90–91
military administration of the B.E.T., 25, 28, 32–33
military aid budget, 96
military intervention in Chad, 46–52, 90, 119,
    123–124, 141(n1), 172–173, 175, 201, 217, 222,
    233–234, 276. *See also* Red Line/Red Zone
military presence in Africa, 25, 148
military presence in Chad, 25, 28–29, 49–52, 85, 94,
    106, 119, 127–128, 170, 172–177, 185–186, 222,
    256, 262, 278
and Niger, 116, 138
1981 meeting of Francophone African states, 154
oil purchases, 78, 136, 176
relations with Deby, 263–265, 268, 276–277
relations with Libya, 78, 106, 109, 123–124, 127,
    136, 149, 151, 169, 172–173, 176, 183–186, 200,
    215, 217, 228–229. *See also* Mitterand, François,
    and Qaddafi
relations with the United States, 31, 52(4), 149, 152,
    165, 170, 173, 176
relations with Tombalbaye, 26–27, 29, 31, 46–47,
    50–51, 85, 88, 90–91, 93, 95–96, 103
Senghor's condemnation of, 133
withdrawals from Chad, 28, 33, 96, 106, 131, 183,
    191
    See also COTONTCHAD; de Gaulle, Charles;
    Foccart, Jacques; Giscard d'Estaing, Valéry;
    Mitterand, François; Pompidou, Georges
Franco-African summit conferences, 95–96, 113–115,
    159, 177–178, 213–215
Franco-Italian Accords (1935), 91, 100(n30), 116
Free Officers (Libya), 74–75
Free Officers (Sudan), 71–72
French Congo, 22
French Equatorial Africa, 10, 14–15, 20, 22, 24, 86. *See
    also* Chad
Front de la Libération Tchadienne (FLT), 39, 40. *See
    also* Front de Libération Nationale du Tchad
Front de Libération Nationale du Tchad (FROLINAT)
    and Abatcha's death, 43
    in Darfur, 65, 148
    dissolutions of, 95, 181
    divisions in, 40–41, 83, 95, 96
    Egyptian support, 61
    forces. *See* First Liberation Army; Forces Armées
        Occidentales; Second Liberation Army; Vulcan
        Force
    Goukouni's appeal to, 151
    IFC's support of, 68
    leadership, 37–38, 40, 82–83, 110, 141. *See also*
        Abatcha, Ibrahim; Djalabo, Abubakr; Siddiq,
        Abba; Taher, Ali Mahamat
    Malloum's appeal rejected, 105

1960s campaigns, 41–45, 60, 63–64
1970s campaigns, 50–51, 90, 95, 115, 119
propaganda, 45, 48
Qaddafi's support for, 76, 83–84, 90, 94, 96, 106,
    108, 111–112, 115, 119
reorganizations, 96, 111–112, 119. *See also* Forces
    Armées Populaires
Sudanese support, 60–61, 63, 72, 111
See also Front de la Libération Tchadienne
Frontiers, 1, 3–5, 14–15
    Chad-Libya frontier, 85–86. *See also* Aozou Strip;
        Borkou-Ennedi-Tibesti Prefecture
    Chad-Sudan frontier, 15–16, 26–27, 30, 44, 60–61,
        63–64, 72–73, 118. *See also* Darfur; Wadai
    defined, 13–14
    government impotence in, 146–147, 264
    Libyan air strikes along Chad-Sudan frontier,
        150–151
    19th-century struggles over, 15–19
    See also Boundaries
Fur people
    ethnic rivalries, 146–147, 204, 238, 243–244, 258
    history, 10, 17, 18
    Libyans distrusted by, 147–148, 206, 254
    and Sudanese rebellion, 70–71
    suppressed by Bashir/RCC, 258, 270
    and Wadai, 57
    See also Darfur

Gabon, 22, 116, 142(n20)
Galopin, Pierre, 98, 125, 185
Garamantean Road (Bilma Trail), 6, 8, 17
Garde Nomade, 32, 34, 44–45, 94
Gaugrang II, *mbang* of Baguirmi, 17
Gendarmerie Nationale (Chad), 94, 96, 118
Geneina, 35, 61, 239–240
Giraud, André, 226, 236
Giscard d'Estaing, Valéry
    elections, 134, 148
    federal solution proposed by, 127
    and Goukouni, 133–134
    intervention in Aozou Strip dispute, 120
    and *L'affaire Claustre*, 97–98, 106, 109
    and the Libyan invasion of Chad, 134, 142(n26)
    and Malloum, 109, 118, 123
    proposal to enlist Acheikh to resolve Chad
        problem, 182
    and Qaddafi, 123–124
    and Tombalbaye, 96, 102
    withdrawals from Chad, 106, 131
Goukouni Oueddi
    and Acheikh, 182, 213, 233
    Acyl blamed for Ati defeat, 119–120
    appeal to FROLINAT, 151
    arrest, 211–213
    Bardai occupation, 115
    battle for Ndjamena, 131–132
    blamed for Libyan withdrawal, 154

in Choua government, 129
control of B.E.T., 125
and Deby, 272
defeat of, 156
demotion, 209–210, 211
and the *Derde*, 41, 90, 109, 111, 112
FAP commanded by, 119, 163, 181. *See also* Forces
   Armées Populaires
and France, 134, 151
and FROLINAT, 111
and Galopin's execution, 98
and GUNT, 129, 130–131, 155–156, 209–210. *See*
   also Gouvernement d'Union Nationale de
   Transition
and Habre, 88–89, 125, 129–130, 219
Habre-Goukani rivalry, 89, 98, 108–109, 112,
   131–132, 150, 160, 177, 182, 236
and the Kano Accords, 128, 129
and *L'affaire Claustre*, 106, 108
Libyan flag raised at Aozou, 96
Libyan withdrawal demanded, 153
and the OAU, 140, 155–156, 177, 210
and Qaddafi, 111–112, 132–135, 140–141, 149, 151,
   158–160, 180–181, 200, 212–213, 236
Red Zone offensive, 175
return to Libya, 226
support in Darfur, 148
vice-president of FAN Command Council, 95
Goura, Ahmad, 224, 227
Gourane people, 65–66, 84, 199, 204, 225. *See also*
   Forces Armées Nationales Tchadiennes
Gourvenac, Camille, 94, 98, 106
Gouvernement d'Union Nationale de Transition
   (GUNT)
   Acheikh's offensive against FANT and Chad,
     200–201
   in Bardai after Habre's victory, 159–160
   battle for Ndjamena, 131. *See also under* Chadian
     civil war
   breakups of, 128, 155–156, 199, 213
   cease-fire (1987), 228
   dissention/factionalism in, 129–130, 150, 153, 163,
     180, 182–183, 209–210, 215
   French assistance, 154
   and Habre, 128–131
   leadership. *See* Acheikh Ibn Oumar; Acyl, Ahmat;
     Goukouni Oueddi; Habre, Hissene; Kamougue,
     Wadal Abdelkader
   Libya denounced by, 126
   and Libyan invasion of Chad, 135, 138, 168–172,
     183
   Libyan support for, 169–171. *See also subhead* and
     Qaddafi
   Libyan withdrawal demanded, 153
   military forces, 150, 155, 168. *See also* Forces
     Armées Populaires; Vulcan Force
   offensive in the Red Zone, 175
   and Qaddafi, 180–183, 209–210, 213, 236

reorganizations of, 129, 130–131, 163, 209–210, 213
   structure and positions, 125, 130, 141, 180–181
Government of National Salvation (Sudan), 245–246.
   See also Bashir, Umar Hasan Ahmad al-
Grand Sanusi. *See* Sanusi al Khattabi al-Idrisi al-
   Hasani, Muhammad ibn Ali al-
Great Britain
   colonial period in Africa, 11, 13–14, 19–21, 44,
     232–233
   financial aid for African peacekeeping force, 148
   and Libya/Qaddafi, 77, 78, 82
   Queen Elizabeth's visit to Sudan, 70–71
Green Book (Qaddafi), 113, 147, 232
Groupe des Officiers des Forces Armées Tchadiennes
   (GOFAT), 105
Guinassou, Taher, 157, 180
Gulf of Sidra, 79, 80(figure), 104, 138, 152, 158, 166

Habre, Hissene
   after Deby's victory, 267, 273–274, 276
   Amnesty International invited to report, 196
   arms needed/acquired, 98, 109–110, 149, 155, 167,
     217, 259
   background and personality, 88–90, 157, 160, 242
   and Bashir, 247–250, 257
   battles, 109, 130–134, 155–157. *See also subhead*
     conflict with Deby
   blood feud with Acyl, 162(n34)
   in Choua government, 129
   concerned by Libyan forces in Darfur, 198, 201,
     235, 248
   concerned by Libya-Sudan alliance, 246–248
   conflict with Deby, 239–242, 249–252, 256–259,
     261–262
   and Deby, 222, 230(n45)
   diplomatic initiatives, 177–178
   disengagement from democracy, 242
   and drought/famine, 191, 260
   and Egypt, 214, 234
   elimination of Codos ordered, 195
   expelled from FROLINAT, 110
   FAN reorganized into FANT, 164. *See also* Forces
     Armées Nationales Tchadiennes
   and France, 118, 138, 169–170, 172–173, 175,
     177–178, 185, 195, 199, 234, 256, 259, 262–263,
     276
   Franco-African summits, 159, 213–215
   French intervention on behalf of, 172–173, 175
   and Galopin's execution, 98, 125, 185
   and Goukouni, 88–89, 125, 129–130, 219
   Goukouni-Habre rivalry, 89, 98, 108–109, 112,
     131–132, 150, 160, 177, 182
   government structure and positions, 157, 163–164,
     228, 239–241. *See also* Conseil de
     Commandement des Forces Armées du Nord;
     Miskene, Idriss
   and GUNT, 125, 128–131
   and the Hadjerai revolt, 226–227, 241

human rights violations, 196, 227, 275
intelligence and secret service, 164, 265, 273
joined by former enemies, 164, 195, 199, 239–241
and the Kano Accords, 128–129
and *L'affaire Claustre*, 97–98, 106, 108–110, 112
leadership of Second Liberation Army, 90. *See also* Second Liberation Army
Libyan flag raised at Aozou, 96
and Libyan-French relations, 184–185
and Malloum, 108, 112, 118–119, 125, 127–128
and Miskene's death, 188(n63)
and Mitterand, 178, 185, 196
1978 address to Chadian people, 126
and the OAU, 132, 177–179, 210
opposed to Giscard's federal solution, 127
pacification of southern Chad, 179, 195–196
political oppression, 164
and Qaddafi/Libya, 4–5, 97, 109–110, 112, 160, 183, 218, 220–221, 223, 236, 248–249
RCC denounced by, 256
rebuilding the FAN, 149
reconquest of B.E.T. planned, 215–216
recovery of, 141
Red Line rejected by, 173, 176–177
retreat to Cameroon, 135, 145, 262
and Sadat, 145
and Sadiq, 223, 235, 242–243, 246
and Siddiq, 88–89, 95
success of, 214
UNIR created, 180. *See also* Union Nationale pour l'Indépendence et la Révolution
and the United States, 138, 152, 157–158, 164–165, 167, 171–173, 179–180, 216, 220, 225, 227–228, 263, 268
urged to use International Court of Justice, 227
Vittel summit (1983), 177–178
Zaghawa shaykhs' authority restored, 241
See also Forces Armées du Nord; Forces Armées Nationales Tchadiennes
Hadi, the Imam al-, 72
Hadjerai, 39–40, 167, 171, 226–227, 237, 267, 271–272, 274. *See also* Mouvement Patriotique du Salut
Haggar, Adoum, 240, 250
Hakim, Aboubakr Abd Al-, 58–59
Haroun, Gody, 226–227
Harrell, Roy, 59, 73(n5)
Heikal, Mohammed, 76
Hernu, Charles, 173, 175, 178, 195
Hessel, Stephane, 106
Hizboulani Party (Senegal), 132
Houphouët-Boigny, 148, 169, 171
Huddleston, Maj. H. J., 21
Hussein, Sid Ahmad al-, 215, 242

Ibrahim, Ahmad, 159
Idris Alawma, 88
Idris, King of Libya, 23, 30, 41, 51, 74, 84, 233
Idris, Muhammad, 90

Innosoro, Battle of, 249–250
International Monetary Fund, 191
Ishkal, Hassan, 75, 153
Islam
history in Africa, 8–11, 16, 17
Islamic constitutions, 68, 70
Islamic reform movements, 9–11. *See also* Mahdi, the; Sanusi al Khattabi al-Idrisi al-Hasani, Muhammad ibn Ali al-; Turabi, Hasan al-
Islamization of Sudan, 192–193, 244–245, 270
jihad. See Jihad
Pan-Islamism, 28–29
Qaddafi's views on, 113. *See also Green Book*
Qaddafi's vision of spreading, 77
Sadiq on, 69
Islamic Charter Front (ICF; Sudan), 68–69
Islamic Conference Organization, 178
Islamic Legion
casualties, 171
conscription and recruitment, 137–138, 147, 205, 206(n7), 233, 250
creation of, 82
in Darfur, 194, 205, 215, 221, 233–236, 243, 249–250, 261
lack of professionalism, 168
and Libyan invasion/occupation of Chad, 135, 163, 195, 198–199, 201, 216–217, 224
reorganized, 240
Isnard, Jacques, 49
Israel, 79, 81–85, 94, 114, 152, 157, 166, 218
Issa Abdalla Muhammad, 181
Issaka, El Hajj, 39, 62, 63
Italian-Egyptian Treaty (1925), 14
Italy, 14–15, 20, 85–86, 91, 111, 116, 233. *See also* Mussolini, Benito
Itno, Ibrahim Muhammad, 175, 217, 239–242

Ja'ali, 18, 21(n8)
Jabal Marra massif, 15
Jabal Uwaynat oasis, 108, 111, 166
Jabir, Abu Bakr Younis al-, 197, 237, 243, 255
Jallaba, 35–36, 146–148
Jalloud, Abd al-Salam, 83, 86, 113–114, 124, 153, 185, 223, 255
Jihad
Chad's civil war proclaimed as, by Qaddafi, 160
declared by Muslims of Chad, 36. *See also* Chadian civil war
the Mahdi's call to, 10–11, 18, 66–67
Sultan of Wadai's call to, 13
Journiac, Rene, 131, 142(n20)

Kamougue, Wadal Abdelkader
alliance with Goukouni, 131
attempt to create Republic of Logone, 151
clashes with FAN, 129–130
concern over Libyan arming of FROLINAT, 94
conflict with Deby's forces, 164

and the coup d'état against Tombalbaye, 108
and GUNT, 125, 129–131, 150, 180, 199, 209–210
and Habre, 119, 196, 219–220, 228
and Kano II conference, 129
and *L'affaire Claustre*, 108–109
and Malloum, 109, 119
move to Abidjan, 199
MRP created, 181
opposed to Libyan occupation of the Aozou Strip,
　112
presence of oil in Chad announced, 112
and Qaddafi/Libya, 128, 130, 180, 213
retirement to south, 131–132, 141
rivalry with Acy's Vulcan Force, 133
See also Codos
Kanami, Shaykh Al-, 218
Kano Accords, 128–129, 142(n16)
Kennedy, John F., 30–32
Kenya, 141. *See also* Moi, Daniel Arap
Khafi, Col. al-, 171
Khalil, Abdallah, 56
Khartoum, 111, 196–197, 202–203
Kheir, Al-Tayib Ibrahim Muhammad, 270–271
Kinga clan, 167
Kinship, 3, 11–12
Kissinger, Henry, 48
Kitchener, Herbert, 1st Earl Kitchener, 4, 67
Koch, Noel, 165, 194
Kolingba, André, 179
Kordofan, 17–18, 27, 205, 233
Kotiga, Alponse, 196, 228
Koue, Issa, 184
Kountche, Seyni, 115–116, 136–138, 158
Kufra oasis, 7, 47, 111
Kufra Road, 7, 9–10, 111, 254
Kusa, Musa, 147, 160, 215–217

Labor movement, in Chad, 45
L'affaire Claustre, 97–98, 106, 108–110, 112
Lagos Peace Accord (1979), 130–131, 137
Lami, Pierre, 50
Lamy, François, 4
Lassou, Gouara, 96, 157, 183, 190, 209, 210, 224
Laval, Pierre, 15, 78, 91
Libya
　agents in Sudan, 147–148, 152, 166, 204, 221
　air strikes along Chad-Sudan frontier, 150–151
　Aozou Strip claimed by, 86, 87(figure), 106–108,
　　111, 158, 167–169, 248, 278
　Aozou Strip occupied by, 6, 91–92, 96, 107–110,
　　113–116, 153, 167–169, 175, 226–227, 278
　arms purchases, 78, 127, 136, 149, 166, 183, 194,
　　218, 224, 230(n30)
　arms sales, 47, 147, 237–238
　B.E.T. occupied by, 164, 172–176, 183–186, 195,
　　201, 212, 216–218, 220
　boundaries. *See* Boundaries
　cease-fire, 228

Chad policy reassessed, 209
Deby supported, 257, 259
disinformation and propaganda, 221
economic assistance to Chad, 90, 93–94, 103
economy, 237. *See also subhead* oil resources and
　revenues
and Egypt, 76, 79, 81–82, 114, 116, 118, 150, 166,
　185, 198, 271
and FROLINAT, 41
geography, 77
and the Gulf of Sidra, 79, 80(figure), 104, 138, 152,
　158
and GUNT, 159–160, 163, 169–170. *See also under*
　Qaddafi, Muammar
invasion/occupation of Chad, 112, 130, 133–141,
　149–154, 161(n28), 169–172, 176, 183–186, 195,
　198–201, 215–221. *See also subheads* Aozou
　Strip occupied by; B.E.T. occupied by
Islamic dissent, 212–213, 219, 229(n11)
Islamization of, 76
Italian imperial period. *See* Italy
Libya-Sudan alliance, 246–248
MPS supported, 227
Mujahidiin/Iranian influx, 270
Muslim Brotherhood in, 74–75, 77, 99(n5). *See also*
　Sanusiyya
19th-century Islamic reform movement. *See* Sanusi
　al Khattabi al-Idrisi al-Hasani, Muhammad ibn
　Ali al-; Sanusiyya
and the OAU, 115–116, 124, 133, 158, 210
oil resources/revenues, 76–77, 82, 136, 201, 218,
　220, 224, 230(n30), 237, 271
political parties, 75
presence in Darfur, 147–148, 194, 198, 201, 205,
　215, 221, 233–239, 243, 249–250, 254, 261
relations with France, 106, 109, 115, 123–124, 127,
　136, 149, 151, 169, 172–173, 175–177, 183–186,
　200, 215, 228–229
relations with Sudan, 197–198, 201–202, 205–206,
　220, 233, 252(n31), 254–256
revolutionary and liberation movements
　supported, 78–79, 137
road construction, 108, 114, 136, 254
and Senegal, 132–133
southern insurgency revived in Chad, 179
and the Soviet Union, 151–152, 166, 183, 194, 203,
　217
subversion in Sudan, 160, 163, 193–194, 198, 202
support for Chadian rebellion, 86, 88, 115, 125
terrorism supported/sponsored by. *See under*
　Qaddafi, Muammar
and Tombalbaye, 30, 49, 102–103
and the Tummo Triangle, 116, 158
and the United Nations, 126, 269
and the United States, 77–79, 152, 160, 164, 166,
　187(n30), 202–203, 209, 226
uranium purchases, 116, 127, 138
withdrawals from Chad, 153–154, 161(n28)

See also Idris, King of Libya; Qaddafi, Muammar
Libyan armed forces
  air force, 6, 166, 167
  army, 224, 237
  casualties/losses, 224–226, 228
  military actions. *See under* Libya
  military strength, 166, 206(n7), 224. *See also* Libya,
    arms purchases
  See also Islamic Legion
Libya-Sudan Integration Charter, 255–256, 261, 271
Lomé Convention, 106, 137

Mahamat Ali Abdallah, 274
Mahdism, 9–11, 18
Mahdists, 39, 69–70, 81, 233, 258. *See also* Ansar;
    Umma
Mahdi, the (Muhammad Ahmad ibn al-Sayyid Abd
    Allah, al-Madhi), 9–11, 57, 60, 232–233
Mahgoub, Muhammad Ahmed, 44, 59–60, 64, 70–71
Malloum, Felix (N'gakoutout Bey'ndi)
  alliances sought, 106
  anti-FROLINAT actions, 42
  and the Aozou Strip, 108, 112
  arrested, 105
  background, 105
  CDR recognized, 120, 123
  Chirac convention signed, 113, 165
  efforts to end rebellion, 105, 108, 112
  and France, 106, 109, 112–113, 118–119, 123–124,
    126–127, 165
  Gourvenac confirmed head of secret service, 106
  governance by, 112
  and Habre, 108, 118–119, 125, 127–128. *See also*
    Gouvernement d'Union Nationale de
    Transition
  and the Kano Accords, 128
  and *L'affaire Claustre*, 106, 108–109
  made Chad's head of state, 105
  and Numayri, 114
  OAU support sought, 124
  and Qaddafi, 113–114, 120
Marion, Pierre, 149
Massaoud, Abd al-Hafiz, 147, 171, 209, 243, 262
Ma'tan as-Sarra oasis, 14, 111, 228
Mengistu Haile Mariam, 168, 177, 192, 194, 204
Middle East Rapid Deployment Force, 164–165
Miskene, Idriss, 132, 167, 171, 178–179, 182, 188(n63),
    226
Missiriya Baggara, 36, 95–96, 147
Mitterand, François
  Acheikh supported, 181–182
  African policies, 148–149, 154, 172
  Chad policies, 148, 151–153, 169–170, 172–173,
    175, 213–214
  confidantes accused of pro-Libyan stance, 169–170
  desire to withdraw from Chad, 177–178, 183, 216
  diplomatic efforts to end Chad-Libyan conflict
    (1987), 227

and Habre, 178, 185, 196
military intervention in Chad, 153, 172–173
1981 meeting of Francophone African states, 154
opposed to French involvement in Chad, 46, 49–50,
    85, 134
and Qaddafi/Libya, 149, 151, 169, 171–173, 175,
    177, 184–185, 200, 217, 219, 263
Red Line agreement, 172–173, 175, 177, 217
and the United States, 149, 152, 165, 173, 203
Vittel summit, 177
Mobutu Sese Seku, 46, 103, 148, 170, 178, 262
Moi, Daniel Arap, 138, 140–141, 156
Moore, George Curtis, 4
Morocco, 138, 145
Moubi people, 36, 52
Moussa, Ahmad, 40–41, 63
Moussa, Hassan, 42
Mouvement National pour la Révolution Culturelle et
    Sociale (MNRCS), 103. *See also* Parti
    Progressiste Tchadienne (PPT)
Mouvement Patriotique du Salut (MPS), 227,
    252(n45), 256–259, 261–262, 272
Mouvement Révolutionnaire du Peuple (MRP), 181
Mubarak al-Fadl al-Mahdi, 243, 245–246, 252(n35)
Mubarak, Hosni, 116, 151, 166, 170, 176, 185, 197–198
Muhammad Ali (Viceroy of Egypt), 18, 66
Muhammad al-Sharif (Sultan of Wadai), 13, 16
Muhammad (the Prophet), 8
Muhammad Zayn. *See* Abu Jummayza
Mukhtar, Sidi Umar al-, 20
Muslim Brotherhood
  in Chad, 42–43
  in Egypt, 67
  in Libya, 74–75, 77, 99(n5). *See also* Sanusiyya
  in Sudan, 39, 67–69, 197, 202
Muslims
  in the B.E.T., 29
  and Chadian civil war. *See* Chadian civil war
  jihad declared by Chadian Muslims, 36
  massacred in central and southern Chad, 125
  See also Arabs; Islam
Mussolini, Benito, 14–15, 20, 82, 85–86, 91, 100(n30),
    111

Nasser, Gamal Abd al-, 4, 25, 41, 55–56, 58, 67, 74–76,
    79
National Assembly (Chad), 27–29, 47, 64, 96–97
National Democratic Alliance (NDA), 245
National Front for the Salvation of Libya (NFSL), 152
National Islamic Front (NIF), 202–204, 244–245, 271
National Political Bureau (PNB), 37
Ndjamena, 27, 95, 157–158, 161(n28), 191, 257–258,
    262
  battles for/in, 128, 131–133, 153–157
  See also Fort Lamy
N'Gakatou, Mosambe, 59
Niger, 92, 107, 115–116, 127–128, 136–138, 158, 168,
    170, 186(n16)

Nigeria, 93, 115–116, 128–130, 136–138, 140–141, 148,
    154, 158, 210, 273–274
Nimr, Adoum, 63
Noel, Cleo A., Jr., 4, 59, 73(n5), 104
Nomadic peoples, 11–12, 28, 32, 36–37
    in the B.E.T., 25–26, 32, 33
    in Chad, 28
    and drought, 35–36, 65–66, 92–93. *See also*
        Drought
    movement of, 32, 35, 57–58, 65–66
    See also Kinship; *specific tribes and peoples*
North Korea, 38, 83
Nouri, Mahamat, 125, 217
Numayri, Jaafar Muhammad al-
    and Baghalani, 110
    and Chadian refugees, 149
    civil war ended, 81, 111, 114
    communist coup attempt against, 81
    concerned by Libyan occupation of Chad, 137–138,
        170
    coup d'état against Mahgoub, 70–71
    and Darfur, 146, 194
    deposed, 196–197
    and Egypt, 114, 152
    government, 72–73
    and Habre, 110, 118, 149
    Islam embraced by, 192
    and Malloum, 114, 118, 120
    and the OAU, 140, 154
    opposed to Khartoum Resolution, 124
    opposition oppressed, 71–72, 81, 83, 193
    and Qaddafi/Libya, 76, 83, 114, 120, 150, 192
    Qaddafi's attempts to overthrow/assassinate, 4, 111,
        113–114, 152, 161(n6), 165–166, 194–195, 204
    and Sadiq, 72, 113–114, 118, 124, 138, 146
    Shari'a law imposed, 192–193
    and Tombalbaye, 72
    and Turabi, 71–72, 118, 124, 138
    and the United States, 4, 165–166, 176, 194–195

Obasanjo, Olusegun, 115–116, 130
Occidental Petroleum, 47, 77, 82, 111
Odingar, Milarew (Noel), 105
Officiers sudannais, 20, 28, 32
Ogier, Commandant, 15, 91, 100(n30)
Oil
    in Chad, 50, 112, 127, 158, 277
    exploration, 47, 158
    Libyan, 76–77, 82, 136, 201, 218, 220, 224,
        230(n30), 237, 271
    prices, 82, 198
Omdurman, 4, 59, 61, 111
1 April Movement, 239–240, 249–251. *See also*
        Mouvement Patriotique du Salut
Operation Épervier, 201, 222, 226, 234, 256, 265, 268,
    278
Operation Manta, 172–173, 199
Operation Tacaud, 124, 128

Organization of African Unity (OAU)
    Chad's complaints to, 88, 91, 115–116, 257
    colonial boundaries enshrined by constitution, 86,
        91
    Committee on Chad, 116, 136–137, 140, 142(n45),
        148, 156, 210
    concern about Libyan imperialism, 132–133
    diplomatic efforts to end Chad-Libyan conflict
        (1987), 219, 226–228
    efforts to resolve Chadian conflict, 128–131,
        177–179
    Kano Accords, 128
    Khartoum Resolution, 124
    peacekeeping force in Chad, 154–157
    principle of noninterference, 61, 156
    and Qaddafi, 137–138, 140–141, 152, 158, 167–168,
        200, 228, 234
    Sadiq's remarks to, 70
    summits, 115–116, 120, 132–133, 140, 158, 168,
        198, 200, 210
    and Tombalbaye, 44, 64
Organization of Saharan States, 136
Ottoman Empire, 12, 14, 16–18
Ouarnang, Ibrahim, 63
Oum Chalouba, battle at, 175
Ounianga Kebir, battle for, 225
Ourada, Yacoub Mohamat, 183

Paillard, Henri, 50–51
Palestinians, 77, 94, 114
Pan American Airlines Flight 103, bombing of, 269
Pan-Arabism, 28–29, 56, 124
    Nasser's, 4, 25, 55, 58, 75
    Qaddafi's, 4, 75–77, 79, 82–83, 111, 160, 215, 218,
        255–256
Pan-Islamism, 28–29. *See also* Pan-Arabism
Papandreou, Andreas, 184–185
Parti Progressiste Tchadienne (PPT), 23, 26–27, 43–44,
        64, 93–94, 103
Pompidou, Georges, 25, 46–48, 52, 78, 90, 93, 96, 103
Popular Defense Force (PDF), 245
Popular Movement for the Liberation of Chad
        (MPLT), 116

Qaddafi, Muammar
    Acheikh arrested, 182–183
    African/Arab opinions of, 168
    African neighbors threatened by, 138
    ambitions, 75, 166, 215, 218. *See also subhead* Pan-
        Arabism of
    Aozou Strip claimed by, 15, 86, 87(figure),
        106–108, 111, 158, 167–169, 248, 278. *See also*
        Libya, Aozou Strip occupied by
    attempts to overthrow/assassinate Numayri, 4, 111,
        113–114, 152, 161(n6), 165–166, 194–195, 204
    background, 84–85, 218–219
    and Bashir, 247, 269–271. *See also* Libya, Libya-
        Sudan alliance

cease-fire, 211, 234
Chad army of national integration proposed, 151, 161(n17)
Chad policy admitted to be mistake, 236–237
command of Libyan invasion assumed, 171
concerned by Islamic fundamentalism in Sudan, 271
and Deby, 240, 242, 256–257, 259, 261, 263, 265, 267–268, 278
domestic reforms, 76–77, 99(n5)
and FAN, 109–110
foreign policy, 75–82, 85–88, 113, 182. *See also specific countries and leaders*
and FROLINAT, 76, 83–84, 90, 94, 96, 106, 108, 111–112, 115, 119
and Giscard, 123–124
and Goukouni, 111–112, 123–125, 140–141, 149, 151, 153, 158–160, 180–181, 200, 212–213
government structure/positions, 74–77
Great Britain ordered to evacuate bases, 77
Green Book, 113, 232
Gulf of Sidra claimed by, 79, 80(figure), 104, 138, 158
and GUNT, 180–183, 209–210, 213, 236. *See also subhead* and Goukouni
and Habre, 4–5, 97, 109–110, 112, 160, 183, 218, 220–221, 223, 236, 248–249
Islamic dissent against, 219, 229(n11)
isolation of, 269
and Kamougue, 128, 130, 213
King Idris overthrown by, 51, 74–75, 233
and *L'affaire Claustre*, 109–110
Libya-Egypt-Sudan unity proposal, 76
Libya-Sudan Integration Charter, 255–256
and Malloum, 113–114, 120
and Mitterand, 169, 172–173, 175, 177, 184–185, 200, 263
and Numayri, 81, 83, 192
and the OAU, 137–138, 140–141, 152, 158, 167–168, 200, 228, 234
oil revenues/finances, 77, 79, 82, 111. *See also under* Libya
Pan-Arabism, 4, 75–77, 79, 82–83, 111, 160, 168, 215, 218, 255–256
peace proposal, 200
personality, 75–76, 83–85, 195, 200, 218, 223, 232, 269
quest for uranium, 92, 107, 116, 121(n14)
Red Line agreement, 172–173, 175, 177
relations with Egypt, 76, 79, 81, 116, 198, 271. *See also subhead* and Sadat
relations with France. *See under* Libya
relations with Sudan, 81, 243, 247, 255–256, 269–271. *See also subhead* and Sadiq
revolutionary and liberation movements supported, 78–79, 137
and Sadat, 76, 79, 81–82, 114, 152
and Sadiq, 110–111, 204, 211, 220, 232–234, 246

Sanusiyya suppressed, 74–75, 77, 99(n5), 233
and Senegal, 132–133
and Siddiq, 89, 96
and the Soviet Union, 203, 226
SPLA supported, 192
support for Chadian rebellion, 89
terrorism supported/sponsored by, 4, 76, 78, 81, 104, 114, 137–138, 160, 166, 195, 202, 209, 269
and Tombalbaye, 84–85, 93–94
Tummo Triangle claimed by, 116
and the United States, 83, 152, 164–165, 202–203, 209
See also Libya

Radio Bardai, 159, 178, 194
Radwan, Radwan Salah, 153
Rahman, Abd al-, 18
Rashid, Sa'id, 160, 202
Reagan, Ronald, 138–139, 151–152, 157, 172, 176, 202
Red Cross, 191
Red Line/Red Zone, 172–178, 174(figure), 216–217, 226
Refugees, 145, 149, 191–192, 196–197, 212, 242, 249, 270–271, 279(n10)
Revolutionary Command Council (RCC; Libya), 74, 199, 261
Revolutionary Command Council (RCC; Sudan), 244–248, 255–256, 260–261, 264, 270–271. *See also* Bashir, Umar Hasan Ahmad al-
Revolutionary Security Guards (Sudan), 245

Sadat, Anwar, 76, 79, 81–82, 114, 145, 151–152, 166
Sadiq al-Mahdi
    Ansar allegiance to, 60, 69, 171, 193
    Arab militias established, 245
    arrested, 72, 193, 246
    attempt to overthrow Numayri, 113–114
    background and personality, 39, 44, 60, 69, 232
    Deby supported by, 242. *See also* Darfur, Deby's forces in
    diplomatic efforts to end Chad-Libyan conflict, 219, 221, 233
    and Egypt, 204
    and Habre, 223, 235, 242–243, 246
    on Islam, 69
    Libyan presence in Sudan denied, 233
    and the Mahdists, 69–70
    negotiations with the SPLA, 239
    and Numayri, 72, 113–114, 118, 124, 138, 146
    Pan-Arabism of, 124
    and Qaddafi, 110–111, 204, 211, 232–234, 243, 246
    self-determination demands classed as treason, 70
    Sudanese elections won, 203
    support for Chadian rebellion, 60–61
    and the United States, 203–206
Sahloul, Ali, 257, 259–260
Said, Mahamat Abba, 141, 163, 183, 213
Saleh, Muhammad, 128

Sand War, 114
Sanoussi, Adam, 39
Sanusi al Khattabi al-Idrisi al-Hasani, Muhammad ibn
    Ali al- (the Grand Sanusi), 7, 9–10, 232–233.
    See also Sanusiyya
Sanusiyya, 7, 9–10, 12, 16, 20, 33, 39, 41, 49, 74–75, 77,
    84, 232–233, 247
Sanussi, Abdalkadar, 141, 213
Sanussi, Hadjaro, 141
Saoun, Mahamat, 63
Sara people, 12–13
Sara Triangle, 14, 111
Sassou-Nguesso, Denis, 210, 219
Saudi Arabia, 158, 179–180, 194
Sayyid Abd al-Rahman al-Madhi, 11, 69
Schultz, George, 165, 216
Second Liberation Army, 89, 92, 95–96, 115, 119.
    See also Forces Armées du Nord; Habre,
    Hissene
Seid, Joseph Brahim, 104
Senegal, 116, 132, 136, 148, 154
Senghor, Leopold, 132–133
Service de Documentation Extérieur et de Contre-
    Espionnage (SDECE), 25, 43, 124, 142(n26),
    149, 272. *See also* France, intelligence service
Shagari, Shehu, 140
Shah, Ahmad, 113
Sharif, Rifi Ali, 199, 216
Shimal, Ali, 258
Siddiq, Dr. Abba, 41, 83–84, 88–90, 92, 95–96,
    100(n29), 105, 111, 129, 136
Slave trade, 6–8, 13, 16–17, 18, 28
Soumaila, Mahamat, 195
Soviet Union, 25, 151–152, 166, 183, 194, 197, 203,
    217, 226
Staewan, Dr. Christian, 97, 98, 110. *See also* L'affaire
    Claustre
State Department (United States), 30–31, 104, 198, 204
States with Saharan Responsibilities, 102
Stevens, Siaka, 137, 138
Sudan
    Abboud government, 55–56
    armed forces, 43, 53(n27), 55–56, 197, 205, 245,
        258
    boundaries. *See* Boundaries
    caravan routes closed by, 114
    Chadian rebels supported by, 37–38, 40, 42–43,
        57–64
    Chadian refugees in, 145, 192, 197, 212, 249,
        279(n10)
    civil war, 23–24, 37–38, 55–57, 60–61, 71–72, 81,
        111, 114
    civil war revived, 192, 239, 255
    constitution, 68, 70, 81
    dependence on the Nile, 194
    diplomatic efforts to end Chad-Libyan conflict
        (1987), 220–221, 227
    drought and famine, 35, 192–194, 260–261, 269

and Egypt, 43, 53(n27), 55–57, 81, 114, 165–166,
    194–195, 197–198
ethnic groups, 12, 67–68, 70–71, 146–147, 204,
    258–259. *See also specific ethnic groups*
famine relief for, 260
FAN supported, 138, 147. *See also* Forces Armées
    du Nord, in Darfur
FANT supplied by, 166
and Habre government, 166, 242
history, 20–21, 66–67, 232–233. *See also* Anglo-
    Egyptian Condominium; Mahdi, the
human rights violations, 245, 258
at independence, 23, 55–56
intelligence service, 56, 193
Islamic reform movement in. *See* Mahdi, the;
    Mahdists; Turabi, Hasan al-
Islamization of, 192–193, 244–245, 255, 270
Libyan agents in, 147–148, 152, 166, 202, 204, 221
Libyan subversion in, 160, 163, 193–194, 198, 202
Libyan troops in, 205, 233. *See also under* Darfur
Mahgoub government. *See* Mahgoub, Muhammad
    Ahmed
Muslim Brotherhood in, 39, 67–69, 197, 202
1985 elections, 203
Numayri government. *See* Numayri, Jaafar
    Muhammad al-
participation in OAU peacekeeping force, 154
political parties, 57, 68–69, 73, 83, 147
and Qaddafi, 81, 111
Queen Elizabeth's visit, 70–71
relations with Libya, 197–198, 201–202, 205–206,
    220, 233, 252(n31), 254–256. *See also* Sadiq al-
    Mahdi, and Qaddafi
relations with the United States, 4, 61, 118, 149,
    152, 161(n24), 165–166, 176, 197, 201–206. *See
    also* Noel, Cleo A., Jr.
Sadiq government. *See* Sadiq al-Mahdi
Swar al-Dahab government, 196–197
terrorist camps in, 271
and Tombalbaye, 30, 37–38, 44, 57, 59–64
transitional government of Sirr al-Khatim al-
    Khalifa, 68
well-drilling programs, 66
See also Darfur; Frontiers, Chad-Sudan frontier
Sudan Communist Party, 83
Sudanese Popular Socialist Front, 147
Sudanese Professionals' Front, 71
Sudan People's Liberation Movement/Army
    (SPLM/SPLA), 192, 197, 239, 245–246
Sudan Socialist Union, 73
Suez Canal, 20, 56
Swar al-Dahab, 196–198, 201–202, 205
Syria, 38, 76, 114

Taha, Mahmoud Muhammad, 193
Taher, Ali Mahamat, 38–40, 44–45
Tahir, Brig. al-Tijani al-, 247, 254, 256
Tayib, Umar Muhammad al-, 193

Tayrab, Muhammad, 17
Teda Toubou, 33, 35–36, 89, 199, 228
Terrorism, international, 4
   French threats to attack terrorism at source, 228
   sponsored/supported by Qaddafi, 4, 76, 78,
      104, 114, 137–138, 160, 166, 195, 202, 209,
      269
Third FROLINAT Army. *See* Forces Armées
     Occidentales
Tibesti. *See* Borkou-Ennedi-Tibesti Prefecture
Togoi, Adoum, 95, 109, 131, 212, 217, 240
Tombalbaye, Ngartha (François)
   actions against rebellion, 42, 45, 48–49
   African authenticity campaign, 102–104
   anti-insurgent propaganda, 45
   and the Aozou Strip, 86, 87(figure), 88, 94. *See also*
     Aozou Strip
   assassinated, 105, 108
   attempted assassination, 86
   background and personality, 25, 27
   and the B.E.T., 25, 32–37
   and the CCT, 93
   cease-fire and peace efforts, 52
   Chadian rebellion acknowledged, 41–42, 45
   "Chadian way" initiative, 29
   and de Gaulle, 26, 31, 46–47
   and the *Derde*, 86
   dictatorship assumed by, 27–28, 43–44, 64
   economic assistance sought, 30, 47, 103–104
   and Egypt, 59
   and Foccart, 27, 29, 47, 95–96, 103
   French military intervention sought, 26, 46–47, 85,
     88
   French withdrawal requested, 96
   and Giscard, 96, 102
   government, 51, 96
   and Israel, 84–85
   and King Idris, 30, 84
   and *L'affaire Claustre*, 98, 104
   and Libya/Qaddafi, 93–94, 103
   military budget, 51
   and Mitterand, 50, 85
   multiple portfolios assumed by, 23
   oil concession granted, 50
   political opposition, 28–29, 102. *See also* Chadian
     civil war
   political oppression by, 27, 32, 48
   political reforms rejected, 47, 50–51
   and Pompidou, 93, 96
   and the PPT. *See* Parti Progressiste Tchadienne
   relations with France, 26–27, 29, 31, 46–47, 50–51,
     85, 88, 90–91, 93, 95–96, 103. *See also* France,
     military intervention in Chad
   relations with Libya/Qadaffi, 49, 86, 88, 102–103.
     See also Aozou Strip
   and "States with Saharan Responsibilities," 102
   and Sudan, 30, 37–38, 44, 57, 59–64, 72
   survival threatened, 43

   and tax collection, 50. *See also* Chad, taxation
Third World and African diplomacy, 30
Toubou appointed to government positions OR
   political appointments, 46
and the United States, 30–31, 85, 103–104
and *yondo*, 102
Toubou, 7–8, 12, 20, 46–47, 98
   arms acquired by, 33, 47, 51
   in the B.E.T., 32, 34, 36, 46, 50, 84
   and the Chadian rebellion, 34, 36, 39, 44–46,
     50–51. *See also* Forces Armées du Nord
   and drought, 35–36, 46, 65, 92–93, 192
   ethnic rivalries, 12, 17, 30, 33, 110
   and Qaddafi/Libya, 84, 108, 160, 212
   See also Daza Toubou; Teda Toubou
Tourgoudi, Ouchar, 159
Toward a United National Liberation Front (Abatcha),
   38
Transitional Military Council (TMC; Sudan), 196–197,
   201, 205
Tripoli Accord, 195
Tripoli Unity Charter, 76
Tuareg, 7–8, 30, 116, 136
Tummo Triangle, 116, 117(figure), 136
Tummo Wells, 116, 158
Turabi, Hasan al-
   Acheikh's appeal to, 249
   and Arab radicals, 270
   background and personality, 67–69, 263
   denouced by Qaddafi, 271
   NIF headed by, 202–203. *See also* National Islamic
     Front
   and Numayri, 71–72, 118, 124, 138
   Pan-Arabism of, 124
   Sudanese Muslim Brotherhood founded, 39
Turayki, Ali al-, 219

Ubaydi, Abd al-Ati, 168, 182
Umma, 57, 69, 71–72, 81, 203, 205
Union Douanière et Economique de l'Afrique Centrale
   (UDEAC), 48, 178
Union Nationale pour l'Indépendence et la Révolution
   (UNIR), 272, 180
Union Nationale Tchadienne (UNT), 38–40
Union Routière Centre-Africaine (UNIROUTE), 93
United Nations, 79, 112, 120, 126, 138, 159, 177, 190,
   212, 260–261, 269
United States
   aerial surveillance, 149–151, 157, 164, 166,
     169–170, 184, 198–199
   African policies, 30–31, 118, 164–165, 198
   alarmed by resurgence of Goukouni/FAP, 163
   ambassador to Sudan assassinated. *See* Noel, Cleo
     A., Jr.
   American evacuation of Sudan, 203
   arms supplied to FANT, 167, 171–173
   discovery of Sudanese support for Chadian
     rebellion, 59, 61

economic assistance to Chad, 157–158, 179–180,
   190. *See also* United States Agency for
   International Development
and Egypt, 118, 149, 151–152, 166, 176
famine relief, 104, 190, 201–202, 260, 268–269
financial aid for peacekeeping troops, 148, 154
and the Gulf of Sidra, 79, 138, 152, 166
Habre government supported, 138, 152, 157–158,
   164–165, 167, 171–173, 179–180, 216, 220, 225,
   227–228, 263, 268
House Intelligence Committee hearing, 179–180
intelligence services. *See* Central Intelligence
   Agency
lack of interest in Chad, 104
Libyan terrorist attacks against US interests, 160
and Libya/Qaddafi, 77–79, 85, 138–139, 152,
   164–166, 176, 187(n30), 202–203, 268–269
Middle East Rapid Deployment Force, 164–165
military operations in North Africa, 78–79, 152,
   165–166, 173, 186(n6), 187(n30), 202–203
and Niger, 158, 186(n16)
Numayri government supported, 165–166,
   194–195
and the OAU, 138, 158
relations with Deby government, 268–269
relations with France, 31, 52(n4), 78, 149, 152, 165,
   170, 173, 176, 203
relations with Sudan, 4, 61, 118, 149, 152,
   161(n24), 165–166, 176, 194–195, 197, 201–206.
   See also Noel, Cleo A., Jr.
report on taxation of nomads, 37
Siddiq's charges against, 83
Soviet Union warned to restrain Libya, 226
terrorism policy, 151
and Tombalbaye, 30–31, 85, 103–104
USCENTCOM, 165
US embassy reports on Chad, 44, 53(n14), 73(n5),
   104
United States Agency for International Development
   (USAID), 31, 59, 73(n5), 158, 201–202, 260
uranium, 50, 91–92, 107, 116, 127, 138

Vixamar, Dr., 102
Vulcan Force

Ahmat Acyl's ("new"), 119, 131, 133
Baghalani's ("old"), 39, 110, 119, 148. *See also*
   Baghalani, Muhammad Al-
commanded by Abdoulaya Adoum Dana, 125
incorporated in FAP under Goukouni, 119

Wadai
   conflict in, 29, 37, 40, 130, 149, 155, 163, 222, 249
   drought, 66, 92–93
   history, 7, 13, 15–19, 26–27, 171
   migration from, 57–58
   See also Frontiers, Chad-Sudan frontier
Wadi Doum, 217, 223–224
Waldheim, Kurt, 112
Walters, Vernon, 165
War of the Tribes, 238–239
Water, 47, 66, 111
Weinberger, Caspar, 164, 173
Wheelus Air Force Base, 78
Wodei Kichidemi. *See Derde*, the
Wori-mi, Allafouza Koni, 250, 252(n45)
World Bank, 126–127, 277

Yom Kippur War, 81–82
Yondo, 102
Yugoslavia, 31

Zaghawa, 12, 146, 175
   armed by Libya, 137
   in the B.E.T., 32, 109
   bombed by Libya, 212
   and Deby's revolt, 239–241
   and drought, 35, 65–66, 145, 192
   ethnic rivalries, 17, 146–147, 204, 274
   in the FAN, 109, 146. *See also* Forces Armées du
      Nord
   Libyans distrusted by, 110
   shaykhs' authority restored by Habre, 241
   suppressed by Bashir/RCC, 270–271
Zaire, 148, 154, 170–171, 187(n27)
Zakariya Idris, Abdallah, 147, 161(n6)
Zouar, battles of, 33–34, 216–217
Zubayr Pasha Rahma Mansur, 18
Zubayr, Rabih, 17, 22